WHAT CAN THIS BOOK DO FOR YOU?

Within a few years, your high school experience will lead you into the work world of adults. This book is designed to give you guidance, ideas, and answers about the many options life offers and the steps you will need to take for each.

WHAT FIRST?

Take a few minutes to claim ownership of this book. Write your name in it. In pencil, lay out your career and life goals as you see them today. Consider the obstacles you may have to overcome in order to achieve your goals. If you don't have a formal plan, that's ok. Answering these questions will spark your imagination and help you make one. The first steps might not be easy, but there are no right or wrong answers. As you continue working through this book, refer to these goals and feel free to fill in any blanks you left or to change your ideas.

WHAT NEXT?

Your needs, goals, ideas, and talents are unique to you. What is right for you may not be right for others. But the steps in the process of choosing a career direction (and understanding what education you might need to get there) are the same whether you aspire to repair car engines or design the next generation of space shuttles.

THINK OF THIS BOOK AS A ROAD MAP

Knowing where you want to go and what roads will lead you there is the first step in the process. You can always change your destination and chart a new course. We're providing the map. The rest is up to you.

GETTI
THE R
SUCCESS

Name ____________________

Age ____________________

Grade ____________________

Date Started ____________________

My current goal after I graduate from high school is to:

____

____

At school, to reach my goal I'll need:

Curriculum planning:

____

____

Clubs, teams, associations:

____

____

Career research:

____

____

Outside of school, to reach my goal I'll need:

Volunteer work:

____

____

Shadowing/mentor program:

____

____

Job experience:

____

____

Extracurricular activities:

____

____

Challenges my goal presents:

____

____

Ideas to overcome these challenges:

____

THOMSON
PETERSON'S

About Thomson Peterson's

Thomson Peterson's (www.petersons.com) is a leading provider of education information and advice, with books and online resources focusing on education search, test preparation, and financial aid. Its Web site offers searchable databases and interactive tools for contacting educational institutions, online practice tests and instruction, and planning tools for securing financial aid. Thomson Peterson's serves 110 million education consumers annually.

For more information, contact Thomson Peterson's, 2000 Lenox Drive, Lawrenceville, NJ 08648; 800-338-3282; or find us on the World Wide Web at www.petersons.com/about.

Editor: Fern A. Oram; Production Editor: Alysha Bullock; Manufacturing Manager: Ray Golaszewski; Composition Manager: Michele Able; Interior Design: Michele Able

ISBN: 0-7689-2003-5 (Middle Atlantic) 0-7689-2004-3 (Midwest)
0-7689-2005-1 (New England) 0-7689-2006-X (South)
0-7689-2007-8 (Texas) 0-7689-2008-6 (West)

Printed in the United States of America

10 9 8 7 6 5 4 3 2 1 07 06 05

Seventh Edition

Dear Student:

Whether graduation seems light-years away or alarmingly close, it's never too early—or too late—to think about what comes after high school. Do you know what your next step will be?

Peterson's Get a Jump! can help you figure that out. This book is designed to help you launch your career, whether this means going on for more education or directly entering the workforce. You have a multitude of options and some crucial choices to make. In the pages that follow, we have tried to give you a jumpstart on planning the future that's right for you.

The book is arranged in five parts. Part 1 has all the guidance you'll need to make the transition to high school. Part 2 provides general introductory information about your options after high school and how to use your high school education to plan for the next phase of your life. Part 3 offers more detailed information about postsecondary education, whether you choose a two-year, four-year, vocational/career college, or the military. Part 4 provides useful information about the workplace and how to handle stress, peer pressure, conflict, and other obstacles you may encounter. Finally, Part 5 contains appendices for each state in your geographic region of the United States, including valuable information on two- and four-year colleges and universities in your area and your state's high school graduation requirements, scholarship and financial aid programs, summer opportunities, and vocational and career colleges.

We hope you find this publication helpful as you begin thinking about the rest of your life. If you have questions or feedback on *Peterson's Get a Jump!*, please contact us at: Editor—Get A Jump!
Thomson Peterson's
2000 Lenox Drive
Lawrenceville, NJ 08648

Sincerely,
Thomson Peterson's Editorial Staff

Contents

Part 1

YOU'RE GOING TO BE A FRESHMAN . . .

YOU KNOW WHAT IT'S SUPPOSED TO BE LIKE—being a freshman in high school should be COOL. But what will it REALLY be like? Will you be able to figure it all out? Of course you will . . . especially since you are reading this! Your high school years will be like nothing else you have experienced and you are going to have questions about everything. Luckily, it's right here that you will be able to get answers. Whether you are wondering about how to keep your "stuff" organized, choosing your classes, or what is a GPA, we are here to help! So, come on, jump in-you're going to be a FRESHMAN!

To Students, Parents, and Counselors:

It was my pleasure to experiment with using Peterson's Get a Jump! *in selected high schools and elementary schools in Chicago. While the logistics of how high school students are scheduled and how they move from class to class made the job of getting the material to them and guiding them through it very challenging, the material was well received by the high schools, and those students who were exposed to the book were excited by all of the information provided in this publication.*

Conversely, the elementary school students, which in Chicago means K-8, especially sixth-eighth graders, are a captive audience and, with assistance from a teacher, were much easier to get together in a group for presentation on a grade by grade and class by class basis. These students were so attentive and curious about high school and what happens there, and I was more than surprised that the students at both the high schools and elementary schools lacked knowledge about such things as: What is a transcript? What is a GPA? What are class ranks? What are honors classes and AP classes?

When I relayed these "discoveries" back to Thomson Peterson's, the idea of adding a special chapter on just these types of questions and issues facing the middle school student getting ready to make the transition to high school was a natural evolution. "The Big Jump to High School" gives parents, guidance counselors, and, most importantly, students the information they need to successfully make that transition—answering not only the questions about transcripts, GPAs, class ranks, and honors and AP classes but also giving advice on participation in extracurricular activities, how to deal with the differences between middle school and high school, setting goals, staying organized, and how to study. And this advice comes not just from Thomson Peterson's, but also from guidance counselors, parents, and students all over the country!

Finally, as a college administrator who has worked with high schools, elementary schools, and junior high schools for more than thirty years, I find Peterson's Get a Jump! *to be a book that has been long overdue. It is an excellent vehicle for young people who seek guidance in planning their educational futures! Best of luck to all of you!*

Nathaniel Thomas, Ph.D.

Chapter 1

THE BIG JUMP TO HIGH SCHOOL

Even if you've never said anything to anyone else, chances are the thought of your first year of high school is totally scary, especially with all these questions whirling around in your head:

Who will I sit with at lunch **What if my best friends don't have lunch when I do** WHERE IS THE VENDING MACHINE How will I find my way around the halls What will I do when I have only four minutes to get to my next class What happens if I get lost ***Will I remember my locker combination*** WHAT HAPPENS IF I CAN'T OPEN MY LOCKER **What happens if there aren't any lockers** How will I carry all those books around in my backpack What if my best friend isn't in the same classes as me **What if I don't know anyone in my classes** *What if I don't know where the bathroom is* **WHAT HAPPENS IF I FORGET WHERE TO GO FOR MY CLASS** What if, what if, what if the seniors are mean to me and treat me like dirt???????

IN MIDDLE SCHOOL, you knew where everything was. You knew exactly who would be sitting next to you at lunch. You knew all the teachers. All the teachers knew you. You were at the top of the heap.

Now you're starting all over again

First of all, take a deep breath, sit back, and realize that it's okay to have the ups and downs, the doubts, and the feelings that zip back and forth between "I can't wait to get into high school" to "I'm hiding under my bed and never coming out." The first few weeks of high school, you're surrounded by a lot of kids who are bigger, who seem to know an awful lot more than you do, and who know exactly where to go. You'll wonder what it will be like, trying out for sports teams or shows and activities with the tenth, eleventh, and twelfth graders.

FROM THE GUIDANCE OFFICE

"Freshmen are afraid the upper class students will pick on them, but honestly, that's not true. Upper class students are not the least bit interested in freshmen."

Helen Erbe
Guidance Counselor
Jackson Memorial High School
Jackson, New Jersey

Second, the friend of a friend's brother who told you he hated ninth grade isn't you. Everyone adjusts to high school in different ways and at different speeds. For some kids, the transition from junior high school/middle school to high school takes a short time, like days or weeks. For others, the adjustment takes longer, especially if they're not admitting to themselves and others what their feelings are and letting others help them get over their insecurities.

ADVICE FROM A SENIOR

Sometimes freshmen give older students too much power. My advice is don't be afraid to be yourself.

Kristen Seghers, Senior
West Windsor-Plainsboro High School South
Princeton Junction, New Jersey

Third, you are not alone. All those big kids ahead of you have gone through the same fears and have had the same feelings, too. They made it through, and you will too. It's most likely that the sophomores, juniors, and seniors are too busy dealing with the problems of being sophomores, juniors, and seniors to be concerned if you forgot your locker combination and have to go slinking off to the school office to find out what it is.

PARENT PERSPECTIVE

"Stephen was nervous about starting ninth grade. It took him only about two to three days to catch on."

Sharon Blumenthal
Parent to Stephen, who is going into the tenth grade.

THE DIFFERENCES: MIDDLE SCHOOL VS. HIGH SCHOOL

There's no getting around it. High school is a different ball game. It's like you're used to playing soccer and all of a sudden in order to score, you're expected to throw the ball, not kick it. Some of the major differences between middle school and high school are:

You are more independent. In middle school, you were part of a group. You did the same things together—ate lunch, took the same classes, goofed off. Same teachers, same schedule. It's a big adjustment to realize that you will have your own schedule of classes that could be very different from your best friend's. You will be in classes with people you don't know because there are different levels of classes. You could be in the middle level of a math class and your friend in the upper level class.

ADVICE FROM A JUNIOR

When I was a freshman, I got into band camp and got to know kids in the band. Then when I was walking through the halls I knew more people other than just the freshmen. If you know people around you then you'll feel comfortable. If you feel comfortable then you'll be more willing to do new things. My high school is a huge high school. The idea is to make as many friends as you can. So talk to everybody.

Matt Wolf, Junior
Doherty High School
Colorado Springs, Colorado

You have to take more responsibility. In middle school you probably had fewer choices about which classes you could take. In high school, there are many more choices about your education, especially as you go into your sophomore year. You'll get to choose some classes, or electives as they're called. As a freshman, the choices you have of electives are limited. Most freshmen can choose only one elective. Sophomores only two. At the junior and senior levels, you'll have more and more choices to make, depending on your goals and interests.

The way you are graded is different in high school. Your teachers in junior high school were probably a lot more lenient when it came to late homework. They were more likely to look at your past record and give you a little leeway. Teachers in high school aren't as likely to accept excuses. "I forgot" won't work. In high school your grades are based on numbers. Two points off if you didn't get your homework done and turned in on time.

You have to speak up for yourself. In middle school, your parents probably helped you if you got into a tough situation, say with a teacher. They were the ones making the phone call or visiting the teacher. In high school, there will be times when you will have to deal with situations on your own, such as speaking with a teacher about homework, or getting your voice heard in clubs and activities even though you're the youngest one there. In high school, you have to develop the ability to get advice from your parents and counselors, figure out how to solve the problem, and then take action.

ADVICE FROM A SENIOR

"Speak up if you have a good idea. In sports or clubs, sometimes younger people have good ideas or strategies and ways to help out, but they don't want to say anything."

Kristen Seghers, Senior
West Windsor-Plainsboro High School South
Princeton Junction, New Jersey

THERE'S SO MUCH TO DO!

Your freshman year is a time for you to explore your interests—what's it like being a crime scene investigator, a computer graphics designer, a veterinarian, etc.

Explore your interests via elective classes. One of the main purposes of high school electives is to allow you to investigate career interests. Though you will be required to take a variety of basic classes like math, English, history, and science, your choice of electives can point you in the direction of a future college major. It could very well be that something you enjoy doing as a freshman could end up being the start of your career.

You can take electives in areas like computers, art, accounting, or music. Say you think you'd like to be in business some day, sitting in an office overlooking the city. You can begin to realize that dream by taking accounting as an elective. You may find out you really like working with numbers. Or, you may find out you'd rather be building high rises instead of sitting in them.

Explore your interests via clubs and activities. In addition to sports, high school offers many clubs and activities outside of what you'll learn in the classroom.

FROM THE GUIDANCE OFFICE

"Some kids that I counsel know what they want to be. Others don't have a clue, and some have an inkling. Your high school courses can help you reach that goal and, if you don't have a goal, can help you explore what you want to do."

Madeleine Wyckoff
Director of Guidance
Port Charlotte High School
Port Charlotte, Florida

You may think these activities are there just so you can have some fun. While that's true, they also give you the opportunity to find out what your interests are. Extracurricular activities can help you find what goals you want to set and then how to reach them.

ADVICE FROM A JUNIOR

I would have definitely joined more clubs and done more activities in my freshman year. Say if you join a drama club as a freshman, you can be at the top when you get to be a junior or senior. If you wait to join when you're a junior, you'll be at the bottom end. Colleges want you to be a leader so you have to start going for the top of activities when you're a freshman.

Matt Wolf, Junior
Doherty High School
Colorado Springs, Colorado

Here's a sample list of clubs and activities in which you can participate. Every school is different, so you'll have to find out what your high school offers, but this list will give you an idea of what you can expect.

- Auto club
- Band
- Bowling club
- Cheerleading
- Choir
- Forensic club
- Math club
- Mock Trial
- Newspaper
- Science club

Explore your interests via volunteer work. High schools often offer opportunities for you to do volunteer work. Are you interested in working with younger kids? In being a lawyer? In helping those who are sick? You can volunteer to help out in a hospital or law office, for instance. By volunteering and working alongside people who are doing the things you may like to do, you can quickly judge if you really do like hospitals or law offices.

TO HONOR OR NOT TO HONOR: CHOOSING CLASSES

One of the most critical decisions you're going to have to make in your first year of high school is whether to take classes on a regular level or on an honors level. You may have heard about AP classes, or Advanced Placement classes. You can't take those until your junior or senior year, but the time to start planning for this high academic level is actually in your freshman year. If your goal is to take college-level courses in high school (that's what AP classes are), you should start in the ninth grade by taking honors classes. AP classes are very competitive with little wiggle room for poor grades or performance as you move from freshman, to sophomore, to junior.

But first you need to know the difference between "regular," honors, and AP classes.

Classes at the "regular" level

Different high schools may have different labels for this level, but basically, if you're in a "regular" level class, you're getting what you need in that subject area to meet the requirements to graduate from high school in four years and go on to college. Do the work expected of you, turn in all your homework, do well on the tests, and you'll get that piece of paper in four years that says you've completed the necessary subjects to become a high school graduate.

Classes at the honors level

Honors level classes require more from you. You'll do more reading and writing that demands more in-depth understanding of the subject matter. Classes at this level develop critical thinking skills by asking you to interpret situations and events. Honors classes are designed to provide you with an in-depth investigation into a subject.

Teachers will expect you to participate in class discussions. You will learn to feel comfortable with a subject so you'll be able to talk about it. For instance, when studying the civil war in an honors class, you'll delve deeper into the conditions that brought the war about, in addition to dates, geographic locations, and famous names. Then you'll look at how the war affected history and learn something about the social and political issues that followed.

Classes at the AP (Advanced Placement) level

In AP classes, you're actually learning at the college level. You are expected to do the assignments and perform on the tests as you would if you were in college. No wonder you can't take AP classes until your junior and senior year. In order to even get into an AP class, you must be a high achiever.

While the hurdles to getting into an AP class are high, the advantages for those who do well in AP classes are huge. The AP exams are given to students across the whole U.S.A. in May and are scored on a level from 1–5, with 5 being tops. If you get a 3, 4, or 5 in the exam of a particular class, you may be able to waive the introductory level of that class in college. Some colleges may even award you college credit!

Not only will this save you time and money, but you'll also impress college admissions offices with the fact that you're taking AP classes. Colleges look favorably on students who worked hard in high school and did well in difficult subjects. During the college admission process, some colleges "weight" the different levels of classes you take. For instance, they'll give you more points for an A in an honors class than they would for an A in a "regular class." An A in a class at a regular level may count as a 4, while an A in an honors level class would count as a 5 and a B in an honors level would count as a 4.

Some things to consider before taking the honors plunge

Many students do well in honors classes. Others struggle, whereas they may have done very well starting off in a "regular" level class. Then, once they've become familiar with the different way classes are taught and what's expected academically of high school students, they may be able to handle an honors class with ease.

You must be honest with yourself and with your parents. Sometimes parents see their kids through rosy glasses and think their sons and daughters are geniuses. Meanwhile, the son or daughter is struggling to cope with the whole change from junior high school to high school, and falls behind. Your mindset has a lot to do with how well you'll do in high school, so it's much better to begin high school at a level that fits you.

If you are terrible at writing, but love science, that's your clue about which honors classes to take and in which sequence. You may take a science honors class your first semester. See how you do. Then you can add an English honors course the second semester.

If you're not confident about you study habits or organizational skills, the first semester of high school is a time to slowly dip your tootsies in the honors pool. Feel the temperature of the water by doing well in a "regular "class, flex your mind muscles, and then dive into honors. The goal is to excel in what you do well and then take the classes that challenge you.

The WORST mistake you can make is to select an honors class because your best friend decided to take it. How well you do in high school determines if many of the doors to your future plans will be open. If you do poorly, you begin to close doors even in your freshman year.

What if you want to be a chef and your parents are determined for you to go to Harvard?

That's a tough situation and the above example is a little on the exaggerated side, but as a freshman, now is the time to address a difference of opinion about your future plans with your parents. So, say you do want to be a chef. You know that honors classes demand a lot more studying and time and that to get into culinary schools or other vocational tracks, you don't need to get As in honors classes. However, your parents know you could get As without too much effort. High school counselors will probably encourage you to take the honors classes. Why not leave your options open? As a freshman, your plans can change a lot before you graduate. If you start out with the plan to be a chef set in concrete and leave no room for change, you could get to your junior year and decide that you hate the smell of burning food. You would rather get a degree in business from a top college. If you'd taken honors classes, you'd be in a good position to go to the university of your choice.

ADVICE FROM A SENIOR

"When you're a freshman, it's hard to see the big picture of your future. I couldn't see it and probably could have done better than I did if I'd talked to some older people or taken a peek at college stuff and seen how important things are."

Kristen Seghers, Senior
West Windsor-Plainsboro High School South
Princeton Junction, New Jersey

Advice for parents

Make sure your child can do well in the honors or AP classes before you start pushing for all As at that level. Each child has different skills. Let's imagine your child takes honors classes in everything that's offered that first year. The child works extremely hard and comes home with a C in science. You're devastated. Your child is devastated. You've never seen a C on a report card. To help your child make the right decisions about honors and AP classes, talk with your child and your child's guidance counselor.

WHAT IN THE WORLD IS A GPA AND WHAT THE HECK IS A TRANSCRIPT?

Your GPA (Grade Point Average). If you haven't already heard about the GPA, those three letters—G, P, and A—are going to mean a lot as you move from freshman to senior. There's no getting around the fact that the GPA is important to your future: what college you can attend, what kind of upper level high school classes you can take (such as those AP classes), what academic and athletic scholarships you may get, or for what special programs you may qualify.

In short, the GPA is the average of all your grades starting from your freshman year. A little planning in your freshman year can go a long way toward a high GPA when you graduate. If you know the impact a GPA can have, you may do things a little differently in your freshman year.

It's good to know how your GPA is computed. Different schools have their own ways to total up a GPA, but this will give you the basic idea.

In general, schools score letter grades as follows:

A = 4 points

B = 3 points

C = 2 points

D = 1 point

F = 0 points

Some schools give higher points for grades earned in honors courses. That's something you would need to check out in the school office. So, let's take a hypothetical student's grades for one semester:

English	A	4 points
History	B	3 points
Music	A	4 points
Math	C	2 points
Spanish	B	3 points
Physical Education	A	4 points

The points total 20 points. Divide that by the number of classes, which is 6, and you get a GPA of 3.33 for one semester.

Let's take the next semester and see how our student did.

English	A	4 points
History	A	4 points
Music	A	4 points
Math	B	3 points
Spanish	C	2 points
Physical Education	A	4 points

That totals 21 points divided by 6, which equals 3.5 GPA. Now, add the total number of points over these last two semesters, which is 41 and divide by the number of classes and you get a 3.42 GPA.

This is a simplified version of how schools score GPAs because some high schools give different points to each class level. For instance, an A in English may be worth more points than an A in physical education.

Your transcript. A transcript goes with you through high school and shows the final grade you received in each of your courses. Your transcript is a history of the classes you took and what grade you achieved in that class. It's what colleges ask for to assess what kind of a student you are.

As a freshman, you need to lay a good foundation academically. Competitive colleges that attract thousands of applications look carefully at your transcript. They're not only looking at your final GPA. They're also looking at how you challenged yourself during your high school years. Did you take courses that stretched you academically, like honors and AP classes, or did you take only those classes you were required to take?

Some important things to know about transcripts

Transcripts differ from school to school. You need to find out what your school records on your transcript. For example, say you got good grades but missed a lot of classes because you just didn't feel like showing up. If your transcript shows the number of times you were not in class, and you're going for a top college or university, your good grades (and high GPA) won't look so good.

- Some schools show how many absences you had for each class.
- Some schools are on the trimester system, which means you'll have three sets of grades for each year.
- Some schools show plus and minus grades, such as a B+ or an A–, and some don't.
- Some schools don't count the freshman year when adding up your GPA.
- Some schools don't show your rank in your class, such as 168 out of 388, but instead use a quartile system, such as ranking you in the top 25% of your class.
- Some schools show your GPA as "weighted," which means that you get an extra credit point for an honors or AP class.
- Some schools show your "citizenship" record in classes. Did you contribute to the class or were you disruptive?
- Some schools will send a profile of your school with your transcript to colleges showing the community in which the school is located, the student population, how many honors and AP classes are offered, the number of periods in a day that classes are offered, etc.

WHAT'S WHAT ON YOUR TRANSCRIPT

A. Your personal information:

Name

Address

Social Security Number or Student ID number (if you don't have a social security number)

Date of Birth

Ethnic Code

NOTE: Parents can request that your social security number, date of birth, and ethnic code be deleted from the transcript when it is sent to various colleges.

B. Abbreviations of the classes you've taken.

C. **Term GPA** is the number of grade points you earn each semester. In the transcript example on the following page, each letter grade is given a number of points, with honors classes getting an extra point:

English 1 Honors (with an extra point for honors)	B	= 4 points
Freehand Drawing 1	A	= 4 points
Spanish 1	B	= 3 points
Algebra 1	B	= 3 points
PE 9	B	= 3 points
Intro to Science 1	C	= 2 points
Government/Law 1	B	= 3 points

Add the points up and you get 22 points. Then divide that total (22) by the number of classes this student took, which is 7. Carry that out to 4 decimal points and you get 3.1429 grade points.

Cumulative GPA is taking the number of grade points from all your previous semesters and adding them up and then dividing them by the number of semesters. Let's look again at this student's transcript for the second semester:

Computer Apps	B	= 3 points
English 2 Honors (with an extra point for honors)	C	= 3 points
Freehand Drawing 1	A	= 4 points
Spanish 1	B	= 3 points
Algebra 1	B	= 3 points
Intro to Science 1	A	= 4 points
Government/Law 1	B	= 3 points

Add the points up and you get 23 points. Then divide that total (23) by 7 (the number of classes) and carry that figure out 4 decimals to get 3.2857 points. Add the two semesters' points (3.1429 and 3.2857) together and divide by the number of semesters, which is 2, and you get the cumulative GPA of 3.2143.

D. Letter grade you earned in each class.

E. Number of absences in each class.

F. Number of credits you earned in each class—you get one credit per class and you need 44 to graduate at this high school. Every school district has a different number of classes you need to graduate or, in some states, every district might be the same.

G. In this transcript, the letter G instead of an A, B, C, D, or F indicates that this course is not taken into account when figuring out your GPA. An "H" would indicate that you dropped the class without a penalty, like an "F". This student didn't drop any classes.

H. **Unofficial Transcript** means that it hasn't been signed or stamped with an official stamp. Transcripts are mailed directly to the school or colleges of your choice. Sometimes they can be transported by the student in a sealed envelope.

I. The date you entered the high school.

J. The date you left the high school.

K. Overall weighted—if your school gives extra points for honors or AP classes when figuring out your GPA, it will be noted here.

L. Your final cumulative GPA.

M. The total amount of credits you attempted.

N. Your class standing and the number of students who were in your senior class when you graduated. This student was 168 out of 388 students in the senior class.

O. Total Credits Earned in High School.

P. Notes about the clubs, sports, and committees in which you participated can be added here with verification from the person responsible for that extracurricular activity.

Q. Signature—the transcript must be signed and have an official seal in order to be accepted as an official transcript.

Colorado Springs Dist 11 (H)

Unofficial Transcript

Doherty High School 719-328-6400
4515 Barnes Rd
Colorado Springs, CO 80917

Entry Date	Counselor	Graduation Date
07/01/1999 (I)		05/20/2003
Exit Date	**Exit Reason**	**Diploma Type**
06/06/2003 (J)	W19-Graduated	High School Diploma

Issued To	Print Date
(A)	09/08/2003 1 of 1

GPA Type	GPA	Crdt Atmpt	Class Rank
Overall Weighted (K)	3.0476 (L)	42.0000 (M)	168 of 388 (N)
Total Credits Earned	44.0000 (O)		

Subject Cd	Course	Mrk1	Abs	Credits
Doherty High School Grd 09 Semester 1 02/00				
EN (B)	English 1, Honors	B	3	1.0000
HU	Frhand Drwng1	A	5	1.0000
HU	Spanish 1	B	4	1.0000
MA	Algebra 1	B	5	1.0000
PE	PE 9	B	7	1.0000
SC	Intro to Science 1	C	6	1.0000
SS	Gov/Law 1	B	5	1.0000
TERM: (C)	**GPA 3.1429**		**CREDITS**	**7.0000**
CUMULATIVE:	**GPA 3.1429**		**CREDITS**	**7.0000**
Doherty High School Grd 09 Semester 2 06/00				
CM	Computer Apps	B	1	1.0000
EN	English 2, Honors	C	1	1.0000
HU	Frhand Drwng2	A (D)	2	1.0000
HU	Spanish 2	B	4	1.0000
MA	Algebra 2	B	1	1.0000
SC	Intro to Science 2	A	1	1.0000
SS	Gov/Law 2	B	3	1.0000
TERM:	**GPA 3.2857**		**CREDITS**	**7.0000**
CUMULATIVE:	**GPA 3.2143**		**CREDITS**	**14.0000**
Doherty High School Grd 10 Semester 1 01/01				
E3	English 3	B	3	1.0000
HL	Health	C	1	1.0000
HU	Spanish 3	B	1	1.0000
MA	Geometry 1	B (E)	1	1.0000
PA	Todays Foods	B	2	1.0000
SC	Biology 1	B	3	1.0000
SS	World & US History 3	C	2	1.0000
TERM:	**GPA 2.7143**		**CREDITS**	**7.0000**
CUMULATIVE:	**GPA 3.0476**		**CREDITS**	**21.0000**
Doherty High School Grd 10 Semester 2 06/01				
E4	English 4	B	11	1.0000
HU	Frhand Drwng3	A	6	1.0000
HU	Spanish 4	B	6	1.0000 (F)
MA	Geometry 2	C	3	1.0000
PE	PE 10	B	7	1.0000
SC	Biology 2	B	7	1.0000
SS	World & US History 4	C	6	1.0000
TERM:	**GPA 2.8571**		**CREDITS**	**7.0000**
CUMULATIVE:	**GPA 3.0000**		**CREDITS**	**28.0000**

Subject Cd	Course	Mrk1	Abs	Credits
Doherty High School Grd 11 Semester 1 01/02				
A1	Hist: US & World 5	C	9	1.0000
E5	English 5	B	9	1.0000
HU	Psychology	B	13	1.0000
MA	Algebra 3	B	10	1.0000
PA	Automotive Tech 1	A	5	1.0000
TERM:	**GPA 3.0000**		**CREDITS**	**5.0000**
CUMULATIVE:	**GPA 3.0000**		**CREDITS**	**33.0000**
Doherty High School Grd 11 Semester 2 05/02				
A2	Hist: US & World 6	B	17	1.0000
E6	English 6	B	21	1.0000
EL	Student Tutor (G)	G	14	1.0000
HU	Psychology, Advanced	A	19	1.0000
MA	Algebra 4	B	14	1.0000
TERM:	**GPA 3.2500**		**CREDITS**	**5.0000**
CUMULATIVE:	**GPA 3.0270**		**CREDITS**	**38.0000**
Doherty High School Grd 12 Semester 1 12/02				
CE	Cons Econ	B	13	1.0000
EN	Creative Writing	A	15	1.0000
EN	Senior Speed Reading 1	B	17	1.0000
PE	PE	A	9	1.0000
PE	Physical Ed	G		1.0000
SC	College Prep Chem 1	C	19	1.0000
TERM:	**GPA 3.2000**		**CREDITS**	**6.0000**
CUMULATIVE:	**GPA 3.0476**		**CREDITS**	**44.0000**

Mrk 1: Course Grade

Student Notes	
(P)	

(Q)

School Official's Signature

TIPS FOR A SMOOTH START

Write down a list of things you want to accomplish. If you have a rough idea of where you're headed, you'll have an easier time getting there. You've already set goals for yourself. Maybe it was to score more points on a video game than the kid down the street. Maybe it was to ride a bike faster or do more maneuvers on a skateboard. When you get into high school, it's important to set goals for yourself from the start. Obviously, the goals will change over time, but having a list of goals—like I want to make the football team; I want to take some honors classes; I want to run for class president; I want to be the editor of the school yearbook—will help you stay motivated and give you something to work toward.

Make your goals specific. For example:

A vague goal is:

I want to be a better student than I was in middle school.

A specific goal is:

The reason I wasn't a good student in middle school is because I didn't turn in my homework. Starting off in high school, I'm going to turn in all my homework on time.

ADVICE FROM A SENIOR

"When I was a freshman, I was intimidated by the older kids' appearance of greatness and their accomplishments. I thought, 'Wow, I can't get to their level.' But don't give up because you think there's too much competition, especially if it's something you really want to do."

Kristen Seghers, Senior
West Windsor-Plainsboro High School South
Princeton Junction, New Jersey

Get involved in clubs and activities immediately. We've already talked about how clubs and activities help narrow your interests and focus you on what you want to do in the future. But extracurricular activities serve another very important purpose for high school freshmen. You'll find friends who like the same things you do. You'll be with older kids so you'll get to know some juniors and seniors. You'll gain confidence in yourself as you work together with other kids. You'll become comfortable with being in high school a lot quicker than if you hang around on the fringes looking in instead of being in the middle of the action, whether it's on a soccer team, chess club, or—whatever!

Get organized. In high school, being organized does not mean showing up in class on time with your teeth brushed. Being organized is brought to a whole different level in high school. Some kids are naturally this way. In junior high school, they knew what homework had to be done, when it was due, and what was required. In high school, the list of things to organize gets longer. You still have to show up on time and whether your teeth are brushed is up to you, but you do have to have all the supplies you need with you.

PARENT PERSPECTIVE

"Every Friday afternoon before leaving school, Jessica gets her locker organized. It's easy for it to get out of control because kids are stuffing things in there all week. Then they can't find something when they need it and the time between classes is so short."

Jodi Domsky
Parent of Jessica, who just started ninth grade and was very organized in middle school.

That sparkly pink pen in your hand won't do to take the test the teacher just handed you. Your teacher specifically told you to bring a blue or black ballpoint. Now where is it? I thought I put it in my backpack. Oh no, here's the sandwich I forgot to eat yesterday on top of my history homework. Your room may be a disaster, but your notebooks, binders, and calendar need to be in tiptop shape.

You're organizing for more classes and carrying around a lot more books and papers than you ever did in middle school. You're going to be involved in sports and clubs. Unless you're organized, you're going to spend more time dealing with chaos and confusion and moldy sandwiches than getting your homework

ADVICE FROM A TEACHER

Typically, middle school students get one big binder with four to five dividers. All their classes' materials are in one binder. It doesn't work that way for high school. They have too much. They can't put homework, notes, handouts and other pieces of paper in one section of the binder. When the binder system fails by mid-October, then they take everything that was in the binder and stuff it in a backpack. Now it's a 15-minute ordeal to find something in the backpack.

Heidi Pimentel
Spanish teacher
Pioneer High School
San Jose, California

done and having all the fun there is to have in high school. Each week in high school goes by at blazing speed and things can get out of control very quickly.

This is what organized students know:

- What was assigned in each class
- When the homework is due
- When the next test is scheduled
- What I need to bring to each class
- Where the supplies I need are located

Organization skills will stay with you the rest of your life. Now's a great time to learn how easy your life will be when you're organized.

ADVICE FROM A JUNIOR

I wasn't very organized and should have been. In middle school, you don't have as many classes as in high school. It's harder to plan for seven classes instead of three or four a day.

Matt Wolf, Junior
Doherty High School
Colorado Springs, Colorado

The way to get organized is to set up a system. It can be someone else's system or your own. The important thing is to have some way to keep track of when assignments are due, when tests are coming, and what nights are taken up with practices or meetings. Each week, go through and set up a new schedule for the coming week. It sounds like a lot of work, but when Thursday hits and your head is spinning, you'll be glad you have a schedule to hang on to. You could have three tests on the same day. Wouldn't it be helpful to know that way ahead of time instead of remembering the day of the tests?

Manage your time. Time management is a term that you've probably heard and put into the "I'll deal with that when I get older" category. Guess what, you're older! You have to take your time and manage it, which means figuring out what you have to do and how much time you have to do it.

It's going to be easy to say, "I'll do my homework after dinner," but you have to take into account that basketball practice doesn't end until 8 p.m., and when you get home you'll want something to eat. So, in reality, you're doing homework until 10 or 11 o'clock, and you have to get up at 6 o'clock.

In high school, your workload increases as you move into the upper classes. If you don't learn how to manage your time, you will only have to struggle that much harder. Plus you have all those other activities eating away at the 24 hours in each day.

Ask questions. You've heard the saying, "No question is a stupid question." Well, kids going into ninth grade seem to forget the "NO" part of that sentence and instead rephrase it as "All my questions are stupid." No matter if you went down the wrong hall and can't find your classroom. No matter if you need help in signing up for a club you really want to join. No matter if you didn't understand what the teacher was saying. The guidance counselors and teachers are there to help you get adjusted and pointed in the right direction.

Take advantage of the help the guidance counselors can give you. You'd be amazed at the number of things you can find in the guidance office—advice on good study habits, advice on planning for college, advice about what to do with that class in which you're having a problem. Use it, because it's there for you.

FROM THE GUIDANCE OFFICE

"As students transition to high school, it is important to develop self-advocacy skills. If you need or want something, you will have to seek out the resources to get the help or support that you desire. If you are struggling academically in a particular subject, you need to seek out your teacher for extra help. Your school counselor is an excellent resource to help you develop your self-advocacy skills and to help problem-solve other situations. Once you are in college, your parents will not be there, so start early so you will feel comfortable approaching the resources available."

Leslie Fisher
Lead Counselor
West Windsor-Plainsboro High School South
Princeton Junction, New Jersey

BEWARE OF THE BLACK HOLE OF THE BACK PACK

It looks like an ordinary backpack (or whatever it is you use to carry your books and school papers), but don't be fooled by its innocent appearance. Somewhere between the time you get out of middle school and into high school, it turns into a black hole—casually destroying finished homework, cheerfully ripping through notes you saved for a test, cunningly hiding the special pen you like.

You may have been organized in junior high school, but once you get into high school, the backpack can turn into an endless pit into which you stuff everything; however, whatever it is you need to find in its endless depths cannot be found without a major search and rescue.

The reason for this dilemma that will suddenly appear in your life is that in high school, you've got a lot more papers to organize. Homework is given in most classes. You're getting handouts that have to be saved for a test that will come up in three weeks, along with that list of notes of supplies you're supposed to bring to science class and the day planner you bought.

You must ramp up the way you keep things organized to keep up with high school. One suggestion is to get a three-subject spiral notebook for each class. Section one is for taking notes in class. Section two is for homework. Section three is for tearing out sheets of paper. You now have everything you need for one subject in one notebook. The pages can't come out unless you tear them out and it's chronological, so you can look back at past notes and tell what was discussed when.

With this system, or any other that suits you best, your backpack will turn into an ordinary useful bag, and when your history teacher asks you to pull out the notes from last week's class, you will know exactly where to find them.

TOP 10 MISTAKES

Everyone makes mistakes, but if you can avoid these TOP 10 as you begin your freshman year, you'll be in much better shape. Drum roll, please. We'll start with the worst.

1. ***My freshman year doesn't count. My senior year is far away. If I mess up, I can always get back on track in the tenth grade.*** While it's true you can make up for bad choices and slip-ups, your freshman year is the foundation upon which the rest of your high school years, and then college, rest. Freshman year isn't practice or a trial period—it's the real thing!

2. ***I'm picking this class because my friend is taking it.*** Your friend picked the class in beginning biology because she's always liked squiggly green bugs. You don't like looking in microscopes. You won't find out what a mistake you've made until you're way behind on homework and have failed several tests, when you could have been getting As in that writing class you wanted to take but didn't.

3. ***I'll just skip this class. One day won't make a difference.*** Not so. In high school, attendance counts. Many schools have policies that cause you to lose credits if you miss class a certain number of times. Even the best of students will miss classes because of illness or other unforeseen events. But remember, much of the teaching in high school is cumulative, meaning that each day is built on what happened in the class the day before. If you get out of the loop, it's really hard to get back in.

4. ***I don't need to write down that assignment. I'll remember it.*** Most likely, you'll only remember the assignment until you leave the classroom, then it's history. By the time you get home, you have a vague recollection of what the teacher said you had to do. Then you have to call someone in the class to ask about the assignment and that person isn't home, so you miss doing the homework.

5. ***I spilled soda on my homework and now I'll be late turning it in if I do it over, so I'll just forget about it.*** You should talk to your teacher about making up lost or forgotten homework. Even though the teacher will probably take off some points, you guarantee getting no points if you don't turn it in at all! So, while the assignment may be late, at least it will be counted. Don't be afraid to ask your teacher about turning in late assignments—better late than never!

6. ***Sorry, I can't join that club, I have to study all the time.*** In your freshman year, it's especially important to become part of the school community. Not only will you get to know other kids who like the same things you do, but you'll also explore what you like to do.

7. ***Everyone else in this class understood what the teacher just said except me, so I won't ask him to explain it.*** You will be surprised to know that if you didn't understand or need more explanation, probably everyone else feels the same way too. Be brave. Ask the question and have everyone else in your class silently thanking you. Plus, most importantly, you'll understand what the teacher was saying.

8. ***I don't want to talk to the teacher about the problems I'm having with her class.*** Teachers aren't mind-readers. They have no clue that you're struggling until they see your work. If you're having problems, it's okay to say, "I just don't get fractions." Teachers love to teach and part of teaching is helping their students understand things.

9. ***There's a situation at school that's making me uncomfortable. I'll just tell my friend about it and not go to the counselor's office.*** Big or small, serious or not, whatever problems you're having or whatever situations are bothering you, your high school counselors are there to help you, protect you, guide you, comfort you. Your best friend may be able to sympathize with your problem, but chances are your friend can't solve the issue as effectively as a counselor or teacher can.

10. ***I really don't need all that much sleep.*** That may have been true during the summer when you could sleep late. Now you're up and out with the sunrise. Trouble is, when you go to bed late, you find yourself nodding off in first period. All that brain power to adjust to high school takes energy. Energy comes from a good night's sleep.

MAKE SURE YOUR PARENTS READ THIS!

Some of you have been through the process of transitioning your son or daughter from middle school to high school. For some of you, it's your first time. Helen Erbe, a guidance counselor at Jackson Memorial High School in Jackson, New Jersey, has been a guidance counselor in middle school, elementary school, and now in high school. She says that having been at all levels, the transitions from elementary to middle and middle to high school are the most traumatic for your kids. The range of emotions swings from fearful to happy and back again. The transition brings out all your child's insecurities. But the cumulative wisdom of other parents and guidance counselors can help you help your children. Here are some tried and tested tips.

- **Find out what tryouts for high school clubs, activities, and sports take place in the summer and see if your child may be interested in joining.**
- **While your child is still in middle school, take her to the high school on casual trips, such as to the library, to the swimming pool, to a play, so she will already be familiar with the building and things to do before ninth grade starts.**
- **Before high school starts, take your child on a test run to walk the halls and meet teachers who are there early to set up their classrooms. Then let him come back by himself for another test run.**
- **Encourage involvement in school activities other than just sports. In general, the students who are involved in extracurriculars enjoy school and have greater academic success. Advise your child to start gradually in the freshman year with a few activities and then add more as she moves toward her senior year.**
- **Help your child set up a system to organize homework assignments, test dates, and other activities.**
- **Give your child space to try things on her own. Get her to advocate for her interests and needs on her own. School administrators and teachers love parent involvement but it's important to let kids deal with some of the issues alone.**
- **Set realistic goals for your child. It's good for children to be challenged but if the goals are too ambitious, children give up reaching any goals.**

Part 2

JUMP-START YOUR FUTURE

COME ON, ADMIT IT. You know that big question—what will I do when I graduate from high school?—is right around the corner. Some of your classmates know what they want to do, but you're freaking out about all of the decisions you still have to make.

You've got a lot of possibilities from which to choose. Maybe you'll attend a two-year or four-year college or a vocational college or a career college. Or you'll join the armed services. Or perhaps you'll go right into the workplace with a full-time job. But before you march across that stage to get your diploma, *Peterson's Get a Jump!* will help you to begin thinking about your options and to open up doors you never knew existed.

Chapter 2

A LOOK AT YOURSELF

Deciding what to do with your life is a lot like flying. Just look at the many ways you can fly and the many directions your life can take.

A TEACHER ONCE asked her students to bring something to class that flies. Students brought kites, balloons, and models of airplanes, blimps, hot-air balloons, helicopters, spaceships, gliders, and seaplanes. But when class began, the teacher explained that the lesson was about career planning, not flying.

She was making the point that your plans for life after high school can take many forms. How you will make the journey is an individual matter. That's why it's important to know who you are and what you want before taking off.

You may not choose your life's career by reading *Peterson's Get a Jump!* (GAJ), but you'll learn how to become part of the decision-making process and find resources that can help you plan your future.

Ready to Fly?

Just having a high school diploma is not enough for many occupations. But, surprise, surprise, neither is a college degree. Different kinds of work require different kinds of training. Knowing how to operate a particular type of equipment, for instance, takes special skills and work experience that you might not learn in college. Employers always want to hire the best-qualified people available, but this does not mean that they always choose those applicants who have the most education. The *type* of education and training you have is just as important as *how much*. Right now, you're at the point in your life where you can choose how much and what kind of education and training you want to get.

If you have a definite career goal in mind, like being a doctor, you probably already know what it will take in terms of education. You're looking at about four years of college, then four years of medical school, and, in most states, one year of residency. Cosmetologists, on the other hand, complete a state-approved training program that ranges from eight to eighteen months.

EDUCATIONAL ATTAINMENT

Highest level of education attained by persons 25 years and older

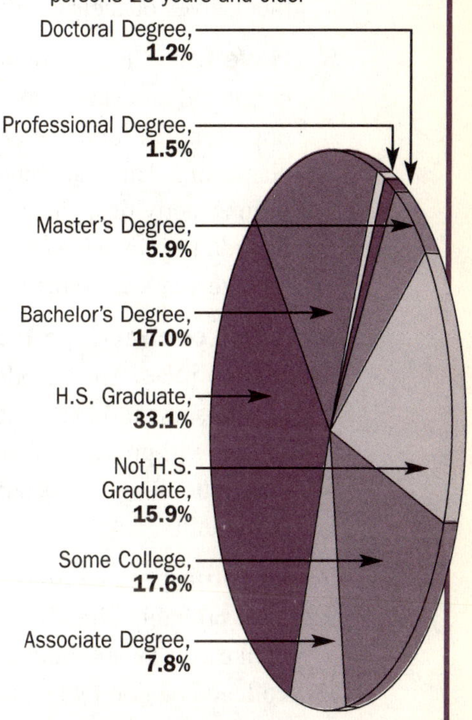

Source: Digest of Educational Statistics, U.S. Department of Commerce, Bureau of the Census, Current Population Survey

But for most of you, deciding what to do after high school is not so easy. Perhaps you haven't chosen a field of work yet. You might just know for certain that you want a job that will give you status and a big paycheck. Or maybe you know what you want to do, but you're not sure what kind of education you'll need. For instance, you may love fixing cars, and the idea of being an auto mechanic sounds great. But you need to decide whether to learn on the job, attend a vocational school, seek an apprenticeship, or pursue a combination of these options.

THE TOP 10 REASONS TO CONTINUE YOUR EDUCATION

Continuing your education after high school is one choice that can give you a good start no matter what your final career decision is. There are many good reasons to do so. If you think college is not for you at all, take a look at this list. It just might change your mind.

10. **Fulfill a dream—or begin one.** Some people hope to become teachers or scientists. For many, continuing their education provides the opportunity to make that wish a reality for themselves or their family.

9. **Have fun.** Classes are an important part of continued education, but there are plenty of opportunities for some great times outside the classroom. There are hundreds of sports, clubs, groups, activities, and associations just waiting for you to join. Many people say that their college years were the best years of their lives.

8. **Make connections that can link you to future jobs.** The friends, professors, supervisors, and classmates you meet after high school will provide valuable ties for future jobs, committees, and associations within the community.

7. **Become part of a cultural stew.** As you have probably already figured out, not everyone is like you. Nor should they be. Being in college is a good way to expose yourself to many types of people from various backgrounds and geographic locations, with different viewpoints and opinions. You may discover that you like people and things you never knew existed.

6. **Meet new people.** By furthering your education, you will widen your circle of friends and, chances are, form meaningful lifelong relationships.

5. **Do what you love doing and get paid for it.** Have you ever taken a test during which everything clicked or played a video game and caught on immediately? This is what happens when you combine education and training with the right job. Work becomes more like play, which is far more satisfying and rewarding than just going through the motions.

4. **Exercise your mind.** Just as physical exercise keeps your body in shape, mental exercise keeps your mind free of cobwebs. No matter what your area of interest, education holds the key to the most interesting and challenging information you can imagine. Explore your outer limits and become a lifelong learner.

3. **Earn a higher income.** Although money isn't everything, it is necessary for survival. A good education prepares you to become a solid member of society. (See the chart below, "Increase Your Earning Power.")

2. **Learn critical-thinking and analytical skills.** More than any other skill, education teaches you to think. Furthering your learning will help you to think critically, organize and analyze information, and write clearly.

1. **You won't get left behind.** In the twenty-first century, you will need to be prepared to change jobs and continually learn new skills in order to keep up with changes in industry, communications, and technology. Education and training will give you that preparation.

INCREASE YOUR EARNING POWER

People with more education tend to earn more money. Look at the average yearly earnings of workers over the age of 25 by education level.

Professional Degree	$80,230
Doctoral Degree	$70,476
Master's Degree	$55,302
Bachelor's Degree	$46,276
Associate Degree	$35,389
Some College	$32,400
High School Diploma	$28,807
Less Than High School Diploma	$21,391

Source: Bureau of the Census; Bureau of Labor Statistics

Breaking Down the Barriers to Continuing Your Education

Some of you may say, "Forget the reasons why I *should* continue my education. I *can't* because (fill in the blank)." Let's see if your objections stand up.

I can't.

Nobody in my family has ever gone to college.

You can!

You can be the first! It's a little scary and not always easy, but just think how great you'll feel being the first person in your family to receive a degree, diploma, or certificate.

I can't.

My grades are not good enough.

You can!

Don't let less-than-perfect grades stand in your way. Different institutions have different requirements, including what grades they accept. Schools also evaluate you for admission as a whole person, including your participation in extracurricular activities; your talents, such as academics and athletics; and your employment and volunteer history. There are also classes that you can take to improve your skills in various subject areas. Get a tutor now or form a study group to improve your grades as much as possible. Talk to your guidance counselor about what the appropriate curriculum for you is so you'll have more options when making decisions about continuing your education.

I can't.

I can't afford it.

You can!

Many families cannot afford to pay education costs completely out of pocket. That's why there are so many opportunities for financial aid, scholarships, grants, and work-study programs. Federal, state, school-sponsored, private, and career-specific financial aid resources are available to students who take the time to look. Talk to a guidance counselor, go to the library, and look on the Internet. Read the "Financial Aid Dollars and Sense" chapter of this guide for more information about how to finance your continued education. Be creative and persistent. It can happen for you.

I can't.

I don't know how to apply or where I want to go.

You can!

Fortunately, there are resources to help you decide which institution to select. Talk to friends, family members, neighbors, your guidance counselor, pastor, coach, or librarian. Take a look at the Appendix at the back of this guide for listings of two-year and four-year colleges, as well as vocational and career colleges in your state.

I can't.

I think it may be too difficult for me.

You can!

Think back to something you have done in your life that seemed too difficult in the beginning. Didn't you find that once you began, put your mind to it, and stuck with it that you succeeded? You can do almost anything if you set your mind to it and are willing to work for it.

I can't.

I'm not sure I'll fit in.

You can!

One of the best things about furthering your education is the chance to meet new people and be part of new experiences in new surroundings. Colleges and other continuing education options attract a wide variety of students from many different backgrounds. Chances are you won't have any problem finding someone else with interests that are similar to yours. Because schools differ in size, location, student body, and lifestyle, you'll surely find one that meets your needs. Advance visits and interviews can help you determine which school is right for you.

FASTEST-GROWING OCCUPATIONS

Want to have a career that's going places? Check out this chart to see which occupations are expected to grow the fastest by the year 2010 and what type of training you'll need to get the job.

Occupation	Expected Openings	Required Education
Computer Software Engineers, applications	760,000	Bachelor's degree
Computer Support Specialists	996,000	Associate degree
Computer Software Engineers, systems software	601,000	Bachelor's degree
Network and Computer Systems Administrators	416,000	Bachelor's degree
Network Systems and Data Communications Analysts	211,000	Bachelor's degree
Desktop Publishers	63,000	Postsecondary Vocational Training
Database Administrators	176,000	Bachelor's degree
Personal and Home Care Aides	672,000	On-the-job training
Computer Systems Analysts	689,000	Bachelor's degree
Medical Assistants	516,000	On-the-job-training
Social and Human Service Assistants	418,000	On-the-job training
Physician Assistants	89,000	Bachelor's degree
Medical Records and Health Information Technicians	202,000	Associate degree
Computer and Information Systems Managers	463,000	Master's degree
Home Health Aides	907,000	On-the-job training
Physical Therapist Aides	53,000	On-the-job training
Occupational Therapist Aides	12,000	On-the-job training
Physical Therapist Assistants	64,000	Associate degree
Audiologists	19,000	Master's degree
Fitness Trainers and Aerobics Instructors	222,000	Postsecondary Vocational Training
Computer and Information Scientists	39,000	Doctoral degree
Veterinary Assistants and Lab Animal Caretakers	77,000	On-the-job training
Occupational Therapist Assistants	23,000	Associate degree
Veterinary Technologists and Technicians	69,000	Associate degree
Speech-language Pathologists	122,000	Master's degree
Mental Health and Substance Abuse Social Workers	116,000	Master's degree
Dental Assistants	339,000	On-the-job training
Dental Hygienists	201,000	Associate degree
Special Education Teachers, grades Pre-K to 6	320,000	Bachelor's degree
Pharmacy Technicians	259,000	On-the-job training

Source: Bureau of Labor Statistics, Occupational Outlook Handbook

I can't.

I don't even know what I want to do with my life.

You can!

Many students don't know this about themselves until they get to experience some of the possibilities. Take the "Self-Assessment Inventory" on page 26 to help you determine what your interests and talents are. Read "Choosing Your Major" on page 97 for a listing of the most popular college majors and their related careers.

I can't.

There is no way I can pursue my education full-time.

You can!

Part-time students are becoming the norm. In fact, a recent study determined that 43 percent of undergraduate students attend school part-time. Most schools offer evening and weekend classes, and many offer work-study opportunities to help students pay for their education. Also, some employers will pay or reimburse you if you are working and want to further your education. If you are enrolled part-time, it does take longer to graduate. But if full-time enrollment is not an option for you, don't give up the opportunity to continue your education. There are many nontraditional ways to achieve your goals.

CHOOSING A CAREER YOU'LL BE HAPPY WITH

Did you know that of the estimated 15 million people searching for employment in the American job market, approximately 12 million are looking for a new occupation or a different employer? That's an awful lot of people who aren't happy with their jobs. Avoid being one of them by taking some time to consider what it is you really want to do now, while you're still in school. Is there a particular type of job you've always dreamed of doing? Or perhaps you're one of the many high school students who say:

"I Kind of Know What I Want, But I'm Not Really Sure."

A good way to gather information about potential occupations is by talking with people who have achieved goals that are similar to yours. Talk to teachers, neighbors, and adult friends about their work experiences. The formal name for that activity is an "informational interview." You're interviewing them about the work they do—not to get a job from them but to gather information about their jobs.

If you don't have any contacts in a field that sparks your interest, do some poking around in the workplace. For instance, if you're interested in a career in nursing, you could visit a hospital, doctor's office, or nursing home. Most people love to talk about themselves, so don't be afraid to ask if they'll chat with you about their profession. Offering to volunteer your services can be the best way to know whether you'll be happy doing that type of work.

"I Don't Have a Clue about What I Want to Do."

If you're completely unsure about what kind of work you'd like to do, contact a career counselor who can help you explore your options and possibly administer some interest and aptitude tests. You also might think about contacting a college career planning and placement office, a vocational school placement office, the counseling services of community agencies, or a private counseling service, which may charge you a fee. Many high schools offer job-shadowing programs, where students actually shadow someone in a particular occupation for an entire day or more. Don't forget that as a high school student, your best resource is your high school guidance counselor. Take a look at the list of the "Fastest-Growing Occupations" on page 24 to get a sampling of the careers with the largest projected job growth in the coming years.

ON THE HUNT FOR INFORMATION

Regardless of how unsure you may be about what you want to do after high school, here's a list of things you can do to get the information you need to head in the right direction. Many people start off thinking they want one career and end up doing something completely different. But this is a good place to begin:

- Investigate careers both in and out of school. Participate in mentoring, job shadowing, and career day opportunities whenever possible.
- Get some on-the-job experience in a field that interests you.
- Research two-year and four-year colleges, vocational/career colleges, and apprenticeship programs.
- Participate in school and state career development activities.
- Prepare for and take aptitude and college entrance tests.

Here are a few Web sites where you can receive valuable direction by completing a career interest questionnaire or by reading about various occupations:

Peterson's

www.petersons.com

On Peterson's Web site, you can read helpful articles about the workplace and search for undergraduate academic and career-oriented degree and certificate programs.

Occupational Outlook Handbook

www.bls.gov/oco

The Bureau of Labor Statistics, an agency within the U.S. Department of Labor, produces this Web site, which offers more information than you'll ever need about specific careers.

SELF-ASSESSMENT INVENTORY

In addition to looking to outside sources for information, there's another rich source of data: yourself. Knowing what you want to do begins with knowing yourself—the real you. The better you understand your own wants and needs, the better you will be able to make decisions about your career goals and dreams. This self-assessment inventory can help.

Who do you admire most, and why?

What is your greatest strength?

What is your greatest talent?

What skills do you already have?

DESCRIBE HOW YOU CURRENTLY USE THESE SKILLS IN YOUR LIFE:

Athletic ability

Mechanical ability

Ability to work with numbers

Leadership skills

Teaching skills

Artistic skills

Analytical skills

CHECK THE AREAS THAT MOST INTEREST YOU.

- ❒ Providing a practical service for people
- ❒ Self-expression in music, art, literature, or nature
- ❒ Organizing and record keeping
- ❒ Meeting people and supervising others
- ❒ Helping others in need, either mentally, spiritually, or physically
- ❒ Solving practical problems
- ❒ Working in forestry, farming, or fishing
- ❒ Working with machines and tools
- ❒ Taking care of animals
- ❒ Physical work outdoors
- ❒ Protecting the public via law enforcement or fire fighting
- ❒ Medical, scientific, or mathematical work
- ❒ Selling, advertising, or promoting

WHAT GIVES YOU SATISFACTION?

Answer the following questions True (T) or False (F).

T F I get satisfaction not from personal accomplishment, but from helping others.

T F I'd like to have a job in which I can use my imagination and be inventive.

T F In my life, money will be placed ahead of job security and personal interests.

T F It is my ambition to have a direct impact on other people's lives.

T F I am not a risk-taker and would prefer a career that offers little risk.

T F I enjoy working with people rather than by myself.

T F I would not be happy doing the same thing all the time.

WHAT MATTERS THE MOST TO YOU?

Rate the items on the list below from 1 to 10, with 10 being extremely important and 1 being not at all important.

___ Good health	___ Seeing the world
___ Justice	___ Love
___ Marriage/family	___ Fun
___ Faith	___ Power
___ Fame	___ Individualism
___ Beauty	___ Charity
___ Safety	___ Honor
___ Friendship	___ Intelligence
___ Respect	___ Wealth
___ Accomplishment	

Mapping Your Future

www.mapping-your-future.org

On this site, you can find out how to choose a career and how to reach your career goals. You can also pick up useful tips on job hunting, resume writing, and job interviewing techniques. This site also provides a ten-step plan for determining and achieving your career goals.

University of Waterloo Career Development Manual

www.cdm.uwaterloo.ca/

This site provides a thorough online career interest survey, and strategies you can use to get the job that's right for you.

LiveCareer

www.livecareer.com

LiveCareer is a San Francisco based company founded by Sigma Assessment Systems, Inc. and a group of leading career professionals and investors. Since 1967, they have developed innovative practical assessment solutions that have helped more than 300,000 people make important career decisions.

HotJobs.com

www.hotjobs.com

Includes information about thousands of job and career fairs, advice on resumes, and much more.

WHAT WOULD YOU DO IF YOU WERE IN A BLIZZARD SURVIVAL SITUATION?

Check the one that would be your most likely role.

- ❐ The leader
- ❐ The one who explains the situation to the others
- ❐ The one who keeps morale up
- ❐ The one who invents a way to keep warm and melt snow for water
- ❐ The one who listens to instructions and keeps the supplies organized
- ❐ The one who positions sticks and rocks to signal SOS

LOOKING AHEAD AND LOOKING BACK

What are your goals for the next five years?

Where would you like to be in ten years?

What was your favorite course, and why?

What was your least favorite course, and why?

Who was your favorite teacher, and why?

What are your hobbies?

What are your extracurricular activities?

What jobs have you held?

What volunteer work, if any, have you performed?

Have you ever shadowed a professional for a day? If so, what did you learn?

Do you have a mentor? If so, who? What have you learned from this person?

Do you want to stay close to home, or would you prefer to travel to another city after high school?

WHAT ARE YOUR CAREER GOALS?

The interests, skills, and knowledge supporting my career goals are:

To fulfill my career goals, I will need additional skills and knowledge in:

I will obtain the additional skills and knowledge by taking part in the following educational activities:

I will need a degree, certification, and/or specialized training in:

When I look in the classified ads of the newspaper, the following job descriptions sound attractive to me:

WHAT ARE YOUR IMMEDIATE PLANS AFTER HIGH SCHOOL?

After high school, I plan to:

- ❐ Work full-time
- ❐ Work part-time and attend school
- ❐ Attend college full-time
- ❐ Attend technical college
- ❐ Enter the military

WHAT WILL YOU NEED TO GET WHERE YOU'RE GOING?

The information I have given indicates that I will be selecting courses that are primarily:

- ❐ College path (Four-year or two-year education that offers liberal arts courses combined with courses in your area of interest.)
- ❐ Vocational path (One or more years of education that include hands-on training for a specific job.)
- ❐ Combination of the two

MY PERFECT JOB WOULD BE ...

Let your imagination run wild You can have any job you want. What's it like? Start by describing to yourself the following job conditions:

Work conditions What hours are you willing to work? Do you feel most satisfied in an environment that is indoors/outdoors, varied/regular, noisy/quiet, or casual/traditional?

Duties What duties do you feel comfortable carrying out? Do you want to be a leader, or do you perform best as a team player?

People Do you want to work with other people or more independently? How much people contact do you want/need?

Education How much special training or education is required? How much education are you willing to seek? Can you build upon the education or experience you have to date? Will you need to gain new education or experience?

Benefits What salary and benefits do you expect? Are you willing to travel?

Disadvantages There are disadvantages with almost any job. Can you imagine what the disadvantages may be? Can you confirm or disprove these beliefs by talking to someone or researching the industry or job further? If these disadvantages really exist, can you live with them?

Personal qualities What qualities do you want in the employer you ultimately choose? What are the most important qualities that you want in a supervisor? In your coworkers?

Look over your responses to this assessment. Do you see recurring themes in your answers that start to show you what kind of career you might like? If not, there are many more places to get information to decide where your interests lie. You can go to your guidance counselor for advice. You can take the Campbell ™ Interest and Skills Inventory, the Strong Interest Inventory, the Self-Directed Search, or other assessment tests that your guidance counselor recommends.

3 Chapter

THE FIRST STEPS TO A CAREER

Don't be too surprised when your summer job turns into your career.

THE WORD "CAREER" has a scary sound to it when you're still in high school. Careers are for college graduates or those who have been in the workplace for years. But unless you grew up knowing for sure that you wanted to fly airplanes or be a botanist, what will you do? You'll be happy to know that interests you have now can very possibly lead to a college major or into a career. A job at a clothing store, for instance, could lead to a career designing clothes. Perhaps those hours you spend chasing Laura Croft, Tomb Raider, will lead to a career creating video games! Maybe you baby-sit and love being around kids, so teaching becomes an obvious choice. Perhaps cars fascinate you, and you find out you want to fix them for a living.

This chapter will show you how you can begin exploring your interests—sort of like getting into a swimming pool starting with your big toe, rather than plunging in. Vocational/career and tech-prep programs, summer jobs, and volunteering are all ways you can test various career paths to decide if you like them.

THE VOCATIONAL/CAREER EDUCATION PATH

If you're looking for a more real-world education, add yourself to the nearly 11 million youths and adults who are getting a taste of the workplace through vocational and career education programs offered in high schools across the nation. These programs are designed to help you develop competency in the skills you'll need in the workplace as well as in school.

What makes this kind of program different is that you learn in the classroom and in the "real world" of the workplace. Not only do you learn the academics in school, but you also get hands-on training by job shadowing, working under a mentor, and actually performing a job outside of school. Your interests and talents are usually taken into consideration, and you can choose from a variety of traditional, high-tech, and service industry training programs. Take a look at the following categories and see what piques your interest.

STUDENT COUNSEL

Q: What do you like about vocational training?

A: I jumped into the tech center my first year when I was a junior because I thought it was a good way to get out of school. But as the year went on, I said, "Hey, this is a good place to be because it's giving me job experience, and I'm learning how to dress and present myself like I was at a real job." I go during the first 3 or last 3 hours out of the school day. When we're in class, we get to do real jobs for people who ask our instructor for help. Then our teacher lets our creative minds go. We just designed a CD cover. One guy here designed a motorcycle and built it, and now he has three people asking him to come and work for them.

Trisha Younk
Tuscola County Tech Center
Reese High School
Reese, Michigan

Agricultural education. These programs prepare students for careers in agricultural production, animal production and care, agribusiness, agricultural and industrial mechanics, environmental management, farming, horticulture and landscaping, food processing, and natural resource management.

Business education. Students prepare for careers in accounting and finance and computer and data processing as well as administrative/secretarial and management/supervisory positions in professional environments (banking, insurance, law, public service).

Family and consumer sciences. These programs prepare students for careers in child care, food management and production, clothing and interiors, and hospitality and facility care. Core elements include personal development, family life and planning, resource management, and nutrition and wellness.

Trade and industrial and health occupations. Students prepare for careers in auto mechanics, the construction trades, cosmetology, electronics, graphics, public safety, and welding. Health occupation programs offer vocational training for careers in dental and medical assisting, practical nursing, home health care, and medical office assisting.

Marketing education. These programs prepare students for careers in sales, retail, advertising, food and restaurant marketing, and hotel management.

There are many vocational/career education programs available; the kinds listed above represent only a few of the possibilities. To find a program that suits your interests and that is located near you, refer to the college and university listings in the Appendix of this book. Or, you can get more information about vocational education programs by calling 202-245-7700 or e-mailing the U.S. Department of Education, Office of Vocational and Adult Education via its Web site, www.ed.gov/about/offices/list/ovae/index.html.

FROM THE GUIDANCE OFFICE

Q: What if going to college is not for me?

A: When adults ask kids what they want to do as a career, kids feel pressured. They think adults want them to identify with one single career. But there are more than 40,000 job titles a person can hold. We tell kids to pick a path first. When you exit high school, there are three paths you can take. One is to the workplace. One leads to the military as a career or as a stepping stone. The third leads to more education—a professional degree, a four-year degree, or a two-year degree. They have to determine which path they'll take.

One of the main selling points about getting career education in high school is that nearly every employer wants you to have some experience before you are hired. In career tech, students are in a workplace environment and can list their time as work experience, and they'll have previous employers who can vouch for them.

Lenore Lemanski
Counselor, Technology Center
Tuscola ISD
Caro, Michigan

THE TECH-PREP PATH

An even more advanced preparation for the workplace and/or an associate degree from a college is called tech-prep. It's an educational path that combines college-prep and vocational/technical courses of study.

During the sequence of courses, the focus is on blending academic and vocational/technical competencies. When you graduate from high school, you'll be able to jump right into the workforce or get an associate degree. But if you want to follow this path, you've got to plan for it starting in the ninth grade. Ask your guidance counselor for more information.

USING THE SUMMER TO YOUR ADVANTAGE

When you're sitting in class, a summer with nothing to do might seem appealing. But after you've listened to all of your CDs, aced all of your video games, hung out at the same old mall, and talked to your friends on the phone about being bored, what's left? How about windsurfing on a cool, clear New England lake? Horseback riding along breathtaking mountain trails? Parlez en français in Paris? Trekking through spectacular canyon lands or living with a family in Costa Rica, Spain, Switzerland, or Japan? Exploring college majors or possible careers? Helping out on an archeological dig or community-service project? Along the way, you'll meet some wonderful people and maybe even make a couple of lifelong friends.

Interested? Get ready to pack your bags and join the 1 million kids and teens who will be having the summer of a lifetime at thousands of terrific camps, academic programs, sports clinics, arts workshops, internships, volunteer opportunities, and travel adventures throughout North America and abroad.

Oh, you don't have the money, you say? Not to worry. There are programs to meet every budget, from $50 workshops to $4,500 world treks and sessions that vary in length from just a couple of hours to a couple of months.

For a list of summer opportunities, take a look at the Appendix in this book. You can also find out about summer opportunities by visiting www.petersons. com.

FROM THE GUIDANCE OFFICE

Q: What options are open to students who take high school career/technology classes and who feel they can't go to college?

A: Students have the opportunity to develop many skills through classes, student organizations, and career/technology classes during high school. These skills form an essential core that they can use to continue on to college, enter the job market, or participate in additional training after graduation. When students can identify those skills and make the connection by applying and expanding their skills as lifelong learners, then the possibilities are endless.

Linda S. Sanchez
Career and Technology Counselor
South San Antonio I.S.D.
Career Education Center
San Antonio, Texas

FLIP BURGERS AND LEARN ABOUT LIFE

A lot of teenagers who are anxious to earn extra cash spend their summers in retail or food service since those jobs are plentiful. If you're flipping burgers or helping customers find a special outfit, you might think the only thing you're getting out of the job is a paycheck. Think again. You will be amazed to discover that you have gained far more.

Being employed in these fields will teach you how to get along with demanding (and sometimes downright unpleasant) customers, how to work on a team, and how to handle money and order supplies. Not only do summer jobs teach you life skills, but they also offer ways to explore potential careers. What's more, when you apply to college or for a full-time job after high school graduation, the experience will look good on your application.

Sometimes, summer jobs become the very thing you want to do later in life. Before committing to a college major, summer jobs give you the opportunity to try out many directions. Students who think they want to be engineers, lawyers, or doctors might spend the summer shadowing an engineer, being a gofer in a legal firm, or volunteering in a hospital.

However, rather than grab the first job that comes along, find out where your interests are and build on what is natural for you. Activities you take for granted provide clues to what you are good at. What about that bookcase you built? Or those kids you love to baby-sit? Same thing with that big party you arranged. The environments you prefer provide other hints, too. Perhaps you feel best in the middle of a cluttered garage or surrounded by people. That suggests certain types of jobs.

Getting a summer job while in high school is the first step in a long line of work experiences to come. And the more experience you have, the better you'll be at getting jobs all your life.

TRY YOUR HAND AT AN INTERNSHIP

Each year, thousands of interns work in a wide variety of places, including corporations, law firms, government agencies, media organizations, interest groups, clinics, labs, museums, and historical sites. How popular are internships? Consider the recent trends. In the early 1980s, only 1 in 36 students completed an internship or other experiential learning program. Compare this to 2000, where one study found that 86 percent of college students had completed internships, with 69 percent reporting having had two or more. And an increasing number of high school students are signing up for internships now, too.

The Employer's Perspective

Employers consider internships a good option in both healthy and ailing economies. In healthy economies, managers often struggle to fill their positions with eager workers who can adapt to changing technologies. Internships offer a low-cost way to get good workers into "the pipeline" without offering them a full-time position up front. In struggling economies, on the other hand, downsizing often requires employers to lay off workers without thinking about who will cover their responsibilities. Internships offer an inexpensive way to offset position losses resulting from these disruptive layoffs.

The Intern's Perspective

If you are looking to begin a career or supplement your education with practical training, internships are a good bet for several reasons.

1. **Internships offer a relatively quick way to gain work experience and develop job skills.** Try this exercise. Scan the Sunday want ads of your newspaper. Choose a range of interesting advertisements for professional positions that you would consider taking. List the desired or required job skills and work experiences specified in the ads. How many of these skills and experiences do you have? Chances are, if you are still in school, you don't have most of the skills and experience that employers require of their new hires. What do you do?

   The growing reality is that many entry-level positions require skills and experiences that schools and part-time jobs don't provide. Sure, you know your way around a computer. You have some customer service experience. You may even have edited your school's newspaper or organized your junior prom. But you still lack the relevant skills and on-the-job experiences that many hiring managers require. A well-chosen internship can offer a way out of this common dilemma by providing you job training in an actual career field. Internships help you take your existing knowledge and skills and apply them in ways that will help you compete for good jobs.

2. **Internships offer a relatively risk-free way to explore a possible career path.** Believe it or not, the best internship may tell you what you *don't* want to do for the next ten or twenty years. Think about it. If you put all your eggs in one basket, what happens if your dream job turns out to be the exact opposite of what you want or who you are? Internships offer a relatively low-cost opportunity to "try out" a career field to see if it's right for *you.*

3. **Internships offer real opportunities to do career networking and can significantly increase your chances of landing a good full-time position.** Have you heard the saying: "It's not what you know, but who you know"? The reality is that who you know (or who knows you) can make a big difference in your job search. Studies show fewer than 20 percent of job placements occur through traditional application methods, including newspaper and trade journal advertisements, employment agencies, and career fairs. Instead, 60 to 90 percent of jobs are found through personal contacts and direct application.

Career networking is the exchange of information with others for mutual benefit. Your career network can tell you where the jobs are and help you compete for them. Isn't it better to develop your networking skills now, when the stakes aren't as high, than later when you are competing with everyone else for full-time jobs? The internship hiring process and the weeks you actually spend on the job provide excellent opportunities to talk with various people about careers, your skills, and ways to succeed.

VOLUNTEERING IN YOUR COMMUNITY

You've probably heard the saying that money isn't everything. Well, it's true, especially when it comes to volunteering and community service. There are a number of benefits you'll get that don't add up in dollars and cents but do add up to open doors in your future.

Community service looks good on a college application. Admissions staff members look for applicants who have volunteered and done community service in addition to grades. You could have gotten top grades, but if that's all that's on your application, you won't come across as a well-rounded person.

Community service lets you try out careers. How will you know you'll like a certain type of work if you haven't experienced it? For instance, you might think you want to work in the health-care field. Volunteering in a hospital will let you know if this is really what you want to do.

Community service is an American tradition. You'll be able to meet some of your own community's needs and join with all of the people who have contributed their talents to our country. No matter what your talents, there are unlimited ways for you to serve your community. Take a look at your interests, and then see how they can be applied to help others.

Here are some ideas to get you started:

- ❑ **Do you like kids?** Volunteer at your local parks and recreation department, for a Little League team, or as a big brother or sister.
- ❑ **Planning a career in health care?** Volunteer at a blood bank, clinic, hospital, retirement home, or hospice. There are also several organizations that raise money for disease research.
- ❑ **Interested in the environment?** Volunteer to assist in a recycling program. Create a beautification program for your school or community. Plant trees and flowers or design a community garden.
- ❑ **Just say no.** Help others stay off drugs and alcohol by volunteering at a crisis center, hotline, or prevention program. Help educate younger kids about the dangers of drug abuse.
- ❑ **Lend a hand.** Collect money, food, or clothing for the homeless. Food banks, homeless shelters, and charitable organizations need your help.
- ❑ **Is art your talent?** Share your knowledge and skills with youngsters, the elderly, or local arts organizations that depend on volunteers to help present their plays, recitals, and exhibitions.
- ❑ **Help fight crime.** Form a neighborhood watch or organize a group to clean up graffiti.
- ❑ **Your church or synagogue may have projects that need youth volunteers.** The United Way, your local politician's office, civic groups, and special interest organizations also provide exceptional opportunities to serve your community. Ask your principal, teachers, or counselors for additional ideas.

For more information on joining in the spirit of youth volunteerism, write to The Consumer Information Center, Dept. 501G, Pueblo, Colorado 81009, and request the *Catch the Spirit* booklet. Also check out the FCIC's Web site at www.pueblo.gsa.gov.

Part 3

THE ROAD TO MORE EDUCATION

SOME PEOPLE WAKE up at age three and announce that they want to be doctors, teachers, or marine biologists—and they do it.

They're the exceptions. Many high school students don't have a clue about what they want to be. They dread the question, "So, what are you going to do after graduation?" Unfortunately, some of those same people are also the ones who end up in careers that don't satisfy them.

You don't have to plan the rest of your life down to the last detail, but you can start to take some general steps toward your future and lay the groundwork. Then, when you do decide what you want to do, you'll be able to seize hold of your dream and go with it.

Chapter 4

PLANNING YOUR EDUCATION IN HIGH SCHOOL

Some people are planners. Then there are the non-planners. Either way, we've got a plan for you!

NON-PLANNERS see the words "plan" and "future" and say, "Yeah, yeah, I know." Meanwhile, they're running out the door for an appointment they were supposed to be at 5 minutes ago.

Unfortunately, when it comes time to really do something about those goals and future hopes, the non-planners often discover that much of what should have been done wasn't done—which is not good when they're planning their future after high school. What about those classes they should have taken? What about those jobs they should have volunteered for? What about that scholarship they could have had if only they'd found out about it sooner?

But there is hope for poor planners. Now that you've thought about yourself and the direction you might want to go after graduating, you can use this chapter to help you plan what you should be doing and when you should be doing it, while still in high school.

Regardless of what type of education you're pursuing after high school, here's a plan to help you get there.

YOUR EDUCATION TIMELINE

Use this timeline to help you make sure you're accomplishing everything you need to accomplish on time.

Ninth Grade

- As soon as you can, meet with your guidance counselor to begin talking about colleges and careers.
- Make sure you are enrolled in the appropriate college-preparatory or tech-prep courses.
- Get off to a good start with your grades. The grades you earn in ninth grade will be included in your final high school GPA and class rank.
- College might seem a long way off now, but grades really do count toward college admission and scholarships.
- Explore your interests and possible careers. Take advantage of Career Day opportunities.
- Get involved in extracurricular activities (both school and non-school-sponsored).
- Talk to your parents about planning for college expenses. Continue or begin a savings plan for college.
- Look at the college information available in your counselor's office and school and public libraries. Use the Internet to check out college Web sites. Visit Peterson's at www.petersons.com to start a list of colleges that might interest you.
- Tour a nearby college, if possible. Visit relatives or friends who live on or near a college campus. Check out the dorms, go to the library or student center, and get a feel for college life.

- Investigate summer enrichment programs. Visit www.petersons.com for some neat ideas about summer opportunities.

Tenth Grade

Fall

- In October, take the Preliminary SAT/National Merit Scholarship Qualifying Test (PSAT/NMSQT) for practice. When you fill out your test sheet, check the box that releases your name to colleges so you can start receiving brochures from them.
- Ask your guidance counselor about the American College Testing program's PLAN (Pre-ACT) assessment program, which helps determine your study habits and academic progress and interests. This test will prepare you for the ACT Assessment next year.
- Take geometry if you have not already done so. Take biology and a second year of a foreign language.
- Become familiar with general college entrance requirements.
- Participate in your school's or state's career development activities.

PARENT PERSPECTIVE

Q: When should parents and their children start thinking about preparing for college?

A: The discussion needs to start in middle school. If parents don't expose their children to these concepts at that time, then it can be too late in the game. Children need to take the right courses in high school. Many kids here end up going to junior colleges because they don't meet the minimum requirements when they graduate. Many universities and private colleges don't count some of the classes kids take in high school. You can't wait until the child is 18 and then say, "Maybe we should do something about getting into college."

Kevin Carr
Parent
Oak Park, California

- Visit Petersons.com for advice on test taking and general college entrance requirements.

Winter

- Discuss your PSAT score with your counselor.
- The people who read college applications aren't looking just for grades. Get involved in activities outside the classroom. Work toward leadership positions in the activities that you like best. Become involved in community service and other volunteer activities.
- Read, read, read. Read as many books as possible from a comprehensive reading list, like the one on pages 42 and 43.
- Read the newspaper every day to learn about current affairs.
- Work on your writing skills—you'll need them no matter what you do.
- Find a teacher or another adult who will advise and encourage you to write well.

Spring

- Keep your grades up so you can have the highest GPA and class rank possible.
- Ask your counselor about postsecondary enrollment options and Advanced Placement (AP) courses.
- Continue to explore your interests and careers that you think you might like.
- Begin zeroing in on the type of college you would prefer (two-year or four-year, small or large, rural or urban). To get an idea of what's available, take a look at college profiles on Petersons.com.
- If you are interested in attending a military academy such as West Point or Annapolis, now is the time to start planning and getting information.
- Write to colleges and ask for their academic requirements for admission.

- Visit a few more college campuses. Read all of the mail you receive from colleges. You may see something you like.
- Attend college fairs.
- Keep putting money away for college. Get a summer job.
- Consider taking SAT Subject Tests in the courses you took this year while the material is still fresh in your mind. These tests are offered in May and June.

Eleventh Grade

Fall

- Meet with your counselor to review the courses you've taken, and see what you still need to take.
- Check your class rank. Even if your grades haven't been that good so far, it's never too late to improve. Colleges like to see an upward trend.
- If you didn't do so in tenth grade, sign up for and take the PSAT/NMSQT. In addition to National Merit Scholarships, this is the qualifying test for the National Scholarship Service and Fund for Negro Students and the National Hispanic Recognition Program.
- Make sure that you have a social security number.
- Take a long, hard look at why you want to continue your education after high school so you will be able to choose the best college or university for your needs.
- Make a list of colleges that meet your most important criteria (size, location, distance from home, majors, academic rigor, housing, and cost). Weigh each of the factors according to their importance to you.
- Continue visiting college fairs. You may be able to narrow your choices or add a college to your list.

PARENT PERSPECTIVE

Q: How involved should parents get in the selection of a college for their children?

A: Parents are getting more involved than ever before in supporting their children in the college process. This phenomenon is due to two factors:

(1) This generation of parents has been much more involved with their children in dealing with the outside world than were their parents.

(2) The investment made by today's parents is much more than that made by parents 20 or 30 years ago. As parents focus on the cost of this big-ticket item, there's interest to be more involved, to get the proper return.

Parents certainly should be involved in the college selection and application process. Studies clearly indicate that parental support in this process and throughout the college years can make a big difference in the success of a student. But this process also should be a learning opportunity in decision making for students. In that regard, parents shouldn't direct the student but provide input and the framework to assist their students.

Parents should not feel uncomfortable making suggestions to help their children through the thought and selection process—especially when it comes to identifying schools that their pocketbooks can accommodate. However, the child must be comfortable with the final decision and must have ultimate responsibility for the selection of the school. When students have made the final decision, it can help in their level of commitment because they've invested in it. They have a responsibility to do well and complete their academics at that location.

Richard Flaherty
President, College Parents of America

- Speak to college representatives who visit your high school.
- If you want to participate in Division I or Division II sports in college, start the certification process. Check with your counselor to make sure you are taking a core curriculum that meets NCAA requirements.
- If you are interested in one of the military academies, talk to your guidance counselor about starting the application process now.

6 STUDY SKILLS THAT LEAD TO SUCCESS

1. **SET A REGULAR STUDY SCHEDULE. No one at college is going to hound you to do your homework. Develop the study patterns in high school that will lead to success in college. Anyone who has ever pulled an all-nighter knows how much you remember when you are on the downside of your fifth cup of coffee and no sleep—not much! Nothing beats steady and consistent study habits.**
2. **SAVE EVERYTHING. To make sure your history notes don't end up in your math notebook and your English papers don't get thrown at the bottom of your friend's locker, develop an organized system for storing your papers. Stay on top of your materials, and be sure to save quizzes and tests. It is amazing how questions from a test you took in March can miraculously reappear on your final exam.**
3. **LISTEN. Teachers give away what will be on the test by repeating themselves. If you pay attention to what the teacher is saying, you will probably notice what is being emphasized. If what the teacher says in class repeats itself in your notes and in review sessions, chances are that material will be on the test. So really listen.**
4. **TAKE NOTES. If the teacher has taken the time to prepare a lecture, then what he or she says is important enough for you to write down. Develop a system for reviewing your notes. After each class, rewrite them, review them, or reread them. Try highlighting the important points or making notes in the margins to jar your memory.**
5. **USE TEXTBOOKS WISELY. What can you do with a textbook besides lose it? Use it to back up or clarify information that you don't understand from your class notes. Reading every word may be more effort than it is worth, so look at the book intelligently. What is in boxes or highlighted areas? What content is emphasized? What do the questions ask about in the review sections?**
6. **FORM A STUDY GROUP. Establish a group that will stay on task and ask one another the questions you think the teacher will ask. Compare notes to see if you have all the important facts. And discuss your thoughts. Talking ideas out can help when you have to respond to an essay question.**

Winter

- Collect information about college application procedures, entrance requirements, tuition and fees, room and board costs, student activities, course offerings, faculty composition, accreditation, and financial aid. The Internet is a good way to visit colleges and obtain this information. Begin comparing the schools by the factors that you consider to be most important.
- Discuss your PSAT score with your counselor.
- Begin narrowing down your college choices. Find out if the colleges you are interested in require the SAT, ACT Assessment, or SAT Subject Tests for admission.
- Register for the SAT and additional SAT Subject Tests, which are offered several times during the winter and spring of your junior year (see the "Tackling the Tests" chapter for a schedule). You can take them again in the fall of your senior year if you are unhappy with your scores.
- Register for the ACT Assessment, which is usually taken in April or June. You can take it again late in your junior year or in the fall of your senior year, if necessary.
- Begin preparing for the tests you've decided to take.
- Have a discussion with your parents about the colleges in which you are interested. Examine financial resources, and gather information about financial aid. Check out the "Financial Aid Dollars and Sense" chapter for a step-by-step explanation of the financial aid process.
- Set up a filing system with individual folders for each college's correspondence and printed materials.

Spring

- Meet with your counselor to review senior-year course selection and graduation requirements.
- Discuss ACT Assessment/SAT scores with your counselor. Register to take the ACT Assessment and/or SAT again if you'd like to try to improve your score.
- Discuss the college essay with your guidance counselor or English teacher.
- Stay involved with your extracurricular activities. Colleges look for consistency and depth in activities.

- Consider whom you will ask to write your recommendations. Think about asking teachers who know you well and who will write positive letters about you. Letters from a coach, activity leader, or an adult who knows you well outside of school (e.g., volunteer work contact) are also valuable.
- Inquire about personal interviews at your favorite colleges. Call or write for early summer appointments. Make necessary travel arrangements.
- See your counselor to apply for on-campus summer programs for high school students. Apply for a summer job or internship. Be prepared to pay for college applications and testing fees in the fall.
- Request applications from schools you're interested in by mail or via the Internet.

Summer

- Visit the campuses of your top-five college choices.
- After each college interview, send a thank-you letter to the interviewer.
- Talk to people you know who have attended the colleges in which you are interested.
- Continue to read books, magazines, and newspapers.
- Practice filling out college applications, and then complete the final application forms or apply on line through the Web sites of the colleges in which you're interested.
- Volunteer in your community.
- Compose rough drafts of your college essays. Have a teacher read and discuss them with you. Polish them, and prepare final drafts. Proofread your final essays at least three times.
- Develop a financial aid application plan, including a list of the aid sources, requirements for each application, and a timetable for meeting the filing deadlines.

ADMISSIONS ADVICE

Q: Other than grades and test scores, what are the most important qualities that you look for in students?

A: We consider the types of classes students have taken. A grade of a B in an honors class is competitive to an A in a regular course. We seek not only academically talented students but those who are well rounded. They need to submit their interests and activities, letters of recommendation, and writing samples in addition to their test scores. We look for someone that's involved in his or her community and high school, someone that holds leadership positions and has a balance of activities outside of academics. This gives us a look at that person as a whole.

Cheyenna Smith
Admission Counselor
University of Houston
Houston, Texas

Twelfth Grade

Fall

- Continue to take a full course load of college-prep courses.
- Keep working on your grades. Make sure you have taken the courses necessary to graduate in the spring.
- Continue to participate in extracurricular and volunteer activities. Demonstrate initiative, creativity, commitment, and leadership in each.
- To male students: you must register for selective service on your eighteenth birthday to be eligible for federal and state financial aid.
- Talk to counselors, teachers, and parents about your final college choices.
- Make a calendar showing application deadlines for admission, financial aid, and scholarships.
- Check resource books, Web sites, and your guidance office for information on scholarships and grants. Ask colleges about scholarships for which you may qualify. Check out Petersons.com for information on scholarships.

- Give recommendation forms to the teachers you have chosen, along with stamped, self-addressed envelopes so your teachers can send them directly to the colleges. Be sure to fill out your name, address, and school name on the top of the form. Talk to your recommendation writers about your goals and ambitions.
- Give School Report forms to your high school's guidance office. Fill in your name, address, and any other required information. Verify with your guidance counselor the schools to which transcripts, test scores, and letters are to be sent. Give your counselor any necessary forms at least two weeks before they are due or whenever your counselor's deadline is, whichever is earlier.
- Register for and take the ACT Assessment, SAT, or SAT Subject Tests, as necessary.
- Be sure you have requested (either by mail or on line) that your test scores be sent to the colleges of your choice.
- Mail or send electronically any college applications for early decision admission by November 1.
- If possible, visit colleges while classes are in session.
- If you plan to apply for an ROTC scholarship, remember that your application is due by December 1.
- Print extra copies or make photocopies of every application you send.

Winter

- Attend whatever college-preparatory nights are held at your school or by local organizations.
- Send midyear grade reports to colleges. Continue to focus on your schoolwork!
- Fill out the Free Application for Federal Student Aid (FAFSA) and, if necessary, the PROFILE®. These forms can be obtained from your guidance counselor or at www.fafsa.ed.gov/ to download the forms or to file electronically. These forms may not be processed before January 1, so don't send them before then.
- Mail or send electronically any remaining applications and financial aid forms before winter break. Make sure you apply to at least one college that you know you can afford and where you know you will be accepted.
- Follow up to make sure that the colleges have received all application information, including recommendations and test scores.
- Meet with your counselor to verify that all forms are in order and have been sent out to colleges.

Spring

- Watch your mail between March 1 and April 1 for acceptance notifications from colleges.
- Watch your mail for notification of financial aid awards between April 1 and May 1.
- Compare the financial aid packages from the colleges and universities that have accepted you.
- Make your final choice, and notify all schools of your intent by May 1. If possible, do not decide without making at least one campus visit. Send your nonrefundable deposit to your chosen school by May 1 as well. Request that your guidance counselor send a final transcript to the college in June.
- Be sure that you have received a FAFSA acknowledgment.
- If you applied for a Pell Grant (on the FAFSA), you will receive a Student Aid Report (SAR) statement. Review this notice, and forward it to the college you plan to attend. Make a copy for your records.
- Complete follow-up paperwork for the college of your choice (scheduling, orientation session, housing arrangements, and other necessary forms).

Summer

- If applicable, apply for a Stafford Loan through a lender. Allow eight weeks for processing.
- Receive the orientation schedule from your college.
- Get residence hall assignment from your college.
- Obtain course scheduling and cost information from your college.
- Congratulations! You are about to begin the greatest adventure of your life. Good luck.

CLASSES TO TAKE IF YOU'RE GOING TO COLLEGE

Did you know that classes you take as early as the ninth grade will help you get into college? Make sure you take at least the minimum high school curriculum requirements necessary for college admission. Even if you don't plan to enter college immediately, take the most demanding courses you can handle.

Review the list of Suggested Courses on this page. Some courses, categories, and names vary from state to state, but this list may be used as a guideline. Talk with your guidance counselor to select the curriculum that best meets your needs and skills.

Of course, learning also occurs outside of school. While outside activities will not make up for poor academic performance, skills learned from jobs, extracurricular activities, and volunteer opportunities will help you become a well-rounded student and will strengthen your college or job application.

SUGGESTED COURSES

College-Preparatory Curriculum

ENGLISH. **Four units, with emphasis on composition (English 9, 10, 11, 12)**

MATHEMATICS. **Three units (algebra I, algebra II, geometry) are essential; trigonometry, precalculus, calculus, and computer science are recommended for some fields of study**

SOCIAL SCIENCE. **Three units (American history, world history, government/economics)**

SCIENCE. **Four units (earth science, biology, chemistry, physics)**

FOREIGN LANGUAGE. **Three units (at least 2 years in the same language)**

FINE ARTS. **One to 2 units**

OTHER. **Keyboarding, computer applications, computer science I, computer science II, physical education, health**

College-Preparatory Curriculum Combined with a Career Education or Vocational Program

ENGLISH. **Four units**

MATHEMATICS. **Three units (algebra I, algebra II, geometry)**

SOCIAL SCIENCE. **Three units (American history, world history, government/economics)**

SCIENCE. **Two units (earth science, biology)**

FOREIGN LANGUAGE. **Three units (at least 2 years in the same language)**

FINE ARTS. **One to 2 units**

OTHER. **Keyboarding, computer applications, physical education, and health and half-days at the Career Center during junior and senior years**

Getting a Head Start on College Courses

You can take college courses while still in high school so that when you're in college, you'll be ahead of everyone else. The formal name is postsecondary enrollment. (In Texas, the formal names are dual credit—academic credit and articulated credit—career and technology credit.) What it means is that some students can take college courses and receive both high school and college credit for the courses taken. It's like a two-for-one deal!

Postsecondary enrollment is designed to provide an opportunity for qualified high school students to experience more advanced academic work. Participation in a postsecondary enrollment program is not intended to replace courses available in high school but rather to enhance the educational opportunities available to students while in high school. There are two options for postsecondary enrollment:

Option A: Qualified high school juniors and seniors take courses for college credit. Students enrolled under Option A must pay for all books, supplies, tuition, and associated fees.

Option B: Qualified high school juniors and seniors take courses for high school and college credit. For students enrolled under this option, the local school district covers the related costs, provided that the student completes the selected courses. Otherwise, the student and parent will be assessed the costs.

Certain preestablished conditions must be met for enrollment, so check with your high school counselor for more information.

SUGGESTED READING LIST FOR GRADES 9 THROUGH 12

Instead of flipping on the TV or putting on those headphones, how about picking up a book instead? Reading not only will take you to wonderful, unexplored worlds through your imagination, but there are practical gains as well. Reading gives you a more well-rounded background. College admissions and future employers pick up on that. And you'll be able to answer the questions, "Did you read that book? What did you think of it?" How many of the books on this list have you read?

Adams, Richard
Watership Down
Aesop
Fables
Agee, James
A Death in the Family
Anderson, Sherwood
Winesburg, Ohio
Anonymous
Go Ask Alice
Asimov, Isaac
Short Stories
Austen, Jane
Emma
Northanger Abbey
Pride and Prejudice
Sense and Sensibility
Baldwin, James
Go Tell It on the Mountain
Balzac, Honore de
Pere Goriot
Beckett, Samuel
Waiting for Godot
Bolt, Robert
A Man for All Seasons
Brontë, Charlotte
Jane Eyre
Brontë, Emily
Wuthering Heights
Brooks, Gwendolyn
In the Mecca
Riot
Browning, Robert
Poems
Buck, Pearl
The Good Earth
Butler, Samuel
The Way of All Flesh
Camus, Albert
The Plague
The Stranger
Cather, Willa
Death Comes for the Archbishop
My Antonia
Cervantes, Miguel
Don Quixote
Chaucer, Geoffrey
The Canterbury Tales
Chekhov, Anton
The Cherry Orchard
Chopin, Kate
The Awakening
Collins, Wilkie
The Moonstone
Conrad, Joseph
Heart of Darkness
Lord Jim
The Secret Sharer
Victory
Crane, Stephen
The Red Badge of Courage
Dante
The Divine Comedy
Defoe, Daniel
Moll Flanders
Dickens, Charles
Bleak House
David Copperfield
Great Expectations
Hard Times
Oliver Twist
A Tale of Two Cities
Dickinson, Emily
Poems
Dinesen, Isak
Out of Africa
Dostoevski, Fyodor
The Brothers Karamazov
Crime and Punishment
Douglas, Frederick
The Life of Frederick Douglas
Dreiser, Theodore
An American Tragedy
Sister Carrie
Early, Gerald
Tuxedo Junction
Eliot, George
Adam Bede
Middlemarch
The Mill on the Floss
Silas Marner
Eliot, T. S.
Murder in the Cathedral
Ellison, Ralph
Invisible Man
Emerson, Ralph Waldo
Essays
Faulkner, William
Absalom, Absalom!
As I Lay Dying
Intruder in the Dust
Light in August
The Sound and the Fury
Fielding, Henry
Joseph Andrews
Tom Jones
Fitzgerald, F. Scott
The Great Gatsby
Tender Is the Night
Flaubert, Gustave
Madame Bovary
Forster, E. M.
A Passage to India
A Room with a View
Franklin, Benjamin
The Autobiography of Benjamin Franklin
Galsworthy, John
The Forsyte Saga
Golding, William
Lord of the Flies
Goldsmith, Oliver
She Stoops to Conquer
Graves, Robert
I, Claudius
Greene, Graham
The Heart of the Matter
The Power and the Glory
Hamilton, Edith
Mythology
Hardy, Thomas
Far from the Madding Crowd
Jude the Obscure
The Mayor of Casterbridge
The Return of the Native
Tess of the D'Urbervilles
Hawthorne, Nathaniel
The House of the Seven Gables
The Scarlet Letter
Hemingway, Ernest
A Farewell to Arms
For Whom the Bell Tolls
The Sun Also Rises
Henry, O.
Stories
Hersey, John
A Single Pebble
Hesse, Hermann
Demian
Siddhartha
Steppenwolf
Homer
The Iliad
The Odyssey
Hughes, Langston
Poems
The Big Sea
Hugo, Victor
Les Misérables
Huxley, Aldous
Brave New World
Ibsen, Henrik
A Doll's House
An Enemy of the People
Ghosts
Hedda Gabler
The Master Builder
The Wild Duck
James, Henry
The American
Daisy Miller
Portrait of a Lady
The Turn of the Screw
Joyce, James
Dubliners
A Portrait of the Artist as a Young Man

Kafka, Franz
- *The Castle*
- *The Metamorphosis*
- *The Trial*

Keats, John
- *Poems*

Kerouac, Jack
- *On the Road*

Koestler, Arthur
- *Darkness at Noon*

Lawrence, Jerome, and Robert E. Lee
- *Inherit the Wind*

Lewis, Sinclair
- *Arrowsmith*
- *Babbitt*
- *Main Street*

Llewellyn, Richard
- *How Green Was My Valley*

Machiavelli
- *The Prince*

MacLeish, Archibald
- *J.B.*

Mann, Thomas
- *Buddenbrooks*
- *The Magic Mountain*

Marlowe, Christopher
- *Dr. Faustus*

Maugham, Somerset
- *Of Human Bondage*

McCullers, Carson
- *The Heart Is a Lonely Hunter*

Melville, Herman
- *Billy Budd*
- *Moby-Dick*
- *Typee*

Miller, Arthur
- *The Crucible*
- *Death of a Salesman*

Monsarrat, Nicholas
- *The Cruel Sea*

Naylor, Gloria
- *Bailey's Cafe*
- *The Women of Brewster Place*

O'Neill, Eugene
- *The Emperor Jones*
- *Long Day's Journey Into Night*
- *Mourning Becomes Electra*

Orwell, George
- *Animal Farm*
- *1984*

Pasternak, Boris
- *Doctor Zhivago*

Poe, Edgar Allan
- *Short Stories*

Remarque, Erich
- *All Quiet on the Western Front*

Rolvaag, O. E.
- *Giants in the Earth*

Rostand, Edmond
- *Cyrano de Bergerac*

Salinger, J. D.
- *The Catcher in the Rye*

Sandburg, Carl
- *Abraham Lincoln: The Prairie Years*
- *Abraham Lincoln: The War Years*

Saroyan, William
- *The Human Comedy*

Sayers, Dorothy
- *The Nine Tailors*

Shakespeare, William
- *Plays and Sonnets*

Shaw, George Bernard
- *Arms and the Man*
- *Major Barbara*
- *Pygmalion*
- *Saint Joan*

Sheridan, Richard B.
- *The School for Scandal*

Shute, Nevil
- *On the Beach*

Sinclair, Upton
- *The Jungle*

Sophocles
- *Antigone*
- *Oedipus Rex*

Steinbeck, John
- *East of Eden*
- *The Grapes of Wrath*
- *Of Mice and Men*

Stowe, Harriet Beecher
- *Uncle Tom's Cabin*

Swift, Jonathan
- *Gulliver's Travels*

Thackeray, William M.
- *Vanity Fair*

Thoreau, Henry David
- *Walden*

Tolstoy, Leo
- *Anna Karenina*
- *War and Peace*

Trollope, Anthony
- *Barchester Towers*

Turgenev, Ivan
- *Fathers and Sons*

Twain, Mark
- *Pudd'nhead Wilson*

Updike, John
- *Rabbit, Run*

Vergil
- *The Aeneid*

Voltaire
- *Candide*

Walker, Alice
- *The Color Purple*
- *Meridian*

Warren, Robert Penn
- *All the King's Men*

Waugh, Evelyn
- *Brideshead Revisited*
- *A Handful of Dust*

Wharton, Edith
- *The Age of Innocence*

White, T. H.
- *The Once and Future King*
- *The Sword in the Stone*

Wilde, Oscar
- *The Importance of Being Earnest*
- *The Picture of Dorian Gray*

Wilder, Thornton
- *Our Town*

Williams, Tennessee
- *The Glass Menagerie*
- *A Streetcar Named Desire*

Wolfe, Thomas
- *Look Homeward, Angel*

Woolf, Virginia
- *Mrs. Dalloway*
- *To the Lighthouse*

Wouk, Herman
- *The Caine Mutiny*

Wright, Richard
- *Black Boy*
- *Native Sun*

Source: The National Endowment for the Humanities.

For more book recommendations, see what college professors suggest in **ARCO Reading Lists for College-Bound Students***, available at your local bookstore.*

5 Chapter

TACKLING THE TESTS

Unless you've been on another planet for the last two or three years, you've probably heard older high school students buzzing about the alphabet soup list of college entrance exams—SAT, ACT Assessment, and PSAT.

SOME OF THE STUDENTS who are getting ready to take one of these tests look like they're in various states of hysteria. Others have been studying for months on end, so when they open their mouths, out pops the definition for "meretricious" or the answer to "What is the ratio of 3 pounds to 6 ounces?" Well, the talk that you've heard about the tests is partly true. They are a big deal and can be crucial to your academic plans. On the other hand, you don't have to walk in cold. Remember that word "planning"? It's a whole lot nicer than the word "panic." Preparing for the tests takes a lot of planning and time, but if you're reading this chapter, you're already ahead of the game.

A FEW FACTS ABOUT THE MAJOR TESTS

The major standardized tests students take in high school are the PSAT, SAT, and ACT Assessment. Colleges across the country use them to get a sense of a student's readiness to enter their ivy-covered halls. These tests, or "boards" as they are sometimes called, have become notorious because of how important they can be. There is a mystique that surrounds them. People talk about the "magic number" that will get you into the school of your dreams.

Beware! There is a lot of misinformation out there. First and foremost, these are not intelligence tests; they are reasoning tests designed to evaluate the way you think. These tests assess the basic knowledge and skills you have gained through your classes in school, and they also gauge the knowledge you have gained through outside experience. The material on these tests is not curriculum-based, but the tests do emphasize those academic experiences that educational institutions feel are good indicators of your probable success in college.

THE ACT ASSESSMENT

The ACT Assessment is a standardized college entrance examination that measures knowledge and skills in English, mathematics, reading, and science reasoning and the application of these skills to future academic tasks. The ACT Assessment consists of four multiple-choice tests.

Test 1: English

- 75 questions, 45 minutes
- Usage and mechanics
- Rhetorical skills

Test 2: Mathematics

- 60 questions, 60 minutes
- Arithmetic
- Elementary algebra
- Intermediate algebra
- Coordinate geometry
- Plane geometry
- Trigonometry

Test 3: Reading

- 40 questions, 35 minutes
- Prose fiction
- Humanities
- Social studies
- Natural sciences

Test 4: Science Reasoning

- 40 questions, 35 minutes
- Data representation
- Research summary
- Conflicting viewpoint

Each section is scored from 1 to 36 and is scaled for slight variations in difficulty. Students are not penalized for incorrect responses. The composite score is the average of the four scaled scores. With the 2004–05 school year, an optional writing component was added to the ACT Assessment.

To prepare for the ACT Assessment, ask your guidance counselor for a free guidebook called *Preparing for the ACT Assessment*. Besides providing general test-preparation information and additional test-taking strategies, this guidebook describes the content and format of the four ACT Assessment subject area tests, summarizes test administration procedures followed at ACT Assessment test centers, and includes a practice test.

STUDENT COUNSEL

Q: What kept you from stressing out about the tests?

A: The best way I found to prepare was to take practice tests to get to know the questions. At first, I'd set the kitchen timer and practice while ignoring the time, just to see what I could do. Practice is the best because they don't really change the type of questions. You read that in every review book, and it's true.

My advice for dealing with the stress on test day? The night before, I watched movies and had popcorn. When you take the test, definitely bring candy. A candy bar in between each section helps.

Theresa-Marie Russo
Edgemont High School
Scarsdale, New York

THE SAT

The SAT measures developed verbal and mathematical reasoning abilities as they relate to successful performance in college. It is intended to supplement the secondary school record and other information about the student in assessing readiness for college. There is one unscored, experimental section on the exam, which is used for equating and/or pretesting purposes and can cover either the mathematics or verbal subject area.

Critical Reading

- 67 questions, 70 minutes
- Sentence completions
- Passages with questions

Math

- 54 questions, 70 minutes
- Multiple choice
- Student-produced responses (grid-ins)

Writing

- 49 questions plus essay, 70 minutes
- Identifying sentence errors
- Improving paragraphs
- Improving sentences
- Essay

Experimental Section

- 15 minutes

Students receive one point for each correct response and lose a fraction of a point for each incorrect response (except for student-produced responses).

WHICH SHOULD I TAKE? THE ACT ASSESSMENT VS. THE SAT

It's not a bad idea to take both. This assures that you will have the test scores required for admission to all schools, because some colleges accept the results of one test and not the other. Some institutions use test results for proper placement of students in English and math courses.

You should take the ACT Assessment and SAT during the spring of your junior year, if not earlier. This enables you to retake the test in the fall of your senior year if you're not satisfied with your scores. Also, this makes it possible for institutions to receive all test scores before the end of January. Institutions generally consider the better score when determining admission and placement. Because most scholarship applications are processed between December and April of the senior year, your best score results can then be included in the application.

These points are totaled to produce the raw scores, which are then scaled to equalize the scores for slight variations in difficulty for various editions of the test. The critical reading, writing, and math scaled scores range from 200–800 per section. The total scaled score range is from 600–2400.

To prepare for the SAT, you should carefully review the pamphlet, *Taking the SAT: Reasoning Test*, which you should be able to get from your guidance counselor. Also, most libraries and bookstores stock a large selection of material about the SAT and other standardized tests.

THE PSAT/NMSQT

The Preliminary SAT/National Merit Scholarship Qualifying Test, better known as the PSAT/NMSQT, is a practice test for the SAT. Many students take the PSAT more than once because scores tend to increase with repetition and because it allows students to become more comfortable with taking standardized tests. During the junior year, the PSAT is also used as a qualifying test for the National Merit Scholarship Program and the National Scholarship Service and Fund for Negro Students. It is also used in designating students for the National Hispanic Scholar Recognition Program. The PSAT includes a writing skills section, which consists entirely of multiple-choice questions. There is, however, no essay section on the PSAT.

Critical Reasoning

- Approximately 80 questions, two 25-minute sections
- Sentence completions
- Critical reading passages

Math

- 56 questions, two 25-minute sections
- Multiple choice
- Grid-in

Writing Skills

- 33 questions, one 30-minute section
- Identifying sentence errors
- Improving sentences
- Improving paragraphs

Students receive a score in each content area (verbal, math, and writing). Each score ranges from 20 to 80 and is totaled with the others for the combined score. The total score ranges from 60 to 240.

RECOMMENDED TEST-TAKING DATES

Sophomore Year	
October	PSAT/NMSQT and PLAN (for practice, planning, and preparation)
May–June	SAT Subject Tests (if necessary)
Junior Year	
October	PSAT/NMSQT (for the National Merit Scholarship Program and practice)
January–June	ACT Assessment and/or SAT, SAT Subject Tests (if necessary—for college admission)
Senior Year	
October–December	ACT Assessment and/or SAT, SAT Subject Tests (if necessary—for college

Selection Index (used for National Merit Scholarship purposes)

- Verbal + Math + Writing
- Score Range: 60 to 240
- Mean Junior Score: 147

National Merit Scholarship Program

- Semifinalist Status: Selection Index of 201 to 222
- Commended Student: Selection Index of 199

SAT SUBJECT TESTS

Subject Tests are required by some institutions for admission and/or placement in freshman-level courses. Each Subject Test measures one's knowledge of a specific subject and the ability to apply that knowledge. Students should check with each institution for its specific requirements. In general, students are required to take three Subject Tests (one English, one mathematics, and one of their choice).

Subject Tests are given in the following areas: biology, chemistry, Chinese, English language proficiency, French, German, Italian, Japanese, Korean, Latin, literature, mathematics, modern Hebrew, physics, Spanish, U.S. history, and world history. These tests are 1 hour long and are primarily multiple-choice tests. Three Subject Tests may be taken on one test date.

Scored like the SAT, students gain a point for each correct answer and lose a fraction of a point for each incorrect answer. The raw scores are then converted to scaled scores that range from 200 to 800.

THE TOEFL TEST

The Test of English as a Foreign Language (TOEFL) is designed to help assess a student's grasp of English if it is not the student's first language. Performance on the TOEFL test may help interpret scores on the verbal section of the SAT. The test consists of four sections: listening, structure, reading, and a writing section. The computer-based test and the paper-based test are given at more than 1,260 centers in 180 countries and are administered by Educational Testing Service (ETS). For further information, visit www.toefl.org.

WHAT OTHER TESTS SHOULD I KNOW ABOUT?

The AP Program

This program allows high school students to try college-level work and build valuable skills and study habits in the process. Subject matter is explored in more depth in AP courses than in other high school classes. A qualifying score on an AP test—which varies from school to school—can earn you college credit or advanced placement. Getting qualifying grades on enough exams can even earn you a full year's credit and sophomore standing at more than 1,400 higher-education institutions. There are

ADMISSIONS ADVICE

Q: What can students who don't have the best grades do to improve their chances of getting into the college of their choice?

A: We encourage students to take the SAT or ACT Assessment more than once and see how they do. There are options for students who may not meet the academic requirements because they've had to work or are gifted in other areas, such as art or athletics, or who perhaps have been through something tragic. We ask them to submit letters or recommendations, a personal statement, and any other documentation that might help support their cases. What were the factors that affected their grades? What else can they offer the university?

We often encourage students who still may not meet the requirements to start at a community college and then transfer. We'll look at their college credit vs. their high school credit. They can prove to us that they can handle a college curriculum.

Cheyenna Smith
Admission Counselor
University of Houston

currently thirty-four AP courses in nineteen different subject areas, including art, biology, and computer science. Speak to your guidance counselor for information about your school's offerings.

College-Level Examination Program (CLEP)

The CLEP enables students to earn college credit for what they already know, whether it was learned in school, through independent study, or through other experiences outside of the classroom. Approximately 2,900 colleges and universities now award credit for qualifying scores on one or more of the 34 CLEP exams. The exams, which are 90 minutes in length and are primarily multiple choice, are administered at participating colleges and universities. For more information, check out the Web site at www.collegeboard.com/clep.

Armed Services Vocational Aptitude Battery (ASVAB)

ASVAB is a career exploration program consisting of a multi-aptitude test battery that helps students explore their interests, abilities, and personal preferences. A career exploration workbook gives students information about the workplace, and a career information resource book helps students match their personal characteristics to the working world. Finally, an occupational outlook handbook describes in detail approximately 250 civilian and military occupations. Students can use ASVAB scores for military enlistment up to two years after they take the test. A student can take the ASVAB as a sophomore, junior, or senior, but students cannot use their sophomore scores to enter the armed forces. Ask your guidance counselor or your local recruiting office for more information. Also, see Chapter 11, "The Military Option."

General Educational Development (GED) Test

If you have not completed your high school education, you may earn an equivalence by taking the GED test, sponsored by your state Department of Education. However, taking the GED test is not a legitimate reason for dropping out of school. In fact, it is more difficult to get into the armed services with only a GED, and some employees have difficulty getting promoted without a high school diploma.

You're eligible to take the GED if you are not enrolled in high school, have not yet graduated from high school, are at least 16 years old, and meet your local requirements regarding age, residency, and length of time since leaving school.

There are five sections to the GED test, covering writing skills, social studies, science, interpreting literature and the arts, and mathematics. Part II of the Writing Skills Test requires writing an essay. The GED costs an average of $35 but can vary from state to state, and the application fee may be waived under certain circumstances. You should contact your local GED office to arrange to take the exam. Call 800-62-MYGED to find your local GED office and for more information.

WHAT CAN I DO TO PREPARE FOR THESE TESTS?

Know what to expect. Get familiar with how the tests are structured, how much time is allowed, and the directions for each type of question. Get plenty of rest the night before the test and eat breakfast that morning.

There are a variety of products, from books to software to videos, available to help you prepare for most standardized tests. Find the learning style that suits you best. As for which products to buy, there are two major categories—those created by the test makers and those created by private companies. The best approach is to talk to someone who has been through the process and find out which product or products he or she recommends.

Some students report significant increases in scores after participating in coaching programs. Longer-term programs (40 hours) seem to raise scores more than short-term programs (20 hours), but beyond 40 hours, score gains are minor. Math scores appear to benefit more from coaching than verbal scores.

Preparation Resources

There are a variety of ways to prepare for standardized tests—find a method that fits your schedule and your budget. But you should definitely prepare. Far too many students walk into these tests cold, either because they find standardized tests frightening or annoying or they just haven't found the time to study. The key is that these exams are standardized. That means these tests are largely the same from administration to administration; they always test the same concepts. They have to, or else you couldn't compare the scores of people who took the tests on different dates. The numbers or words may change, but the underlying content doesn't.

So how do you prepare? At the very least, you should review relevant material, such as math formulas and commonly tested vocabulary words, and know the directions for each question type or test section. You should take at least one practice test and review your mistakes so you don't make them again on test day. Beyond that, you know best how much preparation you need. You'll also find lots of material in libraries or bookstores to help you: books and software from the test makers and from other publishers (including Peterson's) or live courses that range from national test-preparation companies to teachers at your high school who offer classes. Peterson's interactive and personalized SAT Online Course at www.petersonstestprep.com is another resource you'll want to check out.

THE TOP 10 WAYS *NOT* TO TAKE THE TEST

10. **Cramming the night before the test.**
9. **Not becoming familiar with the directions before you take the test.**
8. **Not becoming familiar with the format of the test before you take it.**
7. **Not knowing how the test is graded.**
6. **Spending too much time on any one question.**
5. **Not checking spelling, grammar, and sentence structure in essays.**
4. **Second-guessing yourself.**
3. **Forgetting to take a deep breath to keep from—**
2. **Losing It!**
1. **Writing a one-paragraph essay.**

6 chapter

THE COLLEGE SEARCH

Now that you have examined your interests, talents, wants, and needs in great detail, it's time to start investigating colleges.

THE BEST RESOURCES

There are thousands of colleges and universities in the United States, so before you start filling out applications, you need to narrow down your search. There are a number of sources that will help you do this.

Your Guidance Counselor

Your guidance counselor is your greatest asset in the college search process. He or she has access to a vast repository of information, from college bulletins and catalogs to financial aid applications. He or she knows how well graduates from your high school have performed at colleges across the country, and has probably even visited many of the colleges to get some first-hand knowledge about the places she has sent her students to. The more your guidance counselor sees you and learns about you, the easier it is for her to help you. So make sure you stop by her office often, whether it's to talk about your progress or just to say "hi."

Your Teachers

Use your teachers as resources, too. Many of them have had twenty to thirty years of experience in their field. They have taught thousands of students and watched them go off to college and careers. Teachers often stay in contact with graduates and know about their experiences in college and may be familiar with the schools you are interested in attending. Ask your teachers how they feel about the match between you and your choice of schools and if they think you will be able to succeed in that environment.

Your Family

Your family needs to be an integral part of the college selection process, whether they are financing your education or not. They have opinions and valuable advice. Listen to them carefully. Try to absorb all their information and see if it applies to you. Does it fit with who you are and what you want? What works and what doesn't work for you? Is some of what they say dated? How long ago were their experiences, and how relevant are they today? Take in the information, thank them for their concern, compare what they have said with the information you are gathering, and discard what doesn't fit.

Colleges and Universities

Don't forget to go to college fairs. Usually held in large cities in the evening, they are free and sponsored by your local guidance counselors' association and the National Association of College Admissions Counselors (NACAC). The admissions counselors of hundreds of colleges, vocational/career colleges, and universities attend college fairs each year. Whether your questions are as general as what the overall cost of education is at a particular institution or as specific as how many biology majors had works published last year, the admissions office works to assist you in locating the people who can answer your questions. Bring a shopping bag for all the information you will get.

Admissions officers also visit high schools. Don't forget to attend these meetings during your junior and senior years. In general, college admissions counselors come to a school to get a general sense of the high school and the caliber and personality of the student body. Although it is difficult to make an individual impression at these group sessions, the college counselors do take names on cards for later contact, and you will occasionally see them making notes on the cards when they are struck by an astute questioner. It is helpful to attend these sessions because consistent contact between a student and a college is tracked by colleges and universities. An admissions decision may come down to examining the size of your admissions folder and the number of interactions you have had with the school over time.

College and university brochures and catalogs are a good place to look, too. After reading a few, you will discover that some offer more objective information than others. You will also start to learn what information colleges think is essential to present. That's important. If one college's brochure does not present the same information as most of the other college brochures, you have to ask yourself why. What might this say about the college's academic offerings, athletic or extracurricular programs, or campus life? What does the campus look like? How is the campus environment presented in the brochure? The brochures should present clues to what schools feel are their important majors, what their mission is, and on which departments they are spending their budgets. Take the time to do these informational resources justice. They have a great deal to say to the careful reader.

PARENT PERSPECTIVE

Q: Now that you've been through the process of getting three of your children into college, what's your best advice for parents and teens?

A: Apply early and meet deadlines. Both of our older sons were sitting there after high school graduation wondering why they were on college waiting lists: "I have good grades. I can't figure it out." At eighteen, they don't see tomorrow, much less way down the line, but do you want to deal with their heartbreak at not getting into the college where they want to be? It's their future. It's hard because they're in their senior year and you want it to be fun for them. However, you see the reality out there that they will be facing for the rest of their lives. They don't want to look at it, but you have to keep bringing them back to it—not in a preachy way. If they start earlier than their senior year, it won't be as much of a shock when they become seniors.

Jeanette and Amedee Richard
San Antonio, Texas

A college's Web site can give you a glimpse of campus life that does not appear in the college's brochure and catalog. It is true that the virtual tour will show you the shots that the college marketing department wants you to see, highlighting the campus in the best light, but you can use the home page to see other things, too. Read the student newspaper. Visit college-sponsored chat rooms. Go to the department in the major you are investigating. Look at the Course Bulletin to see what courses are required.

ONLINE HELP

To help you find two-year and four-year colleges or universities in your specific region, take a look at the Appendix in the back of this book for a listing of schools in each state. Then check out the following online resources for additional information on college selection, scholarships, student information, and much more.

Peterson's Undergraduate Channel. Petersons.com provides information and tools that will help you prepare, search, and pay for college. You can search

CRITERIA TO CONSIDER

Depending on your personal interests, the following characteristics should play a role in helping you narrow down the field of colleges you are considering.

AFFILIATION
- Public
- Private, independent
- Private, church affiliated
- Proprietary

SIZE
- Very small (fewer than 1,000 students)
- Small (1,000–3,999 students)
- Medium (4,000–8,999 students)
- Large (9,000–19,999 students)
- Very large (more than 20,000 students)

COMMUNITY
- Rural
- Small town
- Suburban
- Urban

LOCATION
- In your hometown
- Less than 3 hours from home
- More than 3 hours from home

HOUSING
- Dorm
- Off-campus apartment
- Home
- Facilities and services for students with disabilities

STUDENT BODY
- All male
- All female
- Coed
- Minority representation
- Primarily one religious denomination
- Primarily full-time students
- Primarily part-time students
- Primarily commuter students
- Primarily residential students

ACADEMIC ENVIRONMENT
- Majors offered
- Student-faculty ratio
- Faculty teaching reputation
- Instruction by professors versus teaching assistants
- Facilities (such as classrooms and labs)
- Libraries
- Independent study available
- International study available
- Internships available

FINANCIAL AID
- Scholarships
- Grants
- Loans
- Work-study program
- Part-time or full-time jobs

SUPPORT SERVICES
- Academic counseling
- Career/placement counseling
- Personal counseling
- Student health facilities

ACTIVITIES/SOCIAL CLUBS
- Clubs, organizations
- Greek life
- Athletics, intramurals

ATHLETICS
- Division I, II, or III
- Sports offered
- Scholarships available

SPECIALIZED PROGRAMS
- Honors programs
- Services for students with disabilities or special needs

for a school by name or location. In addition to college search and selection tools, the undergraduate channel on Petersons.com also offers tips on financial aid, test preparation, and online applications.

The National Association for College Admission Counseling. This home page offers information for professionals, students, and parents. The Internet address is www.nacac.com.

U.S. Department of Education. This federal agency's National Center for Education Statistics produces reports on every level of education, from elementary to postgraduate. Dozens are available for downloading. You can hook up with these and other links at www.ed.gov/index.jsp.

CAMPUS VISITS

You've heard the old saying, "A picture is worth a thousand words." Well, a campus visit is worth a thousand brochures. Nothing beats walking around a campus to get a feel for it. Some students report that all they needed to know that they loved or hated a campus was to drive through it. Then there is the true story of the guy who applied to a school because it had a prestigious name. Got accepted. Didn't visit, and when he arrived to move into the dorms, discovered to his horror it was an all-male school. A visit would have taken care of that problem.

The best time to experience the college environment is during the spring of your junior year or the fall of your senior year. Although you may have more time to visit colleges during your summer off, your observations will be more accurate when you can see the campus in full swing. Open houses are a good idea and provide you with opportunities to talk to students, faculty members, and administrators. Write or call in advance to take student-conducted campus tours. If possible, stay overnight in a dorm to see what living at the college is really like.

Bring your transcript so that you are prepared to interview with admission officers. Take this opportunity to ask questions about financial aid and other services that are available to students. You can get a good snapshot of campus life by reading a copy of the student newspaper. The final goal of the campus visit is to study the school's personality and decide if it matches yours. Your parents should be involved with the campus visits so that you can share your impressions. Here are some additional campus visit tips:

- Read campus literature prior to the visit.
- Ask for directions, and allow ample travel time.
- Make a list of questions before the visit.
- Dress in neat, clean, and casual clothes and shoes.
- Ask to meet one-on-one with a current student.

- Ask to meet personally with a professor in your area of interest.
- Ask to meet a coach or athlete in your area of interest.
- Offer a firm handshake.
- Use good posture.
- Listen, and take notes.
- Speak clearly, and maintain eye contact with people you meet.
- Don't interrupt.
- Be honest, direct, and polite.
- Be aware of factual information so that you can ask questions of comparison and evaluation.
- Be prepared to answer questions about yourself. Practice a mock interview with someone.
- Don't be shy about explaining your background and why you are interested in the school.
- Ask questions about the background and experiences of the people you meet.
- Convey your interest in getting involved in campus life.
- Be positive and energetic.
- Don't feel as though you have to talk the whole time or carry the conversation yourself.
- Relax, and enjoy yourself.
- Thank those you meet, and send thank-you notes when appropriate.

After you have made your college visits, use the "College Comparison Worksheet" on page 56 to rank the schools in which you're interested. This will help you decide not only which ones to apply to, but also which one to attend once you receive your acceptance letters.

THE COLLEGE INTERVIEW

Not all schools require or offer an interview. However, if you are offered an interview, use this one-on-one time to evaluate the college in detail and to sell yourself to the admission officer. The following list of questions can help you collect the information you may need to know.

WRITING TO A COLLEGE FOR INFORMATION

If neither you nor your guidance counselor has an application for a college that you are interested in, write a brief letter to the college admissions office to request an application.

Date

Your Name
Street Address
City, State, Zip

Office of Admission
Name of College
Street Address
City, State, Zip

To Whom It May Concern:

I am a (freshman, sophomore, junior, senior) at (name of your school) and will graduate in (month) (year).

Please send me the following information about your college: a general information brochure, program descriptions, an admission application, financial aid information, and any other information that might be helpful. I am considering ________________ as my major field of study (optional, if you know your preferred field of study).

I am interested in visiting your campus, taking a campus tour, and meeting with an admission counselor and a financial aid officer. I would also like to meet with an adviser or professor in the (your preferred field of study) department, if possible. I will contact you in a week to set up a time that is convenient.

If you would like to contact me directly, I can be reached at (your phone number with area code and e-mail address). Thank you.

Sincerely,

(Signature)

Your Name

- How many students apply each year? How many are accepted?
- What are the average GPA and average ACT Assessment or SAT score(s) for those accepted?
- How many students in last year's freshman class returned for their sophomore year?
- What is the school's procedure for credit for Advanced Placement high school courses?

(Continued on page 56)

THE MATCHING GAME Read each question and respond by circling Y (Yes), N (No), or C (Combination). Complete all the questions and return to the top. Highlight each action that coordinates with your answer, and then read it. Where you chose C, read both actions. Is there a pattern? Do the questions seem to lead to a certain type of college or university? Certain size? Certain location? Read the suggestions at the end of "The Matching Game" for more ideas.

Question	Yes/No/ Combination	Action
1. Do I have a goal in life?	Y N C	Y: State it.______________________. N: Don't worry, many students start college without knowing what they want to do. Look into colleges that specialize in the arts and sciences.
2. Do I know what I want to achieve with a college diploma?	Y N C	Y: List specifically what your goals are. ______________________ N: Think about what college can offer you.
3. Do I want to broaden my knowledge?	Y N C	Y: Consider a liberal arts college. N: You might need to consider other options or educational opportunities.
4. Do I want specific training?	Y N C	Y: Investigate technical colleges or professional training programs in universities. N: You don't know what you want to study? Don't worry, only 20 pecent of seniors who apply to college are sure.
5. Am I looking for a balanced workload?	Y N C	Y: When you are visiting colleges, ask students about how they handle the workload. N: Check the workload carefully. If no one is on campus on a sunny day, it may not be the school for you
6. Am I self-directed enough to finish a four-year college program?	Y N C	Y: Consider only four-year colleges and universities. N: Maybe a two-year junior or community college is a better way to begin your college experience. Also consider a vocational/career college.
7. Do I know what I do well?	Y N C	Y: Identify majors related to your abilities. ______________________ N: Spend a little more time asking yourself questions about your interests. Speak to your counselor and do an interest inventory.
8. Do I like to spend time learning any one subject more than others?	Y N C	Y: List majors related to that area. ______________________ ______________________ N: Look at your high school courses. Which ones do you like better than others? ______________________
9. Do I know what matters to me and what my values are?	Y N C	Y: Look for the schools that talk about the values on their campus. Do the values confirm or conflict with your values? N: Values are less important to you, so places that really expound their values may seem confining to you.
10. Do I need to be in affluent surroundings?	Y N C	Y: Look at the schools that deliver that package. Check the small, private liberal arts colleges. N: How strong is your reaction against this setting? If it is strong, check larger, more diverse settings, like an urban school.
11. Am I going to college for the financial gains?	Y N C	Y: What majors are going to give you the payback you want? Look at business colleges and professional programs, like premed. N: If a big financial payback does not interest you, look at social service majors, like counseling, teaching, and social work.
12. Am I focused?	Y N C	Y: Search out the programs that will offer you the best options. N: Avoid those schools whose programs are not strong in your focused area.
13. Am I conservative in my views and behavior?	Y N C	Y: The political policies of schools are important. Look into them carefully. You might look at the schools in the Midwest or the South. N: If you're a liberal, look closely at the political climate. Check the schools in the Northeast and on the West Coast.

14. Do I need to be around people who are similar to me?	Y N C	**Y**: If you are African American, check the historically black colleges. If socioeconomic level or a certain look is important to you, study the student populations carefully during campus visits. If it is religious orientation you are interested in, look into religiously sponsored colleges and universities. **N**: Look at large, midsize, and small universities in urban settings.
15. Are the name and prestige of the school important to me?	Y N C	**Y**: Look into the Ivies and the competitive schools to see if you are eligible and what they offer you. Broaden your search to include other colleges and compare their offerings to your specific needs and interests. **N**: Don't exclude the well-known institutions if they fit in every other way.
16. Do I like sports?	Y N C	**Y**: Large universities with Division I teams will give you all the sports you need—as a competitor or a fan. If you do not want to compete at that level, check schools in other divisions. Look at the liberal arts colleges for athletes. **N**: Look into smaller universities and liberal arts colleges with good teams.
17. Am I a techie?	Y N C	**Y**: Check for computer engineering courses at technical universities and large universities near research centers and major computer business areas. Ask about hardwiring, e-mail, and computer packages before you enroll. **N**: It still helps to know what computer services are available where you enroll.
18. Do I need to live in or be near a city?	Y N C	**Y**: How close to a city do you need to be? In the city or an hour away? Do you still want a campus feel? Consider these questions as you visit campuses. **N**: Do you need space, natural beauty, and peaceful surroundings to think? Look into small liberal arts schools in rural and suburban settings. Explore universities in the Midwest and South.
19. Will I need counseling for support?	Y N C	**Y**: Investigate the quality of student services and the mechanism for accessing them. Smaller schools often pride themselves on their services. Look at liberal arts colleges. Universities connected to medical centers often provide extensive services. **N**: It is still good to know what is offered.
20. Do I need an environment in which questioning is important?	Y N C	**Y**: Liberal arts colleges, honors colleges, and smaller universities place an emphasis on academic inquiry. **N**: You like to hear others discuss issues, gather as much information and opinions as you can, and think it over by yourself. Try the university setting.

Suggestions

Here are some ideas for you to consider based on the way you answered the questions.

1. If you answered *no* to numbers 2 and 3, why not investigate apprenticeships, vocational/career colleges, armed services options, and certification or two-year college programs?
2. If you answered *yes* to numbers 4, 11, and 17, technical or professional colleges and universities with hands-on training may give you the education you want.
3. If you answered *yes* to numbers 9, 10, and 20, you are leaning toward a liberal arts setting.
4. If you answered *yes* to numbers 5 and 6, examine the competitive and Ivy League colleges.
5. If you answered *no* to numbers 9, 10, 14, and 20 and yes to 16, 17, and 18, larger universities may offer you the best options.

Once you have completed your self-evaluation, made a decision whether college is for you, have some ideas about your personality and likes and dislikes, and can relate them to the different personalities of colleges, it is time to gather information. It needs to be quality information from the right sources. The quality of information you put into your search now will determine whether your list of colleges will represent a good or a bad match.

- As a freshman, will I be taught by professors or teaching assistants?
- How many students are there per teacher?
- When is it necessary to declare a major?
- Is it possible to have a double major or to declare a major and a minor?
- What are the requirements for the major in which I am interested?
- How does the advising system work?
- Does this college offer study abroad, cooperative programs, or academic honors programs?
- What is the likelihood, due to overcrowding, of getting closed out of the courses I need?
- What technology is available, and what are any associated fees?
- How well equipped are the libraries and laboratories?
- Are internships available?
- How effective is the job placement service of the school?
- What is the average class size in my area of interest?
- Have any professors in my area of interest recently won any honors or awards?
- What teaching methods are used in my area of interest (lecture, group discussion, fieldwork)?
- How many students graduate in four years in my area of interest?
- What are the special requirements for graduation in my area of interest?
- What is the student body like? Age? Sex? Race? Geographic origin?
- What percentage of students live in dormitories? In off-campus housing?
- What percentage of students go home for the weekend?

COLLEGE COMPARISON WORKSHEET

Fill in your top five selection criteria and any others that may be of importance to you. Once you narrow your search of colleges to five, fill in the colleges across the top row. Using a scale of 1 to 5, where 1 is poor and 5 is excellent, rate each college by your criteria. Total each column to see which college rates the highest based upon your criteria.

SELECTION CRITERIA	COLLEGE 1	COLLEGE 2	COLLEGE 3	COLLEGE 4	COLLEGE 5
1.					
2.					
3.					
4.					
5.					
OTHER CRITERIA					
6.					
7.					
8.					
9.					
10.					
TOTAL					

Sample criteria (Use this list as a starting point—there may be other criteria important to you not listed here.): Arts facilities, athletic facilities, audiovisual center, campus setting, class size, classrooms/lecture halls, computer labs, dining hall, dorms, financial aid, fraternity/sorority houses, majors offered, religious facilities, professor profiles, student-faculty ratio, student profile, student union, surrounding community.

STUDENT COUNSEL

Q: How did you choose the college you're attending?

A: I followed my instincts in not going for a big name school. I went where I thought I would get the most out of the school, not necessarily because of its reputation. I considered seven schools, and once I was accepted, I looked at the location and courses they offered and the financial aid I could get.

Chay Linn Park
Pacific University

- What are some of the regulations that apply to living in a dormitory?
- What are the security precautions taken on campus and in the dorms?
- Is the surrounding community safe?
- Are there problems with drug and alcohol abuse on campus?
- Do faculty members and students mix on an informal basis?
- How important are the arts to student life?
- What facilities are available for cultural events?
- How important are sports to student life?
- What facilities are available for sporting events?
- What percentage of the student body belongs to a sorority/fraternity?
- What is the relationship between those who belong to the Greek system and those who don't?
- Are students involved in the decision-making process at the college? Do they sit on major committees?
- In what other activities can students get involved?
- What percentage of students receive financial aid based on need?
- What percentage of students receive scholarships based on academic ability?
- What percentage of a typical financial aid offer is in the form of a loan?
- If my family demonstrates financial need on the FAFSA (and PROFILE®, if applicable), what percentage of the established need is generally awarded?
- How much did the college increase the cost of room, board, tuition, and fees from last year?
- Do opportunities for financial aid, scholarships, or work-study increase each year?
- When is the admission application deadline?
- When is the financial aid application deadline?
- When will I be notified of the admission decision?
- If there is a deposit required, is it refundable?

Keep in mind that you don't need to ask all these questions—in fact, some of them may have already been answered for you in the catalog, on the Web site, or in the interview. Ask only the questions for which you still need answers.

SHOULD YOU HEAD FOR THE IVY LEAGUES?

Determining whether to apply to one of the eight Ivy League schools is something about which you should think long and hard. Sure, it can't hurt to toss your application into the ring if you can afford the application fee and the time you'll spend writing the essays. But if you want to figure out if you'd be a legitimate candidate for acceptance at one of these top-tier schools, you should understand the type of student that they look for and how you compare, says John Machulsky, a guidance counselor at Lawrence High School in New Jersey. Take a look at these statistics:

- Only 30 percent or fewer applicants are accepted at highly competitive colleges each year.
- Most Ivy League students have placed in the top 10 percent of their class.

- Because Ivy League schools are so selective, they want a diverse student population. That means they want students that represent not only the fifty states but also a wide selection of other countries.

Lirio Jimenez, a guidance counselor at New Brunswick High School in New Jersey, says that being accepted by an Ivy League school is a process that starts in the ninth grade. You should select demanding courses and maintain good grades in those courses throughout all four years of high school. Get involved in extracurricular activities as well, and, of course, do well on your standardized tests. When it comes time to apply for college, select at least three schools: one ideal, one possible, and one shoe-in. Your ideal can be an Ivy League if you wish.

Peterson's Get a Jump! certainly doesn't want to discourage you from applying to one of these prestigious schools. We're in your corner and want to see you get the best education possible. However, students are sometimes more concerned about getting accepted than with taking a hard look at what a school has to offer them. Often, a university or college that is less competitive than an Ivy may have exactly what you need to succeed in the future. Keep that in mind as you select the colleges that will offer you what you need.

STUDENT COUNSEL

Q: What made you choose to apply to an Ivy League school?

A: My mother recommended that I apply to Princeton. She said, "Why not just try? What do you have to lose? All they can tell you is no." I was afraid of being rejected. I wasn't a straight-A student, and I thought they weren't going to want me—they get thousands of applications. Through the whole college process I had a whole lot of self-doubt. Looking back, I realize that you won't know if you don't try. Take the chance and fill out the application. If you don't get in, it doesn't mean you're less intelligent. It just wasn't the correct fit.

Zoelene Hill
Princeton University

MINORITY STUDENTS GO TO COLLEGE

African-American, Hispanic, Asian-American, and Native-American high school students have a lot of doors into higher education opening for them. In fact, most colleges want to respond to the social and economic disadvantages of certain groups of Americans. They want to reflect the globalization of our economy. They want their student populations to look like the rest of America, which means people from many different backgrounds and ethnic groups. This isn't just talk either. You'll find that most colleges have at least one member of the admissions staff who specializes in recruiting minorities.

One of the reasons college admissions staff are recruiting minorities and want to accommodate their needs is because there are more minorities thinking of attending college—and graduating. Let's put some numbers to these statements. According to the Department of Education, in 1976, 16 percent of college students were minorities, compared to 27 percent in 1997. Much of the change can be attributed to rising numbers of Hispanic and Asian students. The proportion of Asian and Pacific Islander students rose from 2 percent to 6 percent, and the Hispanic proportion rose from 4 percent to 9 percent during that same time period. The proportion of African-American students fluctuated during most of the early part of the period before rising slightly to 11 percent in 1997, the last year for which data was collected on this subject.

Peterson's Get a Jump! has a lot of information in this section to help you make decisions about college and paying for college. Perhaps the most important information we can give you is that if you want to go to college, you can. There are a lot of organizations ready to assist you. So go for it. See the list of organizations in this section and check with the colleges in which you're interested to connect with the minority affairs office.

Academic Resources for Minority Students

In addition to churches, sororities and fraternities, and college minority affairs offices, minority students can

SHOULD YOU ATTEND A HISTORICALLY BLACK COLLEGE OR UNIVERSITY?

Choosing which college to attend is usually a difficult decision for anyone to make, but when an African-American student is considering attending a historically black college or university (HBCU), a whole other set of family and cultural issues are raised.

There are many valid reasons that favor one or the other. Some are obvious differences. Parents and their children have to be honest with themselves and take a long, hard look at the needs of the student and how the campus environment can fulfill them. To help you decide, here are some questions to ask:

DO I KNOW WHAT'S REALLY IMPORTANT TO ME?

Look at the reasons why you want a degree and what you want to achieve with it. Is the choice to attend an HBCU yours or your family's? Do you have a particular field of study you want to pursue? Sometimes students can get so caught up in applying to a particular institution, they don't realize it doesn't even offer their major.

HOW WILL THIS CAMPUS FIT MY PLANS FOR THE FUTURE?

There's no substitute for doing your homework about the campuses you're seriously considering. Know the reputation of those campuses in the community and among employers and the general population. Find out about student retention, graduation, and placement rates.

DOES THIS CAMPUS HAVE THE FACILITIES AND LIVING CONDITIONS THAT SUIT MY COMFORT LEVEL?

Finding a campus where you're comfortable is a big factor in choosing a college. What do you want in campus facilities and living conditions? For instance, if you currently attend a small private high school in a suburban setting, perhaps you wouldn't like living on a large urban campus with peers who don't mirror your kind of background.

WHAT LEVEL OF SUPPORT WILL I GET ON CAMPUS?

Students considering institutions where few people are like them should look at the available support systems and organizations that will be available to them. Parents need to feel comfortable with the contact person on campus.

When all the factors that determine the choice of a college are laid out, the bottom line is which institution best meets your needs. For some African-American students, an HBCU is the best choice. For others, it's not. African-American students reflect many backgrounds, and there is no single decision that will be right for everyone.

receive information and assistance from the following organizations:

ASPIRA

ASPIRA's mission is to empower the Puerto Rican and Latino community through advocacy and the education and leadership development of its youth.

1444 Eye Street, NW, Suite 800
Washington, D.C. 20005
202-835-3600
www.aspira.org

INROADS

A national career-development organization that places and develops talented minority youth (African-American, Hispanic-American, and Native-American) in business and industry.

10 South Broadway, Suite 700
St. Louis, Missouri 63102
314-241-7488
www.inroads.org

National Action Council for Minorities in Engineering (NACME)

An organization that aims to provide leadership and support for the national effort to increase the representation of successful African-American, American Indian, and Latino women and men in engineering and technology and math- and science-based careers.

440 Hamilton Avenue, Suite 302
White Plains, New York 10601-1813
914-539-4010
www.nacme.org

National Association for the Advancement of Colored People (NAACP)

The purpose of the NAACP is to improve the political, educational, social, and economic status of minority groups; to eliminate racial prejudice; to keep the public aware of the adverse effects of racial discrimination; and to take lawful action to secure its elimination, consistent with the efforts of the national organization.

4805 Mt. Hope Drive
Baltimore, Maryland 21215
877-NAACP-98 (toll-free)
www.naacp.org

STUDENT COUNSEL

Q: How did you make the decision to attend a historically black college or university?

A: Selecting a college was one of the hardest decisions I've ever had to make. As a recipient of the National Achievement Scholarship and a National History Day winner, I was offered scholarships to a number of colleges across the country, including many HCBUs. I tried to figure out which institution would be able to give me the most help in achieving my goals. I finally decided on Florida A&M University (FAMU) in my hometown of Tallahassee.

There are many pluses to attending college in my hometown. By living on campus, I have the freedom to make my own decisions and live as a young adult while being close to the loving support of my parents. Also, FAMU will help me succeed in my objective of obtaining a bachelor's degree in broadcast journalism. As I look back, I am glad that I, unlike some of my high school peers, did not rush to judgment during the process of choosing a college. I am very happy with my decision.

Larry Rivers
Florida A&M University

The National Urban League

The Campaign for African-American Achievement of the National Urban League provides services for African-Americans and economically disadvantaged people. These services include basic academic development, GED test preparation for youths and adults, after-school tutoring for children, parent training classes, scholarships, an annual tour of historically black colleges and universities, and summer employment for youths.

120 Wall Street
New York, New York 10005
212-558-5300
www.nul.org

United Negro College Fund (UNCF)

The UNCF serves to enhance the quality of education by raising operating funds for its 39 member colleges and universities, providing financial assistance to deserving students, and increasing access to technology for students and faculty at historically black colleges and universities.

8260 Willow Oaks Corporate Drive
P.O. Box 10444
Fairfax, Virginia 22031-8044
800-331-2244 (toll-free)
www.uncf.org

The American Indian Higher Education Consortium (AIHEC)

AIHEC's mission is to support the work of tribal colleges and the national movement for tribal self-determination through four objectives: maintain commonly held standards of quality in American Indian education; support the development of new tribally controlled colleges; promote and assist in the development of legislation to support American Indian higher education; and encourage greater participation by American Indians in the development of higher education policy.

121 Oronoco Street
Alexandria, Virginia 22314
703-838-0400
www.aihec.org

The Gates Millennium Scholars (GMS)

The Gates Millennium Scholars, funded by a grant from the Bill & Melinda Gates Foundation, was established in 1999 to provide outstanding African-American, American-Indian/Alaska Natives, Asian-Pacific Islander Americans, and Hispanic-American students with an opportunity to complete an undergraduate college education in all discipline areas and a graduate education for those students pursuing studies in mathematics, science, engineering, education, or library science. The goal of GMS is to promote academic excellence and to provide an opportunity for thousands of outstanding students with significant financial need to reach their fullest potential.

P.O. Box 10500
Fairfax, Virginia 22031-8044
877-690-4677 (toll-free)
www.gmsp.org

Hispanic Association of Colleges and Universities (HACU)

The Hispanic Association of Colleges and Universities is a national association representing the accredited colleges and universities in the United

States where Hispanic students constitute at least 25 percent of the total student enrollment. HACU's goal is to bring together colleges and universities, corporations, government agencies, and individuals to establish partnerships for promoting the developing Hispanic-serving colleges and universities; improving access to and the quality of postsecondary education for Hispanic students; and meeting the needs of business, industry, and government through the development and sharing of resources, information, and expertise.

4204 Gardendale Street, Suite 216
San Antonio, Texas 78229
512- 692-3805
www.buscapique.com/latinusa/buscafile/sud/hacu.htm

Hispanic Scholarship Fund (HSF)

The Hispanic Scholarship Fund is the nation's leading organization supporting Hispanic higher education. HSF was founded in 1975 with a vision to strengthen the country by advancing college education among Hispanic Americans. In support of its mission, HSF provides the Latino community with college scholarships and educational outreach support.

55 Second Street, Suite 1500
San Francisco, California 94105
877-473-4636 (toll-free)
www.hsf.net/about/index.htm

STUDENTS WITH DISABILITIES GO TO COLLEGE

The Americans with Disabilities Act (ADA) requires educational institutions at all levels, public and private, to provide equal access to programs, services, and facilities. Schools must be accessible to students, as well as to employees and the public, regardless of any disability. To ensure such accessibility, they must follow specific requirements for new construction, alterations or renovations, academic programs, and institutional policies, practices, and procedures. Students with specific disabilities have the right to request and expect accommodations, including auxiliary aids and services that enable them to participate in and benefit from all programs and activities offered by or related to a school.

TIPS FOR STUDENTS WITH DISABILITIES

- **Document your disability with letters from your physician(s), therapist, case manager, school psychologist, and other service providers.**
- **Get letters of support from teachers, family, friends, and service providers that detail how you have succeeded despite your disability.**
- **Learn the federal laws that apply to students with disabilities.**
- **Research support groups for peer information and advocacy.**
- **Visit several campuses.**
- **Look into the services available, the pace of campus life, and the college's programs for students with disabilities.**
- **Ask about orientation programs, including specialized introductions for, or about, students with disabilities.**
- **Ask about flexible, individualized study plans.**
- **Ask if the school offers technology such as voice synthesizers, voice recognition, and/or visual learning equipment to its students.**
- **Ask about adapted intramural/social activities.**
- **Ask to talk with students who have similar disabilities to hear about their experiences on campus.**
- **Once you select a college, get a map of the campus and learn the entire layout.**
- **If you have a physical disability, make sure the buildings you need to be in are accessible to you. Some, even though they comply with the ADA, aren't as accessible as others.**
- **Be realistic. If you use a wheelchair, for example, a school with an exceptionally hilly campus may not be your best choice, no matter what other accommodations it has.**

To comply with ADA requirements, many high schools and universities offer programs and information to answer questions for students with disabilities and to assist them both in selecting appropriate colleges and in attaining full inclusion once they enter college. And most colleges and universities have disabilities services offices to help students negotiate the system. When it comes time to apply to colleges, write to the ones that you're interested in to find out what kinds of programs they have in place. When it comes time to narrow down your choices, make a request for a visit.

What Is Considered a Disability?

A person is considered to have a disability if he or she meets at least one of three conditions. The individual must:

1. have a documented physical or mental impairment that substantially limits one or more major life activities, such as personal self-care, walking, seeing, hearing, speaking, breathing, learning, working, or performing manual tasks;
2. have a record of such an impairment; or
3. be perceived as having such an impairment.

Physical disabilities include impairments of speech, vision, hearing, and mobility. Other disabilities, while less obvious, are similarly limiting; they include diabetes, asthma, multiple sclerosis, heart disease, cancer, mental illness, mental retardation, cerebral palsy, and learning disabilities.

Learning disabilities refer to an array of biological conditions that impede a person's ability to process and disseminate information. A learning disability is commonly recognized as a significant deficiency in one or more of the following areas: oral expression, listening comprehension, written expression, basic reading skills, reading comprehension, mathematical calculation, or problem solving. Individuals with learning disabilities also may have difficulty with sustained attention, time management, or social skills.

If you have a disability, you will take the same steps to choose and apply to a college as other students, but you should also evaluate each college based on your special need(s). Get organized, and meet with campus specialists to discuss your specific requirements. Then, explore whether the programs, policies, procedures, and facilities meet your specific situation.

It is usually best to describe your disability in a letter attached to the application so the proper fit can be made between you and the school. You will probably need to have your psychoeducational evaluation and testing record sent to the school. Some colleges help with schedules and offer transition courses, reduced course loads, extra access to professors, and special study areas to help address your needs.

Remember, admission to college is a realistic goal for any motivated student. If you invest the time and effort, you can make it happen.

STUDENT COUNSEL

The following quotes are from students who attend a college that offers services for learning disabled students.

"I have delayed development. I need help getting things done, and I need extra time for tests. As long as I'm able to go up to teachers and ask questions, I do well on tests."

—Anita

"I have dyslexia. I thought the term 'disabilities services' was for people with visual and hearing impairments. But when I got here, I found it covered a variety of disabilities. It was like Christmas. You got everything you wanted and more."

—Debra

"I am hard of hearing. I was always afraid I wouldn't be able to hear what [teachers] said. It's hard to read lips and listen at the same time. With note takers, I still get what I need even if the teacher moves around. They want you to make it through."

—Jeannette

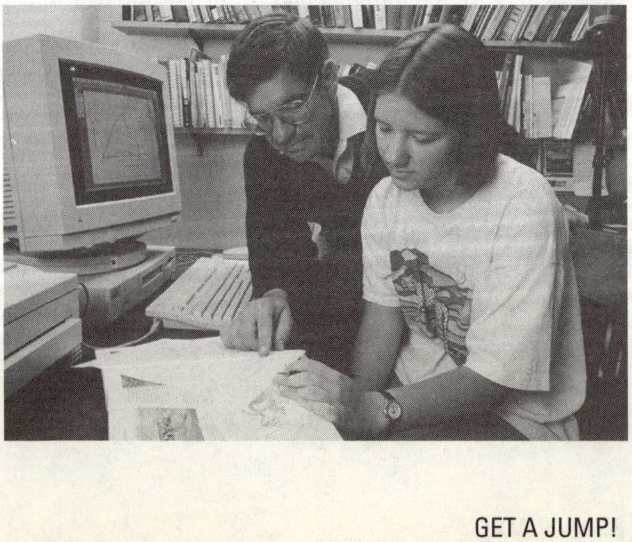

DIRECTORY FOR STUDENTS WITH DISABILITIES

The following resources can help students, families, and schools with the legal requirements for accommodating disabilities. They can also link you with other groups and individuals that are knowledgeable in students' rights and the process of transition into post-secondary education.

Also, there are special interest, education, support, and advocacy organizations for persons with particular disabilities. Check with your counselor or contact one of the following organizations for information:

ACT Assessment Administration

Standard-Time National Testing with Accommodations

ACT Test Administration
P.O. Box 168
Iowa City, Iowa 52243-0168
319-337-1510

Extended-Time National Testing (up to 5 hours testing time or 5 hours, 45 minutes if taking the Writing Test)

ACT Registration
P.O. Box 414
Iowa City, Iowa 52243-0414
319-337-1815

Association on Higher Education and Disability (AHEAD)
P.O. Box 540666
Waltham, Massachusetts 02454
781-788-0003
www.ahead.org

Attention Deficit Disorder Association (ADDA)
P.O. Box 543
Pottstown, Pennsylvania 19464
484-945-2101
www.add.org

Children and Adults with Attention-Deficit/ Hyperactivity Disorders (CHADD)
8181 Professional Place,
Suite 150
Landover, Maryland 20785
800-233-4050 (toll-free)
www.chadd.org

Council for Learning Disabilities
P.O. Box 4014
Leesburg, Virginia 20177
www.cldinternational.org

HEATH Resource Center National Clearinghouse on Postsecondary Education for Individuals with Disabilities

The George Washington University
HEATH Resource Center
2121 K Street, NW, Suite 220
Washington, D.C. 20037
800-544-3284 (toll-free)
www.heath.gwu.edu

International Dyslexia Association
The Chester Building, Suite 382
8600 LaSalle Road
Baltimore, Maryland 21286-2044
410-296-0232
www.interdys.org

Learning Disabilities Association of America (LDA)
4156 Library Road
Pittsburgh, Pennsylvania 15234
412-341-1515
www.ldanatl.org

National Center for Learning Disabilities (NCLD)

381 Park Avenue South,
Suite 1401
New York, New York 10016
888-575-7373 (toll-free)
www.ncld.org

National Dissemination Center for Children with Disabilities

P.O. Box 1492
Washington, D.C. 20013
800-695-0285 (toll-free)
www.nichcy.org

Recording for the Blind & Dyslexic

20 Roszel Road
Princeton, New Jersey 08540
866-RFBD-585
www.rfbd.org

SAT Services for Students with Disabilities

The College Board Services for Students with Disabilities
P.O. Box 6226
Princeton, New Jersey
08541-6226
609-771-7137
www.collegeboard.com

7 Chapter

APPLYING TO COLLEGE

The big moment has arrived. It's time to make some decisions about where you want to apply.

ONCE YOUR LIST IS FINALIZED, the worst part is filling out all the forms accurately and getting them in by the deadlines. Because requirements differ, you should check with all the colleges that you are interested in attending to find out what documentation is needed and when it is due.

WHAT SCHOOLS LOOK FOR IN PROSPECTIVE STUDENTS

As if you were sizing up the other team to plan your game strategy, you'll need to understand what admissions committees want from you as you assemble all the pieces of your application.

PARENT PERSPECTIVE

Q: How did you help your daughter get into college?

A: The key is to start early, like in the junior year. We didn't do that. At this point in the fall of our daughter's senior year, deadlines are coming up, and we haven't really looked at any colleges yet or gone on visits. It's kind of like choosing a house to buy without going to the house. The parent's role is to ask a lot of questions to get your child to figure out exactly what it is he or she wants to do. It's a big decision.

We hired a financial aid consultant who is helping us look at different colleges. The biggest worry is the FAFSA form. If you get it wrong, and they send it back to you—you have to start all over again. In the meantime, you're behind and others are getting grants. The whole process is very confusing, and there's no one to walk you through it. We've looked at different colleges on the Internet, and college fairs are a good resource. Plus, our daughter has done a lot on her own.

Doug and Judy Ames
Colorado Springs, Colorado

Academic record: Admission representatives look at the breadth (how many), diversity (which ones), and difficulty (how challenging) of the courses on your transcript.

Grades: You should show consistency in your ability to work to your potential. If your grades are not initially good, colleges look to see that significant improvement has been made. Some colleges have minimum grade point averages that they are willing to accept.

Class rank: Colleges may consider the academic standing of a student in relation to the other members of his or her class. Are you in the top 25 percent of your class? Top half? Ask your counselor for your class rank.

Standardized test scores: Colleges look at test scores in terms of ranges. If your scores aren't high but you did well academically in high school, you shouldn't be discouraged. There is no set formula for admission. Even at the most competitive schools, some students' test scores are lower than you would think.

Extracurricular activities: Colleges look for depth of involvement (variety and how long you participated), initiative (leadership), and creativity demonstrated in activities, service, or work.

Recommendations: Most colleges require a recommendation from your high school guidance counselor. Some ask for references from teachers or other adults. If your counselor or teachers don't know you well, you should put together a student resume, or brag sheet, that outlines what you have done during your four years of high school. In this chapter, you'll find a worksheet that will help you put together your resume.

College interview: Required by most colleges with highly selective procedures. For further information, see "The College Interview" in the previous chapter.

ADMISSION PROCEDURES

Your first task in applying is to get application forms. That's easy. You can get them from your high school's guidance department, at college fairs, or by calling or writing to colleges and requesting applications. (See "Writing to a College for Information" in the previous chapter.) The trend, however, is leaning toward online applications, which you can do at the school's Web site. Admission information can also be gathered from college representatives, catalogs, Web sites, and directories; alumni or students attending the college; and campus visits. Take a look at "Do's and Don'ts for Filling out Your Applications" on page 70 for some guidelines.

PARENT PERSPECTIVE

Q: What can parents do to help their children make decisions about colleges?

A: Parents and teens should visit college campuses early and trust their gut feelings about whether the campus feels right. Above all, don't be blinded by name-brand colleges and the strong peer pressure that seems to steer your teen in the direction of prestigious colleges. Just as in shopping for clothing: Would you rather have a name brand or something that fits you well and makes you feel comfortable?

Ask your teen some questions. Do you really want to live in a pressure-cooker for the next four years? Some students thrive in a highly competitive environment, but many do not—even if they are excellent students. Before making a final decision, a teen should spend three or four days at the two colleges that interest him or her the most.

Senior year in high school is a time when teens go through many changes and experiment with many different roles. This can be bewildering to parents. Be patient. Realize that the time is equally bewildering to your son or daughter. Parents can be supportive and understanding, even though their teen may seem to be pushing them away. Offer guidance about choosing the right college, even though your teen might seem to be rejecting it. Teens hear everything, though they might not show it.

Marilyn Wedge, Ph.D.
Parent, family therapist, and educational consultant
Agoura Hills, California

Which Admissions Option Is Best for You?

One of the first questions you will be asked on applications for four-year colleges and universities is which admission option you want. What they're talking about is whether you want to apply early action, early decision, deferred admission, etc.

Four-year institutions generally offer the following admissions options:

Early admission: A student of superior ability is admitted into college courses and programs before completing high school.

Early decision: A student declares a first choice college, requests that the college decide on acceptance early (between November and January), and agrees to enroll if accepted. Students with a strong high school record who are sure they want to attend a certain school should consider early decision admission. (See "More on Early Decision," on the next page.)

Early action: Similar to early decision, but if a student is accepted, he or she has until the regular admission deadline to decide whether or not to attend.

Early evaluation: A student can apply under early evaluation to find out if the chance of acceptance is good, fair, or poor. Applications are due before the regular admission deadline, and the student is given an opinion between January and March.

Regular admission: This is the most common option offered to students. A deadline is set for when all applications must be received, and all notifications are sent out at the same time.

Rolling admission: The college accepts students who meet the academic requirements on a first-come, first-served basis until it fills its freshman class. No strict application deadline is specified. Applications are reviewed and decisions are made immediately (usually within two to three weeks). This method is commonly used at large state universities, so students should apply early for the best chance of acceptance.

Open admission: Virtually all high school graduates are admitted, regardless of academic qualifications.

Deferred admission: An accepted student is allowed to postpone enrollment for a year.

If you're going to a two-year college, these options also apply to you. Two-year colleges usually have an "open-door" admission policy, which means that high school graduates may enroll as long as space is available. Sometimes vocational/career colleges are somewhat selective, and competition for admission may be fairly intense for programs that are highly specialized.

More on Early Decision

Early decision is a legally binding agreement between you and the college. If the college accepts you, you pay a deposit within a short period of time and sign an agreement stating that you will not apply to other colleges. To keep students from backing out, some colleges mandate that applicants' high school counselors cannot send transcripts to other institutions.

STUDENT COUNSEL

Q: What made you want to apply to college early decision?

A: I visited lots of schools in Pennsylvania, but the minute I walked on the campus at Gettysburg, I knew I wanted to come here. I liked the way the campus was set up. It was small, and everything was together. The student-teacher ratio was low, and it had a good political science program. It had everything that I wanted.

But if you want to go early decision, you have to visit the schools to be able to compare and contrast the different campuses. Many of the schools will have the same things, like small class size, but the way you feel about the campus is the largest factor because that's where you will be living. I visited Gettysburg four times, so when I went early decision, I was confident about it. I realized it was a huge step and knew I had to be sure. But after visiting here so many times, I knew I'd be unhappy anywhere else.

Kelly Keegan
Gettysburg College

In many ways, early decision is a win-win for both students and colleges. Students can relax and enjoy their senior year of high school without waiting to see if other colleges have accepted them. And colleges know early in the year who is enrolled and can start planning the coming year.

When Is Early Decision the Right Decision?

For good and bad reasons, early decision is a growing trend, so why not just do it? Early decision is an excellent idea that comes with a warning. It's not a good idea unless you have done a thorough college search and know without a shred of doubt that this is the college for you. Don't go for early decision unless you've spent time on the campus, in classes and dorms, and you have a true sense of the academic and social climate of that college.

Early decision can get sticky if you change your mind. Parents of students who have signed agreements and then want to apply elsewhere get angry at high school counselors, saying they've taken away their rights to choose among colleges. They try to force them to send out transcripts even though their children have committed to one college. To guard against this scenario, some colleges ask parents and students to sign a statement signifying their understanding that early decision is a binding plan. Some high schools now have their own form for students and parents to sign acknowledging that they completely realize the nature of an early decision agreement.

The Financial Reason Against Early Decision

Another common argument against early decision is that if an institution has you locked in, there's no incentive to offer applicants the best financial packages. The consensus seems to be that if you're looking to play the financial game, don't apply for early decision.

However, some folks argue that the best financial aid offers are usually made to attractive applicants. In general, if a student receives an early decision offer, they fall into that category and so would get "the sweetest" financial aid anyway. That doesn't mean that there aren't colleges out there using financial incentives to get students to enroll. A strong candidate who applies to six or eight schools and gets admitted to them all will look at how much money the colleges throw his or her way before making a decision.

Before You Decide...

If you're thinking about applying for early decision at a college, ask yourself these questions first. You'll be glad you did.

- Why am I applying early decision?
- Have I thoroughly researched several colleges and do I know what my options are?
- Do I know why I'm going to college and what I want to accomplish there?
- Have I visited several schools, spent time in classes, stayed overnight, and talked to professors?
- Do the courses that the college offers match my goals?
- Am I absolutely convinced that one college clearly stands out above all others?

MORE MUMBO JUMBO

Besides confusing terms like deferred admission, early decision, and early evaluation, just discussed, you'll most likely stumble upon some additional terms that might bamboozle you. Here, we explain a few more:

Academic Calendar

Traditional semesters: Two equal periods of time during a school year.

Early semester: Two equal periods of time during a school year. The first semester is completed before Christmas.

Trimester: Calendar year divided into three equal periods of time. The third trimester replaces summer school.

Quarter: Four equal periods of time during a school year.

4-1-4: Two equal terms of about four months separated by a one-month term.

Accreditation

Accreditation is recognition of a college or university by a regional or national organization, which indicates that the institution has met its objectives and is maintaining prescribed educational standards. Colleges may be accredited by one of six regional associations of schools and colleges and by any one of many national specialized accrediting bodies.

Specialized accreditation of individual programs is granted by national professional organizations. This is intended to ensure that specific programs meet or exceed minimum requirements established by the professional organization. States may require that students in some professions that grant licenses graduate from an accredited program as one qualification for licensure.

Accreditation is somewhat like receiving a pass/fail grade. It doesn't differentiate colleges and universities that excel from those that meet minimum requirements. Accreditation applies to all programs within an institution, but it does not mean that all programs are of equal quality within an institution. Accreditation does not guarantee transfer recognition by other colleges. Transfer decisions are made by individual institutions.

Affiliation

Not-for-profit colleges are classified into one of the following categories: state-assisted, private/independent, or private/church-supported. The institution's affiliation does not guarantee the quality or nature of the institution, and it may or may not have an effect on the religious life of students.

State-assisted colleges and universities and private/independent colleges do not have requirements related to the religious activity of their students. The influence of religion varies among private/church-supported colleges. At some, religious services or study are encouraged or required; at others, religious affiliation is less apparent.

Articulation Agreement

Articulation agreements facilitate the transfer of students and credits among state-assisted institutions of higher education by establishing transfer procedures and equitable treatment of all students in the system.

One type of articulation agreement links two or more colleges so that students can continue to make progress toward their degree, even if they must attend different schools at different times. For example, some states' community colleges have agreements with their state universities that permit graduates of college parallel programs to transfer with junior standing.

A second type of articulation agreement links secondary (high school) and postsecondary institutions to allow students to gain college credit for relevant vocational courses. This type of agreement saves students time and tuition in the pursuit of higher learning.

Because articulation agreements vary from school to school and from program to program, it is recommended that students check with their home institution and the institution they are interested in attending in order to fully understand the options available to them and each institution's specific requirements.

Cross-Registration

Cross-registration is a cooperative arrangement offered by many colleges and universities for the purpose of increasing the number and types of courses offered at any one institution. This arrangement allows students to cross-register for one or more courses at any participating host institution. While specific cross-registration program requirements may vary, typically a student can cross-register without having to pay the host institution additional tuition.

If your college participates in cross-registration, check with your home institution concerning any additional tuition costs and request a cross-registration form. Check with your adviser and registrar at your home institution to make sure that the course you plan to take is approved, and then contact the host institution for cross-registration instructions. Make sure that there is space available in the course you want to take at the host institution, as some host institutions give their own students registration priority.

To participate in cross-registration, you may need to be a full-time student (some programs allow part-time student participation) in good academic and financial standing at your home institution. Check with both colleges well in advance for all of the specific requirements.

THE COMPLETE APPLICATION PACKAGE

Freshman applications can be filed any time after you have completed your junior year of high school. Colleges strongly recommend that students apply by April (at the latest) of their senior year in order to be considered for acceptance, scholarships, financial aid, and housing. College requirements may vary, so always read and comply with specific requirements. In general, admission officers are interested in the following basic materials:

- A completed and signed application and any required application fee.
- An official copy of your high school transcript, including your class ranking and grade point average. The transcript must include all work completed as of the date the application is submitted. Check with your guidance counselor for questions about these items. If you apply on line, you must inform your guidance counselor and request that he or she send your transcript to the schools to which you are applying. Your application will not be processed without a transcript.
- An official record of your ACT Assessment or SAT scores.
- Other items that may be required include letters of recommendation, an essay, the

(Continued on page 70)

COLLEGE APPLICATION CHECKLIST Keep track of your applications by inserting a check mark or the completion date in the appropriate column and row.

	College 1	College 2	College 3	College 4
Campus visit				
Campus interview				
Letters of recommendation				
NAME:				
Date requested				
Follow-up				
NAME:				
Date requested				
Follow-up				
NAME:				
Date requested				
Follow-up				
Counselor recommendation form to counselor				
Secondary school report form to counselor				
Test scores requested				
Transcripts sent				
Application completed				
Essay completed				
All signatures collected				
Financial aid forms enclosed				
Application fee enclosed				
Copies made of all forms and documentation enclosed in application packet				
Postage affixed/return address on envelope				
Letters of acceptance/denial/wait list received				
Colleges notified of intent				
Tuition deposit sent				
Housing and other forms submitted to chosen college				
Orientation scheduled				

secondary school report form and midyear school report (sent in by your guidance counselor after you fill out a portion of the form), and any financial aid forms required by the college.

Use the "College Application Checklist" on the previous page to make sure you have what you need before you send everything off.

Filling out the Forms

Filling out college applications can seem like a daunting task, but there are six easy steps to follow for the successful completion of this part of the process.

Step 1: Practice Copies

Make a photocopy of each application of each college to which you plan to apply. Since the presentation of your application may be considered an important aspect in the weighting for admission, you don't want to erase, cross out, or use white-out on your final application. Make all your mistakes on your copies. When you think you have it right, then transfer the information to your final original copy or go on line to enter it on the college's electronic application. Remember, at the larger universities, the application packet may be the only part of you they see.

Step 2: Decide on Your Approach

What is it about your application that will grab the admission counselor's attention so that it will be pulled out of the sea of applications on his or her desk for consideration? Be animated and interesting in what you say. Be memorable in your approach to your application, but don't overdo it. You want the admissions counselor to remember you, not your Spanish castle made of popsicle sticks. Most importantly, be honest and don't exaggerate your academics and extracurricular activities. Approach this process with integrity every step of the way. First of all, it is the best way to end up in a college that is the right match for you. Second, if you are less than truthful, the college will eventually learn about it.

DO'S AND DON'TS FOR FILLING OUT YOUR APPLICATIONS

One of the most intimidating steps of applying for admission to college is filling out all the forms. This list of do's and don'ts will help you put your best foot forward on your college applications.

DO

- **Read applications and directions carefully.**
- **Make sure that everything that is supposed to be included is enclosed.**
- **Make copies of applications, and practice filling one out before you complete the original.**
- **Fill out your own applications. Type the information yourself to avoid crucial mistakes.**
- **Start with the simple applications and then progress to the more complex ones.**
- **Type or neatly print your answers, and then proofread the applications and essays several times for accuracy. Also ask someone else to proofread them for you.**
- **If asked, describe how you can make a contribution to the schools to which you apply.**
- **Be truthful, and do not exaggerate your accomplishments.**
- **Keep a copy of all forms you submit to colleges.**
- **Be thorough and on time.**

DON'T

- **Use correction fluid. If you type your application, use a correctable typewriter or the liftoff strips to correct mistakes. Better yet, fill out your application on line.**
- **Write in script. If you don't have access to a computer or typewriter, print neatly.**
- **Leave blank spaces. Missing information may cause your application to be sent back or delayed while admission officers wait for complete information.**
- **Be unclear. If the question calls for a specific answer, don't try to dodge it by being vague.**
- **Put it off!**

How will they know? You have to supply support materials to accompany your application, things like transcripts and recommendations. If you tell one story and they tell another, the admissions office will notice the disparity—another red flag!

Step 3: Check the Deadlines

In September of your senior year, organize your applications in chronological order. Place the due dates for your final list of schools next to their names on your stretch, target, and safety list and on your "College Application Checklist." Work on the earliest due date first.

Step 4: Check the Data on You

You need to make sure that the information you will be sending to support your applications is correct. The first thing to double-check is your transcript. This is an important piece because you must send a transcript with each application you send to colleges. Take a trip to the guidance office and ask for a "Transcript Request Form." Fill out the request for a formal transcript indicating that you are requesting a copy for yourself and that you will pick it up. Pay the fee if there is one.

When you get your transcript, look it over carefully. It will be several pages long and will include everything from the titles of all the courses that you have taken since the ninth grade along with the final grade for each course to the community service hours you have logged each year. Check the information carefully. It is understandable that with this much data, it is easy to make an input error. Because this information is vital to you and you are the best judge of accuracy, it is up to you to check it. Take any corrections or questions you have back to your guidance counselor to make the corrections. If it is a questionable grade, your counselor will help you find out what grade should have been posted on your transcript. Do whatever needs to be done to make sure your transcript has been corrected no later than October 1 of your senior year.

Step 5: List Your Activities

When you flip through your applications, you will find a section on extracurricular activities. It is time to hit your computer again to prioritize your list of extracurricular activities and determine the best approach for presenting them to your colleges. Some students will prepare a resume and include this in every application they send. Other students will choose to develop an "Extracurricular, Academic, and Work Experience Addendum" and mark those specific sections of their application as "See attached Addendum."

If you are a powerhouse student with a great deal to say in this area, it will take time to prioritize your involvement in activities and word it succinctly yet interestingly. Your "Brag Sheet" will help (see "The Brag Sheet" on page 72). Put those activities that will have the strongest impact, show the most consistent involvement, and demonstrate your leadership abilities at the top of the list. This will take time, so plan accordingly. If you feel you have left out important information because the form limits you, include either an addendum or your resume as a back-up.

Step 6: Organize Your Other Data

What other information can you organize in advance of sitting down to fill out your applications?

The Personal Data Section

Most of this section is standard personal information that you will not have any difficulty responding to, but some items you will need to think about. For example, you may find a question that asks, "What special college or division are you applying to?" Do you have a specific school in mind, like the College of Engineering? If you are not sure about your major, ask yourself what interests you the most and then enter that college. Once you are in college and have a better sense of what you want to do, you can always change your major later.

The application will provide an optional space to declare ethnicity. If you feel you would like to declare an area and that it would work to your advantage for

(Continued on page 73)

THE BRAG SHEET

At the beginning of this chapter, we described how a student resume can help your guidance counselors and teachers write their letters of recommendation for you. Putting together a list of your accomplishments will also help you organize all of the information you will need to include when you fill out your college applications.

ACADEMICS

GPA (Grade Point Average) ______________________

THE HONORS COURSES I HAVE TAKEN ARE:

English ______________________

History ______________________

Math ______________________

Science ______________________

Language ______________________

Electives ______________________

THE AP COURSES I HAVE TAKEN ARE:

English ______________________

History ______________________

Math ______________________

Science ______________________

Language ______________________

Electives ______________________

STANDARDIZED TEST SCORES

PSAT ______________________

1st SAT ______________________

2nd SAT ______________________

ACT Assessment ______________________

SAT SUBJECT TESTS

Test 1 __________ **Score** __________

Test 2 __________ **Score** __________

Test 3 __________ **Score** __________

SPECIAL TALENTS

I have received the following academic awards:

____

____

____

____

I have performed in these theatrical productions: __________

____

I am lettered in the following sports: ______________________

____

I have played on the following traveling teams: ______________________

____

____

I am a member of the following musical groups: ______________________

____

EXTRACURRICULAR ACTIVITIES

I participate on a regular basis in the following extracurricular activities: ______________________

____

I have held the following offices: ______________________

____

____

I have established the following extracurricular organizations:

____

____

I have held the following after-school and summer jobs: __________

____

____

GOALS

I plan to major in the following area in college: ______________________

____

admission, consider completing this section of the application.

You are also going to need your high school's College Entrance Examination Board (CEEB) number. That is the number you needed when you filled out your test packets. It is stamped on the front of your SAT and ACT Assessment packets, or, if you go to the guidance department, they'll tell you what it is.

The Standardized Testing Section

Applications ask you for your test dates and scores. Get them together accurately. All your College Board scores should be recorded with the latest test results you have received. Your latest ACT Assessment record will only have the current scores unless you asked for all your past test results. If you have lost this information, call these organizations or go to your guidance department. Your counselor should have copies. Be sure the testing organizations are sending your official score reports to the schools to which you're applying. If you are planning to take one of these tests in the future, the colleges will want those dates, too; they will wait for those scores before making a decision. If you change your plans, write the admissions office a note with the new dates or the reason for canceling.

The Senior Course Load Section

Colleges will request that you list your present senior schedule by semester. Set this information up in this order: List any AP or honors-level full-year courses first, as these will have the most impact. Then list other required full-year courses and then required semester courses, followed by electives. Make sure you list first-semester and second-semester courses appropriately. Do not forget to include physical education if you are taking it this year.

Your Recommendation Writers

Most schools will require you to submit two or three letters of recommendation from adults who know you well.

Guidance Counselor Recommendations

Nearly all colleges require a letter of recommendation from the applicant's high school guidance counselor. Some counselors will give students an essay question that they feel will give them the background they need in order to structure a recommendation. Other counselors will canvass a wide array of individuals who know a student in order to gather a broader picture of the student in various settings. No one approach is better than the other. Find out which approach is used at your school. You will probably get this information as a handout at one of those evening guidance programs or in a classroom presentation by your school's guidance department. If you are still not sure you know what is expected of you or if the dog has eaten those papers, ask your guidance counselor what is due and by what date. Make sure that you complete the materials on time and that you set aside enough of your time to do them justice.

Teacher Recommendations

In addition to the recommendation from your counselor, colleges may request additional recommendations from your teachers. Known as formal recommendations, these are sent directly to the colleges by your subject teachers. Most colleges require at least one formal recommendation in addition to the counselor's recommendation. However, many competitive institutions require two, if not three, academic recommendations. Follow a school's directions regarding the exact number. A good rule-of-thumb is to have recommendations from teachers in two subject areas (e.g., English and math).

Approach your recommendation writers personally to request that they write for you. If they agree, provide them with a copy of your Brag Sheet. On the other hand, you may be met with a polite refusal on the order of "I'm sorry, but I'm unable to write for you. I've been approached by so many seniors already that it would be difficult for me to accomplish your recommendation by your due dates." This teacher may really be overburdened with requests for recommendations, especially if this is a senior English teacher, or the teacher may be giving you a signal that someone else may be able to write a stronger piece for you. Either way, accept the refusal politely, and seek another recommendation writer.

How do you decide whom to ask? Here are some questions to help you select your writers:

- How well does the teacher know you?
- Has the teacher taught you for more than one course? (A teacher who taught you over a two- to three-year period has seen your talents and skills develop.)
- Has the teacher sponsored an extracurricular activity in which you made a contribution?
- Do you get along with the teacher?
- Does the college/university indicate that a recommendation is required or recommended from a particular subject-area instructor?
- If you declare an intended major, can you obtain a recommendation from a teacher in that subject area?

Other Recommendation Writers

Consider getting recommendations from your employer, your rabbi or pastor, the director of the summer camp where you worked for the last two summers, and so on—but only if these additional letters are going to reveal information about you that will have a profound impact on the way a college will view your candidacy. Otherwise, you run the risk of overloading your application with too much paper.

FROM THE GUIDANCE OFFICE

Q: Why are essays so important to the college application?

A: Students focus more on grades than anything else. They think grades are the be-all and end-all and that an SAT score will get them in. For most selective schools, that's just one piece of the pie. Many of the schools in the upper 20 percent of competitive schools consider the essay more heavily. Essays show whether the student is a thinker, creative, and analytical. They're looking for the type of personality that can shine rather than one that simply can spit out names and dates. When everyone has high SATs in a pool of applicants, the essay is what makes one student stand out over another.

Patsy Lovelady
Counselor
MacArthur High School
San Antonio, Texas

Writing the Application Essay

Application essays show how you think and how you write. They also reveal additional information about you that is not in your other application material. Not all colleges require essays, and those that do often have a preferred topic. Make sure you write about the topic that is specified and keep to the length of pages or words. If the essay asks for 300 words, don't submit 50 or 500. Some examples of essay topics include:

Tell us about yourself. Describe your personality and a special accomplishment. Illustrate the unique aspects of who you are, what you do, and what you want out of life. Share an experience that made an impact on you, or write about something you have learned from your parents.

Tell us about an academic or extracurricular interest or idea. Show how a book, experience, quotation, or idea reflects or shapes your outlook and aspirations.

Tell us why you want to come to our college. Explain why your goals and interests match the programs and offerings of that particular school. This question requires some research about the school. Be specific.

Show us an imaginative side of your personality. This question demands originality but is a great opportunity to show off your skills as a writer. Start writing down your thoughts and impressions well before the essay is due. Think about how you have changed over the years so that if and when it comes time to write about yourself, you will have plenty of information. Write about something that means a lot to you, and support your thoughts with reasons and examples. Then explain why you care about your topic.

The essay should not be a summary of your high school career. Describe yourself as others see you, and use a natural, conversational style. Use an experience to set the scene in which you will illustrate something about yourself. For example, you might discuss how having a disabled relative helped you to appreciate life's simple pleasures. Or you may use your athletic experiences to tell how you learned the value of teamwork. The essay is your chance to tell something positive or enriching about yourself, so highlight an experience that will make the reader interested in you.

Outline in the essay what you have to offer the college. Explain why you want to attend the institution and how your abilities and goals match the strengths and offerings at the university. Write, rewrite, and edit. Do not try to dash off an essay in one sitting. The essay will improve with time and thought. Proofread and concentrate on spelling, punctuation, and content. Have someone else take a look at your essay. Make copies and save them after mailing the original.

Admission officers look for the person inside the essay. They seek students with a breadth of knowledge and experiences, someone with depth and perspective. Inner strength and commitment are admired, too. Not everyone is a winner all the time. The essay is a tool you can use to develop your competitive edge. Your essay should explain why you should be admitted over other applicants.

As a final word, write the essay from the heart. It should have life and not be contrived or one-dimensional. Avoid telling them what they want to hear; instead, be yourself.

SPECIAL INFORMATION FOR ATHLETES

If you weren't a planner before, but you want to play sports while in college or go to college on an athletic scholarship, you'd better become a planner now. There are many regulations and conditions you need to know ahead of time so that you don't miss out on possible opportunities.

First, think about whether or not you have what it takes to play college sports. It's a tough question to ask, but it's a necessary one. In general, playing college sports requires both basic skills and natural

SAMPLE APPLICATION ESSAY

Here is one student's college application essay. She answered the question, "Indicate a person who has had a significant influence on you, and describe that influence."

Mrs. Morrone did not become my guidance counselor until my sophomore year of high school. During my first meeting with her, I sat across from her in an uncomfortable vinyl chair and refused to meet her eyes as I told her about my long and painful shyness, how I detested oral reports, and how I feared raising my hand in class or being called on to answer a question—all because I didn't want to be the center of attention.

She did not offer me advice right away. Instead, she asked me more about myself—my family, my friends, what kinds of music, books, and movies I liked. We talked easily, like old friends, and it was not long before I began to look forward to our weekly meetings. Her office was one of the few places where I felt like I could be myself and let my personality shine through, where I knew that I was accepted and liked unconditionally.

In November of that year, the drama club announced auditions for the spring play, The Glass Menagerie. I had studied it in English class and it was one of my favorites; not surprisingly, I identified strongly with the timid Laura. I talked with Mrs. Morrone about the play and how much I liked theater. At one point I sighed, "I'd love to play Laura."

"Why don't you try out for the show?" Mrs. Morrone suggested.

The very idea of performing, onstage, in a spotlight, in front of dozens of people frightened me. She did not press the matter, but at the end of the session she encouraged me to bring a copy of the play to our next few meetings and read some of the character's lines, "just for fun." I did, and found myself gradually transforming into Laura as I recited her lines with increasing intensity.

After a couple of these amateur performances, she told me that I was genuinely good as Laura, and she would love to see me at least audition for the part. "I would never force you to do it," she said, "but I would hate to see you waste your potential." I insisted that I was too frightened, but she promised that she would come and watch my audition. She told me to pretend she was the only person in the audience.

A week later, I did read for the part of Laura. Mrs. Morrone beamed with pride in the back of the auditorium. I discovered that I truly enjoyed acting; slipping into another character cracked the shell that I had built around myself. I did not get the part, but I had found a passion that enriched my life in immeasurable ways. I owe Mrs. Morrone so much for putting me on the path to becoming a professional actress and for helping me to finally conquer my shyness. Without her quiet support and strength, none of this would have come to pass.

FROM THE GUIDANCE OFFICE

Q: What's a big mistake high school athletes make when thinking about college?

A: Some athletes think that their athletic ability alone will get them a scholarship and do not believe that their academics must be acceptable. The Division I or II schools cannot offer scholarships if the student has not met the academic standards required by the school for admission. Our counselors start reminding students in the freshman year and every year after that the courses they take do make a difference in how colleges view their transcripts. Students can't start preparing in their senior year of high school.

Sue Bradshaw
Guidance Counselor
Sterling High School
Baytown, Texas

ability, a solid knowledge of the sport, overall body strength, speed, and sound academics. Today's athletes are stronger and faster because of improved methods of training and conditioning. They are coached in skills and techniques, and they begin training in their sport at an early age. Remember, your talents will be compared with those from across the U.S. and around the world.

Second, know the background. Most college athletic programs are regulated by the National Collegiate Athletic Association (NCAA), an organization that has established rules on eligibility, recruiting, and financial aid. The NCAA has three membership divisions: Division I, Division II, and Division III. Institutions are members of one or another division according to the size and scope of their athletic programs and whether they provide athletic scholarships.

If you are planning to enroll in college as a freshman and you wish to participate in Division I or Division II athletics, you must be certified by the NCAA Initial-Eligibility Clearinghouse (www.ncaaclearinghouse.net). The Clearinghouse was established as a separate organization by the NCAA member institutions to ensure consistent interpretation of NCAA initial-eligibility requirements for all prospective student athletes at all member institutions.

You should start the certification process when you are a junior in high school. Check with your counselor to make sure you are taking a core curriculum that meets NCAA requirements. Also, register to take the ACT Assessment or SAT as a junior. Submit your Student Release Form (available in your guidance counseling office) to the Clearinghouse by the beginning of your senior year.

Initial Eligibility of Freshman Athletes for Division I and II

Students who plan to participate in NCAA Division I or II college sports must obtain the Student Release Form from their high school, complete it, and send it to the NCAA Clearinghouse. This form authorizes high schools to release student transcripts, including test scores, proof of grades, and other academic information, to the Clearinghouse. It also authorizes the Clearinghouse to release this information to the colleges that request it. The form and corresponding fee must be received before any documents will be processed. (Fee waivers are available for economically disadvantaged students. Check with your counselor for fee waiver information.)

Students must also make sure that the Clearinghouse receives ACT Assessment and/or SAT score reports. Students can have score reports sent directly to the Clearinghouse by entering a specific code (9999) printed in the ACT Assessment and SAT registration packets.

Once a year, high schools will send an updated list of approved core courses, which lists each course offering that meets NCAA core course requirements. The Clearinghouse personnel will validate the form. Thereafter, the Clearinghouse will determine each student's initial eligibility. Collegiate institutions will request information from the Clearinghouse on the initial eligibility of prospective student-athletes. The Clearinghouse will make a certification decision and report it directly to the institution.

Three types of eligibility are possible:

1. Certification of eligibility for expense-paid campus visits.
2. Preliminary certification of eligibility to participate in college sports (appears likely to meet all NCAA requirements but not yet graduated).

ATHLETIC RESUME

Name ______________________

Address ______________________

____

High school address and phone number

____

____

____

Coach's name ______________________

Height/weight ______________________

Foot speed (by specific event) ______________________

Position played ______________________

Weight classification ______________________

GPA ______________________

Class rank ______________________

ACT Assessment or SAT scores (or when you plan to take them)______________________

____

Athletic records held______________________

____

All-state teams ______________________

Special awards ______________________

Off-season accomplishments ______________________

Weightlifting exercises ______________________

Vertical jumps ______________________

Push-ups ______________________

Bench jumps ______________________

Shuttle run ______________________

Leadership characteristics ______________________

Former successful athletes from your high school

____

Outstanding capabilities______________________

Citizenship ______________________

Alumni parents/relatives ______________________

Include the following with your resume:

- Team schedule with dates and times
- Videotape with jersey number identified
- Newspaper clippings about you and/or your team

3. Final certification granted when proof of graduation is received.

Additional information about the Clearinghouse can be found in the *Guide for the College-Bound Student-Athlete*, published by the NCAA. To get a copy of this guide, call 800-638-3731 (toll-free). You can also visit the NCAA Web site at www2.ncaa.org.

National Association of Intercollegiate Athletics (NAIA) Regulations

The National Association of Intercollegiate Athletics (NAIA) has different eligibility requirements for student-athletes. To be eligible to participate in intercollegiate athletics as an incoming freshman, two of the following three requirements must be met:

1. Have a 2.0 (C) or higher cumulative final grade point average in high school.
2. Have a composite score of 18 or higher on the ACT Assessment or an 860 total score or higher on the SAT on a single test administered on a national test date.
3. Have a top-half final class rank in his or her high school graduating class.

Student-athletes must also have on file at the college an official ACT Assessment or SAT score report from the appropriate national testing center. Results reported on the student's high school transcript are not acceptable. Students must request that their test scores be forwarded to the college's admission office.

If you have additional questions about NAIA eligibility, contact them at:

NAIA
23500 W. 105 Street
P.O. Box 1325
Olathe, Kansas 66051
913-791-0044
www.naia.org

AUDITIONS AND PORTFOLIOS

If you decide to study the arts, such as theater, music, or fine arts, you may be required to audition or show your portfolio to admissions personnel. The following tips will help you showcase your talents and skills when preparing for an audition or portfolio review.

STUDENT COUNSEL

Q: What's it like going to an art school?

A: This is not your normal college experience. You totally immerse yourself in art and commit all your time to it. It's intense and can be stressful. The teachers are great. Most are working professionals. The student body is impressive. I have people in my class who are 35 and have gone to a regular college.

Coming from high school, it's hard to get into an art school. You're disadvantaged because you haven't worked. I suggest going to the portfolio days in high school where schools will evaluate your portfolio and you can get an idea of where you want to go. Since my sophomore year in high school, I kept in touch with the admissions person I talked to at portfolio day. She followed me along and saw my interest.

Eric Davidson
Art Center
Pasadena, California

Music Auditions

High school students who wish to pursue a degree in music, whether it is vocal or instrumental, typically must audition. If you're a singer, prepare at least two pieces in contrasting styles. One should be in a foreign language, if possible. Choose from operatic, show music, or art song repertories, and make sure you memorize each piece. If you're an instrumentalist or pianist, be prepared to play scales and arpeggios, at least one etude or technical study, and a solo work. Instrumental audition pieces need not be memorized. In either field, you may be required to do sight-reading.

When performing music that is sight-read, you should take time to look over the piece and make certain of the key and time signatures before proceeding with the audition. If you're a singer, you should bring a familiar accompanist to the audition.

"My advice is to ask for help from teachers, try to acquire audition information up front, and know more than is required for the audition," says one student. "It is also a good idea to select your audition time and date early."

"Try to perform your solo in front of as many people as you can as many times as possible," says another student. "You may also want to try to get involved in a high school performance."

Programs differ, so students are encouraged to call the college and ask for audition information. In general, music departments seek students who demonstrate technical competence and performance achievement.

Admission to music programs varies in degree of competitiveness, so you should audition at a minimum of three colleges and a maximum of five to amplify your opportunity. The degree of competitiveness varies also by instrument, especially if a renowned musician teaches a certain instrument. Some colleges offer a second audition if you feel you did not audition to your potential. Ideally, you will be accepted into the music program of your choice, but keep in mind that it's possible to not be accepted. You must then make the decision to either pursue a music program at another college or consider another major at that college.

Dance Auditions

At many four-year colleges, an open class is held the day before auditions. A performance piece that combines improvisation, ballet, modern, and rhythm is taught and then students are expected to perform the piece at auditions. Professors look for coordination, technique, rhythm, degree of movement, and body structure. The dance faculty members also assess your ability to learn and your potential to complete the curriculum. Dance programs vary, so check with the college of your choice for specific information.

Art Portfolios

A portfolio is simply a collection of your best pieces of artwork. The pieces you select to put in your portfolio should demonstrate your interest and aptitude for a serious education in the arts. A well-developed portfolio can help you gain acceptance into a prestigious art college and increase your chances of being awarded a scholarship in national portfolio competitions. The pieces you select should show diversity in technique and variety in subject matter. You may show work in any medium (oils, photography, watercolors, pastels, etc.) and in either black-and-white or color. Your portfolio can include classroom assignments as well as independent projects. You can also include your sketchbook.

Specialized art colleges request that you submit an average of ten pieces of art, but remember that quality is more important than quantity. The admission office staff will review your artwork and transcripts to assess your skill and potential for success. Usually, you will present your portfolio in person; however, some schools allow students to mail slides if distance is an issue. There is no simple formula for success other than hard work. In addition, there is no such thing as a "perfect portfolio," nor any specific style or direction to achieve one.

Tips for Pulling Your Portfolio Together:

- Try to make your portfolio as clean and organized as possible.
- It is important to protect your work, but make sure the package you select is easy to handle and does not interfere with the viewing of the artwork.
- Drawings that have been rolled up are difficult for the jurors to handle and view. You may shrink-wrap the pieces, but it is not required.
- Avoid loose sheets of paper between pieces.
- If you choose to mount or mat your work (not required), use only neutral gray tones, black, or white.
- Never include framed pieces or three smudge.
- A slide portfolio should be presented in a standard 8 × 11 plastic slide sleeve, which can be purchased at any photo or camera supply store.
- Be sure paintings are completely dry before you place them in your portfolio.
- Label each piece with your name, address, and high school.

Theater Auditions

Most liberal arts colleges do not require that students who audition be accepted into the theater department unless the college offers a Bachelor of Fine Arts (B.F.A.) degree in theater. You should apply to the college of your choice prior to scheduling an audition. You should also consider spending a full day on campus so that you may talk with theater faculty members and students, attend classes, meet with your admission counselor, and tour the facilities.

Although each college and university has different requirements, you should prepare two contrasting monologues taken from plays of your choice if you're auditioning for a B.F.A. acting program. Musical theater requirements generally consist of one up-tempo musical selection and one ballad, as well as one monologue from a play or musical of your choice. The total of all your pieces should not exceed 5 minutes. Music for the accompanist, a resume of your theater experience, and a photo are also required.

Tips to Get You Successfully through an Audition:

- Choose material suitable for your age.
- If you choose your monologue from a book of monologues, you should read the entire play and be familiar with the context of your selection.
- Select a monologue that allows you to speak directly to another person; you should play only one character.
- Memorize your selection.
- Avoid using characterization or style, as they tend to trap you rather than tapping deeper into inner resources.

8 Chapter

FINANCIAL AID DOLLARS AND SENSE

Getting financial aid can be intimidating—but don't let that stop you.

FINDING THE MONEY you need to attend a two- or four-year institution or vocational/career college is a challenge, but you can do it if you devise a strategy well before you actually start applying to college. Financial aid comes from a lot of different sources. But this is where GAJ comes in. You'll find lots of help in this guide in locating those sources and where to get advice. Financial aid is available to help meet both direct educational costs (tuition, fees, books) and personal living expenses (food, housing, transportation).

Times have changed to favor the student in the financial aid process. Because the pool of potential traditional college students is somewhat limited, colleges and universities are competing to attract the top students to their school. In fact, some colleges and universities not only use financial aid as a method to help students fund their college education but often as a marketing and recruitment tool. This puts students and families at an advantage, one that should be recognized and used for bargaining power.

PROJECTED COLLEGE EXPENSES

The following chart estimates the cost of one year of college education, including tuition, room, and board. Estimates are based on a 6 percent annual increase.

School Year	Public 4-Year	Private 4-Year
2004–2005	$11,354	$27,516
2007–2008	13,400	32,500
2010–2011	15,450	37,420
2014–2015	18,200	44,025

Source: The College Entrance Examination Board, "Trends in College Pricing, 2004"

It used to be that colleges and universities offered need-based and merit-based financial aid to only needy and/or academically exceptional students. Now some schools offer what might be called incentive or tuition discount aid to encourage students to choose them over another college. This aid, which is not necessarily based on need or merit, is aimed at students who meet the standards of the college but who wouldn't necessarily qualify for traditional kinds of aid.

A BIRD'S-EYE VIEW OF FINANCIAL AID

You and your family should be assertive in negotiating financial aid packages. It used to be that there was no room for such negotiation, but in today's environment, it is wise to be a comparison shopper. Families should wait until they've received all of their financial offers and then talk to their first-choice college to see if the college can match the better offers from other colleges.

To be eligible to receive federal/state financial aid, you must maintain satisfactory academic progress toward a degree or certificate. This criterion is established by each college or university. You'll also need a valid social security number, and all male students must register for selective service on their eighteenth birthday.

You apply for financial aid during your senior year. Every school requires the Free Application for

FINANCIAL AID GLOSSARY

ASSETS. The amount a family has in savings and investments. This includes savings and checking accounts, a business, a farm or other real estate, and stocks, bonds, and trust funds. Cars are not considered assets, nor are such possessions as stamp collections or jewelry. The net value of the principal home is counted as an asset by some colleges in determining their own awards but is not included in the calculation for eligibility for federal funds.

CITIZENSHIP/ELIGIBILITY FOR AID. To be eligible to receive federally funded college aid, a student must be one of the following:

1. A United States citizen;
2. A non-citizen national;
3. A permanent resident with an I-151 or I-551 without conditions;
4. A participant in a suspension of deportation case pending before Congress; or
5. A holder of an I-94 showing one of the following designations: "Refugee," "Asylum Granted," "Indefinite Parole" and/or "Humanitarian Parole," "Cuban/Haitian Entrant, Status Pending," or "Conditional Entrant" (valid if issued before April 1, 1980).

Individuals in the U.S. on an F1 or F2 visa or on a J1 or J2 exchange visa cannot get federal aid.

COOPERATIVE EDUCATION. A program offered by many colleges in which students alternate periods of enrollment with periods of employment, usually paid, and that can lengthen the usual baccalaureate program to five years.

EXPECTED FAMILY CONTRIBUTION (EFC). A figure determined by a congressionally mandated formula that indicates how much of a family's resources should be considered "available" for college expenses. Factors such as taxable and nontaxable income and the value of family assets are taken into account to determine a family's financial strength. Allowances for maintaining a family and future financial needs are then taken into consideration before determining how much a family should be able to put toward the cost of college.

INDEPENDENT STUDENT. A student who reports only his or her own income and assets (and that of a spouse, if relevant) when applying for federal financial aid. Students are automatically considered independent at 24 years of age. Students who are under 24 will be considered independent if they are:

- married as of the date of filing the FAFSA.
- provide more than half the support of a legal dependent other than a spouse.
- a veteran of the U.S. Armed Forces.
- an orphan or ward of the court.
- classified as independent by a college's financial aid administrator because of other unusual circumstances.
- a graduate or professional student.

MERIT-BASED AID. Any form of financial aid awarded on the basis of personal achievement or individual characteristics without reference to financial need.

SUBSIDIZED LOAN. While enrolled at least half-time, this loan does not accure interest. For Subsidized Federal Stafford and/or Direct Loans, the government pays the interest to the lender on behalf of the borrower while the student is in college and during approved grace periods.

Federal Student Aid (FAFSA), which cannot be filed until after January 1 of your senior year. Your application will be processed in about 4 weeks if you use the paper application or about one week if you apply on line at www.fafsa.ed.gov. You'll then receive a Student Aid Report (SAR), which will report the information from the FAFSA and show your calculated Expected Family Contribution (EFC—the number used in determining your eligibility for federal student aid). Each school you listed on the application, as well as your state of legal residence, will also receive your FAFSA information. If you are applying to higher cost colleges or some scholarship programs, you also may have to file the PROFILE® application. This should be completed in September or October of your senior year. More information on the PROFILE is available from your high school guidance office or on the Web at www.collegeboard.org. There is a fee charged with the PROFILE.

COLLEGE FUNDS AVAILABLE

Use this chart to estimate resources that will be available for college expenses. Check your progress at the end of your sophomore and junior years to see if your plans for seeking financial aid need to be revised.

YOUR RESOURCES	Estimated amount available	Actual amount: 11 grade	Actual amount: 12th grade
Savings and other assets			
Summer earnings			
Part-time work during school year			
Miscellaneous			
PARENTS' RESOURCES			
From their current income			
From college savings			
Miscellaneous (insurance, annuities, stocks, trusts, home equity, property assets)			
TOTAL			

Source: American College Testing Program

You must reapply for federal aid every year. Also, if you decide to transfer to another school, your aid doesn't necessarily go with you. Check with your new school to find out what steps you must take to continue receiving aid. You should plan any transfer at least three months in advance.

Once you've decided to which schools you want to apply, talk to the financial aid officers of those schools. There is no substitute for getting information from the source when it comes to understanding your financial aid options. That personal contact can lead you to substantial amounts of financial aid.

If you qualify for admission, don't let the sticker price of the college or program scare you away, because you may get enough financial assistance to pay for the education you want. Don't rule out a private institution until you have received the financial aid package from the school. Private colleges, in order to attract students from all income levels, offer significant amounts of financial aid. Public-supported institutions tend to offer less financial aid because the lower tuition acts as a form of assistance (see "Projected College Expenses"). In addition, students attending school in their home state often have more aid possibilities than if they attend an out-of-state college. Use the "College Funds Available" chart to determine how much you and your family can contribute to your education and the "College Cost Comparison Worksheet" to figure out which schools best suit you financially.

TYPES OF FINANCIAL AID

Be sure that you understand the differences between the types of financial aid so you are fully prepared to apply for each. One or more of these financial resources may make it possible to pursue the education you want.

Grants: Grants are usually given to students with financial need. But the term is also used for athletics (Division I only), academics, demographics, and special talents. Grants do not have to be repaid.

Scholarships: Scholarships, also called "merit aid," are awarded for academic excellence or other special talents or abilities. Repayment is not required.

Loans: Student loans, which have very favorable terms and conditions, are sponsored by the federal government, state governments, and through commercial lending institutions. The Financial Aid Office is the best source of information on student loans. These must be repaid, generally after you graduate or leave school.

College Work-Study: College Work-Study is a federally sponsored program that enables colleges to hire students for employment. If eligible, students work a limited number of hours throughout the school year. Many colleges use their own funds to hire students to work in the many departments and offices on campus. If you do not receive a federal work-study grant, you should contact the Student Employment Office or the Financial Aid Office to help locate nonfederal work-study positions that may be available.

Financial Aid Programs: The federal government is the single largest source of financial aid for students, making more than an estimated $81 billion available in loans, grants, and other aid to millions of students. In addition, a number of sources of financial aid are available to students from state governments, private lenders, foundations, and private sources, and the colleges and universities themselves.

FEDERAL GRANTS

The federal government offers a number of educational grants, which are outlined below:

Federal Pell Grant

The Federal Pell Grant is the largest grant program in the nation; about 5.1 million students receive awards annually. This grant is intended to be the base or starting point of assistance for lower-income families. Eligibility for a Federal Pell Grant depends on the EFC, or Expected Family Contribution. (See the "Financial Aid Glossary" for a description of commonly used terms.) The actual Pell Grant award amounts depend on how much funds are appropriated by Congress each year. The maximum for the 2005–06 school year is $4,050. How much you will receive depends not only on your EFC, but also on your cost of attendance and whether you're a full-time or part-time student.

Federal Supplemental Educational Opportunity Grant (FSEOG)

As its name implies, the Federal Supplemental Educational Opportunity Grant (FSEOG) provides additional need-based federal grant money to supplement the Federal Pell Grant. Each participating college is given funds to award to especially needy students. The maximum award is $4,000 per year, but the amount a student receives depends on the college's policy, the availability of FSEOG funds, the total cost of education, and the amount of other aid awarded.

COLLEGE COST COMPARISON WORKSHEET

Chart your course to see which college or university best fits your financial resources. Your totals in expenses and funds available should be the same amount. If not, you have a funding gap, meaning that you have more expenses than funds available.

	College 1	College 2	College 3	College 4
EXPENSES				
Tuition and fees	$	$	$	$
Books and supplies	$	$	$	$
Room and board	$	$	$	$
Transportation	$	$	$	$
Miscellaneous	$	$	$	$
TOTAL	$	$	$	$
FUNDS AVAILABLE				
Student and parent contributions	$	$	$	$
Grants	$	$	$	$
Scholarships	$	$	$	$
Work-study	$	$	$	$
TOTAL	$	$	$	$
Funding gap	$	$	$	$

FEDERAL SCHOLARSHIPS

The following comprise the scholarships available through the federal government:

ROTC Scholarships

The Armed Forces (Army, Air Force, Navy, Marines) may offer up to a four-year scholarship that pays full college tuition plus a monthly allowance; however, these scholarships are very competitive and based upon GPA, class rank, ACT Assessment or SAT scores, and physical qualifications. Apply as soon as possible before December 1 of your senior year. Contact the headquarters of each of the armed forces for more information: Army, 800-USA-ROTC; Air Force, 800-423-USAF; Navy, 800-USA-NAVY; Marines, 800-MARINES (all numbers are toll-free).

Scholarships from Federal Agencies

Federal agencies, such as the CIA, NASA, Department of Agriculture, and Office of Naval Research, offer an annual stipend as well as a scholarship. In return, the student must work for the agency for a certain number of years or else repay all the financial support. See your counselor for more information.

Robert C. Byrd Honors Scholarship

To qualify for this scholarship, you must demonstrate outstanding academic achievement and excellence in high school as indicated by class rank, high school grades, test scores, and leadership activities. Award amounts of $1,500 are renewable for four years. Contact your high school counselor for application information. Deadlines may vary per state, so also contact your state's Department of Education.

FINANCIAL AID ADVICE

Q: What do you wish students and their parents knew about financial aid?

A: They don't know they should get their financial application filed early enough, so if we run into snags, it can be corrected. They make mistakes, such as not answering the question about the amount of taxes paid the previous year. A lot of parents think that if they didn't send in a check to the IRS, they didn't pay taxes. Something as simple as that causes a lot of problems. If their financial information is recorded incorrectly, it can really mess them up. They should read all the information on the financial aid form, and if they have questions, they should ask someone. Speaking from my experience, if you can't get in touch with the college you're child is thinking of attending, then call a local college. Any time an application doesn't go through the system smoothly, it can cause major problems.

Now that you can apply over the Internet, the applications are much simpler and worded in layman's terms. If applicants miss filling in some information, that will trigger a warning that they omitted something. I realize that not all students have access to the Internet, but they can go to the public library and look into getting onto the Internet there.

Trudy Masters, Financial Aid Officer
Lee College
Baytown, Texas

FEDERAL LOANS

Following are methods through which you may borrow money from the federal government:

Federal Perkins Loan

This loan provides low-interest (5 percent) aid for students with exceptional financial need. The Federal Perkins Loans are made through the college's Financial Aid Office—that is, the college is the lender. For undergraduate study, you may borrow a maximum of $4,000 per year for up to five years of undergraduate study and may take up to ten years to repay the loan, beginning nine months after you graduate, leave school, or drop below half-time status. No interest accrues while you are in school and, under certain conditions (e.g., if you teach in a low-income area, work in law enforcement, are a full-time nurse or medical technician, or serve as a Peace Corps or VISTA volunteer), some or all of your loans may be either partially paid or cancelled in full. Payments also can be deferred under certain conditions, such as unemployment.

FFEL Stafford Loan

A Federal Family Education (FFEL) Stafford Loan may be borrowed from a participating commercial lender, such as a bank, credit union, or savings and loan association. This is a variable rate loan, capped at a maximum of 8.25 percent. If you qualify for a need-based subsidized FFEL Stafford Loan, the interest is paid by the federal government while you are enrolled in school. There is also an unsubsidized FFEL Stafford Student Loan that is not based on need and for which you are eligible, regardless of your family income.

The maximum amount you may borrow as a dependent student is $2,625 for freshman, $3,500 for sophomores, and $5,500 for juniors and seniors, with a maximum of $23,000 for your undergraduate program. The maximum amount for independent students is $6,625 for freshman, $7,500 for sophomores, and $10,500 for juniors and seniors, with a maximum of $46,000 for your undergraduate program. (The subsidized amount for independent students is the same as for dependent students, based on financial need.) There may be up-front origination fees charged for these loans that are deducted from the loan proceeds.

To apply for an FFEL Stafford Student Loan, you must first complete a FAFSA to determine eligibility for the subsidized amount of your loan. You should contact your school's Financial Aid Office to determine the most efficient method of selecting a lender, since many schools have established a preferred lender list. If your school does not have a preferred lender list, contact any local financial institution in your area or your state's Department of Higher Education for assistance. The lender will help you through the process, including a one-time signing of a promissory note. The proceeds of the loan, less any fees, will be sent to your college to be credited to your account.

If you qualify for a subsidized Stafford Loan, you don't have to pay interest while in school. For an unsubsidized Stafford Loan, you will be responsible for paying the interest from the time the loan is disbursed. However, most FFEL lenders will permit you to delay making payments and will add the interest to your loan. Once the repayment period starts, you should contact the lender and/or your school's Financial Aid Office to discuss repayment options. For many students, it is wise to consider consolidating all of your student loans into one loan program.

William D. Ford Federal Direct Loans

The Federal Direct Loan program is very similar to the FFEL Stafford Loan program except that the school serves as the lender. There is no need to contact a private financial institution for your student loans. About 30 percent of all U.S. colleges participate in the Direct Loan program. The terms and conditions of the two loan programs are essentially the same. There are many repayment plans available to meet your needs, and these will be explained to you during your "exit interview" during your final term of school.

FINANCIAL AID RESOURCES

You can use these numbers for direct access to federal and state agencies and processing services.

FEDERAL STUDENT AID INFORMATION CENTER

Provides duplicate student aid reports and aid applications to students. Also answers questions on student aid, mails Department of Education publications, makes corrections to applications, and verifies college federal aid participation. Call 800-4-Fed-Aid (toll-free) or visit their Web site at www.studentaid.ed.gov

VETERANS BENEFITS ADMINISTRATION

Provides dependent education assistance for children of disabled veterans. College-bound students should call the VBRO to determine whether or not they qualify for assistance, what the benefits are, and if a parent's disability qualifies them for benefits. Call 800-827-1000 (toll-free) or visit their Web site at www.gibill.va.gov.

ACT FINANCIAL AID NEED ESTIMATOR (FANE)

Mails financial tabloids to students, provides information on filling out financial aid forms, and estimates financial aid amounts. Also mails financial need estimator forms. Forms are also accessible on line. Go to www.ACT.org or call 319-337-1000.

COLLEGE SCHOLARSHIP SERVICE (PROFILE)

Provides free applications and registration forms for federal student aid. Helps students fill out applications. Call 305-829-9793 or visit http://profileonline.collegeboard.com/index.jsp.

COLLEGE FOR TEXANS

Here is everything a Texan needs to know about preparing for, applying for and paying for college or technical school. And it's all in one up-to-date, easy-to-navigate site as big as the state itself. And remember $3 billion is available every year to help Texans attend college. Go to www.collegefortexans.com for more information.

Parent Loans for Undergraduate Students (PLUS)

The PLUS loans are for parents of dependent students and are designed to help families with cash-flow problems. There is no needs test to qualify, and the loans are made by FFEL lenders or directly by the Department of Education. The loan has a variable interest rate that cannot exceed 9 percent, and there is no specific yearly limit; parents can borrow up to the cost of your education, less other financial aid received. Repayment begins sixty days after the money is advanced. There may be an origination fee of up to 4 percent charged for these loans. Parent borrowers must generally have a good credit record to qualify for PLUS loans.

The PLUS loan will be processed under either the Direct or the FFEL system, depending on the type of loan program for which the college has contracted.

Nursing Student Loan Program

These loans are awarded to nursing students with demonstrated financial need. This loan has a 5 percent interest rate, repayable after completion of studies. Repayment is to be completed within ten years. Contact your college's Financial Aid Office for deadline and other information, including maximum borrowing amounts.

THINKING AHEAD TO PAYING BACK YOUR STUDENT LOAN

More than ever before, loans have become an important part of financial assistance. The majority of students find that they must borrow money to finance their education. If you accept a loan, you are incurring a financial obligation. You will have to repay the loan in full, along with all of the interest and any additional fees (collection, legal, etc.). Since you will be making loan payments to satisfy the loan obligation, carefully consider the burden your loan amount will impose on you after you leave college. Defaulting on a student loan can jeopardize your financial future. Borrow intelligently.

Some Repayment Options

A number of repayment options are available to borrowers of federally guaranteed student loans.

The Standard Repayment Plan requires fixed monthly payments (at least $50) over a fixed period of time (up to ten years). The length of the repayment period depends on the loan amount. This plan usually results in the lowest total interest paid because the repayment period is shorter than under the other plans.

The Extended Repayment Plan allows loan repayment to be extended over a period from generally twelve to thirty years, depending on the total amount borrowed. Borrowers still pay a fixed amount each month (at least $50), but usually monthly payments will be less than under the Standard Repayment Plan. This plan may make repayment more manageable; however, borrowers usually will pay more interest because the repayment period is longer.

The Graduated Repayment Plan allows payments to start out low and increase every two years. This plan may be helpful to borrowers whose incomes are low initially but will increase steadily. A borrower's monthly payments must be at least half but may not be more than one-and-a-half times what he or she would pay under Standard Repayment. As in the Extended Repayment Plan, the repayment period will usually vary from twelve to thirty years, depending on the total amount borrowed. Again, monthly payments may be more manageable at first because they are lower, but borrowers will pay more interest because the repayment period is longer.

The Income Contingent Repayment Plan bases monthly payments on adjusted gross income (AGI) and the total amount borrowed. This is currently only available to students who participate in Direct Loans; however, some FFEL lenders and guaranty agencies provide income-sensitive repayment plans. As income rises or falls each year, monthly payments will be adjusted accordingly. The required monthly payment will not exceed 20 percent of the borrower's discretionary income as calculated under a published formula. Borrowers have up to twenty-five years to repay; after that time, any unpaid amount will be discharged, and borrowers must pay taxes on the amount discharged. In other words, if the federal government forgives the balance of a loan, the amount is considered to be part of the borrower's income for that year.

OTHER FEDERAL PROGRAMS

The following programs offer alternative ways to earn money for college:

Federal Work-Study (FWS)

The Federal Work Study program provides both on- and off-campus jobs to students who have financial need. Funding for this program is from federal grants to the institutions, plus a partial match from the employer. Students work on an hourly basis and are paid at least the minimum wage. Students are allowed to work up to the amount of the grant authorized by the college. Contact the Financial Aid Office for more information.

AmeriCorps

AmeriCorps is a national service program for a limited number of students. Participants work in a public or private nonprofit agency that provides service to the community in one of four priority areas: education, human services, the environment, and public safety. In exchange, they earn a stipend for living expenses and up to $4,725 a year to apply toward college expenses. Students can work either before, during, or after they go to college and can use the funds to either pay current educational expenses or repay federal student loans. If you successfully complete one full-time term of service (at least 1,700 hours over one year or less), you will be eligible for an award of $4,725. If you successfully complete one part-time term of service (at least 900 hours over two years or less), you will be eligible for an award of $2,362.50. You should speak to your college's Financial Aid Office for more details about this program and any other initiatives available to students or visit the Web at www.americorps.org.

FROM THE GUIDANCE OFFICE

Q: Why might higher-priced institutions still be affordable?

A: Parents and students ask what college is going to cost and how they will pay for it. I tell them to start early and keep looking. Don't discount a school because of cost. Private schools have a higher price tag, but they do have financial aid packages that are bigger than you might expect.

Kids need some help to initiate searches for scholarships. Get them on the Internet. Each year, we have a group of students who start early and get their applications in and recommendations written. Then there's the group of procrastinators who miss out on opportunities of getting into the college of their choice. It can be a big disappointment.

Nadine Boyer
Counselor
East Richland High School
Olney, Illinois

FAMILIES' GUIDE TO TAX CUTS FOR EDUCATION

Many new tax benefits for adults who want to return to school and for parents who are sending or planning to send their children to college will be available due to the balanced budget that was signed into law in 1997. These tax cuts effectively make the first two years of college universally available, and they give many more working Americans the financial means to go back to school if they want to choose a new career or upgrade their skills. Millions of families are eligible for the Hope and Lifetime Learning tax credits each year, as well as the taxable income deduction allowed for tuition and fees.

HOPE Scholarship Tax Credit

The HOPE Scholarship tax credit helps make the first two years of college or career school universally available. Students receive a 100 percent tax credit for the first $1,000 of tuition and required fees and a 50 percent credit on the second $1,000. This credit is available for tuition and required fees minus grants, scholarships, and other tax-free educational assistance.

The credit is gradually reduced for families with Adjusted Gross Incomes between $41,000 and $51,000 if single, or between $83,000 and $103,000 if married. These limits are adjusted for inflation every year. The credit can be claimed in two years for students who are in their first two years of college or career school and who are enrolled on at least a half-time basis in a degree or certificate program for any portion of the year. The taxpayer can claim a credit for his own tuition expense or for the expenses of his or her spouse or dependent children.

The Lifetime Learning Tax Credit

This tax credit is targeted at adults who want to go back to school, change careers, or take a course or two to upgrade their skills and to college juniors, seniors, graduate, and professional degree students. A family will receive a 20 percent tax credit for tuition and required fees paid each year and for the first $10,000 with the minimum credit being $2,000. Just like the HOPE Scholarship tax credit, the Lifetime Learning tax credit is available for tuition and required fees minus grants, scholarships, and other tax-free educational assistance. The maximum credit is determined on a per-taxpayer (family) basis, regardless of the number of postsecondary students in the family, and is phased out at the same income levels as the HOPE Scholarship tax credit. Families will be able to claim the Lifetime Learning tax credit for some members of their family and the HOPE Scholarship tax credit for others who qualify in the same year.

Tuition and Fees Tax Deduction

The Tuition and Fees Tax Deduction can reduce the amount of your taxable income by as much as $4,000 per year. This deduction is subtracted from your income, which means you can claim this deduction even if you do not itemize your deductions on Schedule A of Form 1040. This deduction may benefit you if you do not qualify for the Hope or Lifetime Learning Tax Credits because your income is too high. This program is available for four years, 2002 through 2005. Participating in the Hope and/or Lifetime Tax credits does not preclude participation in this program, as long as the same student is not used as the basis for each deduction, credit, or exclusion and the family does not exceed the Lifetime Learning maximum per family. The income cut-off for single tax payers is $65,000 (Modified Adjusted Gross Income) and $13,000 for married filers. Check with the IRS or your accountant for more information.

APPLYING FOR FINANCIAL AID

Applying for financial aid is a process that can be made easier when you take it step by step.

1. You must complete the Free Application for Federal Student Aid (FAFSA) to be considered for federal financial aid. Pick up the FAFSA from your high school guidance counselor or college financial aid office or download it from the Department of Education's Web site at www.fafsa.ed.gov. The FAFSA can be filed after January 1 of the year you will be attending school. Submit the form as soon as possible but never before the first of the year. If you need to estimate income tax information, it is easily amended later in the year.
2. Apply for any state grants. Most states use the FASFA for determining state aid, but be sure to check out the specific requirements with your state Higher Education Assistance agency. Your high school guidance office can answer most questions about state aid programs.
3. Some schools (usually higher cost private colleges) require an additional form know as the PROFILE®. This application is needed for institutional grants and scholarships controlled by the school. Check to see if the schools you are applying to require the PROFILE form. Additional information is available from your high school guidance office or online through the College Board at www.collegeboard.com. There is a fee associated with this form.

CHECKLIST FOR SENIORS

Applying for financial aid can become confusing if you don't record what you've done and when. Use this chart to keep track of important information. Remember to keep copies of all applications and related information.

COLLEGE APPLICATIONS	COLLEGE 1	COLLEGE 2	COLLEGE 3	COLLEGE 4
Application deadline				
Date sent				
Official transcript sent				
Letters of recommendation sent				
SAT/ACT Assessment scores sent				
Acceptance received				
INDIVIDUAL COLLEGE FINANCIAL AID AND SCHOLARSHIP APPLICATIONS				
Application deadline				
Date sent				
Acceptance received				
FREE APPLICATION FOR FEDERAL STUDENT AID (FAFSA), FINANCIAL AID FORM (FAF), AND/OR PROFILE®				
Form required				
Date sent				
School's priority deadline				
PROFILE® ACKNOWLEDGMENT (if filed)				
Date received				
Correct (Y/N)				
Date changes made, if needed				
Date changes were submitted				
STUDENT AID REPORT				
Date received				
Correct (Y/N)				
Date changes made, if needed				
Date changes were submitted				
Date sent to colleges				
FINANCIAL AWARD LETTERS				
Date received				
Accepted (Y/N)				

Source: The Dayton-Montgomery County Scholarship Program

Some schools may require an institutional aid application. This is usually found with the admission application. Contact each college you are considering to be sure you have filed the required forms.

4. Complete individual colleges' required financial aid application forms on time. These deadlines are usually before March 15, but check to be sure.
5. Make sure your family completes the required forms during your senior year of high school.
6. Always apply for grants and scholarships before applying for student loans. Grants and scholarships are essentially free money. Loans must be repaid with interest.

Use the "Checklist for Seniors" above to keep track of the financial aid application process.

NATIONAL, STATEWIDE, AND LOCAL SCHOLARSHIPS

Without a doubt, the best source for up-to-date information on private scholarships is the Internet. There are a variety of excellent Web sites to explore, including www.petersons.com, among others. The most important thing to be careful about is scholarship scams, where you are asked either to pay for a scholarship search by an independent organization or pay a "processing fee" to a particular organization to receive their scholarship.

State and Local Scholarships

It is not possible within the scope of this book to list all of the sources of state and local scholarship dollars. The following are excellent resources for seeking financial assistance:

- Your guidance counselor
- A high school teacher or coach
- Your high school and elementary school PTA (yes, many elementary school PTAs award scholarships to alumni)
- The local librarian
- College admissions office
- Your parents' alma mater
- Your employer
- Your parents' employer
- Professional and social organizations in your community
- The local Financial Aid Office of a college in your area
- Your state Higher Education Assistance Agency

SCHOLARSHIPS FOR MINORITY STUDENTS

The following is just a sample of the many scholarships available to minority students.

Bureau of Indian Affairs Higher ED Grant Programs
1849 C Street, NW/MS 3512-MIB
Washington, D.C. 20240-001
www.oiep.bia.edu

The Gates Millennium Scholars
P.O. Box 10500
Fairfax, Virginia 22031-5044
www.gmsp.org

Hispanic Scholarship Fund College Scholarship Program
55 Second Street, Suite 1500
San Francisco, California 94105
877-473-4636
www.hsf.net

National Achievement Scholarship Program
1560 Sherman Avenue, Suite 200
Evanston, Illinois 60201-4897
847-866-5100
www.nationalmerit.org

National Association of Minority Engineering Program Administrators National Scholarship Fund
1133 West Morse Boulevard, Suite 201
Winter Park, Florida 32789
407-647-8839
www.namepa.org

Jackie Robinson Foundation Scholarship
3 West 35th Street, 11th Floor
New York, New York 10001
212-290-8600
www.jackierobinson.org

APPLYING FOR SCHOLARSHIPS

Here are some tips to help make a success of your scholarship hunt.

1. **Start early.** Your freshman year is not too early to plan for scholarships by choosing extracurricular activities that will highlight your strengths, and getting involved in your church and community—all things that are important to those who make scholarship decisions.

2. **Search for scholarships.** The best source of scholarships can be found on the Internet. There are many great Web sites that are free, including www.petersons.com. For more information, you should also check www.finaid.org and www.ed.gov/studentaid. Scholarship information is also available at your local library.

TYPES OF ATHLETIC SCHOLARSHIPS

Colleges and universities offer two basic types of athletic scholarships: **the institutional grant, which is an agreement between the athlete and the college, and the conference grant, which also binds the college to the athlete. The difference is that the athlete who signs an institutional grant can change his or her mind and sign with another team. The athlete who signs a conference contract cannot renegotiate another contract with a school that honors conference grants. Here are the various ways that a scholarship may be offered:**

Full four-year. **Also known as full ride, these scholarships pay for room, board, tuition, and books. Due to the high cost of awarding scholarships, this type of grant is being discouraged by conferences around the country in favor of the one-year renewable contract or the partial scholarship.**

Full one-year renewable contract. **This type of scholarship, which has basically replaced the four-year grant, is automatically renewed at the end of each school year for four years if the conditions of the contract are met. The recruiter will probably tell you in good faith that the intent is to offer a four-year scholarship, but he is legally only allowed to offer you a one-year grant. You must ask the recruiter as well as other players what the record has been of renewing scholarships for athletes who comply athletically, academically, and socially. Remember—no athlete can receive more than a full scholarship.**

One-year trial grant (full or partial). **A verbal agreement between you and the institution that at the end of the year, your renewal will be dependent upon your academic and athletic performance.**

Partial scholarship. **The partial grant is any part of the total cost of college. You may be offered room and board but not tuition and books, or you may be offered just tuition. The possibility exists for you to negotiate to a full scholarship after you complete your freshman year.**

Waiver of out-of-state fees. **This award is for out-of-state students to attend the college or university at the same fee as an in-state student.**

3. **Apply, apply, apply.** One student applied for nearly sixty scholarships and was fortunate enough to win seven. "Imagine if I'd applied for five and only gotten one," she says.
4. **Plan ahead.** It takes time to get transcripts and letters of recommendation. Letters from people who know you well are more effective than letters from prestigious names who you know.
5. **Be organized.** In the homes of scholarship winners, you can often find a file box where all relevant information is stored. This method allows you to review deadlines and requirements every so often. Computerizing the information, if possible, allows you to change and update information quickly.
6. **Follow directions.** Make sure that you don't disqualify yourself by filling the forms out incorrectly, missing the deadline, or failing to supply important information. Type your applications, if possible, and have someone proofread them.

WHAT YOU NEED TO KNOW ABOUT ATHLETIC SCHOLARSHIPS

Whether you're male or female or interested in baseball, basketball, crew, cross-country, fencing, field hockey, football, golf, gymnastics, lacrosse, sailing, skiing, soccer, softball, swimming and diving, tennis, track and field, volleyball, or wrestling, there may be scholarship dollars available for you. But, here's that word again—planning. You must plan ahead if you want to get your tuition paid for in return for your competitive abilities.

At the beginning of your junior year, ask your guidance counselor to help you make sure that you take the required number and mix of academic courses and to inform you of the SAT and ACT Assessment score minimums that must be met to play college sports. Also ask your counselor about academic requirements, because you must be certified by the NCAA Clearinghouse, and this process must be started by the end of your junior year.

But before you do all that, think. Do you want and need an athletic scholarship? Certainly, it is prestigious to receive an athletic scholarship, but some athletes compare having an athletic scholarship to having a job at which you are expected to perform. Meetings, training sessions, practices, games, and (don't forget!) studying take away from social and leisure time. Also, with very few full-ride scholarships available, you will most likely receive a partial scholarship or a one-year renewable contract. If your scholarship is not renewed, you may be left scrambling for financial aid. So ask yourself if you are ready for the demands and roles associated with accepting an athletic scholarship.

If you decide that you want an athletic scholarship, you need to market yourself to beat the stiff competition. Think of yourself as a newly designed sports car, and you're selling the speed, look, and all those other goodies to a waiting public. The point is that you're going to have to sell, or market, your abilities to college recruiters. You're the product, and the college recruiter is the buyer. What makes you stand out from the rest?

College recruiters look for a combination of the following attributes when awarding athletic scholarships: academic excellence, a desire to win, self-motivation, ability to perform as a team player, willingness to help others, cooperation with coaching staff, attitude in practice, attitude in games/matches, toughness, strength, optimal height and weight, and excellence.

In order to successfully sell your skills to a college or university, you'll need to take three main steps: 1) locate the colleges and universities that offer scholarships in your sport, 2) contact the institution in a formal manner, and 3) follow up each lead.

Finding and Getting Athletic Scholarships

Ask your coach or assistant coaches for recommendations; learn about the conference or institution from newspaper or television coverage; ask your guidance counselor; review guidebooks, reference books, and the Internet; ask alumni; or attend a tryout or campus visit. You can also call the NCAA to request a recruiting guide for your sport. The following steps can help you snag that scholarship:

1. **Contact the school formally.** Once you make a list of schools in which you are interested, get the names of the head coaches and write letters to the top twenty schools on your list. Then compile a factual resume of your athletic and academic accomplishments. Put together 10 to 15 minutes of video highlights of your athletic performance (with your jersey number noted), get letters of recommendation from your high school coach and your off-season coach, and include a season schedule.
2. **Ace the interview.** When you meet a recruiter or coach, exhibit self-confidence with a firm handshake, by maintaining eye contact, and by making sure that you are well groomed. According to recruiters, the most effective attitude is quiet confidence, respect, sincerity, and enthusiasm.
3. **Ask good questions.** Don't be afraid to probe the recruiter by getting answers to the following questions: Do I qualify athletically and academically? If I am recruited, what would the parameters of the scholarship be? For what position am I being considered? It's okay to ask the recruiter to declare what level of interest he or she has in you.
4. **Follow up.** Persistence pays off when it comes to seeking an athletic scholarship, and timing can be everything. There are four good times when a follow-up letter from your coach or a personal letter from you is extremely effective: prior to your senior season, during or just after the senior season, just prior to or after announced conference-affiliated signing dates or national association signing dates, and mid- to late summer, in case other scholarship offers have been withdrawn or declined.

To sum up, you know yourself better than anyone, so you must look at your skills—both athletic and academic—objectively. Evaluate the skills you need to improve, and keep the desire to improve alive in your heart. Develop your leadership skills, and keep striving for excellence with your individual achievements. Keep your mind open as to what school you want to attend, and keep plugging away, even when you are tired, sore, and unsure. After all, athletes are trained to be winners!

MYTHS ABOUT SCHOLARSHIPS AND FINANCIAL AID

The scholarship and financial aid game is highly misunderstood by many high school students. And high school guidance counselors often lack the time to fully investigate scholarship opportunities and to inform students about them. The myths and misconceptions persist while the truth about scholarships remains hidden, the glittering prizes and benefits unknown to many teenagers.

Myth 1: Scholarships are rare, elusive awards won only by valedictorians, geniuses, and whiz kids.

The truth is that with proper advice and strategies, private scholarships are very much within the grasp of high school students who possess talent and ability in almost any given field. Thousands of high school students like you compete and win.

Myth 2: My chances of being admitted to a college are reduced if I apply for financial aid.

The truth is that most colleges have a policy of "need-blind" admissions, which means that a student's financial need is not taken into account in the admission decision. However, there are a few colleges that do consider ability to pay before deciding whether or not to admit a student. There are a few more that look at ability to pay of those whom they placed on a waiting list to get in or those students who applied late. Some colleges will mention this in their literature, others may not. In making decisions about the college application and financing process, however, families should apply for financial aid if the student needs the aid to attend college.

Myth 3: All merit scholarships are based on a student's academic record.

The truth is that many of the best opportunities are in such areas as writing, public speaking, leadership, science, community service, music and the arts, foreign languages, and vocational-technical skills. So that means you don't always have to have a 3.99 GPA to win if you excel in a certain area.

Myth 4: You have to be a member of a minority group to get a scholarship.

The truth is that there are indeed some scholarships that are targeted toward women and minority students. There are also scholarships for which you must be a member of a specific national club or student organization (such as 4-H and the National Honor Society), which makes these scholarships just as exclusive. But most scholarship opportunities are not exclusive to any one segment of the population.

Myth 5: If you have need for and receive financial aid, it's useless to win a scholarship from some outside organization because the college will just take away the aid that the organization offered.

It's true that if you receive need-based aid, you can't receive more than the total cost of attendance (including room and board, books, and other expenses, not just tuition). If the financial aid that you've been awarded meets the total cost and you win an outside scholarship, colleges have to reduce something. But usually, they reduce the loan or work-study portion of your financial aid award before touching the grant portion that they've awarded you. This means that you won't have to borrow or earn as much. Also, most colleges don't meet your full financial need when you qualify for need-based financial aid. So, if you do win an outside scholarship, chances are that your other aid will not be taken away or reduced.

SCHOLARSHIP SCAMS

Although most scholarship sponsors and most scholarship search services are legitimate, schemes that pose as either legitimate scholarship search services or scholarship sponsors have cheated thousands of families.

These fraudulent businesses advertise in campus newspapers, distribute flyers, mail letters and postcards, provide toll-free phone numbers, and even have sites on the Web. The most obvious frauds operate as scholarship search services or scholarship clearinghouses. Another quieter segment sets up as a scholarship sponsor, pockets the money from the fees and charges that are paid by thousands of hopeful scholarship seekers, and returns little, if anything, in proportion to the amount it collects. A few of these frauds inflict great harm by gaining access to individuals' credit or checking accounts with the intent to extort funds.

The Federal Trade Commission (FTC), in Washington, D.C., has a campaign called Project $cholar$cam to confront this type of fraudulent activity. There are legitimate services; however, a scholarship search service cannot truthfully guarantee that a student will receive a scholarship, and students almost always will fare as well or better by doing their own homework using a reliable scholarship information source, such as *Peterson's Scholarships, Grants & Prizes* or www.petersons.com, than by wasting money and time with a search service that promises a scholarship.

The FTC warns you to be alert for these six warning signs of a scam:

1. **"This scholarship is guaranteed or your money back."** No service can guarantee that it will get you a grant or scholarship. Refund guarantees often have impossible conditions attached. Review a service's refund policies in writing before you pay a fee.
2. **"The scholarship service will do all the work."** Unfortunately, nobody else can fill out the personal information forms, write the essays, and supply the references that many scholarships may require.
3. **"The scholarship will cost some money."** Be wary of any charges related to scholarship information services or individual scholarship applications, especially in significant amounts. Before you send money to apply for a scholarship, investigate the sponsor.
4. **"You can't get this information anywhere else."** In addition to Peterson's, scholarship directories from other publishers are available in any large bookstore, public library, or high school guidance office.
5. **"You are a finalist" or "You have been selected by a national foundation to receive a scholarship."** Most legitimate scholarship programs almost never seek out particular applicants. Most scholarship sponsors will contact you only in response to an inquiry because they generally lack the budget to do anything more than this. Should you think that there is any real possibility that you may have been selected to receive a scholarship, before you send any money, investigate first to be sure that the sponsor or program is legitimate.
6. **"The scholarship service needs your credit card or checking account number in advance."** Never provide your credit card or bank account number on the telephone to the representative of an organization that you do not know. Get information in writing first. An unscrupulous operation does not need your signature on a check. It will scheme to set up situations that will allow it to drain a victim's account with unauthorized withdrawals.

In addition to the FTC's six signs, here are some other points to keep in mind when considering a scholarship program:

- Fraudulent scholarship operations often use official-sounding names, containing words such as *federal, national, administration, division, federation,* and *foundation.* Their names are often a slight variant of the name of a legitimate government or private organization. Do not be fooled by a name that seems reputable or official, an official-looking seal, or a Washington, D.C., address.

- If you win a scholarship, you will receive written official notification by mail, not by telephone. If the sponsor calls to inform you, it will follow up with a letter in the mail. If a request for money is made by phone, the operation is probably fraudulent.
- Be wary if an organization's address is a box number or a residential address. If a bona fide scholarship program uses a post office box number, it usually will include a street address and telephone number on its stationery.
- Beware of telephone numbers with a 900-area code. These may charge you a fee of several dollars a minute for a call that could be a long recording that provides only a list of addresses or names.
- Watch for scholarships that ask you to "act now." A dishonest operation may put pressure on an applicant by saying that awards are on a "first-come, first-serve" basis. Some scholarship programs will give preference to the earlier qualified applications. However, if you are told, especially on the telephone, that you must respond quickly but that you will not hear about the results for several months, there may be a problem.
- Be wary of endorsements. Fraudulent operations will claim endorsements by groups with names similar to well-known private or government organizations. The Better Business Bureau (BBB) and government agencies do not endorse businesses.
- Don't pay money for a scholarship to an organization that you've never heard of before or whose legitimacy you can't verify. If you have already paid money to such an organization and find reason to doubt its authenticity, call your bank to stop payment on your check, if possible, or call your credit card company and tell it that you think you were the victim of consumer fraud.

To find out how to recognize, report, and stop a scholarship scam, you may write to the Federal Trade Commission's Consumer Response Center at 600 Pennsylvania Avenue NW, Washington, D.C. 20580. On the Web, go to www.ftc.gov, or call 877-FTC-HELP (toll-free). You can also check with the Better Business Bureau (BBB), which is an organization that maintains files of businesses about which it has received complaints. You should call both your local BBB office and the BBB office in the area of the organization in question; each local BBB has different records. Call 703-276-0100 to get the telephone number of your local BBB, or look at www.bbb.org for a directory of local BBBs and downloadable BBB complaint forms.

FINANCIAL AID ON THE WEB

A number of good financial aid resources exist on the Web. It is quick and simple to access general financial aid information, links to relevant Web sites, loan information, employment and career information, advice, scholarship search services, interactive worksheets, forms, and free expected family contribution (EFC) calculators.

Also visit the Web sites of individual colleges to find more school-specific financial aid information.

FAFSA Online

The Free Application for Federal Student Aid (FAFSA) can be filed on the Web at www.fafsa.ed.gov. You can download a worksheet from this Web site, since the questions are formatted differently from the paper application. FAFSA on the Web is a much quicker process and helps eliminate errors. To file electronically, the student and one parent will need an electronic signature Personal Identification Number (PIN). To get a PIN, go to www.pin.ed.gov. The pin number will be sent to you within 24 hours.

FIND MONEY FOR COLLEGE

Don't have enough money to pay for college? Afraid your family makes too much and you can't get financial aid? Regardless of your financial situation, BestCollegeDeals® helps you quickly and easily identify each college's unique financial aid packages—student loans, grants, discounts, scholarships—and little-known financial deals you've probably never even heard of.

How does it work? It's simple!

1. **Provide financial information about your family in a safe, secure environment that ensures your privacy.**
2. **Calculate, with help from BestCollegeDeals®, your Estimated Expected Family Contribution (EFC), the amount of money you may be expected to pay toward your college education.**
3. **Choose location, enrollment size, and whether you're interested in a public, private, all-women's, or all-men's college or university.**
4. **Get a list of colleges, and information about their financial aid offerings, that match your preferences.**
5. **Discover great need- and merit-based (merit awards include scholarships, grants, and prizes that are given for academic achievement) financial deals that you can't find anywhere else!**

No matter what your level of income, BestCollegeDeals® gives your family personalized support. BestCollegeDeals® helps you and your family better understand the financial aid process. Go to www.bestcollegedeals to learn more!

The Education Resource Institute (TERI)

TERI is a private, not-for-profit organization that was founded to help middle-income Americans afford a college education. This site contains a database describing programs that aim to increase college attendance from underrepresented groups. (The target population includes students from low-income families and those who are the first in their family to pursue postsecondary education.) Visit TERI's Web site at www.teri.org.

FinAid

This Web site offers numerous links to valuable financial aid information, including scholarship search engines. You can find the site at www.finaid.org.

Mapping Your Future

This site is sponsored by a group of guaranty agencies that participate in the Federal Family Education Loan Program (FFELP). They are committed to providing information about higher education and career opportunities. Information is available to help parents of middle school students plan for college and for adults returning to higher education to learn new skills. You can find this site at www.mapping-your-future.org.

Student Financial Assistance Information, U.S. Department of Education

This page takes you to some of the major publications on student aid, including the latest edition of *The Student Guide*. Visit www.ed.gov/finaid.html.

Petersons.com

Get advice on finding sources to pay for college and search for scholarships at www.petersons.com/finaid.

AES

American Education Services (AES) is a division of PHEAA, which has grown from a small student loan guarantor with a volume of only 4,600 student loans in 1964, to one of the largest, full-service financial aid organizations in the nation. AES helps students succeed by giving them the tools to plan for higher education and find money for school, as well as allowing them to manage student loan accounts online. Visit them at www.aessuccess.org.

Chapter 9

WHAT TO EXPECT IN COLLEGE

If you were going on a long trip, wouldn't you want to know what to expect once you reached your destination? The same should hold true for college.

G*ET A JUMP!* CAN'T FILL IN all the details of what you'll find once you begin college. However, we can give you information about some of the bigger questions you might have, such as how to choose your classes or major and how you can make the most of your life outside the classroom.

CHOOSING YOUR CLASSES

College is designed to give you freedom, but at the same time, it teaches you responsibility. You will probably have more free time than in high school, but you will also have more class material to master. Your parents may entrust you with more money, but it is up to you to make sure there's enough money in your bank account when school fees are due. The same principle applies to your class schedule: You will have more decision-making power than ever, but you also need to know and meet the requirements for graduation.

To guide you through the maze of requirements, all students are given an adviser. This person, typically a faculty member, will help you select classes that meet your interests and graduation requirements. During your first year or two at college, you and your adviser will choose classes that meet general education requirements and select electives, or non-required classes, that pique your interests. Early on, it is a good idea to take a lot of general education classes. They are meant to expose you to new ideas and help you explore possible majors. Once you have selected a major, you will be given an adviser for that particular area of study. This person will help you understand and meet the requirements for that major.

In addition to talking to your adviser, talk to other students who have already taken a class you're interested in and who really enjoyed how a professor taught the class. Then try to get into that professor's class when registering. Remember, a dynamic professor can make a dry subject engaging. A boring professor can make an engaging subject dry.

As you move through college, you will notice that focusing on the professor is more important than focusing on the course title. Class titles can be cleverly crafted. They can sound captivating. However, the advice above still holds true: "Pop Culture and Icons" could turn out to be awful, and "Beowulf and Old English" could be a blast.

When you plan your schedule, watch how many heavy reading classes you take in one semester. You don't want to live in the library or the dorm study lounge. In general, the humanities, such as history, English, philosophy, and theology, involve a lot of reading. Math and science classes involve less reading; they focus more on solving problems.

Finally, don't be afraid to schedule a fun class. Even the most intense program of study will let you take a few electives. So take a deep breath, dig in, and explore!

CHOOSING YOUR MAJOR

You can choose from hundreds of majors—from accounting to zoology—but which is right for you? Should you choose something traditional or select a major from an emerging area? Perhaps you already know what career you want, so you can work backward to decide which major will best help you achieve your goals.

If you know what you want to do early in life, you will have more time to plan your high school curriculum, extracurricular activities, jobs, and community service to coincide with your college major. Your college selection process may also focus upon the schools that provide strong academic programs in a certain major.

Where Do I Begin?

Choosing a major usually starts with an assessment of your career interests. Once you have taken the self-assessment test in Part 1, you should have a clearer understanding of your interests, talents, values, and goals. Then review possible majors, and try several on for size. Picture yourself taking classes, writing papers, making presentations, conducting research, or working in a related field. Talk to people you know who work in your fields of interest and see if you like what you hear. Also, try reading the classified ads in your local newspaper. What jobs sound interesting to you? Which ones pay the salary that you'd like to make? What level of education is required in the ads you find interesting? Select a few jobs that you think you'd like and then consult the following list of majors to see which major(s) coincide. If your area of interest does not appear here, talk to your counselor or teacher about where to find information on that particular subject.

Majors and Related Careers

Agriculture

Many agriculture majors apply their knowledge directly on farms and ranches. Others work in industry (food, farm equipment, and agricultural supply companies), federal agencies (primarily in the Departments of Agriculture and the Interior), and state and local farm and agricultural agencies. Jobs might be in research and lab work, marketing and sales, advertising and public relations, or journalism and radio/TV (for farm communications media). Agriculture majors also pursue further training in biological sciences, animal health, veterinary medicine, agribusiness management, vocational agriculture education, nutrition and dietetics, and rural sociology.

Architecture

Architecture and related design fields focus on the built environment as distinct from the natural environment of the agriculturist or the conservationist. Career possibilities include drafting, design, and project administration in architectural, engineering, landscape design, interior design, industrial design, planning, real estate, and construction firms; government agencies involved in construction, housing, highways, and parks and recreation; and government and nonprofit organizations interested in historic or architectural preservation.

Area/Ethnic Studies

The research, writing, analysis, critical thinking, and cultural awareness skills acquired by area/ethnic studies majors, combined with the expertise gained in a particular area, make this group of majors valuable in a number of professions. Majors find positions in administration, education, public relations, and communications in such organizations as cultural, government, international, and (ethnic) community agencies; international trade (import-export); social service agencies; and the communications industry (journalism, radio, and TV). These studies also provide a good background for further training in law, business management, public administration, education, social work, museum and library work, and international relations.

Arts

Art majors most often use their training to become practicing artists, though the settings in which they work vary. Aside from the most obvious art-related career—that of the self-employed artist or craftsperson—many fields require the skills of a visual artist. These include advertising; public relations; publishing; journalism; museum work; television, movies, and theater; community and social service agencies concerned with education, recreation, and entertainment; and teaching. A background in art is also useful if a student wishes to pursue art therapy, arts or museum administration, or library work.

Biological Sciences

The biological sciences include the study of living organisms from the level of molecules to that of populations. Majors find jobs in industry; government agencies; technical writing, editing, or illustrating; science reporting; secondary school teaching (which usually requires education courses); and research and laboratory analysis and testing. Biological sciences are also a sound foundation for further study in medicine, psychology, health and hospital administration, and biologically oriented engineering.

Business

Business majors comprise all the basic business disciplines. At the undergraduate level, students can major in a general business administration program or specialize in a particular area, such as marketing or accounting. These studies lead not only to positions in business and industry but also to management positions in other sectors. Management-related studies include the general management areas (accounting, finance, marketing, and management) as well as special studies related to a particular type of organization or industry. Management-related majors may be offered in a business school or in a department dealing with the area in which the management skills are to be applied. Careers can be found throughout the business world.

Communication

Jobs in communication range from reporting (news and special features), copywriting, technical writing, copyediting, and programming to advertising, public relations, media sales, and market research. Such positions can be found at newspapers, radio and TV stations, publishing houses (book and magazine), advertising agencies, corporate communications departments, government agencies, universities, and firms that specialize in educational and training materials.

Computer, Information, and Library Sciences

Computer and information science and systems majors stress the theoretical aspects of the computer and emphasize mathematical and scientific disciplines. Data processing, programming, and computer technology programs tend to be more practical; they are more oriented toward business than to scientific applications and to working directly with the computer or with peripheral equipment. Career possibilities for computer and information science majors include data processing, programming, and systems development or maintenance in almost any setting: business and industry, banking and finance, government, colleges and universities, libraries, software firms, service bureaus, computer manufacturers, publishing, and communications.

STUDENT COUNSEL

Q: Why did you choose a seven-year premed program instead of a traditional four-year college program?

A: I'm one of those people who knew what I wanted to do since I was very little, so that made choosing easier. If I was not 100 percent sure that I wanted to go into medicine, I would not be in this seven-year program. For students who are interested but not really sure that they want to go into medicine, they should pick a school they will enjoy, get a good education, and then worry about medical school. That way, if they decide in their junior year that medicine is not for them, they have options.

Elliot Servais
Premed
Boston University

STUDENT COUNSEL

Q: What advice do you have for high school students who are considering going into engineering?

A: In high school, take AP courses in a lot of different areas. That gives you an idea of what those subjects will be like in college. I knew I was good at science and math but didn't know which direction would really interest me. I took an AP English course and didn't do so well. Then I took a chemistry course and knew I could see myself digging deeper. An AP course will give you an idea if that subject is something you want to pursue as a major.

Most engineering majors don't have to decide on what engineering discipline they want until their sophomore year. As a freshman, you can take courses and not really know what type of engineering you want. I took an introduction to engineering course, and it convinced me that this is what I want to do. Your freshman year will give you a flavor for different engineering majors so you don't end up in your junior year and realize you don't like that major. The first semester here is totally an adjustment period.

Michael Romano
Chemical Engineering
Cornell University

Library science gives preprofessional background in library work and provides valuable knowledge of research sources, indexing, abstracting, computer technology, and media technology, which is useful for further study in any professional field. In most cases, a master's degree in library science is necessary to obtain a job as a librarian. Library science majors find positions in public, school, college, corporate, and government libraries and research centers; book publishing (especially reference books); database and information retrieval services; and communications (especially audiovisual media).

Education

Positions as teachers in public elementary and secondary schools, private day and boarding schools, religious and parochial schools, vocational schools, and proprietary schools are the jobs most often filled by education majors. However, teaching positions also exist in noneducational institutions, such as museums, historical societies, prisons, hospitals, and nursing homes, as well as jobs as educators and trainers in government and industry. Administrative (nonteaching) positions in employee relations and personnel, public relations, marketing and sales, educational publishing, TV and film media, test development firms, and government and community social service agencies also tap the skills and interests of education majors.

Engineering and Engineering Technologies

Engineering and science technology majors prepare students for practical design and production work rather than for jobs that require more theoretical, scientific, and mathematical knowledge. Engineers work in a variety of fields, including aeronautics, bioengineering, geology, nuclear engineering, and quality control and safety. Industry, research labs, and government agencies where technology plays a key role, such as in manufacturing, electronics, construction communications, transportation, and utilities, hire engineering as well as engineering technology and science technology graduates regularly. Work may be in technical activities (research, development, design, production, testing, scientific programming, or systems analysis) or in nontechnical areas where a technical degree is needed, such as marketing, sales, or administration.

Foreign Language and Literature

Knowledge of foreign languages and cultures is increasingly recognized as important in today's international world. Language majors possess a skill that is used in organizations with international dealings as well as in career fields and geographical areas where languages other than English are prominent. Career possibilities include positions with business firms with international subsidiaries; import-export firms; international banking; travel agencies; airlines; tourist services; government and international agencies dealing with international affairs, foreign trade, diplomacy, customs, or immigration; secondary school foreign language teaching and bilingual education (which usually require education courses); freelance translating and

(Continued on page 103)

MAKING THAT MAJOR DECISION: REAL-LIFE ADVICE FROM COLLEGE SENIORS

Somewhere between her junior and senior year in high school, Karen Gliebe got the psychology bug. When choosing a major in college, she knew just what she wanted. Justin Bintrim, on the other hand, did a complete 180. He thought he'd study physics, then veered toward philosophy. It wasn't until he took survey courses in literature that he found where his heart really lay, and now he's graduating with a degree in English.

You might find yourself at either end of this spectrum when choosing a major. Either you'll know just what you want or you'll try on a number of different hats before finally settling on one. To give you a taste of what it could be like for you, meet four college seniors who have been through the trials and errors of choosing their majors. Hopefully you'll pick up some pointers from them or at least find out that you don't have to worry so much about what your major will be.

From Grove City College, a liberal arts school in Pennsylvania, meet Karen Gliebe, who will graduate with a degree in psychology, and English major Justin Bintrim. From Michigan State University, meet computer engineering major Seth Mosier and Kim Trouten, who is finishing up a zoology degree. Here's what they had to say:

HOW THEY CHOSE THEIR MAJORS

Karen: During high school, I volunteered at a retirement center, and my supervisor gave me a lot of exposure to applied psychology. After my freshman year in college, I talked to people who were using a psychology degree. You put in a lot of work for a degree and can wonder if it's worth all the work. It helps to talk to someone who has gone through it so you can see if that's what you want to be doing when you graduate.

Justin: I wasn't sure about what my major would be. One professor told me to take survey courses to see if I was interested in the subject. I took English literature, math, psychology, and philosophy. I liked English the best and did well in it. The next semester, I took two English courses and decided to switch my major. My professors told me not to worry about choosing a major. They said to get my feet wet and we'll talk about your major in two years. I decided that if they're not worried about a major, I wouldn't be either, but I still had it on my mind. I was around older students who were thinking about their careers, so I talked to them about the jobs they had lined up.

Seth: I liked computers in high school. In college, I started out in computer science but got sick of coding. My interest in computers made me pick computer science right off the bat. I didn't know about computer engineering until I got to college.

Kim: I wanted to be a veterinarian but after two years decided that I didn't want to go to school for that long. I was still interested in animals and had two options. One was in animal science, which is working more with farm animals, or going into zoology. I decided to concentrate on zoo and aquarium science. Besides being a vet, the closest interaction with animals would be being a zookeeper.

THE ELECTIVES THEY TOOK AND WHY

Karen: My adviser told me to take different classes, so I took philosophy, art, religion, and extra psychology classes that weren't required.

Justin: I was planning to do a double major, but my professors said to take what interested me. English majors have lots of freedom to take different courses, unlike science majors.

Seth: Because I'm in computer engineering, I don't get to take a lot of electives. I am taking a swimming class right now and took a critical incident analysis class where we looked at major accidents. I wanted something that wasn't computer engineering-related but extremely technical.

Kim: I took some kinesiology classes, which was pretty much an aerobics class. I needed to work out and figured I could get credit for it. I also took sign language because I'm interested in it.

WHAT THEY'RE GOING TO DO WITH THEIR DEGREES

Karen: I want to go to graduate school and hopefully get some experience working with kids.

Justin: I'm applying to graduate school in English literature and cultural studies. I want to do research and become a college professor.

Seth: I'm going to work for the defense department. It's not the highest offer I've gotten, but it will be the most fun, which is more important to me than the money.

Kim: My goals have changed again. I don't plan on using my degree. I just got married a year ago, and my husband and I want to go into full-time ministry. I'll work for a while, and then we'll go overseas.

THE CHANGES THEY WOULD MAKE IN THE CLASSES THEY TOOK IF THEY COULD

Karen: There are classes I wouldn't necessarily take again. But even though I didn't learn as much as I wanted to, it was worth it. I learned how to work and how to organize my efforts.

Justin: I should have worried less about choosing a major when I first started college. I didn't have the perspective as to how much time I had to choose.

Seth: I have friends who would change the order in which they took their humanities classes. I was lucky enough to think ahead and spread those classes out over the entire time. Most [engineering] students take them their freshman year to get them all out of the way. Later on, they're locked in the engineering building all day. Because I didn't, it was nice for me to get my mind off engineering.

Kim: Something I can't change are the labs. They require a lot of work, and you only get one credit for 3 hours. Some labs take a lot of work outside of class hours. I had a comparative anatomy lab, which kept me busy over entire weekends. I suggest you don't take a lot of classes that require labs all at once.

THEIR ADVICE FOR YOU

Karen: You don't have to know what you want to do with the rest of your life when you get to college. Most people don't even stay with the major they first choose. Colleges recognize that you will see things you may have not considered at first. Some high school students say they won't go to college unless they know what they want to do.

Justin: If it's possible, take a little of this and a little of that. If you're an engineering student, you'll have it all planned out [for you], but if you're a liberal arts major and are not sure, you probably can take something from each department.

Seth: If possible, take AP exams in high school. You'll be able to make a decision about a major. Freshmen who think they want to do engineering suffer through math and physics classes. Then by their sophomore or junior year, they realize they don't want to be engineers. If they'd taken AP classes, they'd know by their freshman year.

Kim: When I changed my major, I was worried that I might have spent a year in classes that wouldn't count toward my new major. But you shouldn't be scared to change majors because if you stick with something you don't like, you'll have to go back and take other classes anyway.

Though these four seniors arrived at a decision about which major they wanted in different ways, they had similar things to say:

- **It's okay to change your mind about what you want out of college.**
- **To find out which major you might want, start with what you like to do.**
- **Talk to professionals who have jobs in the fields that interest you.**
- **Ask your professors about what kinds of jobs you could get with the degree you're considering.**
- **Talk to seniors who will be graduating with a degree in the major you're considering.**
- **Take electives in areas that interest you, even though they may have nothing to do with your major.**
- **College is a time to explore many different options, so take advantage of the opportunity.**

interpreting (high level of skill necessary); foreign language publishing; and computer programming (especially for linguistics majors).

Health Sciences

Health professions majors, while having a scientific core, are more focused on applying the results of scientific investigation than on the scientific disciplines themselves. Allied health majors prepare graduates to assist health professionals in providing diagnostics, therapeutics, and rehabilitation. Medical science majors, such as optometry, pharmacy, and the premedical profession sequences, are, for the most part, preprofessional studies that comprise the scientific disciplines necessary for admission to graduate or professional school in the health or medical fields. Health service and technology majors prepare students for positions in the health fields that primarily involve services to patients or working with complex machinery and materials. Medical technologies cover a wide range of fields, such as cytotechnology, biomedical technologies, and operating room technology.

Administrative, professional, or research assistant positions in health agencies, hospitals, occupational health units in industry, community and school health departments, government agencies (public health, environmental protection), and international health organizations are available to majors in health fields, as are jobs in marketing and sales of health-related products and services, health education (with education courses), advertising and public relations, journalism and publishing, and technical writing.

Home Economics and Social Services

Home economics encompasses many different fields—basic studies in foods and textiles as well as consumer economics and leisure studies—that overlap with aspects of agriculture, social science, and education. Jobs can be found in government and community agencies (especially those in education, health, housing, or human services), nursing homes, child-care centers, journalism, radio/TV, educational media, and publishing. Types of work also include marketing, sales, and customer service in consumer-related industries, such as food processing and packaging, appliance manufacturing, utilities, textiles, and secondary school home economics teaching (which usually requires education courses).

Majors in social services find administrative positions in government and community health, welfare, and social service agencies, such as hospitals, clinics, YMCAs and YWCAs, recreation commissions, welfare agencies, and employment services. See the "Law and Legal Studies" section for information on more law-related social services.

Humanities (Miscellaneous)

The majors that constitute the humanities (sometimes called "letters") are the most general and widely applicable and the least vocationally oriented of the liberal arts. They are essentially studies of the ideas and concerns of human kind. These include classics, history of philosophy, history of science, linguistics, and medieval studies. Career possibilities for humanities majors can be found in business firms, government and community agencies, advertising and public relations, marketing and sales, publishing, journalism and radio/TV, secondary school teaching in English and literature (which usually requires education courses), freelance writing and editing, and computer programming (especially for those with a background in logic or linguistics).

Law and Legal Studies

Students of legal studies can use their knowledge of law and government in fields involving the making, breaking, and enforcement of laws; the crimes, trials, and punishment of law breakers; and the running of all branches of government at local, state, and federal levels. Graduates find positions of all types in law firms, legal departments of other organizations, the court or prison system, government agencies (such as law enforcement agencies or offices of state and federal attorneys general), and police departments.

Mathematics and Physical Sciences

Mathematics is the science of numbers and the abstract formulation of their operations. Physical sciences involve the study of the laws and structures of physical matter. The quantitative skills acquired through the study of science and mathematics are especially useful for computer-related careers. Career possibilities include positions in industry (manufacturing and processing companies, electronics firms, defense contractors, consulting firms); government agencies (defense, environmental protection, law enforcement); scientific/technical writing, editing, or illustrating; journalism (science reporting); secondary school teaching (usually requiring education courses); research and laboratory analysis and testing; statistical analysis; computer programming; systems analysis; surveying and mapping; weather forecasting; and technical sales.

Natural Resources

A major in the natural resources field prepares students for work in areas as generalized as environmental conservation and as specialized as groundwater contamination. Jobs are available in industry (food, energy, natural resources, and pulp and paper companies), consulting firms, state and federal government agencies (primarily the Departments of Agriculture and the Interior), and public and private conservation agencies. See the "Agriculture" and "Biological Sciences" sections for more information on natural resources-related fields.

Psychology

Psychology majors involve the study of behavior and can range from the biological to the sociological. Students can study individual behavior, usually that of humans, or the behavior of crowds. Students of psychology do not always go into the obvious clinical fields, the fields in which psychologists work with patients. Certain areas of psychology, such as industrial/organizational, experimental, and social, are not clinically oriented. Psychology and counseling careers can be in government (such as mental health agencies), schools, hospitals, clinics, private practice, industry, test development firms, social work, and personnel. The careers listed in the "Social Sciences" section are also pursued by psychology and counseling majors.

Religion

Religion majors are usually seen as preprofessional studies for those who are interested in entering the ministry. Career possibilities for religion also include casework, youth counseling, administration in community and social service organizations, teaching in religious educational institutions, and writing for religious and lay publications. Religious studies also prepare students for the kinds of jobs other humanities majors often pursue.

Social Sciences

Social sciences majors study people in relation to their society. Thus, social science majors can apply their education to a wide range of occupations that deal with social issues and activities. Career opportunities are varied. People with degrees in the social sciences find careers in government, business, community agencies (serving children, youth, and senior citizens), advertising and public relations, marketing and sales, secondary school social studies teaching (with education courses), casework, law enforcement, parks and recreation, museum work (especially for anthropology, archaeology, geography, and history majors), preservation (especially for anthropology, archaeology, geography, and history majors), banking and finance (especially for economics majors), market and survey research, statistical analysis, publishing, fundraising and development, and political campaigning.

Technologies

Technology majors, along with trade fields, are most often offered as two-year programs. Majors in technology fields prepare students directly for jobs; however, positions are in practical design and production work rather than in areas that require more theoretical, scientific, and mathematical knowledge.

Engineering technologies prepare students with the basic training in specific fields (e.g., electronics, mechanics, or chemistry) that are necessary to become technicians on the support staffs of engineers. Other technology majors center more on maintenance and repair. Work may be in technical activities, such as production or testing, or in nontechnical areas where a technical degree is needed, such as marketing, sales, or administration. Industries, research labs, and government agencies in which technology plays a key role—such as in manufacturing, electronics, construction, communications, transportation, and utilities—hire technology graduates regularly.

Still Unsure?

Relax! You don't have to know your major before you enroll in college. More than half of all freshmen are undecided when they start school and prefer to get a feel for what's available at college before making a decision. Most four-year colleges don't require students to formally declare a major until the end of their sophomore year or beginning of their junior year. Part of the experience of college is being exposed to new subjects and new ideas. Chances are your high school never offered anthropology. Or marine biology. Or applied mathematics. So take these classes and follow your interests. While you're fulfilling your general course requirements, you might stumble upon a major that appeals to you, or maybe you'll discover a new interest while you're volunteering or involved with other extracurricular activities. Talking to other students might lead to new options you'll want to explore.

Can I Change My Major If I Change My Mind?

Choosing a major does not set your future in stone, nor does it necessarily disrupt your life if you need to change your major. However, there are advantages to choosing a major sooner rather than later. If you wait too long to choose, you may have to take additional classes to satisfy the requirements, which may cost you additional time and money.

THE OTHER SIDE OF COLLEGE: HAVING FUN!

There is more to college than writing papers, reading books, and sitting through lectures. Your social life plays an integral part in your college experience.

Meeting New People

The easiest time to meet new people is at the beginning of something new. New situations shake people up and make them feel just uncomfortable enough to take the risk of extending their hand in friendship. Fortunately for you, college is filled with new experiences. There are the first weeks of being the newest students. This can be quickly followed by being a new member of a club or activity. And with each passing semester, you will be in new classes with new teachers and new faces. College should be a time of constantly challenging and expanding yourself, so never feel that it is too late to meet new people.

But just how do you take that first step in forming a relationship? It's surprisingly easy. The first few weeks of school will require you to stand in many lines. Some will be to buy books; others will be to get meals. One will be to get a student I.D. card. Another will be to register for classes. While standing in line, turn around and introduce yourself to the person behind you. Focus on what you have in common and try to downplay the differences. Soon you will find the two of you have plenty to talk about. When it is time to leave the line, arrange to have coffee later or to see a movie. This will help you form relationships with the people you meet.

Be open to the opportunities of meeting new people and having new experiences. Join clubs and activities. Investigate rock-climbing. Try ballet. Write for the school paper. But most of all, get involved.

Campus Activities

College life will place a lot of demands on you. Your classes will be challenging. Your professors will expect more from you. You will have to budget and manage your own money. But there is a plus side you probably haven't thought of yet: college students do have free time.

The average student spends about three hours a day in class. Add to this the time you will need to spend studying, eating, and socializing, and you will still have time to spare. One of the best ways to use this time is to participate in campus activities.

Intramural Sports

Intramurals are sports played for competition between members of the same campus community. They provide competition and a sense of belonging without the same level of intensity in practice schedules. Anyone can join an intramural sport. Often there are teams formed by dormitories, sororities, or fraternities that play team sports such as soccer, volleyball, basketball, flag-football, baseball, and softball. There are also individual intramural sports such as swimming, golf, wrestling, and diving. If you want to get involved, just stop by the intramural office. Usually it is located near the student government office.

Student Government

Student government will be set up in a way that is probably similar to your high school. Students form committees and run for office. However, student government in college has more power than in high school. The officers address all of their class's concerns directly to the President of the college or university and the Board of Trustees. Most student governments have a branch responsible for student activities that brings in big name entertainers and controversial speakers. You may want to get involved to see how such contacts are made and appearances negotiated.

Community Service

Another aspect of student life is volunteering, commonly called community service. Many colleges offer a range of opportunities. Some allow you to simply commit an afternoon to a cause, such as passing out food at a food bank. Others require an ongoing commitment. For example, you might decide to help an adult learn to read every Thursday at 4 p.m. for three months. Some colleges will link a service commitment with class credit. This will enhance your learning, giving you some real-world experience. Be sure to stop by your community service office and see what is available.

Clubs

There are a variety of clubs on most college campuses spanning just about every topic you can imagine. Amnesty International regularly meets on most campuses to write letters to help free prisoners in foreign lands. Most college majors band together in a club to discuss their common interests and career potential. There are also clubs that are based on the use of certain computer software or that engage in outdoor activities like sailing or downhill skiing. The list is endless. If you cannot find a club for your interest, consider starting one of your own. Stop by the student government office to see what rules you will need to follow. You will also need to find a location to hold meetings and post signs to advertise your club. When you hold your first meeting, you will probably be surprised at how many people are willing to take a chance and try a new club.

Greek Life

A major misconception of Greek life is that it revolves around wild parties and alcohol. In fact, the vast majority of fraternities and sororities focus on instilling values of scholarship, friendship, leadership, and service in their members. From this point forward, we will refer to both fraternities and sororities as fraternities.

Scholarship

A fraternity experience helps you make the academic transition from high school to college. Although the classes taken in high school are challenging, they'll be even harder in college. Fraternities almost always require members to meet certain academic standards. Many hold mandatory study times, keep old class notes and exams on file for study purposes, and personal tutors are often available. Members of a fraternity have a natural vested interest in seeing that other members succeed academically, so older members often assist younger members with their studies.

Friendship

Social life is an important component of Greek life. Social functions offer an excellent opportunity for freshmen to become better acquainted with others in the chapter. Whether it is a Halloween party or a formal dance, there are numerous chances for members to develop poise and confidence. By participating in these functions, students enrich friendships and build memories that will last a lifetime. Remember, social functions aren't only parties; they can include such activities as intramural sports and Homecoming.

Leadership

Because fraternities are self-governing organizations, leadership opportunities abound. Students are given hands-on experience in leading committees, managing budgets, and interacting with faculty members and administrators. Most houses have as many as ten officers, along with an array of committee members. By becoming actively involved in leadership roles, students gain valuable experience that is essential for a successful career. Interestingly, although Greeks represent less than 10 percent of the undergraduate student population, they hold the majority of leadership positions on campus.

Service

According to the North-American Interfraternity Council, fraternities are increasingly becoming involved in philanthropies and hands-on service projects. Helping less fortunate people is a major focus of Greek life. This can vary from work with Easter Seals, blood drives, and food pantry collections to community upkeep, such as picking up trash, painting houses, or cleaning up area parks. Greeks also get involved in projects with organizations such as Habitat for Humanity, the American Heart Association, and Children's Miracle Network. By being involved in philanthropic projects, students not only raise money for worthwhile causes, but they also gain a deeper insight into themselves and their responsibility to the community.

ROOMMATES

When you arrive on campus, you will face a daunting task: to live peacefully with a stranger for the rest of the academic year.

To make this task easier, most schools use some type of room assignment survey. This can make roommate matches more successful. For example, two people who prefer to stay up late and play guitar can be matched, while two people who prefer to rise at dawn and hit the track can be a pair. Such differences are easy to ask about on a survey and easy for students to report. However, surveys cannot ask everything, and chances are pretty good that

HOMESICKNESS

Homesickness in its most basic form is a longing for the stuff of home: your parents, friends, bedroom, school, and all of the other familiar people and objects that make you comfortable. But on another level, homesickness is a longing to go back in time. Moving away to college forces you to take on new responsibilities and begin to act like an adult. This can be scary.

While this condition is often described as a "sickness," no pill will provide a quick fix. Instead, you need to acknowledge that your feelings are a normal reaction to a significant change in your life. Allow yourself to feel the sadness of moving on in life and be open to conversations about it that may crop up in your dorm or among your new friends. After all, everyone is dealing with this issue. Then, make an effort to create a new home and a new life on campus. Create new habits and routines so that this once-strange place becomes familiar. Join activities and engage in campus life. This will help you to create a feeling of belonging that will ultimately be the key to overcoming homesickness.

something about your roommate is going to get on your nerves.

In order to avoid conflict, plan ahead. When you first meet, work out some ground rules. Most schools have roommates write a contract together and sign it during the first week of school. Ground rules help eliminate conflict from the start by allowing each person to know what is expected. You should consider the following areas: privacy, quiet time, chores, and borrowing.

When considering privacy, think about how much time alone you need each day and how you and your roommate will arrange for private time. Class schedules usually give you some alone time. Be aware of this; if your class is cancelled, consider going for a cup of coffee or a browse in the bookstore instead of immediately rushing back to your room. Privacy also relates to giving your roommate space when he or she has had a bad day or just needs time to think. Set up clear hours for quiet time. Your dorm will already have some quiet hours established. You may choose to simply reiterate those or add additional time. Just be clear.

Two other potentially stormy issues are chores and borrowing. If there are cleaning chores that need to be shared, make a schedule and stick to it. No one appreciates a sink full of dirty dishes or a dingy shower. Remember the golden rule: do your chores as you wish your roommate would. When it comes to borrowing, set up clear rules. The safest bet is to not allow it; but if you do, limit when, for how long, and what will be done in case of damage.

Another issue many students confront is whether or not to live with a best friend from high school who is attending the same college. Generally, this is a bad idea for several reasons. First, you may think you know your best friend inside and out, but you may be surprised by her personal living habits. There is nothing like the closeness of a dorm room to reveal the annoying routines of your friend. Plus, personalities can change rapidly in college. Once you are away from home, you may be surprised at how you or your friend transforms from shy and introverted to late night partygoer. This can cause conflict. A final downfall is that the two of you will stick together like glue in the first few weeks and miss out on opportunities to meet other people.

Armed with this information, you should have a smooth year with your new roommate. But just in case you are the exception, most colleges will allow students who absolutely cannot get along to move. Prior to moving, each student must usually go through a dispute resolution process. This typically involves your Resident Adviser, you, and your roommate trying to work through your problems in a structured way.

Living with a roommate can be challenging at times, but the ultimate rewards—meeting someone new, encountering new ideas, and learning how to compromise—will serve you well later in life. Enjoy your roommate and all the experiences you will have, both good and bad, for they are all part of the college experience.

COMMUTING FROM HOME

For some students, home during the college years is the same house in which they grew up. Whether you are in this situation because you can't afford to live on campus or because you'd just rather live at home with your family, some basic guidelines will keep you connected with campus life.

By all means, do not just go straight home after class. Spend some of your free time at school. Usually there is a student union or a coffee shop where students gather and socialize. Make it a point to go there and talk to people between classes. Also, get involved in extracurricular activities, and visit classmates in the dorms.

If you drive to school, find other students who want to carpool. Most schools have a commuters' office or club that will give you a list of people who live near you. Sharing a car ride will give you time to talk and form a relationship with someone else who knows about the challenges of commuting.

Commuters' clubs also sponsor a variety of activities throughout the year—give them a try! Be sure also to consider the variety of activities open to all members of the student body, ranging from student government to community service to intramural sports. You may find this takes a bit more effort on your part, but the payoff in the close friendships you'll form will more than make up for it.

WHAT IF YOU DON'T LIKE THE COLLEGE YOU PICK

In the best of all worlds, you compile a list of colleges, find the most compatible one, and are accepted. You have a great time, learn a lot, graduate, and head off to a budding career. However, you may find the college you chose isn't the best of all worlds. Imagine these scenarios:

1. Halfway through your first semester of college, you come to the distressing conclusion that you can't stand being there for whatever reason. The courses don't match your interests. The campus is out in the boonies, and you don't ever want to see another cow. The selection of extracurricular activities doesn't cut it.
2. You have methodically planned to go to a community college for two years and move to a four-year college to complete your degree. Transferring takes you nearer to your goal.
3. You thought you wanted to major in art, but by the end of the first semester, you find yourself more interested in English lit. Things get confusing, so you drop out of college to sort out your thoughts and now you want to drop back in, hoping to rescue some of those credits.
4. You didn't do that well in high school—socializing got in the way of studying. But you've wised up, have gotten serious about your future, and two years of community college have brightened your prospects of transferring to a four-year institution.

Circumstances shift, people change, and, realistically speaking, it's not all that uncommon to transfer. Many people do. The reasons why students transfer run the gamut, as do the institutional policies that govern them. The most common transfers are students who move from a two-year to a four-year university or the person who opts for a career change midstream.

Whatever reasons you might have for wanting to transfer, you will be doing more than just switching academic gears. Aside from potentially losing credits, time, and money, transferring means again adjusting to a new situation. This affects just about all transfer students, from those who made a mistake in choosing a college to those who planned to go to a two-year college and then transferred to a four-year campus. People choose colleges for arbitrary reasons. That's why admissions departments try to ensure a good match between the student and campus before classes begin. Unfortunately, sometimes students don't realize they've made a mistake until it's too late.

The best way to avoid transferring is to extensively research a college or university before choosing it. Visit the campus and stay overnight, talk to admissions and faculty members, and try to learn as much as you can.

10 Chapter

OTHER OPTIONS AFTER HIGH SCHOOL

Years ago, most young people went directly to work after high school. Today, most young people first go to school for more training, but the majority don't go to traditional four-year colleges.

According to Shannon McBride, Director of the Golden Crescent Tech Prep Partnership in Victoria, Texas, "Only 40 percent of high school graduates attempt to go to a four-year college, and of those, only 25 percent get their degree. And of that 25 percent, only 37 percent use the degree they got in that area."

So why aren't the remaining 60 percent of students choosing a traditional four-year college? The reasons are as varied as the students. Life events can often interfere with plans to attend college. Responsibilities to a family may materialize that make it impossible to delay earning an income for four years. One may have to work and go to school. And traditional colleges demand certain conventions, behaviors, and attitudes that don't fit every kind of person. Some people need a lot of physical activity to feel satisfied, while others just aren't interested in spending day after day sitting, reading, memorizing, and analyzing. Years of strict time management and postponed rewards are more than they can stand.

If any of these reasons ring true with you, there are still postsecondary options for you, all of which will not only allow you to pursue further education but also will train you for a career. Let's take a look at some of these educational directions you can follow.

DISTANCE LEARNING

As a future college student, can you picture yourself in any of these scenarios?

1. You need some information, but the only place to find it is at a big state university. Trouble is, it's hundreds of miles away. No problem. You simply go to your local community college and hook up electronically with the university. Voilà! The resources are brought to you.
2. That ten-page paper is due in a few days, but you still have some last-minute questions to ask the professor before you turn it in. Only one problem: you won't be able to see the professor until after the paper is due. Being a night owl, you also want to work on it when your roommate is asleep. Not to worry. Since you have the professor's e-mail address, just like all the other students in the class, you simply e-mail your question to her. She replies. You get your answer, finish the paper, and even turn it in electronically.
3. After graduating from high school, you can't go to college right away, but your employer has a neat hook up with a college that offers courses via the Internet. During your lunch hours, you and several of your work buddies log in to a class and get college credit.

Not too long ago, if you'd offered these scenarios to high school graduates as real possibilities, they would have thought you were a sci-fi freak. Distance education was not common at all—or if it was, it usually meant getting courses via snail mail or on videotape. Well, today you are in the right place at the right time. Distance education is a reality for countless high school graduates.

What distance education now means is that you can access educational programs and not have to physically be in a classroom on a campus. Through such technologies as cable or satellite television, videotapes and audiotapes, fax, computer modem, computer conferencing and videoconferencing, and other means of electronic delivery, the classroom comes to you—sometimes even if you're sitting in your room in your bunny slippers and it's 2 in the morning.

Distance learning expands the reach of the classroom by using various technologies to deliver university resources to off-campus sites, transmit college courses into the workplace, and enable you to view class lectures in the comfort of your home.

Where and How Can I Take Distance Learning Courses?

The technology for new, cheaper telecommunications technology is getting better all the time, and there is a growing demand for education by people who can't afford either the time or money to be a full-time, on-campus student. To fill that demand, educational networks also are growing and changing how and when you can access college courses.

Most states have established new distance learning systems to advance the delivery of instruction to schools, postsecondary institutions, and state government agencies. Colleges and universities are collaborating with commercial telecommunication entities, including online information services, such as America Online and cable and telephone companies, to provide education to far-flung student constituencies. Professions such as law, medicine, and accounting, as well as knowledge-based industries, are utilizing telecommunications networks for the transmission of customized higher education programs to working professionals, technicians, and managers.

Ways in Which Distance Learning May Be Offered:

- **Credit courses.** In general, if these credit courses are completed successfully, they may be applied toward a degree.
- **Noncredit courses and courses offered for professional certification.** These programs can help you acquire specialized knowledge in a concentrated, time-efficient manner and stay on top of the latest developments in your field. They provide a flexible way for you to prepare for a new career or study for professional licensure and certification. Many of these university programs are created in cooperation with professional and trade associations so that courses are based on real-life workforce needs, and the practical skills learned are immediately applicable in the field.

The Way Distance Learning Works

Enrolling in a distance learning course may simply involve filling out a registration form, making sure that you have access to the equipment needed, and paying the tuition and fees by check, money order, or credit card. In these cases, your applications may be accepted without entrance examinations or proof of prior educational experience.

Other courses may involve educational prerequisites and access to equipment not found in all geographic locations. Some institutions offer detailed information about individual courses, such as a course outline, upon request. If you have access to the Internet and simply wish to review course descriptions, you may be able to peruse an institution's course catalogs electronically by accessing the institution's home page on the Web.

Time Requirements

Some courses allow you to enroll at your convenience and work at your own pace. Others closely adhere to a traditional classroom schedule. Specific policies and time limitations pertaining to withdrawals, refunds, transfers, and renewal periods can be found in the institutional catalog.

Admission to a Degree Program

If you plan to enter a degree program, you should consult the academic advising department of the institution of your choice to learn about entrance requirements and application procedures. You may find it necessary to develop a portfolio of your past experiences and accomplishments that may have resulted in college-level learning.

How Do I Communicate with My Instructor?

Student-faculty exchanges occur using electronic communication (through fax and e-mail). Many institutions offer their distance learning students access to toll-free numbers so students can talk to their professors or teaching assistants without incurring any long-distance charges.

Responses to your instructor's comments on your lessons, requests for clarification of comments, and all other exchanges between you and your instructor will take time. Interaction with your instructor—whether by computer, phone, or letter—is important, and you must be willing to take the initiative.

What Else Does Distance Learning Offer?

Distance learning comes in a variety of colors and flavors. Along with traditional college degrees, you can earn professional certification or continuing education units (CEUs) in a particular field.

College Degrees

There are opportunities for you to earn degrees at a distance at the associate, baccalaureate, and graduate levels. Two-year community college students are now able to earn baccalaureate degrees—without relocating—by transferring to distance learning programs offered by four-year universities. Corporations are forming partnerships with universities to bring college courses to worksites and encourage employees to continue their education. Distance learning is especially popular among people who want to earn their degree part-time while continuing to work full-time. Although on-campus residencies are sometimes required for certain distance learning degree programs, they generally can be completed while employees are on short-term leave or vacation.

Professional Certification

Certificate programs often focus on employment specializations, such as hazardous waste management or electronic publishing, and can be helpful to those seeking to advance or change careers. Also, many states mandate continuing education for professionals such as teachers, nursing home administrators, or accountants. Distance learning offers a convenient way for many individuals to meet professional certification requirements. Health care, engineering, and education are just a few of the many professions that take advantage of distance learning to help their professionals maintain certification.

Many colleges offer a sequence of distance learning courses in a specific field of a profession. For instance, within the engineering profession, certificate programs in computer-integrated manufacturing, systems engineering, test and evaluation, waste management education, and research consortium are offered via distance learning.

Business offerings include distance learning certification in information technology, total quality management, and health services management.

Within the field of education, you'll find distance learning certificate programs in areas such as early reading instruction and special education for the learning handicapped.

Continuing Education Units (CEUs)

If you choose to take a course on a noncredit basis, you may be able to earn continuing education units (CEUs). The CEU system is a nationally recognized system to provide a standardized measure for accumulating, transferring, and recognizing participation in continuing education programs. One CEU is defined as 10 contact hours of participation in an organized continuing education experience under responsible sponsorship, capable direction, and qualified instruction.

COMMUNITY COLLEGES

Two-year colleges or community colleges, are often called "the people's colleges." With their open-door policies (admission is open to individuals with a high school diploma or its equivalent), community colleges provide access to higher education for millions of Americans who might otherwise be excluded from higher education. Community college students are diverse, of all ages, races, and economic backgrounds. While many community college students enroll full-time, an equally large number attend on a part-time basis so they can fulfill employment and family commitments as they advance their education.

Today, there are more than 1,800 community colleges in the United States. They enroll more than 7.4 million students, who represent more than 50 percent of all undergraduates in the United States. As you can see, millions of first-time freshmen begin their higher education in a community college.

Community colleges are also referred to as either technical or junior colleges, and they may either be under public or independent control. What unites all two-year colleges is that they are regionally accredited, postsecondary institutions, whose highest credential awarded is the associate degree. With few exceptions, community colleges offer a comprehensive curriculum, which includes transfer, technical, and continuing education programs.

Important Factors in a Community College Education

The student who attends a community college can count on receiving quality instruction in a supportive learning community. This setting frees the student to pursue his or her own goals, nurture special talents, explore new fields of learning, and develop the capacity for lifelong learning.

From the student's perspective, four characteristics capture the essence of community colleges:

- They are community-based institutions that work in close partnership with high schools, community groups, and employers in extending high-quality programs at convenient times and places.
- Community colleges are cost effective. Annual tuition and fees at public community colleges average approximately half those at public four-year colleges and less than 15 percent of private four-year institutions. In addition, since most community colleges are generally close to their students' homes, these students can also save a significant amount of money on the room, board, and transportation expenses traditionally associated with a college education.
- They provide a caring environment, with faculty members who are expert instructors, known for excellent teaching and for meeting students at the point of their individual needs, regardless of age, sex, race, current job status, or previous academic preparation. Community

A SCHOLARSHIP FOR CAREER COLLEGE STUDENTS

The Imagine America Scholarship can help those who dream of a career but might not be able to achieve it through traditional college education.

What is the Imagine America Scholarship?

Introduced in 1998 by the Career College Foundation, the *Imagine America* Scholarship aims to reduce the growing "skills gap" in America. Any graduating high school senior can be considered for selection for one of the three scholarships awarded to his or her high school. The *Imagine America* Scholarship gives thousands of graduating high school seniors scholarships of $1,000 to be used at more than 400 participating career colleges and schools across the country.

You are eligible for the Imagine America Scholarship if:

- **You attend any private postsecondary institution that is accredited by an agency recognized by the U.S. Department of Education.**
- **You are graduating from high school this year.**

To find out more about the Imagine America Scholarship Program, talk to your high school counselor or visit www.imagine-america.org for more information.

colleges join a strong curriculum with a broad range of counseling and career services that are intended to assist students in making the most of their educational opportunities.

- Many offer comprehensive programs, including transfer curricula in such liberal arts programs as chemistry, psychology, and business management, that lead directly to a baccalaureate degree and career programs that prepare students for employment or assist those already employed in upgrading their skills. For those students who need to strengthen their academic skills, community colleges also offer a wide range of developmental programs in mathematics, languages, and learning skills, designed to prepare the student for success in college studies.

Getting to Know Your Two-Year College

The best way to learn about your college is to visit in person. During a campus visit, be prepared to ask a lot of questions. Talk to students, faculty members, administrators, and counselors about the college and its programs, particularly those in which you have a special interest. Ask about available certificates and associate degrees. Don't be shy. Do what you can to dig below the surface. Ask college officials about the transfer rate to four-year colleges. If a college emphasizes student services, find out what particular assistance is offered, such as educational or career guidance. Colleges are eager to provide you with the information you need to make informed decisions.

MOST POPULAR MAJORS FOR COMMUNITY COLLEGE GRADS

The American Association of Community Colleges conducted a survey in the year 2000 to see what the most popular majors for community college students were. The top 15 majors and their average starting salaries follow:

MAJOR	AVERAGE STARTING SALARY
1. Registered Nursing	$32,757
2. General Computer Technologies	$34,242
3. Computer Networking	$38,767
4. Engineering–Electric/Electronics	$29,464
5. Computer Technician/Networking	$36,092
6. Manufacturing Technology	$30,291
7. Radiology Technology	$32,478
8. Digital Media	$35,409
9. Computer Programming	$30,838
10. General Skilled Trades	$25,598
11. Law Enforcement	$27,975
12. Dental Hygiene	$41,907
13. Computer-Aided Design	$27,968
14. Automotive	$29,305
15. General Allied Health	$24,781

The Money Factor

For many students, the decision to attend a community college is often based on financial factors. If you aren't sure what you want to do or what talents you have, community colleges allow you the freedom to explore different career interests at a low cost. For those students who can't afford the cost of university tuition, community colleges let them take care of their basic classes before transferring to a four-year institution. Many two-year colleges can now offer you instruction in your own home through cable television or public broadcast stations or through home study courses that can save both time and money. Look into all your options, and be sure to add up all the costs of attending various colleges before deciding which is best for you.

Working and Going to School

Many two-year college students maintain full-time or part-time employment while they earn their degrees. Over the past decades, a steadily growing number of students have chosen to attend community colleges while they fulfill family and employment responsibilities. To enable these students to balance the demands of home, work, and school, most community colleges offer classes at night and on weekends.

For the full-time student, the usual length of time it takes to obtain an associate degree is two years. However, your length of study will depend on the course load you take: the fewer credits you earn each term, the longer it will take you to earn a degree. To assist you in moving more quickly toward your degree, many community colleges now award credit through examination or for equivalent knowledge gained through relevant life experiences. Be certain to find out the credit options that are available to you at the college in which you are interested. You may discover that it will take less time to earn a degree than you first thought.

Preparation for Transfer

Studies have repeatedly shown that students who first attend a community college and then transfer to a four-year college or university do at least as well academically as the students who entered the four-year institutions as freshmen. Most community colleges have agreements with nearby four-year institutions to make transfer of credits easier. If you are thinking of transferring, be sure to meet with a counselor or faculty adviser before choosing your courses. You will want to map out a course of study with transfer in mind. Make sure you also find out the credit-transfer requirements of the four-year institution you might want to attend.

New Career Opportunities

Community colleges realize that many entering students are not sure about the field in which they want to focus their studies or the career they would like to pursue. Community colleges have the resources to help students identify areas of career interest and to set challenging occupational goals.

Once a career goal is set, you can be confident that a community college will provide job-relevant, quality occupation and technical education. About half of the students who take courses for credit at community colleges do so to prepare for employment or to acquire or upgrade skills for their current job. Especially helpful in charting a career path is the assistance of a counselor or a faculty adviser, who can discuss job opportunities in your chosen field and help you map out your course of study.

In addition, since community colleges have close ties to their communities, they are in constant contact with leaders in business, industry, organized labor, and public life. Community colleges work with these individuals and their organizations to prepare students for direct entry into the world of work. For example, some community colleges have established partnerships with local businesses and industries to provide specialized training programs. Some also provide the academic portion of apprenticeship training, while others offer extensive job-shadowing and cooperative education opportunities. Be sure to examine all of the career-preparation opportunities offered by the community colleges in which you are interested.

VOCATIONAL/CAREER COLLEGES

Career education is important for every employee as technology continues to change. From the largest employers, such as the U.S. military, defense contractors, IBM, aviation, and health care, down to the company with one and two employees, issues of keeping up with technology and producing goods and services cheaper, faster, and at less cost requires—indeed demands—a skilled, world-class workforce. In good or bad economic times, you will always have a distinct advantage if you have a demonstrable skill and can be immediately productive while continuing to learn and improve. If you know how to use technology, work collaboratively, and find creative solutions, you will always be in demand.

Career colleges offer scores of opportunities to learn the technical skills required by many of today's and tomorrow's top jobs. This is especially true in the areas of computer and information technology, health care, and hospitality (culinary arts, travel and tourism, and hotel and motel management). Career colleges range in size from those with a handful of students to universities with thousands enrolled. They are located in every state in the nation and share one common objective—to prepare students for a successful career in the world of work through a focused, intensive curriculum.

America's career colleges are privately owned and operated for-profit companies. Instead of using tax support to operate, career colleges pay taxes. Because

SNAPSHOT OF A CAREER COLLEGE STUDENT

Katrina Dew
Network Systems Administration
Silicon Valley College
Fremont, California

ABOUT KATRINA

Right after high school, Katrina headed for junior college, but she felt like she was spinning her wheels. She wanted something that was goal-oriented. Community college offered too many options. She needed to be focused in one direction.

At first, Katrina thought she would become a physical therapist. Then she realized how much schooling she would need to begin working. Turning to the computer field, she saw some definite benefits. For one, she had messed around with them in high school. She could get a degree and get out in two years. She saw that computer careers are big and getting bigger. Plus, there weren't a lot of women in that field, which signaled more potential for her. But before she switched schools, she visited the career college, talked to students, and sat in on lectures. She really liked the way the teachers related to their students. Along with her technical classes, she's taken algebra, psychology, English composition, and management communication.

WHAT I LIKE ABOUT BEING A CAREER STUDENT

"Career colleges are for fast-track-oriented students who want to get out in the work field and still feel that they have an appropriate education."

Nicholas Cecere
Automotive Techniques Management
Education America/Vale Technical Institute
Blairsville, Pennsylvania

ABOUT NICHOLAS

Nicholas has completely repainted his 1988 Mercury Topaz, redone all the brakes, put in a brand-new exhaust system, and lots of smaller stuff here and there. But he says that's nothing compared to the completely totaled cars some of his classmates haul into the school. Talk about hands-on: they're able to completely restore them while going through the program.

Nicholas didn't always have gasoline running through his veins. In fact, he just recently discovered how much he likes automotives. After graduating from high school, he went to a community college, and after one semester, he left to work at a personal care home. Standing over a sink of dirty dishes made him realize he wanted more than just a job. He started thinking about what he wanted to do and visited a few schools and the body shop where his brother worked. Where others saw twisted car frames, Nicholas saw opportunity and enrolled in the program.

WHAT I LIKE ABOUT BEING A CAREER STUDENT

"I compare career college to a magnifying glass that takes the sun and focuses it. You learn just what you need to learn."

career colleges are businesses, they must be responsive to the workforce needs of their communities or they will cease to exist.

Generally, career colleges prepare you for a specific career. Some will require you to take academic courses such as English or history. Others will relate every class you take to a specific job, such as computer-aided drafting or interior design. Some focus specifically on business or technical fields. Bob Sullivan, a career counselor at East Brunswick High School in East Brunswick, New Jersey, points out that the negative side to this kind of education is that if you haven't carefully researched what you want to do, you could waste a lot of time and money. "There's no room for exploration or finding yourself as opposed to a community college where you can go to find yourself and feel your way around," he explains.

So how do you find the right career college for you? A good place to start is knowing generally what you want to do. You don't have to know the fine details of your goals, but you should have a broad idea, such as a career in allied health or business or computing.

After you've crossed that hurdle, the rest is easy. Since professional training is the main purpose of career colleges, its graduates are the best measure of a school's success. Who hires the graduates? How do their jobs relate to the education they received? Career colleges should be able to provide that data to prospective students. "Career colleges have a different customer than other institutions," notes Stephen Friedheim, President of ESS College of Business in Dallas, Texas. In addition to focusing on the needs of their students, career colleges also want to ensure they meet the needs of the employers who are hiring their graduates. "The assumption is that if you can please the employer, you will please the student," Friedheim explains.

Checking the credentials of a career college is one of the most important steps you should take in your career college search. Though not every career college has to be accredited, it is a sign that the college has gone through a process that ensures quality. It also means that students can qualify for federal grant and loan programs. Furthermore, you should see if the college has met the standards from professional training organizations. In fields such as court reporting and health-related professions, those criteria are paramount.

FINANCIAL AID OPTIONS FOR CAREER AND COMMUNITY COLLEGES

The financial aid process is basically the same for students attending a community college, a career college, or a technical institute as it is for students attending a four-year college. However, there are some details that can make the difference between getting the maximum amount of financial aid and only scraping by.

As with four-year students, the federal government is still your best source of financial aid. Most community colleges and career and technical schools participate in federal financial aid programs. To get detailed information about federal financial aid programs and how to apply for them, read through Chapter 8: "Financial Aid Dollars and Sense." In the meantime, here are some quick tips on where to look for education money.

Investigate federal financial aid programs. You should definitely check out a Federal Pell Grant, which is a need-based grant available to those who can't pay the entire tuition themselves. The Federal Supplemental Educational Opportunity Grant (FSEOG) is for those students with exceptional financial need. You also can take advantage of the Federal Work-Study programs that provide jobs for students with financial aid eligibility in return for part of their tuition. Many two-year institutions offer work-study, but the number of jobs tends to be limited. Also, federal loans make up a substantial part of financial aid for two-year students. Student loans, which have lower interest rates, may be sponsored by the institution or federally sponsored, or they may be available through commercial financial institutions. They are basically the same as those for the traditional four-year college student, such as the Federal Perkins Loan and the Direct Stafford Loan and the Federal Family Education Stafford Loan. In fact, some private career colleges and technical institutes only offer federal loans. You also can find more specific information about federal loans in Chapter 8.

WHAT TO LOOK FOR IN A CAREER COLLEGE

A tour of the college is a must! While visiting the campus, do the following:

- **Get a full explanation of the curriculum, including finding out how you will be trained.**
- **Take a physical tour of the classrooms and laboratories and look for cleanliness, modern equipment/computers, and size of classes. Observe the activity in classes: Are students engaged in class, and are lectures dynamic?**
- **Ask about employment opportunities after graduation. What are the placement rates (most current) and list of employers? Inquire about specific placement assistance: resume preparation, job leads, etc. Look for "success stories" on bulletin boards, placement boards, and newsletters.**
- **Find out about tuition and other costs associated with the program. Ask about the financial aid assistance provided to students.**
- **Find out if an externship is part of the training program. How are externships assigned? Does the student have any input as to externship assignment?**
- **Ask if national certification and registration in your chosen field is available upon graduation.**
- **Inquire about the college's accreditation and certification.**
- **Also find out the associations and organizations to which the college belongs. Ask what awards or honors the college has had bestowed.**
- **Ask if the college utilizes an advisory board to develop employer relationships.**
- **Ask about the rules and regulations. What GPA must be maintained? What is the attendance policy? What are grounds for termination? What is the refund policy if the student drops or is terminated? Is there a dress code? What are the holidays of the college?**

Source: Arizona College of Allied Health, Phoenix, Arizona

Don't overlook scholarships. What many two-year students don't realize is that they could be eligible for scholarships. Regrettably, many make the assumption that scholarships are only for very smart students attending prestigious universities. You'd be surprised to learn how many community and career colleges offer scholarships. It's critical to talk to the financial aid officer of each school you plan to attend to find out what scholarships might be available.

Two-year students should find out how their state of residence can help them pay for tuition. Every state in the union has some level of state financial aid that goes to community college students. The amounts are dependent on which state you live in, and most aid is in the form of grants.

APPRENTICESHIPS

Some students like working with their hands and have the skill, patience, and temperament to become expert mechanics, carpenters, or electronic repair technicians. If you think you'd enjoy a profession like this and feel that college training isn't for you, then you might want to think about a job that requires apprenticeship training.

To stay competitive, America needs highly skilled workers. But if you're looking for a soft job, forget it. An apprenticeship is no snap. It demands hard work and has tough competition, so you've got to have the will to see it through. An apprenticeship is a program formally agreed upon between a worker and an employer where the employee learns a skilled trade through classroom work and on-the-job training. Apprenticeship programs vary in length, pay, and intensity among the various trades. A person completing an apprenticeship program generally becomes a journeyperson (skilled craftsperson) in that trade.

The advantages of apprenticeships are numerous. First and foremost, an apprenticeship leads to a lasting lifetime skill. As a highly trained worker, you can take your skill anywhere you decide to go. The more creative, exciting, and challenging jobs are put in the hands of the fully skilled worker, the all-around person who knows his or her trade inside out.

Skilled workers advance much faster than those who are semiskilled or whose skills are not broad enough to equip them to assume additional responsibilities in a career. Those who complete an apprenticeship have also acquired the skills and judgment that are necessary to go into business for themselves if they choose.

What to Do If You're Interested in an Apprenticeship

If you want to begin an apprenticeship, you have to be at least 16 years old, and you must fill out an application for employment. These applications may be available year-round or at certain times during the year, depending on the trade in which you're interested.

Federal regulations prohibit anyone under the age of 16 from being considered for an apprenticeship. Some programs require a high school degree or certain course work. Other requirements may include passing certain aptitude tests, proof of physical ability to perform the duties of the trade, and possession of a valid driver's license.

Once you have met the basic program entrance requirements, you'll be interviewed and awarded points on your interest in the trade, your attitude toward work in general, and personal traits, such as appearance, sincerity, character, and habits. Openings are awarded to those who have achieved the most points.

Because an apprentice must be trained in an area where work actually exists and where a certain pay scale is guaranteed upon completion of the program, the wait for application acceptance may be pretty long in areas of low employment. This standard works to your advantage, however. Just think: You wouldn't want to spend one to six years of your life learning a job where no work exists or where the wage is the same as, or just a little above, that of an unskilled or semiskilled laborer.

If you're considering an apprenticeship, the best sources of assistance and information are vocational or career counselors, local state employment security agencies, field offices of state apprenticeship agencies, and regional offices of the Bureau of Apprenticeship and Training (BAT). Apprenticeships are usually registered with the BAT or a state apprenticeship council. Some apprenticeships are not registered at all, although that doesn't necessarily mean that the program isn't valid. To find out if a certain apprenticeship is legitimate, contact your state's apprenticeship agency or a regional office of the BAT. Addresses and phone numbers for these regional offices are listed on the following page. You can also visit the Bureau's Web site at www.doleta.gov/atels_bat/bat.cfm.

BUREAU OF APPRENTICESHIP AND TRAINING OFFICES

NATIONAL OFFICE
Employment and Training Agency
U.S. Department of Labor
Frances Perkins Building
200 Constitution Avenue, NW
Washington, DC 20210
Phone: 877-US-2JOBS (toll-free)

REGION I - BOSTON

Douglas F. Small
U.S. Department of Labor/ETA
J.F.K. Federal Building, Room E-350
Boston, MA 02203
Phone: 617-788-0170
Fax: 617-788-0101
E-mail: RO1-RA-BOS@dol.gov

- Connecticut
- Maine
- Massachusetts
- New Hampshire
- New Jersey
- New York
- Rhode Island
- Vermont
- Puerto Rico
- Virgin Islands

REGION II - PHILADELPHIA

Lenita Jacobs-Simmons
U.S. Department of Labor/ETA
Suite 825 East
The Curtis Center
170 South Independence Mall West
Philadelphia, PA 19106
Phone: 215-861-5200

- Delaware
- Washington DC
- Maryland
- Pennsylvania
- Virginia
- West Virginia

REGION III - ATLANTA

Helen Parker
Regional Administrator
U.S. Department of Labor/ETA
Atlanta Federal Center
61 Forsyth Street, Room 6M12
Atlanta, GA 30303
Phone: 404-562-2092
Fax: 404-562-2149

- Alabama
- Florida
- Georgia
- Kentucky
- Mississippi
- North Carolina
- South Carolina
- Tennessee

REGION IV - DALLAS

Joseph Juarez
Regional Administrator
U.S. Department of Labor/ETA
525 Griffin Street, Room 317
Dallas, TX 75202
Phone: 214-767-8263
Fax: 214-767-5113

- Arkansas
- Louisiana
- New Mexico
- Oklahoma
- Colorado
- Montana
- North Dakota
- South Dakota
- Texas
- Utah
- Wyoming

REGION V - CHICAGO

Byron Zuidema
Regional Administrator
U.S. Department of Labor/ETA
230 South Dearborn Street, 6th Floor
Chicago, IL 60604
Phone: 312-596-5400

- Illinois
- Indiana
- Michigan
- Minnesota
- Ohio
- Iowa
- Kansas
- Missouri
- Nebraska
- Wisconsin

REGION VI - SAN FRANCISCO

Richard Trigg
Regional Administrator
U.S. Department of Labor/ETA
P.O. Box 193767
71 Stevenson Street, Suite 830
San Francisco, CA 94119-3767
Phone: 415-975-4610
Fax: 415-975-4612

- Arizona
- California
- Hawaii
- Nevada
- Alaska
- Idaho
- Oregon
- Washington
- Guam

11 Chapter

THE MILITARY OPTION

Bet you didn't know that the United States military is the largest employer in the country. There's got to be a good reason that so many people get their paychecks from Uncle Sam.

SHOULD I OR SHOULDN'T I WORK FOR THE LARGEST EMPLOYER IN THE U.S.?

Every year, thousands of young people pursue a military career and enjoy the benefits it offers. Yet thousands more consider joining the military and decide against it. Their reasons vary, but many choose not to enlist because they lack knowledge of what a career in the military can offer. Others simply mistrust recruiters based on horror stories they've heard. Sadly, many make the decision against joining the military without ever setting foot in the recruiting office.

But if you are an informed "shopper," you will be able to make an informed choice about whether the military is right for you.

People rarely buy anything based on their needs: Instead, they buy based on their emotions. We see it on a daily basis in advertising, from automobiles to soft drinks. We rarely see an automobile commercial that gives statistics about how the car is engineered, how long it will last, the gas mileage, and other technical specifications. Instead, we see people driving around and having a good time.

The reason for this is that advertising agencies know that you will probably buy something based on how you feel rather than what you think. Because of this tendency to buy with emotion rather than reason, it is important to separate the feelings from the facts. That way, you can base your decision about whether to join the military primarily on the facts.

There are two big questions that you must answer before you can come to any conclusions. First, is the military right for me, and second, if the first answer is yes, which branch is right for me?

Suppose that you have to decide whether to buy a new car or repair your current car. The first choice you make will determine your next course of action. You will have to weigh the facts to determine if you will purchase a new car or not. Once you've decided to buy a car rather than repair your old one, you must then decide exactly what make and model will best suit your needs.

NO HYPE, JUST THE FACTS

So you didn't wake up one morning and know for sure that you're going to join the Navy. One minute you think you'd like the Army, but then you talk to your cousin who convinces you to follow him into the Air Force. But then the neighbor down the street is a Marine, and he's gung ho for you to join up with them. What to do?

Well, a helpful Web site is the answer. Go to www.spear.navy.mil/profile for some really straightforward and non-partisan information about each branch of the military. You'll be able to compare the benefits that each service offers plus pick up other helpful tips and information. The Web site is designed specifically for high school students considering the military.

"Normally the first question we get from people interested in the Air Force is 'What does the Air Force have to offer me?' But I back off and ask them about their qualifications. Sometimes it's easier to go to an Ivy League school than to join the Air Force because of our stringent requirements."

Master Sergeant Timothy Little
United States Air Force

You should make a list of the reasons why you want to join the military before you ever set foot in the recruiter's office. Whether your list is long—containing such items as money for college, job security, opportunity to travel, technical training, and good pay—or contains only one item, such as having full-time employment, the number of items on your list is not what's important. What is important is that you are able to satisfy those reasons, or primary motivators.

Whatever your list contains, the first course of action is to collect your reasons to join the military and put them in order of importance to you. This process, known as rank-ordering, will help you determine if you should proceed with the enlistment process.

"Take two people with the same qualifications who are looking for jobs. The person with the Army background will be that much more competitive. That's due to the fact that he or she is disciplined and knows how to act without being told what to do."

Staff Sergeant Max Burda
United States Army

Rank-ordering your list is a simple process of deciding which motivators are most important to you and then listing them in order of importance. List your most important motivator as number one, your next most important as number two, and so on.

If we apply the car-buying scenario here, your primary motivators may be finding a car that costs under $20,000, gets at least 30 miles to the gallon, has leather interior, is available in blue, and has a sunroof. If you put those motivators in rank order, your list might look something like this:

1. Costs under $20,000
2. Gets at least 30 mpg
3. Has a sunroof
4. Has leather interior
5. Available in blue

You'll notice that the number one, or most important, motivator in this case is cost, while the last, or least important, motivator is color. The more important the motivator, the less likely you'll be willing to settle for something different or to live without it altogether.

After you've rank-ordered your motivators, go down your list and determine whether those motivators can be met by enlisting in the military. If you find that all your motivators can be met by enlisting, that's great; but even if only some of your motivators can be met, you may still want to consider enlisting. Seldom does a product meet all our needs and wants.

CHOOSING WHICH BRANCH TO JOIN

"If you like to travel, we offer more than anyone else. The longest you're underway is generally two to three weeks, with three to four days off in every port and one day on the ship. Prior to pulling in, you can even set up tours."

Chief Petty Officer Keith Horst
United States Navy

If you are seriously considering joining the military, you probably have checked out at least two of the branches. Check them all out, even if it means just requesting literature and reviewing it. A word of caution though: Brochures do not tell the complete story, and it is very difficult to base your decision either for or against a military branch on the contents of a brochure alone. Would you buy a car based solely on the information contained in a brochure? Probably not!

"I tell people that you get paid the same in all the services, and the benefits are the same. What's different about each branch is the environment."

Sergeant Ian Bonnell, Infantry Sergeant
United States Marines

The process of choosing the right branch of the military for you is basically the same process that you used to determine if joining the military was right for you. You should start with your list of primary

I'M JOINING THE AIR FORCE

It didn't take Brian Filipek long to decide he wanted to join the Air Force. But that's if you don't count the times he talked to people who had served in the Air Force or the research he did on the Internet to gather information—and that was before he even set foot inside the recruiter's office. By the time an Air Force recruiter responded to a card Brian had sent in, he was pretty sure he liked what he'd seen so far. "The recruiter didn't have to do any work to convince me," says Brian. After that, it was a matter of going through the pre-qualifying process, like whether he met the height and weight qualifications, and the security forms he had to fill out.

After he enlisted, Brian didn't stop gathering information. Long before he was sent to Basic Training, he found out about Warrior Week, which is held on one of the last weeks in Basic Training. He was already looking forward to it. "I'm an outdoors kind of person," he says. "I want to do the obstacle course and ropes course."

Though the idea of testing his endurance and strength appeals to him, being away from family will be hard. "Granted, your food is cooked for you, but you're still on your own," he says. However, he knows that it's worth it to achieve his goal of education and free job training. Brian acknowledges that the military is not for everyone, but as far as he's concerned, he's sure he's made the right choice.

Brian Filipek, Enlistee
U.S. Air Force

motivators and use the "yes/no" method to determine whether each branch can meet all or some of those motivators. Once you've determined which branch or branches can best meet your motivators, it's time to compare those branches. Remember to look for the negative aspects as well as the motivators of each of the branches as you compare.

After making your comparisons, you may still find yourself with more than one choice. What do you do then? You could flip a coin, but that's not the wisest idea! Instead, look at some of these factors:

Length of enlistment—Some branches may require a longer term for offering the same benefits that you could receive from another branch.

Advanced pay grade—You may be entitled to an advanced rank in some branches based on certain enlistment options.

"In the Army, you can get training in everything from culinary arts to truck driving and all the way to aviation mechanics, military intelligence, and computer networking."
Staff Sergeant Max Burda
United States Army

Length and type of training—How long will your training take? Usually the longer the training, the more in-depth and useful it is. You'll also want to consider how useful the training will be once you've left the military.

Enlistment bonuses—Be careful when using an enlistment bonus as the only factor in deciding which branch to choose. If it comes down to a tie between two branches and only one offers a bonus, it's not a bad reason to choose that branch.

Additional pay and allowances—There may be additional pay you'd be entitled to that can only be offered by a particular branch. For instance, if you join the Navy, you may be entitled to Sea Pay and Submarine Pay, something obviously not available if you join the Air Force.

Ability to pursue higher education—While all the military branches offer educational benefits, you must consider when you will be able to take advantage of these benefits. If your job requires 12-hour shifts and has you out in the field a lot, when will you be able to attend classes?

"Everyone in the Navy learns how to fight a fire. You get qualified in First Aid and CPR. That's mandatory for every sailor. The only jobs we don't have in the Navy are veterinarians, forest rangers, and rodeo stars."
Chief Petty Officer Keith Horst
United States Navy

Once you have considered these factors, and perhaps some of your own, you should be able to decide which branch is right for you. If you still haven't been able to select one branch over another, though, consider the following:

- Ask your recruiter if you can speak to someone who has recently joined.
- If there is a base nearby, you may be able to get a tour to look at its facilities.
- If you are well versed in Internet chat rooms, you may want to look for ones that cater to military members—then ask a lot of questions.
- Talk to friends and family members who are currently serving in the military. Be careful, however, not to talk to people who have been out of the military for a while, as they probably aren't familiar with today's military. Also, avoid people who left the military under less-than-desirable conditions (for example, someone who was discharged from Basic Training for no compatibility).

If you choose to continue with processing for enlistment, your next step will probably be to take the Armed Services Vocational Aptitude Battery (ASVAB).

THE ASVAB

The ASVAB, a multiple-aptitude battery designed for use with students in their junior or senior year in high school or in a postsecondary school, as well as those seeking military enlistment, was developed to yield results useful to both students and the military. The military uses the results to determine the qualifications of candidates for enlistment and to help place them in military occupational programs. Schools use ASVAB test results to assist their students in developing future educational and career plans.

Frequently Asked Questions about the ASVAB

What is the Armed Services Vocational Aptitude Battery (ASVAB)?

The ASVAB, sponsored by the Department of Defense, is a multi-aptitude test battery consisting of nine short individual tests covering Word Knowledge, Paragraph Comprehension, Arithmetic Reasoning, Mathematic Knowledge, General Science, Auto and Shop Information, Mechanical Comprehension, Electronics Information, and Assembling Objects. Your ASVAB results provide scores for each individual test, as well as three academic composite scores—Verbal, Math, and Academic Ability—and two career exploration composite scores.

Why should I take the ASVAB?

As a high school student nearing graduation, you are faced with important career choices. Should you go on to college, technical, or vocational school? Would it be better to enter the job market? Should you consider a military career? Your ASVAB scores are measures of aptitude. Your composite scores measure your aptitude for higher academic learning and give you ideas for career exploration.

When and where is the ASVAB given?

ASVAB is administered annually or semiannually at more than 14,000 high schools and postsecondary schools in the United States.

Is there a charge or fee to take the ASVAB?

ASVAB is administered at no cost to the school or to the student.

How long does it take to complete the ASVAB?

ASVAB testing takes approximately 3 hours. If you miss class, it will be with your school's approval.

If I wish to take the ASVAB but my school doesn't offer it (or I missed it), what should I do?

See your school counselor. In some cases, arrangements may be made for you to take it at another high school. Your counselor should call 800-323-0513 (toll-free) for additional information.

How do I find out what my scores mean and how to use them?

Your scores will be provided to you on a report called the ASVAB Student Results Sheet. Along with your scores, you should receive a copy of *Exploring Careers: The ASVAB Workbook*, which contains information that will help you understand your

ASVAB results and show you how to use them for career exploration. Test results are returned to participating schools within thirty days.

What is a passing score on the ASVAB?

No one "passes" or "fails" the ASVAB. The ASVAB enables you to compare your scores to those of other students at your grade level.

If I take the ASVAB, am I obligated to join the military?

No. Taking the ASVAB does not obligate you to the military in any way. You are free to use your test results in whatever manner you wish. You may use the ASVAB results for up to two years for military enlistment if you are a junior, a senior, or a postsecondary school student. The military services encourage all young people to finish high school before joining the armed forces.

If I am planning to go to college, should I take the ASVAB?

Yes. ASVAB results provide you with information that can help you determine your capacity for advanced academic education. You can also use your ASVAB results, along with other personal information, to identify areas for career exploration.

Should I take the ASVAB if I plan to become a commissioned officer?

Yes. Taking the ASVAB is a valuable experience for any student who aspires to become a military officer. The aptitude information you receive could assist you in career planning.

Should I take the ASVAB if I am considering entering the Reserve or National Guard?

Yes. These military organizations also use the ASVAB for enlistment purposes.

What should I do if a service recruiter contacts me?

You may be contacted by a service recruiter before you graduate. If you want to learn about the many opportunities available through military service, arrange for a follow-up meeting. However, you are under no obligation to the military as a result of taking the ASVAB.

Is the ASVAB administered other than in the school testing program?

Yes. ASVAB is also used in the regular military enlistment program. It is administered at approximately sixty-five Military Entrance Processing Stations located throughout the United States. Each year, hundreds of thousands of young men and women who are interested in enlisting in the uniformed services (Army, Navy, Air Force, Marines, and Coast Guard) but who did not take the ASVAB while in school are examined and processed at these military stations.

Is any special preparation necessary before taking the ASVAB?

Yes. A certain amount of preparation is required for taking any examination. Whether it is an athletic competition or a written test, preparation is a *must* in order to achieve the best results. Your test scores reflect not only your ability but also the time and effort in preparing for the test. The uniformed services use ASVAB to help determine a person's qualification for enlistment and to help indicate the vocational areas for which the person is best suited. Achieving your maximum score will increase your vocational opportunities. So take practice tests to prepare.

BASIC TRAINING: WHAT HAVE I GOTTEN MYSELF INTO?

The main objective of Basic Training is to transform civilians into well-disciplined military personnel in a matter of weeks. Performing such a monumental task takes a lot of hard work, both mentally and physically. For most people, Basic Training ends with a parade on graduation day. For others, though, it ends somewhere short of graduation. It is those "horror stories" that make Basic Training the one biggest fear, or anxiety-inducer, for those considering military enlistment.

Unlike the boot camp you may have heard about from your Uncle Louie or seen on television, today's Basic Training doesn't include the verbal and physical abuse of yesterday. All of the military branches are ensuring that new enlistees are treated fairly and with dignity. Not that enlistees aren't yelled at (because they are); however, the vulgarity and demeaning verbal attacks are a thing of the past. There are, from time to time, incidents involving instructors who contradict the military's policies. These violations, however, receive a lot of attention, are thoroughly investigated, and usually end up with disciplinary action taken against those involved in the abuse.

> *"A lot of kids are worried about Marine boot camp. They've seen movies or heard stories. Boot camp is not set up to make you fail. It's challenging, but that's the purpose of it. You're learning that no matter what life throws at you, you will be able to improvise, adapt, and overcome."*
>
> **Sergeant Ian Bonnell, Infantry Sergeant**
> **United States Marines**

I SURVIVED BASIC TRAINING

Although Michael Hipszky was eager to join the Navy, it didn't take long for doubts about his decision to hit him. While he was riding the bus to the Navy's Basic Training facility, he asked himself THE QUESTION—"Why am I putting myself through this mess?" Recalls Michael, "It crosses everyone's mind. As far as I know, in my division, everyone had the same thought. 'I want to go home.' Those first few days are intense."

He figures it's because you lose control the minute you walk through the door on the first day of Basic Training. Someone's telling you (in a very loud voice) how to stand at attention, how to stand in line, how to do just about everything. "So many things go through your head," says Michael. He soon found that if he followed three rules, life got a whole lot easier:

1. KEEP YOUR MOUTH SHUT. **"Your mouth is your biggest problem," he warns, "talking when you aren't supposed to and saying dumb things."**
2. PAY ATTENTION TO DETAIL. **"They'll say things like, 'Grab the door knob, turn it half to the right, and go through.' A lot of people will just pull it open and get yelled at. They teach you how to fold your clothes and clean the head (toilet). Everything is paying attention to detail," Michael advises.**
3. DON'T THINK FOR YOURSELF. **"Wait to be told what to do," Michael says, recalling the time his group was handed a form and told to wait until ordered to fill it out. Many saw that the form was asking for information like name, date, and division and began filling it out, only to get in trouble because they didn't wait.**

Having been through Basic Training, Michael now knows that every little thing—from folding T-shirts the exact way he'd been told to do (arms folded in), to sweeping the floor, to marching—is all part of the training process. "You don't realize it until you're done," he says.

Despite all the yelling and push-ups, Michael values the training he got in the classes. He learned how to put out different kinds of fires, how to manage his money, how to identify aircraft—even etiquette. And that's just for starters.

His lowest point was about halfway through Basic, which, he found out, usually happens for everyone at the same time. "The first half of Basic, everything is so surreal. Then you get halfway through, and finishing up Basic seems so far away. You're always busy, whether you're stenciling your clothes or marching. You march a lot," he says. But then he reached his highest point, which was pass-in review at the end of the training and winning awards. He knew he'd done well. Looking into his future with the Navy, Michael says, "I want to see the world and have the experiences that the Navy can give you." Having finished Basic Training, he's well on his way.

Airman Michael Hipszky
United States Navy

If you are still uncertain of which branch you'd like to join, do not allow the type of Basic Training you'll receive to be your only deciding factor. If, for example, the Marine Corps meets all your needs and is clearly your first choice, do not select the Air Force because its Basic Training seems easier. Conversely, if the Air Force is clearly your first choice, do not select the Marine Corps because it has the "toughest" Basic Training, and you want to prove you are up to the challenge. Basic Training is a means of your transformation from civilian life to military life. It happens in a relatively short period of time compared to the entire length of your enlistment.

Some Words on Getting through Basic Training

No matter what you may have heard or read elsewhere, there are no secrets to getting through Basic Training; only common sense and preparation will get you through. Here are some do's and don'ts that should help you survive Basic Training for any of the services. Although following these guidelines will not ensure your success at Basic Training, your chances for success will be greatly improved by following them.

Before Arriving at Basic Training

DO:

- Start an exercise program.
- Maintain a sensible diet.
- Stay out of trouble (pay any traffic fines promptly before leaving for Basic Training).
- Ensure that all of your financial obligations are in order.
- Bring the required items that you are told to bring.
- Give up smoking.

DON'T:

- Skip preparing yourself physically because you think that Basic Training will whip you into shape.
- Abuse drugs and/or alcohol.
- Have a big send-off party and get drunk the night before you leave for Basic Training.
- Leave home with open tickets, summonses, or warrants.
- Get yourself into heavy debt (such as buying a new car).
- Bring any prohibited items.
- Have your hair cut in a radical manner. (This includes having your head shaved. Men will receive a "very close" haircut shortly after arriving at Basic Training.)
- Have any part of your body pierced, tattooed, or otherwise altered.

PAYING FOR COLLEGE THROUGH THE ARMED SERVICES

You can take any of the following three paths into the armed services—all of which provide opportunities for financial assistance for college.

Enlisted Personnel

All five branches of the armed services offer college-credit courses on base. Enlisted personnel can also take college courses at civilian colleges while on active duty.

> *"In the Air Force, you're not only getting an education, but also experience. You could go to school for a degree in avionics technology, but in the Air Force, you get the teaching and the experience—real-world, hands-on experience—that makes your education marketable."*
>
> **Master Sergeant Timothy Little**
> **United States Air Force**

ROTC

More than 40,000 college students participate in Reserve Officers' Training Corps (ROTC). Two-, three-, and four-year ROTC scholarships are available to outstanding students. You can try ROTC at no obligation for two years or, if you have a four-year scholarship, for one year. Normally, all ROTC classes, uniforms, and books are free. ROTC graduates are required to serve in the military for a set period of time, either full-time on active duty or part-time in the Reserve or National Guard. Qualifying graduates can delay their service to go to graduate or professional school first.

U.S. Service Academics

Openings at the U.S. service academies are few, so it pays to get information early. Every student is on a full scholarship, but free does not mean easy—these intense programs train graduates to meet the demands of leadership and success.

West Point. The U.S. Military Academy (Army) offers a broad-based academic program with forty-two majors in various fields of study. Extensive training and leadership experience go hand in hand with academics. *www.usma.edu*

Annapolis. The U.S. Naval Academy is a unique blend of tradition and state-of-the-art technology. Its core curriculum includes nineteen major fields of study, and classroom work is supported by practical experience in leadership and professional operations. *www.usna.edu*

Air Force Academy. The U.S. Air Force Academy prepares and motivates cadets for careers as Air Force officers. The academy offers a B.S. degree in thirty-two majors. Graduates receive a reserve commission as a second lieutenant in the Air Force. *www.usfa.edu*

Coast Guard Academy. This broad-based education, which leads to a B.S. degree in eight technical or professional majors, includes a thorough grounding in the professional skills necessary for the Coast Guard's work. *www.cga.edu*

WHAT'S MY JOB?—OH, I JUST DRIVE AN ARMORED CARRIER AROUND

Justin Platt thought maybe he would join the Army, but first he had a few doubts to overcome. A big one was his reluctance to be away from friends and family. Another one was the overseas duty—something he definitely didn't want. But his desire to get his foot in the door of medical training won out. When he found out that he could get an education in the Army to become a nurse, his fears flew out the window, and Justin joined the Army. He's glad he did.

Stationed at Fort Carson in Colorado, Justin's been through Basic Training and is on his first stint of active duty working in—you guessed it—the medical field. "I work in an aid station, which is like a mini hospital," he says. He's the one who does the screening for anyone in his battalion who comes into sick call. Okay, it's from 5 a.m. to 7 p.m., but Justin doesn't mind.

Justin's job on active duty doesn't just consist of handing out Band-Aids and cough drops. He's also learning how to drive an armored carrier—not your usual medical training. But in the field, Army medics have to be able to pick up the wounded, which means knowing how to drive what he describes as a souped-up SUV—only instead of tires, it has tracks.

Justin plans to get enough rank to go from green to gold—enlisted to officer. "I'll have to take additional college courses to get a four-year degree," he says. It'll take him about seven years, including his Army duty. Not bad for someone who once had doubts about joining the military.

Private First Class Justin Platt
Fort Carson, Colorado

Financing Higher Education through the U.S. Armed Forces

The U.S. military provides a number of options to help students and their parents get financial aid for postsecondary education.

The Active Duty Montgomery GI Bill

The Active Duty Montgomery GI Bill, called "ADMGIB" for short, provides up to 36 months of education benefits to eligible veterans for college, business, technical or vocational courses, correspondence courses, apprenticeship/job training, and flight training. You may be an eligible veteran if you got an Honorable Discharge, you have a High School Diploma or GED, or, in some cases, 12 hours of college credit, AND you meet the necessary requirements related to military service. You MUST have elected to participate in the ADMGIB, which involves giving up $100 of your pay per month for the first twelve months of military service. The monthly benefit paid to you is based on the type of training you take, length of your service, your category, and if the Department of Defense put extra money in your *MGIB* Fund (called "kickers"). You usually have ten years to use your *MGIB* benefits, but the time limit can be less, in some cases, and longer under certain circumstances.

The Selected Reserve Montgomery GI Bill

The Selected Reserve Montgomery GI Bill (SRMGIB) may be available to you if you are a member of the Selected Reserve. The Selected Reserve includes the Army Reserve, Navy Reserve, Air Force Reserve, Marine Corps Reserve and Coast Guard Reserve, and the Army National Guard and the Air National Guard. You may use this education assistance program for degree programs, certificate or correspondence courses, cooperative training, independent study programs, apprenticeship/on-the-job training, and vocational flight training programs. Remedial, refresher, and deficiency training are available under certain circumstances. Eligibility for this program is determined by the Selected Reserve components. VA makes the payments for this program. You may be entitled to receive up to 36 months of education benefits. Your benefit entitlement ends fourteen years from the date of your eligibility for the program, or on the day you leave the Selected Reserve.

Call toll-free 1-888-GI-BILL-1 for more information, or visit the Web site at www.gibill.va.gov/education/benefits.htm.

The Department of Defense

The U.S. Department of Defense offers a large number of education benefits to those enrolled in the U.S. military or employed by the Department of Defense, including scholarships, grants, tuition assistance, and internships. Visit their Web site at http://web.lmi.org/edugate for complete information.

Tuition Assistance

All branches of the military pay up to 75 percent of tuition for full-time, active-duty enlistees who take courses at community colleges or by correspondence during their tours of duty. Details vary by service.

The Community College of the Air Force

Enlisted Air Force personnel can convert their technical training and military experience into academic credit, earning an associate degree, an occupational instructor's certificate, or a trade school certificate. Participants receive an official transcript from this fully accredited program. You can visit the Community College of the Air Force on line at www.au.af.mil/au/ccaf.

Educational Loan-Repayment Program

The Armed Services can help repay government-insured and other approved loans. Each of the services is free to offer such programs, but individual policies differ.

Other Forms of Tuition Assistance

Each branch of the military offers its own education incentives. To find out more, check with a local recruiting office.

Part 4

YOU AND THE WORKPLACE

SOME OF YOU WILL GO TO COLLEGE first and then look for jobs. Some of you might work for a few years and then go to college. And many of you will go immediately into the workplace and bypass college altogether. Whenever you become an employee, you'll want to know what you can do to succeed on the job and move to both higher levels of responsibility and more pay.

Chapter 12

JUMP INTO WORK

Almost everyone ends up in the workplace at some point. No matter when you plan to receive that first full-time paycheck, there are some things you'll need to do to prepare yourself for the world of work.

AT EACH GRADE LEVEL, there are specific steps you should take regardless of whether or not you plan to attend college immediately following high school. In fact, college and career timelines should coincide, according to guidance counselors and career specialists, and students should take college-preparatory courses, even if they aren't planning on attending college.

THE CAREER TIMELINE

The following timeline will help you meet college requirements and prepare you for work. In an effort to make sure that you are adequately preparing for both school and work, incorporate these five steps into your career/college timeline:

1. **Take an aptitude test.** You can do this as early as the sixth grade, but even if you do this in high school, it's not too late. By doing so, you will begin to get a feel for what areas you might be good at and enjoy. Your guidance counselor should have a test in his or her office for you to take, or you can try the ASVAB (see page 123). Thousands of high school students take this test every year to discover possible career paths—and taking the ASVAB doesn't require you to join the military!
2. **Beginning in middle school, you should start considering what your options are after high school.** However, if you're only starting to think about this in high school, that's okay, too. Keep a notebook of information gathered from field trips, job-shadowing experiences, mentoring programs, and career fairs to help you make sense of the possibilities open to you. This process should continue through high school. Many schools offer job shadowing and internship programs for students to explore different vocational avenues. Take advantage of these opportunities if you can. Too often, students don't explore the workplace until after they've taken the courses necessary to enter a particular profession, only to discover it wasn't the career they dreamed of after all.
3. **No later than the tenth grade, visit a vocational center to look at the training programs offered.** Some public school systems send students to vocational and career program centers for career exploration.

TAKING A BREAK BETWEEN HIGH SCHOOL AND COLLEGE

Because of the soaring costs of college tuition today, college is no longer a place to "find yourself." It is a costly investment in your future. The career you choose to pursue may or may not require additional education; your research will determine whether or not it's required or preferred. If you decide not to attend college immediately after high school, however, don't consider it to be a closed door. Taking some time off between high school and college is considered perfectly acceptable by employers. Many students simply need a break after thirteen years of schooling. Most experts agree that it's better to be ready and prepared for college; many adults get more out of their classes after they've had a few years to mature.

Source: Street Smart Career Guide: A Step-by-Step Program for Your Career Development.

4. **During your junior and senior years, be sure to create a portfolio of practice resumes, writing samples, and a list of work skills.** This portfolio should also include your high school transcript and letters of recommendation. It will serve as a valuable reference tool when it comes time to apply for jobs.

5. **By tenth or eleventh grade, you should begin focusing on a specific career path.** More employers today are looking for employees who have both the education and work experience that relates to the career field for which they're interviewing. If you are looking for part-time employment, you should consider jobs that pertain to your field of study. Until you start interacting with people in the field, you won't have a realistic feel of what's involved in that profession. If you're planning on heading into the workplace right after high school, take a look at the following pages for a list of careers that don't require a four-year degree.

WRITING YOUR RESUME

Resumes are a critical part of getting a job. A resume is an introduction of your skills to a potential employer. For that reason, your resume must stand out in a crowd because some employers receive dozens of resumes each week. A resume that is too long, cluttered, or disorganized may find its way to the "circular file," also known as the trash can. You can avoid this hazard by creating a resume that is short, presentable, and easy to read.

Remember that a resume is a summary of who you are and an outline of your experiences, skills, and goals. While writing it, you may discover some talents that you weren't aware you had and that will help boost your confidence for the job search.

Begin by collecting facts about yourself, including where you went to high school, your past and present jobs, activities, interests, and leadership roles. Next to the individual activities, write down what responsibilities you had. For example, something as simple as babysitting requires the ability to settle disagreements and supervise others.

Next, decide on how you would like to format your resume. Most hiring managers expect to see one of two types of resumes: chronological or functional. The chronological resume is the most traditional, supplying the reader with a sequential listing (from present to past) of your accomplishments. Because the emphasis here is on past employment experience, high school and college students with little or no employment history might want to avoid this resume type. A functional resume, on the other hand, highlights a person's abilities rather than his or her work history. Entry-level candidates who want to focus on skills rather than credentials should consider using a functional resume.

CAREERS WITHOUT A FOUR-YEAR DEGREE

Some students spend a few years in the workplace before going to college. Others begin their career with a high school diploma, a vocational certificate, or up to two years of education or training after high school.

With that in mind, sometimes it's easier to know what you don't want rather than what you do want. Take a look at the list below, and check off the careers that interest you. Perhaps you've thought of something you'd like to do that isn't on this list. Well, don't dump your hopes. There are many different levels of training and education that can lead you to the career of your dreams. Since this list is not all-inclusive, you should check with your high school counselor or go on line to research the training you'll need for the job or career you want—without a four-year degree. Then talk to your guidance counselor, teacher, librarian, or career counselor for more information about the careers on the list below or those you've researched on your own.

AGRICULTURE AND NATURAL RESOURCES

High school/vocational diploma

- ❑ Fisher
- ❑ Groundskeeper
- ❑ Logger
- ❑ Pest Controller

Up to two years beyond high school

- ❑ Fish and Game Warden
- ❑ Tree Surgeon

APPLIED ARTS (VISUAL)

High school/vocational diploma

- ❑ Floral Arranger
- ❑ Merchandise Displayer
- ❑ Painter (artist)

Up to two years beyond high school

- ❑ Cartoonist
- ❑ Commercial Artist
- ❑ Fashion Designer
- ❑ Interior Decorator
- ❑ Photographer

APPLIED ARTS (WRITTEN AND SPOKEN)

High school/vocational diploma

- ❑ Proofreader

Up to two years beyond high school

- ❑ Advertising copywriter
- ❑ Legal assistant

BUSINESS MACHINE/COMPUTER OPERATION

High school/vocational diploma

- ❑ Data Entry
- ❑ Statistical Clerk
- ❑ Telephone Operator
- ❑ Typist

Up to two years beyond high school

- ❑ Computer Operator
- ❑ Motion Picture Projectionist

CONSTRUCTION AND MAINTENANCE

High school/vocational diploma

- ❑ Bricklayer
- ❑ Construction Laborer
- ❑ Elevator Mechanic
- ❑ Floor Covering Installer
- ❑ Heavy Equipment Operator
- ❑ Janitor
- ❑ Maintenance Mechanic

Up to two years beyond high school

- ❑ Building Inspector
- ❑ Carpenter
- ❑ Electrician
- ❑ Insulation Worker
- ❑ Lather
- ❑ Painter (construction)
- ❑ Pipefitter
- ❑ Plumber
- ❑ Roofer
- ❑ Sheet Metal Worker
- ❑ Structural Steel Worker
- ❑ Tile Setter

CRAFTS AND RELATED SERVICES

High school/vocational diploma

- ❑ Baker/Cook/Chef
- ❑ Butcher
- ❑ Furniture Upholsterer
- ❑ Housekeeper (hotel)
- ❑ Tailor/Dressmaker

Up to two years beyond high school

- ❑ Dry Cleaner
- ❑ Jeweler
- ❑ Locksmith
- ❑ Musical Instrument Repairer

CREATIVE/PERFORMING ARTS

High school/vocational diploma

- ❑ Singer
- ❑ Stunt Performer

Up to two years beyond high school

- ❑ Actor/Actress
- ❑ Dancer/Choreographer
- ❑ Musician
- ❑ Writer/Author

EDUCATION AND RELATED SERVICES

High school/vocational diploma

- ❑ Nursery School Attendant
- ❑ Teacher's Aide

ENGINEERING AND RELATED TECHNOLOGIES

High school/vocational diploma

- ❑ Biomedical Equipment Technician
- ❑ Laser Technician

Up to two years beyond high school

- ❑ Aerospace Engineer Technician
- ❑ Broadcast Technician
- ❑ Chemical Laboratory Technician
- ❑ Civil Engineering Technician
- ❑ Computer Programmer
- ❑ Computer Service Technician
- ❑ Electronic Technician
- ❑ Energy Conservation Technician
- ❑ Industrial Engineering Technician
- ❑ Laboratory Tester
- ❑ Mechanical Engineering Technician
- ❑ Metallurgical Technician
- ❑ Pollution Control Technician
- ❑ Quality Control Technician
- ❑ Robot Technician
- ❑ Surveyor (land)
- ❑ Technical Illustrator
- ❑ Tool Designer
- ❑ Weather Observer

FINANCIAL TRANSACTIONS

High school/vocational diploma

- ❑ Accounting Clerk
- ❑ Bank Teller
- ❑ Cashier
- ❑ Payroll Clerk
- ❑ Travel Agent

Up to two years beyond high school

- ❑ Bookkeeper
- ❑ Loan Officer

HEALTH CARE (GENERAL)

High school/vocational diploma

- ❑ Dental Assistant
- ❑ Medical Assistant
- ❑ Nursing/Psychiatric Aide

Up to two years beyond high school

- ❑ Dietetic Technician
- ❑ Nurse (practical)
- ❑ Nurse (registered)
- ❑ Optometric Assistant
- ❑ Physical Therapist's Assistant
- ❑ Physician's Assistant
- ❑ Recreation Therapist

HEALTH-CARE SPECIALTIES AND TECHNOLOGIES

High school/vocational diploma

- ❑ Dialysis Technician

Up to two years beyond high school

- ❑ Dental Hygienist
- ❑ Dental Laboratory Technician
- ❑ EEG Technologist
- ❑ EKG Technician
- ❑ Emergency Medical Technician
- ❑ Medical Laboratory Technician
- ❑ Medical Technologist
- ❑ Nuclear Medicine Technologist
- ❑ Operating Room Technician
- ❑ Optician
- ❑ Radiation Therapy Technologist
- ❑ Radiologic Technologist
- ❑ Respiratory Therapist
- ❑ Sonographer

HOME/BUSINESS EQUIPMENT REPAIR

High school/vocational diploma

- ❑ Air-Conditioning/Refrigeration/ Heating Mechanic
- ❑ Appliance Servicer
- ❑ Coin Machine Mechanic

Up to two years beyond high school

- ❑ Communications Equipment Mechanic
- ❑ Line Installer/Splicer
- ❑ Office Machine Servicer
- ❑ Radio/TV Repairer
- ❑ Telephone Installer

INDUSTRIAL EQUIPMENT OPERATIONS AND REPAIR

High school/vocational diploma

- ❑ Assembler
- ❑ Blaster
- ❑ Boilermaker
- ❑ Coal Equipment Operator
- ❑ Compressor House Operator
- ❑ Crater
- ❑ Dock Worker
- ❑ Forging Press Operator
- ❑ Furnace Operator
- ❑ Heat Treater
- ❑ Machine Tool Operator
- ❑ Material Handler
- ❑ Miner
- ❑ Sailor
- ❑ Sewing Machine Operator

Up to two years beyond high school

- ❑ Bookbinder
- ❑ Compositor/Typesetter
- ❑ Electronic Equipment Repairer
- ❑ Electroplater
- ❑ Firefighter
- ❑ Instrument Mechanic
- ❑ Lithographer
- ❑ Machine Repairer
- ❑ Machinist
- ❑ Millwright
- ❑ Molder
- ❑ Nuclear Reactor Operator
- ❑ Patternmaker
- ❑ Photoengraver
- ❑ Power House Mechanic
- ❑ Power Plant Operator
- ❑ Printing Press Operator
- ❑ Stationery Engineer
- ❑ Tool and Die Maker
- ❑ Water Plant Operator
- ❑ Welder
- ❑ Wire Drawer

MANAGEMENT AND PLANNING

High school/vocational diploma

- ❑ Administrative Assistant
- ❑ Food Service Supervisor
- ❑ Postmaster
- ❑ Service Station Manager

Up to two years beyond high school

- ❑ Benefits Manager
- ❑ Building Manager
- ❑ Caterer
- ❑ Contractor
- ❑ Credit Manager
- ❑ Customer Service Coordinator
- ❑ Employment Interviewer
- ❑ Executive Housekeeper
- ❑ Funeral Director
- ❑ Hotel/Motel Manager
- ❑ Importer/Exporter
- ❑ Insurance Manager
- ❑ Manager (small business)
- ❑ Office Manager
- ❑ Personnel Manager
- ❑ Restaurant/Bar Manager
- ❑ Store Manager
- ❑ Supermarket Manager

MARKETING AND SALES

High school/vocational diploma

- ❑ Auctioneer
- ❑ Bill Collector
- ❑ Driver (route)
- ❑ Fashion Model
- ❑ Product Demonstrator
- ❑ Salesperson (general)
- ❑ Sample Distributor

Up to two years beyond high school

- ❑ Claims Adjuster
- ❑ Insurance Worker
- ❑ Manufacturer's Representative
- ❑ Real Estate Agent
- ❑ Sales Manager
- ❑ Travel Agent
- ❑ Travel Guide

PERSONAL AND CUSTOMER SERVICE

High school/vocational diploma

- ❑ Barber
- ❑ Bartender
- ❑ Beautician
- ❑ Child-Care Worker
- ❑ Counter Attendant
- ❑ Dining Room Attendant
- ❑ Electrologist
- ❑ Flight Attendant
- ❑ Host/Hostess
- ❑ Houseparent
- ❑ Manicurist
- ❑ Parking Lot Attendant
- ❑ Porter
- ❑ Private Household Worker
- ❑ Waiter/Waitress

RECORDS AND COMMUNICATIONS

High school/vocational diploma

- ❑ Billing Clerk
- ❑ Clerk (general)
- ❑ File Clerk
- ❑ Foreign Trade Clerk
- ❑ Hotel Clerk
- ❑ Meter Reader
- ❑ Postal Clerk
- ❑ Receptionist
- ❑ Stenographer

Up to two years beyond high school

- ❑ Court Reporter
- ❑ Legal Secretary
- ❑ Library Assistant
- ❑ Library Technician
- ❑ Medical Records Technician
- ❑ Medical Secretary
- ❑ Personnel Assistant
- ❑ Secretary
- ❑ Travel Clerk

SOCIAL AND GOVERNMENT

High school/vocational diploma

- ❑ Corrections Officer
- ❑ Police Officer
- ❑ Security Guard
- ❑ Store Detective

Up to two years beyond high school

- ❑ Detective (police)
- ❑ Hazardous Waste Technician
- ❑ Recreation Leader
- ❑ Personal/Customer Services

STORAGE AND DISPATCHING

High school/vocational diploma

- ❑ Dispatcher
- ❑ Mail Carrier
- ❑ Railroad Conductor
- ❑ Shipping/Receiving Clerk
- ❑ Stock Clerk
- ❑ Tool Crib Attendant
- ❑ Warehouse Worker

Up to two years beyond high school

- ❑ Warehouse Supervisor

VEHICLE OPERATION AND REPAIR

High school/vocational diploma

- ❑ Automotive Painter
- ❑ Bus Driver
- ❑ Chauffeur
- ❑ Diesel Mechanic
- ❑ Farm Equipment Mechanic
- ❑ Forklift Operator
- ❑ Heavy Equipment Mechanic
- ❑ Locomotive Engineer
- ❑ Railroad Braker
- ❑ Refuse Collector
- ❑ Service Station Attendant
- ❑ Taxicab Driver
- ❑ Truck Driver

Up to two years beyond high school

- ❑ Aircraft Mechanic
- ❑ Airplane Pilot
- ❑ Auto Body Repairer
- ❑ Automotive Mechanic
- ❑ Garage Supervisor
- ❑ Motorcycle Mechanic

Parts of a Resume

At the very least, your resume should include the following components:

Heading: Centered at the top of the page should be your name, address, phone number, and e-mail address.

Objective: In one sentence, tell the employer the type of work for which you are looking.

Education: Beginning with your most recent school or program, include the date (or expected date) of completion, the degree or certificate earned, and the address of the institution. Don't overlook any workshops or seminars, self-study, or on-the-job training in which you have been involved. If any courses particularly lend themselves to the type of work for which you are applying, include them. Mention grade point averages and class rank when they are especially impressive.

Skills and abilities: Until you've actually listed these on paper, you can easily overlook many of them. They may be as varied as the ability to work with computers or being captain of the girl's basketball team.

Work experience: If you don't have any, skip this section. If you do, begin with your most recent employer and include the date you left the job, your job title, the company name, and the company address. If you are still employed there, simply enter your start date and "to present" for the date. Include notable accomplishments for each job. High school and college students with little work experience shouldn't be shy about including summer, part-time, and volunteer jobs, such as lifeguarding, babysitting, delivering pizzas, or volunteering at local parks.

Personal: Here's your opportunity to include your special talents and interests as well as notable accomplishments or experiences.

References: Most experts agree that it's best to simply state that references are available upon request. However, if you do decide to list names, addresses, and phone numbers, limit yourself to no more than three. Make sure you inform any people whom you have listed that they may be contacted.

SAMPLE FUNCTIONAL RESUME

Michele A. Thomas
3467 Main Street
Atlanta, Georgia 30308
404-555-3423
E-mail: mthomas_987654321@yahoo.com

OBJECTIVE

Seeking a sales position in the wireless phone industry

EDUCATION

High School Diploma, June 2005

John F. Kennedy High School, Atlanta, Georgia

SKILLS

Computer literate, IBM: MS Works, MS Word, WordPerfect, Netscape; Macintosh: MS Word, Excel

ACTIVITIES/LEADERSHIP

Student Government secretary, 2004–2005

Key Club vice president, 2003–2004

Future Business Leaders of America

AWARDS

Varsity Swim Club (Captain; MVP Junior, Senior; Sportsmanship Award)
Outstanding Community Service Award, 2004

EXPERIENCE

Sales Clerk, The Limited, Atlanta, Georgia; part-time, September 2004 to present

Cashier, Winn-Dixie Supermarkets, Atlanta, Georgia, Summers 2002 and 2003

INTERESTS

Swimming, reading, computers

REFERENCES

Available upon request

SAMPLE COVER LETTER

Take a look at how this student's cover letter applied the facts outlined in her resume to the job to which she's applying. You can use this letter to help you get started on your own cover letters. Text that appears in all caps below indicates the kind of information you need to include in that section. Before you send your letter, proofread it for mistakes and ask a parent or friend you trust to look it over as well.

(DATE)
June 29, 2005

(YOUR ADDRESS)
3467 Main Street
Atlanta, Georgia 30308
Phone: 404-555-3423
E-mail: mthomas_987654321@yahoo.com

(PERSON—BY NAME—TO WHOM YOU'RE SENDING THE LETTER)
Mr. Charles E. Pence
Manager, Human Resources
NexAir Wireless
20201 East Sixth Street
Atlanta, Georgia 30372

Dear Mr. Pence:

(HOW YOU HEARD OF THE POSITION)
Your job announcement in the *Atlanta Gazette* for an entry-level sales position asked for someone who has both computer and sales skills. (SOMETHING EXTRA THAT WILL INTEREST THE READER) My training and past job experience fit both of those categories. I also bring an enthusiasm and desire to begin my career in a communications firm such as NexAir.

(WHAT PRACTICAL SKILLS YOU CAN BRING TO THE POSITION)
A few weeks ago, I graduated from John F. Kennedy High School here in Atlanta. While in school, I concentrated on gaining computer skills on both IBM and Macintosh machines and participated in organizations such as the Key Club, in which I was vice president, and the Future Business Leaders of America.

(RELATE PAST EXPERIENCE TO DESIRED JOB)
As you will see from my resume, I worked as a cashier at Winn-Dixie Supermarket for two summers and am currently employed as a sales clerk at The Limited. From these two positions, I have gained valuable customer service skills and an attention to detail, qualities which I am sure are of utmost importance to you as you make your hiring decision.

I would very much like to interview for the position and am available at your convenience. I look forward to hearing from you soon.

Sincerely,

Michele A. Thomas

Resume-Writing Tips

These tips will help as you begin constructing your resume:

- Keep the resume short and simple. Although senior executives may use as many as two or three pages, recent graduates should limit themselves to one page.
- Capitalize headings.
- Keep sentences short; avoid writing in paragraphs.
- Use language that is simple, not flowery or complex.
- Be specific, and offer examples when appropriate.
- Emphasize achievements.
- Be honest.
- Don't include information about salary or wages unless specifically requested.
- Use high-quality, white, beige, or gray, 8 ½" × 11" paper.
- Make good use of white space by leaving adequate side and top margins on the paper.
- Make what you write presentable and use good business style.
- Because your resume should be a reflection of your personality, write it yourself.
- Avoid gimmicks such as colored paper, photos, or clip art.
- Make good use of bullets or asterisks, underlining, and bold print.
- Proofread your work, and have someone you trust proofread it also.
- Be neat and accurate.
- Never send a resume without a cover letter.

The Cover Letter

Every resume should be accompanied by a cover letter. This is often the most crucial part of your job search because the letter will be the first thing that a potential employer reads. When you include a cover letter, you're showing the employer that you care enough to take the time to address him or her personally and that you are genuinely interested in the job.

Always call the company and verify the name and title of the person to whom you are addressing the letter. Although you will want to keep your letter brief, introduce yourself and begin with a statement that will catch the reader's attention. Indicate the position you are applying for and mention if someone referred you or if you are simply responding to a newspaper ad. Draw attention to yourself by including something that will arouse the employer's curiosity about your experience and accomplishments. A cover letter should request something, most commonly an interview. Sign and date your letter. Then follow up with a phone call a few days after you're sure the letter has been received. Persistence pays!

JOB HUNTING 101

High school is a time for taking classes and learning, developing relationships with others, becoming involved in extracurricular activities that teach valuable life skills, and generally preparing for college or a job. Regardless of where you're headed after high school, you need to learn how to create a favorable impression. That can mean setting some clear, attainable goals for yourself, putting them down on paper in the form of a resume and cover letter, and convincing interviewers that you are, indeed, the person for whom they are looking. In short, learn how to sell yourself. A brief course in Job Hunting 101 will help you do just that.

Marketing Yourself

You can use several approaches to market yourself successfully. Networking, the continual process of contacting friends and relatives, is a great way to get information about job openings. Seventy-five percent of the job openings in this country are not advertised but are filled by friends, relatives, and acquaintances of current employees. From the employer's perspective, there is less risk associated with hiring someone recommended by an employee than hiring someone unknown. Networking is powerful. Everyone has a primary network of people they know and talk to frequently. Those acquaintances know and talk to networks of their own, thereby creating a secondary network for you and multiplying the number of individuals who know what you're looking for in a job.

Broadcasting is another marketing method in which you gather a list of companies that interest you and then mail them letters asking for job interviews. Although the rate of return on your mailings is small, two thirds of all job hunters use this approach, and half of those who use it find a job. You will increase your response rate by addressing your letter to a particular person—the one who has the power to hire you—and by following up with a phone call a few days after the letter has been received. To obtain the manager's name, simply call the company and ask the receptionist for the person's name, job title, and correct spelling. Good resources for finding potential employers include referrals, community agencies, job fairs, newspaper ads, trade directories, trade journals, state indexes, the local chamber of commerce, the Yellow Pages, and the Web. The following tips can help as you begin hunting for the perfect job:

- Job-hunting is time-intensive. Do your homework and take it seriously by using every opportunity available to you.
- Prepare yourself for the fact that there will be far more rejections than acceptances.
- Consider taking a temporary job while you continue the job hunt. It will help pay the bills and give you new skills to boost your resume at the same time.
- Research the activities of potential employers and show that you have studied them when you're being interviewed.
- Keep careful records of all contacts and follow-up activities.
- Don't ignore any job leads—act on every tip you get.
- Stay positive.

With all these thoughts in mind, you should be ready to begin the process of making people believe in you, and that's a major part of being successful in your job hunt.

THE JOB INTERVIEW

You can prevent some of the preinterview jitters by adequately preparing. Remember that you have nothing to lose and that you, too, are doing the choosing. Just as you are waiting and hoping to be offered a job, you have the option of choosing whether or not to accept an offer. It's all right to feel somewhat anxious, but keep everything in perspective. This is an adventure, and you are in control. Most important, remember to be yourself. With all of this in mind, consider some of the following points of the interview process:

- Speak up during the interview, and furnish the interviewer with the information he or she needs in order to make an informed decision. It is especially impressive if you can remember the names of people to whom you've been introduced. People like to be called by name, and it shows that you took the initiative to remember them.
- Always arrive a few minutes early for the interview, and look your best. The way you act and dress tells the interviewer plenty about your attitude and personality. Sloppy dress, chewing gum, and cigarettes have no place at an interview and will probably cut your interview short. Instead, dress professionally and appropriately for the job. Avoid heavy makeup, short skirts, jeans, and untidy or flashy clothing of any kind.

The best way to prepare for the interview is to practice. Have a friend or relative play the role of the interviewer, and go over some of the most commonly asked questions. Learn as much as you can about the company you're interviewing with—it pays to do your homework. When you show a potential employer that you've taken the time and initiative to learn about his or her company, you're showing that you will be a motivated and hardworking employee. Employers fear laziness and minimal effort, looking instead for workers who don't always have to be told what to do and when to do it.

Here is a list of interview questions you can expect to have to answer:

- **Tell me a little bit about yourself.** This is your chance to pitch your qualifications for the job in 2 minutes. Provide a few details about your education, previous jobs you've held, and extracurricular activities that relate to the position for which you're interviewing.
- **Are you at your best when working alone or in a group?** The safest answer is "Both." Most companies today cluster their employees into work groups, so you will need strong interpersonal skills. However, on occasion, you may be required to work on projects alone.
- **What did you like the most about your last job? What did you dislike the most about it?** Always accentuate the positives in an interview, so focus primarily on what you liked. Also be honest about what you disliked, but then explain how facing the negatives helped you grow as an employee.
- **What are your career goals?** Be sure you've done some research on the company and industry before your interview. When this question comes up, talk realistically about how far you believe your skills and talents will take you and what actions you plan to take to ensure this happens, such as pursuing more education.

Take the time to prepare some answers to these commonly asked questions. For instance, if you haven't set at least one career goal for yourself, do it now. Be ready to describe it to the interviewer. Likewise, you should be able to talk about your last job, including what you liked the most and the least. Adapt your answers so they apply to the job for which you are presently interviewing. Other questions that might be asked include:

- What qualifications do you have?
- Why do you want to work for us?
- Do you enjoy school? Why or why not?

FINDING JOBS ON THE WEB

As mentioned, you can find jobs through your network of friends, family, and acquaintances; through classified ads in the newspaper; and through career Web pages. Here is a listing of popular Web sites that not only offer job search technology but also information on resume writing, interviewing, and other important career advice.

www.monster.com	**www.careerbuilder.com**
www.hotjobs.com	**www.vault.com**

- Do you plan to continue your education?
- What do you plan to be doing five years from now?
- What motivates you to do a good job?

If you are seeking a job as a manager, you might respond by saying you liked the varied responsibilities of your past job. Recall that you enjoyed the unexpected challenges and flexible schedule. And when describing what you liked least, make sure you respond with some function or area of responsibility that has nothing to do with the responsibilities of the job you hope to get.

More than likely, you'll be asked to tell the interviewer something about yourself. This is your chance to "toot your horn," but don't ramble. You might ask the interviewer specifically what he or she would like to hear about: your educational background or recent experiences and responsibilities in your present or last job. After he or she chooses, stick to the basics; the next move belongs to the interviewer.

When asked about personal strengths and weaknesses, given that the question is two parts, begin with a weakness so you can end on a strong note with your strengths. Again, try to connect your description of a strength or weakness with the requirements for the job. Naturally, it wouldn't be wise to reveal a serious weakness about yourself, but you can mention how you have changed your shortcomings. You might say, "I like to get my work done fast, but I consciously try to slow down a little to make sure I'm careful and accurate." When it comes to strengths, don't exaggerate, but don't sell yourself short either.

Asking Questions

You can ask questions, too. In fact, the interviewer expects you to ask questions to determine if the job is right for you, just as he or she will be trying to find out if you'll be successful working for his or her company. When you ask questions, it shows that you're interested and want to learn more. When the type of question you ask indicates that you've done your homework regarding the job and the company, your interviewer will be impressed. Avoid asking questions about salary or fringe benefits, anything adversarial, or questions that show you have a negative opinion of the company. It's all right to list your questions on a piece of paper; it's the quality of the question that's important, not whether you can remember it. Here are a few sample questions that you should consider asking if the topics don't come up in your interview:

- What kind of responsibilities come with this job?
- How is the department organized?
- What will be the first project for the new hire to tackle?
- What is a typical career advancement path for a person in this position?
- Who will the supervisor be for this position, and can I meet him or her?
- What is the office environment like? Is it casual or corporate?
- When do you expect to reach a hiring decision?

Following Up

After the interview, follow up with a thank-you note to the interviewer. Not only is it a thoughtful gesture, it triggers the interviewer's memory about you and shows that you have a genuine interest in the job. Your thank-you note should be written in a business letter format and should highlight the key points in your interview.

During the interview process, remember that you will not appeal to everyone who interviews you. If your first experience doesn't work out, don't get discouraged. Keep trying.

SAMPLE THANK-YOU LETTER

After you've interviewed for a job, it's important to reiterate your interest in the position by sending a thank-you letter to those who interviewed you. Take a look at Michele's letter to the manager she interviewed with at NexAir. You can use this letter as a model when the time comes for you to write some thank-you letters.

July 17, 2005

Michele A. Thomas
3467 Main Street
Atlanta, Georgia 30308
Phone: 404-555-3423
E-mail: mthomas_987654321@yahoo.com

Mr. Charles E. Pence
Manager, Human Resources
NexAir Wireless
20201 East Sixth Street
Atlanta, Georgia 30372

Dear Mr. Pence:

It was a pleasure meeting with you Monday to discuss the sales opportunity at NexAir's downtown location. After learning more about the position, it is clear to me that with my background and enthusiasm, I would be an asset to your organization.

As we discussed, my experiences as a cashier at Winn-Dixie Supermarket and as a sales clerk at The Limited have provided me with the basic skills necessary to perform the responsibilities required of a sales representative at NexAir. I believe that with my ability to learn quickly and communicate effectively, I can help NexAir increase sales of its wireless products.

Thank you for the opportunity to interview with your organization. If there is any additional information I can provide about myself, please do not hesitate to call me. I look forward to hearing your decision soon.

Sincerely,

Michele A. Thomas

WHAT EMPLOYERS EXPECT FROM EMPLOYEES

As part of the National City Bank personnel team in Columbus, Ohio, Rose Graham works with Cooperative Business Education (CBE) coordinators in the area who are trying to place high school students in the workplace. When asked what skills she looks for in potential employees, she quickly replies that basic communication skills are at the top of her list. She stresses, "The ability to construct a sentence and put together words cannot be overemphasized." She cites knowledge of the personal computer, with good keyboarding skills, as essential.

In an article published in the *Nashville Business Journal*, Donna Cobble of Staffing Solutions outlined these basic skills for everyday life in the workplace:

Communication. Being a good communicator not only means having the ability to express oneself properly in the English language, but it also means being a good listener. If you feel inferior in any of these areas, it's a good idea to sign up for a public speaking class, read books on the subject, and borrow techniques from professional speakers.

Organization. Organization is the key to success in any occupation or facet of life. The ability to plan, prioritize, and complete a task in a timely fashion is a valuable skill. Check out Chapter 13 for tips on improving your time-management skills.

Problem solving. Companies are looking for creative problem solvers, people who aren't afraid to act on a situation and follow through with their decision. Experience and practice play a major role in your ability to determine the best solution. You can learn these techniques by talking with others about how they solve problems as well as observing others in the problem-solving process.

Sensitivity. In addition to being kind and courteous to their fellow workers, employees need to be sensitive to a coworker's perspective. That might mean putting yourself in the other person's shoes to gain a better understanding of that person's feelings. Employers look for individuals who are able to work on a team instead of those concerned only with their own personal gain.

Judgment. Although closely related to problem solving, good judgment shows up on many different levels in the workplace. It is the ability of a person to assess a situation, weigh the options, consider the risks, and make the necessary decision. Good judgment is built on experience and self-confidence.

Concentration. Concentration is the ability to focus on one thing at a time. Learning to tune out distractions and relate solely to the task at hand is a valuable asset for anyone.

Cooperation. Remember that you're being paid to do a job, so cooperate.

Honesty. Dishonesty shows up in many different ways, ranging from stealing time or property to divulging company secrets. Stay honest.

Initiative. Don't wait to be told exactly what to do. Show some initiative and look around to see what needs to be done next.

Willingness to learn. Be willing to learn how things are done at the company instead of doing things the way you want to do them.

Dependability. Arrive at work on time every day and meet your deadlines.

Enthusiasm. Although not every task you're assigned will be stimulating, show enthusiasm for your work at all times.

Acceptance of criticism. Constructive criticism is necessary for any employee to learn how things should be done. Employees who view criticism as a way to improve themselves will benefit from it.

Loyalty. There is no place for negativity in the workplace. You simply won't be happy working for an employer to whom you're not loyal.

Never fail to show pride in your work, the place where you work, and your appearance. By making these traits a part of your personality and daily performance, you will demonstrate that you are a cut above other employees with equal or better qualifications.

JUMPING ON THE SALARY FAST-TRACK

So the job offer comes, and it's time to talk about money. Unless you are an undiscovered genius, you most likely will start near the bottom of the salary scale if you're heading straight to the workplace after graduating from high school. There's not much room to negotiate a salary since you probably won't be able to say, "Well, I've done this, this, and this. I know what my experience is worth." You will find that most people hiring first-time employees will have a "take-it-or-leave-it" attitude about salary offers. However, according to Amryl Ward, a human resources consultant who has been hiring employees for more than twenty-five years in various human resource positions, there are some things that entry-level employees can do to make themselves more easily hired and, once hired, to get themselves on the fast-track toward more pay:

- **As you interview for the job, be prepared to tell a potential employer why you're worth hiring.** "Bring your skills to the table," says Ward. For instance, you might not think that the job you had during the summer at that big office supply store did anything more than earn you spending money. On the contrary, you learned valuable skills, such as how to be part of a team and how to deal with customers. What about that after-school office job you had? You learned how to answer the phones and how to work with certain software. Think carefully about the jobs you had in high school and what you learned from them. Those are called transferable skills.
- **Once you're hired, be willing to do more than just what the job requires.** Sure, you may be frying fries at the start. But if you come in early and stay late, if you pitch in to help another employee with his or her job, or if you voluntarily clean up the counters and sweep the floor, that says to management, "This employee is a winner. Let's keep him or her in mind the next time a promotion comes up." Soon, you might be managing a crew, then the store.

ON THE JOB

Once you snag that perfect job, there's no time to rest easy. You need to keep your manager happy and instill trust in your coworkers. And at the same time you're doing this, you'll want to watch out for yourself, keep yourself happy, and stay ahead of the learning curve. Here are some ways for you to do just that.

Minding Your Office Etiquette

Okay, so maybe you didn't know which was the salad fork at your cousin Sally's wedding reception. Most likely, though, you can name a few basic rules of etiquette, like not chewing with your mouth open at the dinner table. Now, what about when it comes to the manners you're supposed to have in the workplace? That usually draws a blank if you've never worked in an office setting. How would you know what's the right way to answer the phone or talk to your boss or customers?

Shannon McBride, of the Golden Crescent Tech-Prep Partnership in Victoria, Texas, has seen many students come through his program and land good jobs. He's also seen many of them succeed because they knew how to present themselves in a professional situation. Unfortunately, he can also relate stories of high school graduates who had no clue how to act in the workplace. They didn't realize that when they're working in an office with a group of people, they have to go out of their way to get along and follow the unwritten rules of that workplace. McBride says that means you'll have to size up how others are dressing and match what the office is geared to. For instance, if you work in a business office, most likely you'd wear slacks and a button-down shirt or a nice skirt and top. If you worked in a golf pro shop, you'd wear a golf shirt and shorts. "As much as you want to be an individual," says McBride, "you have to fit in when you're in a business setting. If you want an adult job, you have to act like an adult."

A lot of young people don't grasp how important office etiquette is and blow it off as just some silly rules imposed by adults. But McBride cautions that not following the norms of office etiquette can make or break a job. You can have all the technical talent and know all the latest software applications, but if you're not up on how people dress, talk, and conduct business, your job probably won't last very long. When it comes to getting a job, McBride warns, "First impressions are so important. Bad office etiquette can hurt that first impression." The best advice that we can give is that if you're not sure what the policy is about answering phones, using e-mail or the Internet on the job, or dress codes, ask your boss. He or she won't steer you wrong and will be pleased that you were concerned enough to ask.

Finding a Friendly Face at Work

There you are on the first day of a new job. Everyone looks like they know what they're doing while you stand there feeling really dumb. Even for the most seasoned employee, those first few weeks on the job are tough. Of course, everyone else looks like they know what they're doing because they've been doing it for quite some time. Wouldn't it be nice, though, if you had someone to help you adjust? Someone who would give you those little inside tips everyone else learns with experience. Someone to caution you about things that could go wrong or give you a heads-up when you're doing something that could lead to a reprimand. If you look around the office, you'll find such a person, says Robert Fait, Career Counselor and Instructional Specialist, who is associated with Career and Technology Education in the Katy Independent School district in Katy, Texas.

You might not realize that such a person is a mentor, but in the strict definition of the word, that's what he or she is. Or, as Fait puts it, "Mentors are role models who are willing to assist others with personal education and career goal setting and planning. This caring person shares a listening ear, a comforting shoulder, and an understanding heart." In other words, a mentor is someone who will make you feel comfortable in a new working environment, show you the procedures, and, in the end, help you become more productive.

Unless the company you're working for has a formal mentoring program, mentors don't come with huge signs around their necks that read, "Look here. I'm a mentor. Ask me anything." You have to look for them. Fait advises new employees to look closely at their coworkers and take notice of who demonstrates positive behavior, has strong work habits, and seems trustworthy. Those are the people to approach. "Such workers are usually willing to share their knowledge and insights with others," says Fait.

Who knows? Given some time, you could become a mentor yourself after you've been on the job for a while. Maybe you'll be able to help some new employee who looks kind of bewildered and in need of a friendly hand because you'll remember what it was like to be that new person.

13 Chapter

SURVIVAL SKILLS

Whether you're headed to college or work, you're going to come face to face with some intimidating stuff after graduation.

YOUR LEVEL OF STRESS will most likely increase due to the demands of your classes or job and your exposure to alcohol or drugs. Various forms of conflict will arise, and you're going to have to keep up with your own health and nutrition. Seem daunting? It's really not if you keep a level head about you and stick to your core values. This chapter will help you work through the muddier side of life after high school.

SKILLS TO MAKE YOU STRESS-HARDY

Jump out of bed and into the shower. What to wear? Throw that on. Yuck—what's that stain? "Mom, where are my clean socks?" Tick, tock. No time to grab a bite if you want to make the homeroom bell. Skid around the corner and race for the classroom just as the final bell rings. Whoops, forgot your bio book. Sports, clubs, job, homework, friends on the internet, and finally (sigh) sleep.

Sound like your life? If you're like most high school students, that description probably hits pretty close to home. So now we'll take your already hectic schedule and throw in the fact that you'll soon be graduating and have to figure out what to do with your life. Can you say "stress"?

Some people say that stress actually motivates them to perform better, but we won't talk about those perfect people. For most of you, stress means that you may snap at the dog, slam a few doors, get mad at your dad, and feel down. Maybe you'll even have physical symptoms—upset stomach, rapid heartbeat, sweaty palms, dizziness. The list goes on. Not a good place to be when you're dealing with a huge list of things to do, plus graduation staring you in the face.

How to handle stress has been written about countless times, but out of all the advice that's out there, a few simple pointers can really help you prevent the sweaty palms and nauseated feeling in the pit of your stomach.

- **French fries out, good food in.** Eat at least one hot, balanced meal a day. Healthy, as in veggies, fruits, meats, cheese, grains. Read further along in this chapter for more information about nutrition and health.
- **Sleep.** 7, 8, 10 hours a day. Easier said than done, but well worth it. Sleep will not only get you through high school but also your college and career lives, and it will help you stop feeling like such a frazzled bunch of nerve endings.
- **Hug your dog, cat, rabbit, friend, or mom.** Loneliness breeds stress because then all you've got is yourself and those stressed-out thoughts zooming around in your head.
- **Hang out with friends.** That takes time, but being with people you like and doing fun things eases stress—as long as you don't overdo it.
- **Exercise.** This does not include running down the hall to make the bell. We're talking 20

minutes of heart-pounding perspiration at least three times a week. It's amazing what a little sweat can do to relax you. Believe it or not, good posture helps too.

- **Don't smoke, drink, or use excessive amounts of caffeine.** Whoever told you that partying is the way to relieve stress got it all wrong. Nicotine and alcohol actually take away the things your body needs to fight stress.
- **Simplify your expenses.** Money can be a big stress factor. Think of ways to eliminate where you're spending money so that the money you have doesn't have to be stretched so far. Be creative. Share resources. Sell items you no longer use. Maybe put off buying something you've been wanting.
- **Let your feelings out of your head.** It takes time and energy to keep them bottled up inside. Have regular conversations with your parents and siblings so that minor annoyances can be solved when they're still small.
- **Organize your time.** As in prioritizing and dealing with one small part of your life instead of trying to solve everything in one shot. Read on for more information about time management.
- **Lighten up.** When you've graduated and are into whatever it is you'll end up doing, you'll look back and realize that this was a teensy little part of your life. So look on the bright side. The decisions you'll be making about your future are heavy, but they won't be cut in stone. You can change them if they don't work out.

Stress Busters

Most people get stressed when things are out of control—too many things to do, too many decisions to make, or too much information to digest. If you add not having enough time, enough money, or enough energy to get it all done, you have the perfect recipe for stress.

In the space below, identify what's causing you stress:

____

____

____

____

____

____

Then, choose from these three stress-busting options:

1. **Alter the situation.** Some things you can't control, some things you can. Change the ones you can. If you have too much on your plate and can't possibly do it all, push a few things aside. There's got to be something on the list you can get rid of. (And no, homework is not a choice.) Maybe you need to be able to say no to extra demands. Concentrate on what is important. Make a list of your priorities from the most important to the least, and work your way down.
2. **Avoid the situation—for now.** Step back and ask, "Is this really a problem? Do I really need to solve it now?" This doesn't mean you should procrastinate on things that need to get done. Think of this stress buster as buying some time, taking a break, catching your breath, getting advice, and airing out the situation so that you can deal with it when you're better prepared to handle it.
3. **Accept the situation.** How you perceive your circumstances has a lot to do with how you make decisions about them. Put whatever is stressing you in the perspective of the big picture. How will this really affect me next year or even ten years from now? Look at your circumstances through the lens of your personal values. Think about what feels right to you, not someone else.

Quick Fixes for Stressful Moments

So, you've done all the things we talked about and you're still feeling like you're being pulled in a million directions. If your stress thermometer has hit the top, use these quick fixes to help you calm down.

- Make the world slow down for a bit. Take a walk. Take a shower. Listen to some soothing music.
- Breathe deeply. Get in tune with the rhythm of your own breathing. Lie or sit down for 15 minutes and just concentrate on relaxing.
- Relax those little knots of tension. Start at your head and work down to your toes.
- Close your eyes and clear your mind. Oops, there comes that nagging thought. Out, out, out. Get rid of the clutter. Imagine yourself in your favorite place: the beach, under a tree, whatever works.
- Close the door to your bedroom, and let out a blood-curdling scream. Walt Whitman knew what he was talking about when he said, "I sound my barbaric yawp over the roofs of the world." Just let your family know what you're doing so they don't come running to your room in fear. You'll be amazed at how much better you feel.
- When all else fails, watch a funny movie. Read the comics. Get in a giggly frame of mind. Those big challenges will quickly be brought down to size.

WINNING THE TIME MANAGEMENT GAME

What is the value of time? Eight dollars an hour? The price of a scholarship because the application is a day late? Time can be a very expensive resource or something you can use to your advantage. Even if you recognize the value of time, managing it is a challenge.

When you live with enough time, life is relaxed and balanced. In order to find that balance, you have to prioritize and plan. Decide what you want and what is important to you. Organize logically and schedule realistically. Overcome obstacles. Change bad habits. Simplify and streamline. Save time when you can. Sound impossible? It's not easy, but you can do it. The secret is held in a Chinese proverb: The wisdom of life is the elimination of nonessentials.

It's All about Control

The good thing about time is that much of it is yours to do with as you wish. You may feel out of control and as if you must run to keep up with the conflicting demands and expectations of your life. But we all have the same number of hours in each day. The key is in how we spend them. The following tips are designed to help you spend your time wisely and to keep you in control of your life.

Prepare a list of your goals and the tasks necessary to accomplish them. This could be by day, week, month, semester, or even year. You may also want to break the list into sections, such as friends and family, school, work, sports, health and fitness, home, personal development, and college preparation.

Prioritize based on time-sensitive deadlines. Use a grading system to code how important each task is. A is "Do It Now," B is "Do It Soon," C is "Do It Later." Understand the difference between "important" and "urgent."

Be realistic about how much you can really do. Analyze how you spend your time now. What can you cut? How much time do you truly need for each task?

Think ahead. How many times have you underestimated how long it will take to do something? Plan for roadblocks, and give yourself some breathing space.

Accept responsibility. Once you decide to do something, commit yourself to it. That doesn't mean that a task that was on the "A" list can't be moved to the "C" list. But be consistent and specific about what you want to accomplish.

Divide and conquer. You may need to form a committee, delegate tasks to your parents, or ask for help from a friend. That is why it is called time management.

Take advantage of your personal prime time. Don't schedule yourself to get up and do homework at 6 a.m.

if you are a night owl. It won't work. Instead, plan complex tasks when you are most efficient.

Avoid procrastination. There are a million ways to procrastinate. And not one of them is a good reason if you really want to get something done. Have you ever noticed that you always find time to do the things you enjoy?

Do the most unpleasant task first. Get it over with. Then it will be all downhill from there.

Don't over-prepare. That is just another way to procrastinate.

Learn to say no to the demands on your time that you cannot afford.

Be enthusiastic, and share your goals with others.

If you set too many goals at once, you will overwhelm yourself from the start. Remember, what is important is the quality of the time you spend on a task, not the quantity. It doesn't make any difference if you study for 10 hours if you don't recall a thing you've reviewed. The overall goal is to be productive, efficient, and effective, not just busy. You'll also need to pace yourself. All work and no play makes for an unbalanced person.

Use all the benefits of modern technology to help you manage time. You can save lots of time by using a fax, e-mail, or voice mail. If you don't already use a day planner or calendar, you would be wise to invest in one. Write in all the important deadlines, and refer to it often. Block out commitments you know you have so you won't over-schedule yourself. When you do over-schedule yourself or underestimate the time it takes to accomplish a task, learn from your mistakes. But don't get too down on yourself. Give yourself a pep talk every now and then to keep yourself positive and motivated.

MOVING OUT ON YOUR OWN?

As you consider moving away from home either to a college dorm or your own place, some pretty wonderful expectations of what it will be like no doubt will come floating into your head. No more parental rules. On your own. Making your own decisions. Hamburgers forever. Coming and going when you want to. Wait, what's this? Looks like you're out of clothes to wear. No more cereal bowls—they're all in the sink, and they're dirty. Out of milk and the refrigerator's empty. Yikes! What happened to all those warm, fuzzy thoughts about freedom?

Sure, it's nice to be able to come and go as you please, but before you get too far into that pleasant—and unrealistic—mind mode, here are some thoughts you might want to consider as you make plans to become independent. Ozzie Hashley, a guidance counselor at Clinton Community Schools in Clinton, Michigan, works with juniors and seniors in high school. Here is what he says to inform students about six realities of independent life.

1. If you rent your own place, have you thought about the extra charges in addition to the rent? Says Hashley, "Many students think only of paying the rent. They don't realize that they'll be responsible for utilities in many cases. Or the money it will take to wash and dry their clothes."
2. Subsisting on hamburgers and fries sounds yummy, but as you watch a fast food diet eat its way into your paycheck, you'll most likely think about cooking up something yourself. What will you cook? Who will buy the food? More importantly, who will do the dishes? Dividing up the responsibilities of preparing food is a big aspect of being on your own, especially when sharing a living space.
3. Medical insurance may not be on your mind as you prepare to graduate—you're probably on your parents' insurance plans right now. However, once you are established as independent at age 18 and you're living on your own, insurance becomes a big consideration. If you need health care and don't have medical insurance, the bills will be big. So when you get a job,

make sure that you have medical coverage. If you're going off to college after high school, you'll most likely be covered under your parents' insurance until age 23.

4. There's no one to tell you when to come home when you're on your own. There's also no one to tell you that you're really disorganized when it comes to managing your time. Time management might not sound like a big deal now, but when you have to juggle all the facets of being independent—your job, taking care of your living space and car, your social life—then being able to manage time becomes an important part of life.

5. Managing your money moves into a whole other realm when you are on your own. You have to make sure you have enough to pay the rent, your car loan, and insurance, not to mention that movie you wanted to see, the CD you wanted to buy, or those jeans you saw at the mall last week. If you want to eat at the end of the month, budgeting will become an important part of your new independent vocabulary. Ask your parents or an adult you trust to help you set up your budget. Also learn how to balance your checkbook. It's a lot easier to manage your money when you keep track of how much you have in your bank account and how much you spend!

DRUGS AND ALCOHOL: ARE YOU AT RISK?

At risk? Wait a minute. How could you be at risk when the legal drinking age in all fifty states is 21? Chances are, if you're reading this, you're not 21 yet. It's also illegal to smoke or buy any tobacco product before age 18, and possession of any drug for recreational use is illegal, period. So if you drink alcohol before age 21; smoke or buy cigarettes, cigars, or chewing tobacco before age 18; or take any illegal drugs, you could:

- be arrested for driving under the influence (DUI);
- be convicted;
- be required to pay steep fines;
- have your driving privileges suspended;
- get kicked out of school (that's any kind of school, college included);
- get fired;
- go to jail; and/or
- have a criminal record.

A criminal record . . . so what?

Consider this true story. A 29-year-old man who recently received his graduate degree in business was offered a job with a major Fortune-100 corporation. We're talking big bucks, stock options, reserved parking space—the whole nine yards. When the company did a background check and found that he was arrested for a DUI during his freshman year of college, they rescinded their offer. The past can and will come back to haunt you. Let's not even think about what would happen down the line if you decide to run for public office.

Think about why you might want to try drinking or doing drugs. For fun? To forget your troubles? To be cool? Are your reasons good enough? Remember the consequences before you make a decision.

How Can I Say No Without Looking Like a Geek?

"It takes a lot more guts to stay sober, awake, and aware than to just get high, get numb, and learn nothing about life," says one former user. "Laugh at people who suggest you drink or take drugs, and then avoid them like the plague."

Friends worth having will respect your decision to say no. And girls—if a guy pressures you to drink or get high, ditch him pronto. You can vice-versa that for guys, too. According to the National Institute on Drug Abuse (NIDA), alcohol and club drugs like GHB or Rohypnol (roofies) make you an easy target for date rape.

The Nitty Gritty

Along with the temporary pleasure they may give you, all drugs (including club drugs, alcohol, and nicotine) have a downside. Alcohol, for example, is a depressant. Even one drink slows down the part of your brain that controls your reasoning. So your judgment gets dull just when you're wondering, "Should I drive my friends home? Should I talk to this guy? Should I have another drink?"

Your body needs about an hour to burn up the alcohol in one drink. Nothing, including coffee, will sober you up any faster. Here's what "one drink" means: one shot of hard liquor (straight or mixed in a cocktail), one glass of wine, or one 12-ounce beer.

Alcohol helps smart people make bad decisions. In fact, many drugs make you believe that you're thinking even more clearly than usual. Well, guess what? You aren't. Depending on what drug you take, how much, and what you do while you're on it, you're also risking confusion, nausea, headache, sleep problems, depression, paranoia, rape (especially "date rape"), unwanted pregnancy, sexually transmitted diseases (STDs) ranging from herpes to HIV/AIDS, having a baby with a birth defect, memory impairment, persistent psychosis, lung damage, cancer, injuring or killing someone else, and death.

Take a moment now, when your brain is razor sharp, to decide if those consequences are worth the escape you get for 20 minutes one night. You may be saying, "Oh, come on. Only addicts have problems like that." Getting drunk or high doesn't necessarily mean that you're an alcoholic or an addict—but it always means a loss of control.

"So much of addiction is about denial," says one member of Alcoholics Anonymous. "I just didn't think I looked or acted or thought or smelled or lied or cheated or failed like an alcoholic or addict. It was when the drugs and alcohol use started to cause problems in multiple areas of my life that I began to think the problem might reside with me. Friends leaving—in disgust—was what opened my eyes."

DID YOU KNOW...

... **that nicotine is as addictive as cocaine and heroin, according to the American Cancer Society?**

... **that drinking a lot of alcohol fast can kill you on the spot, according to Keystone College?**

... **that MDMA (Ecstasy, X, Adam, Clarity, Lover's Speed), according to NIDA, may permanently damage your memory?**

DO I HAVE A PROBLEM?

Take the quiz below to see if you're in real trouble with drugs or alcohol.

1. **Do you look forward to drinking or using drugs?**
2. **Do most of your friends drink or do drugs?**
3. **Do you keep a secret supply of alcohol or drugs?**
4. **Can you drink a lot without appearing drunk?**
5. **Do you "power-hit" to get high faster, by binge-drinking, funneling, or slamming?**
6. **Do you ever drink or do drugs alone, including in a group where no one else is doing so?**
7. **Do you ever drink or use drugs when you hadn't planned to?**
8. **Do you ever have blackouts where you can't remember things that happened when you were drunk or high?**

If you answered yes to any of these questions, you probably need help. If you have a friend who fits the picture, find a respectful way to bring up your concerns. Don't be surprised if he or she tells you to back off—but don't give up, either. If someone in your family has an alcohol or drug problem, be aware that you may be prone to the same tendency.

Source: Keystone College, La Plume, Pennsylvania

Where Can I Get Help?

If you think you have a problem, or if you think a friend has a problem, try Alcoholics Anonymous or Narcotics Anonymous. If you're not sure, ask yourself the questions in "Do I Have a Problem?" on the top of this page.

Talk to any adult you trust: maybe your doctor, a clergy member, a counselor, or your parents. Health clinics and hospitals offer information and treatment. The American Cancer Society can help you quit smoking. These are only a few places to turn—check out the Yellow Pages and the Web for more.

Alcoholics Anonymous
212-870-3400
www.aa.org

American Cancer Society
800-ACS-2345
www.cancer.org

Narcotics Anonymous
818-773-9999
www.na.org

So, that's the straight stuff. You're at a tough but wonderful age, when your life is finally your own and your decisions really matter. Think about what you value most—and then make your choices.

CONFLICT: HOW TO AVOID IT AND DEFUSE IT

You're walking along and you see a group of kids up ahead . . . and suddenly you're afraid. Or you're about to talk to someone you have a disagreement with, and already you're tense. Or your boyfriend's jealousy is spooking you. What should you do?

All of these situations involve potential conflicts that could get out of hand. Even if you never get into a violent situation, you'll face conflicts with others, as we all do. Learning to spot the warning signs of violence and to handle conflicts well will bring you lifelong benefits.

What's Your Style?

What do you do when you're faced with a potential conflict? Do you try to get away, no matter what? Do you find yourself bowing to pressure from others? Do you feel like you have to stand and fight, even if you don't want to? Do you wish you had some new ways to handle conflict?

Different situations call for different strategies. First, let's talk about situations where violence is a real possibility. Most of us get a bad feeling before things get violent, but too often, we ignore the feeling. Trust your gut feeling! And whether you're on the street or in school, Fred Barfoot of the Crime Prevention Association of Philadelphia suggests that you keep in mind these tips for avoiding violence:

- Walk like you're in charge and you know where you're going.
- Stick to lighted areas.
- Travel with a trusted friend when possible. On campus, get an escort from security at night. Loners are targets.
- If a person or group up ahead makes you nervous, cross the street immediately—and calmly—as if you'd intended to anyway.
- Call out to an imaginary friend, "Hey, Joe! Wait up!" and then run toward your "friend," away from whoever is scaring you.
- Go right up to the nearest house and ring the bell. Pretend you're expected: "Hey Joe, it's me!" You can explain later.
- If someone threatens you physically, scream.
- If someone assaults you, scream, kick where it hurts, scratch—anything.
- Don't ever get in a car with someone you don't know well or trust, even if you've seen that person around a lot.
- Strike up a conversation with an innocent bystander if you feel threatened by someone else, just to make yourself less vulnerable for a few minutes.
- Wear a whistle around your neck or carry a personal alarm or pepper spray.
- If someone mugs you, hand over your purse, wallet, jewelry—whatever he or she asks for. None of it is worth your life.
- Don't go along with something your gut says is wrong, no matter who says it's okay.

Remember that it's not a sign of weakness to back down if someone's egging you on to fight. Bill Tomasco, principal of Furness High School in Philadelphia, says that pressure from other kids to fight creates much of the violence in schools. If you're being pushed to fight, show true strength: Know that your opponent has a good side too, speak only to that good side, and don't give in to the pressure of the crowd.

Are You Safe at Home?

Locking doors and windows makes sense—but sometimes the danger lies within. A lot of violence occurs in abusive relationships, says Amy Gottlieb, a marriage family therapist intern at the California Family Counseling Center in Encino. To find out if you're at risk, ask yourself whether your partner, roommate, or family member:

- Uses jealousy to justify controlling you
- Puts you down, humiliates you, or pulls guilt trips on you
- Threatens to reveal your secrets or tells lies about you
- Makes all the decisions
- Frightens you, especially if it's on purpose
- Threatens you in any way
- Makes light of abusive behavior or says you provoked it

If any of these things are going on in your relationship, talk about it to an adult you trust, and ask for help.

Talking It Out

If your instincts tell you to get away from a situation, do it. But you can resolve many actual or potential conflicts face to face and gracefully so that everyone walks away feeling good. Read on for some tips on handling conflict from Kare Anderson, a communications expert in Sausalito, California.

Most of us make the mistake of reacting quickly, thinking only of our own needs, and not listening, says Anderson. Try doing the opposite. First and foremost, think about what you really want from the situation, and keep your goal in mind the whole time. But bring up the other person's concerns first. Then, discuss how the situation affects you both. Offer a solution that will benefit you both—and only then talk about how your solution addresses your own needs.

When the other person is talking, really listen—don't just come up with retorts in your head. Always show that you've heard the person before you give your response, especially if you're talking with someone of a different sex, size, or race. Those differences can distract us so much that we actually hear less. If you're female, you may need to s-l-o-w yourself down. Say less than you think you need to. Guys, don't shut down altogether—keep the communication going.

Even if the other person acts like a jerk, be gracious and respectful. Ask questions instead of criticizing. Let someone save face instead of looking like a fool. If you insult or embarrass someone, you may never have that person's full attention again. In short, treat the other person as you'd like to be treated.

What should you do if you're really angry? One teen said, "Thinking about things calms me down." Another said, "Once in a while, we have to cool off for a day and then come back to the discussion." Anger almost always covers up fear. What are you afraid of? Is the reward you want out of this negotiation bigger than your fear? Focus on that reward. Don't forget to breathe—long, slow breaths.

Think about these strategies often, so you'll be more likely to use them when a situation gets hot, instead of just reacting blindly. Use them to plan for negotiations ahead of time, too. Learning to resolve problems with people takes most of us a lifetime—get a jump on it now!

THE LOWDOWN ON SEXUAL HARASSMENT

Has someone ever looked at you, talked to you, or touched you in a way that gave you the creeps, made you self-conscious about your body, or created a sexual mood when it wasn't appropriate? And did you begin to dread seeing this person because he or she just wouldn't quit?

If so, you've encountered sexual harassment. Sexual harassment is inappropriate behavior that

- is happening to you because of your sex,
- is unwanted (you don't like it),
- is objectively offensive (to a hypothetical "reasonable" man or woman),
- is either severe, persistent, or pervasive, and
- interferes with your work or school experience.

Paul Edison, a domestic and sexual violence prevention educator in Portland, Oregon, says that mostly—just as with crimes like rape—men harass women. But teenage girls are a bit more likely than older women to sexually harass someone, more girl-on-girl harassment goes on with teens, and guys get harassed, too. In some of the most brutal cases coming to light, gay men (or men perceived to be gay) are the targets.

People who sexually harass others fall into three camps, says Edison. Some just seem to be misguided and insensitive. Others get turned on by harassing someone. And a third group does it to intimidate—for example, to drive someone away from a job or just to make him or her feel bad about himself or herself.

So What Do I Do if Someone's Harassing Me?

Experts in self-defense say the best technique is to name the behavior that's bugging you and request that it stop. You might say, "Your hand is on my knee. Please remove it." If the person doesn't quit, you might try writing a letter spelling out what's bothering you and requesting that the person stop—this way, you've confronted the situation directly and you also have a record of your complaint.

But here's the good news, says Edison: You are not expected to handle harassment on your own, especially if the person harassing you is in a position of authority over you, such as a teacher, sergeant, or boss. The authorities at your school or your job should handle it—but they can't do that unless you tell them what's going on.

If you file a complaint, be prepared to describe what happened, when, and where. And make sure you report your concerns to someone who has clear authority to handle sexual harassment complaints, such as the principal or the personnel director.

Often, the person harassing you will stop as soon as he or she gets the clear message that the behavior isn't okay with you, especially if your complaint goes to someone higher up as well. Edison notes that most harassment cases don't end up involving lawyers and lawsuits. You may choose, in serious cases, to register your complaint with the Office of Civil Rights (if you're being harassed at school) or the Equal Employment Opportunity Commission (if you're being harassed at work). You can also file your complaint on different levels at the same time: for example, with your school and the police.

You have the legal right to a school and workplace free from discrimination based on your race, color, religion, sex, national origin, and—depending on where you live, as state and local laws vary—your sexual orientation. You have the right to protection from retaliation if you file a complaint of harassment. So don't be afraid to report a situation if it truly offends you and interferes with your life.

What If I'm Just Being Hypersensitive?

If someone's words or actions make you uncomfortable, that's all the reason you need to ask that person to stop the behavior, no matter how innocent the behavior may be. Trust your feelings—especially if you find you're trying to convince yourself that nothing is wrong.

What Will Happen to the Person Who Has Been Harassing Me?

If your complaint is successfully handled, says Edison, the main thing that will happen is that the person will stop harassing you. People aren't "charged" with sexual harassment unless their behavior includes criminal conduct. But your harasser may face disciplinary action, loss of privileges, suspension, expulsion, lawsuits, or criminal action, depending on the severity of his or her behavior.

How Can I Avoid Harassing Someone?

Sometimes the line between harmless flirting, joking, or complimenting and harassment is pretty thin. How can you stay on the right side of that line?

First, pay attention to your own motives. Be honest with yourself. Do you enjoy watching someone get uncomfortable when you say or do certain things? Do you feel angry with the person for some reason? Do you enjoy exercising your authority over this person in some way? Do you find yourself obsessing about the person? If any of these are true, whatever you're saying or doing probably isn't harmless.

Even if your motives seem harmless to you, be extraordinarily careful about whom and how you touch. You may be comfortable touching people casually—perhaps you'll touch someone's hand or shoulder in conversation—but remember that other people's boundaries may differ from yours.

Pay attention to the person's reactions to you. Are you getting clear green signals when you do or say things around this person, or does the person seem to shrink away from you? Does the person shut down or seem upset when you do or say certain things? If someone's told you clearly that she or he doesn't like it when you do or say certain things, apologize and stop at once. And remember, no means no.

So, if you're faced with something that feels like sexual harassment, remember to trust your feelings, convey them clearly, and get help promptly if you need it.

STAYING HEALTHY IN SPITE OF YOURSELF

When someone—like your mom—asks if you're eating right, do you ever want to say, "Hey, have you looked at my life lately? Do you see a lot of time there for eating right?" Well, how about exercise—are you getting enough? "Yeah, right. I bench-press my backpack when I'm not doing wind sprints to my next class," may be how you reply.

If you're feeling like you can't escape your stress and fatigue, you might be surprised by how much better you'll feel if you keep active and don't just eat junk. Your workload will seem easier. You'll sleep better. You'll look fantastic. And you can stay healthy—even if time and money are in short supply.

But Really, Who Has Time to Exercise?

As one teen says, "Schoolwork gets in the way, and then I want to relax when I have a moment that isn't filled with schoolwork." You can make time for anything, if you choose to. But if you aren't athletic by nature or school or work keeps you going nonstop, exercise is the first thing to go out the window.

However, you don't have to become a gym rat or run miles to get enough exercise. Longer workouts are great if you do them consistently, but you're better off getting little bits of regular exercise than just doing a huge workout every so often or never doing anything. And by "little bits," we mean 15- to 20-minute chunks. Add that to a fast walk to the bus, a frenzied private dance session in your room, or running up the stairs instead of taking the elevator, and you're exercising!

Regardless of how you choose to pump that muscle in the middle of your chest, the important thing is that you're doing something. You'll not only feel better about yourself, but you'll have increased energy to do other things, like study, go to work, or go out with friends.

What Does "Eating Right" Mean Anyway?

Eating right means eating a balance of good foods in moderate amounts. Your diet needn't be complicated or expensive. Dr. Michele Wilson, a specialist in adolescent medicine at the Children's Hospital of Philadelphia, notes that a teen's diet should be heavy in grains—especially whole grains—and light in sugars and fats. It should include a lot of fruits and vegetables and provide you with plenty of protein, calcium, vitamin A, B vitamins, iron, and zinc. Sound complicated?

Well, what's complicated about a bean burrito with cheese? How about pasta with vegetables, meat, or both in the sauce? A banana or some cantaloupe? Stir-fried vegetables with tofu? Carrot sticks with peanut butter? Yogurt? Cereal with milk and fruit? All of these are cheap, quick to make, and great for you.

One teen swears by microwaveable veggie burgers and adds, "Staying away from deep-fried anything is a good plan." Try to avoid things like chips and sweets, says Dr. Wilson, adding that if you're a vegetarian—and especially if you don't eat dairy products or fish—you should make sure you're getting enough protein and iron. And no matter what your diet, drink water—eight glasses a day.

As Long as I'm in Control of What I Eat, I'm Okay, Right?

That depends. Of course, having no control over what you eat is a problem. But "in control" can be good or bad. How severely do you control what and how you eat? Are you obsessed with getting thinner? Do people who love you tell you that you're too thin, and do you take that as a compliment? Do you ever binge secretly or make yourself throw up after a meal? If any of these are true, you may be suffering from anorexia or bulimia.

According to the National Association of Anorexia Nervosa and Associated Disorders (ANAD), eating disorders affect about 7 million women and 1 million men in this country and can lead to serious health problems—even death. "The thing that convinced me to get help was fear—I had to be hospitalized, as I was literally dying from my anorexia," says one woman. Most Americans who are anorexic or bulimic developed their eating disorders in their teens.

We asked some women being treated for eating disorders what they used to see when they looked in the mirror. "Total ugliness," said one. "The smallest dimple in my flesh looked immense," said another. And a third said, "I got rid of the mirrors because they would set me off to where I wouldn't eat for days." Their advice to teens struggling with an eating disorder? "Treat yourself as you wish your parents had treated you," "Ask people you feel close to not to discuss your weight with you," and "Find ways outside of yourself to feel in control." Above all—get help! That means going to someone you trust, whether it be a parent, relative, sibling, friend, doctor, or teacher. Or call ANAD's national hotline at 847-831-3438 for a listing of support groups and referrals in your area.

So if I Eat Right and Exercise, I'm Healthy?

Well, probably. But Dr. Wilson suggests that you keep a few other things in mind too. If you smoke, drink, or do drugs, you're asking for trouble. Aside from their many scarier side effects, all these habits can steal nutrients that you need. If all this sounds like the recipe for a dull and totally uncool life, remember that feeling and looking great are never boring and that vomiting (or dying) after downing the most tequilas in the fastest time looks really uncool. If you're making short-term decisions that will hurt you in the long run, take some time to figure out why. Good health is priceless—just ask any grandparent.

Part 5

APPENDICES

NOW THAT YOU HAVE DECIDED what types of opportunities you wish to pursue after graduation, you need a jumping-off point for getting more information. The **Appendices** that follow will provide you with a sampling of additional data to help you with your decision-making process.

NOTE: Because of Thomson Peterson's comprehensive editorial review and because all material comes directly from institution or organization officials, we believe that the information presented in these **Appendices** is accurate. Nonetheless, errors and omissions are possible in a data collection and processing endeavor of this scope. You should check with the specific institution or organization at the time of application to verify pertinent data that may have changed since the publication of this book.

MIDWEST REGION

HIGH SCHOOL DIPLOMA TEST REQUIREMENTS

Illinois

In the fall of 2004, the Prairie State Achievement Examination (PSAE) will become a requirement for graduation. The test measures reading, mathematics, writing, science, and social studies. It is given to all students in grade 11. For more information, call the Illinois Dept. of Education at 217-782-4823 or go to their Web site at www.isbe.net/assessment.

Indiana

Students in grades 3, 6, 8, and 10 are required to take ISTEP+, Indiana's state achievement test. ISTEP+ is a criterion-referenced test, which measures a student's obtained knowledge. These tests are cumulative and are directly linked to the Indiana Academic Standards. For example, the grade 10 test measures what students have learned from kindergarten through the ninth grade.

The grade 10 test is also known as the Graduation Qualifying Examination (GQE). All Indiana students who wish to obtain a state-recognized diploma must take the GQE and receive passing scores in English/language arts and mathematics or meet all waiver requirements. In addition, there is an optional norm-referenced component. School corporations have the option of choosing if they wish to give the norm-referenced portion of the test; however, this decision must be made by the superintendent and be implemented on a corporation-wide basis. Members of the class of 2007 took the new GQE in the fall of 2004. The new GQE will test English/language arts, mathematics, and Algebra I. For more information, call the Indiana Department of Education, Division of Assessment at 317-232-9050 or go to their Web site at www.doe. state.in.us.

Iowa

Iowa currently does not require high school students to pass a proficiency test in order to receive a high school diploma.

Kansas

Kansas currently does not require school students to pass a proficiency test in order to receive a high school diploma.

Michigan

Michigan currently does not require high school students to pass a proficiency test in order to receive a high school diploma.

Minnesota

Minnesota's Graduation Standards have two components: the Basic Standards and the High Standards. The Basic Standards are a "safety net" to make sure that no student graduates without learning the basic skills needed to live and work in today's society. Students must pass tests in reading, mathematics, and writing to show they meet the Basic Standards and in order to be eligible to graduate from a public high school. The reading and mathematics exam is first given in the eighth grade, and the written composition exam is first given in the tenth grade. Students must pass to graduate from a public high school in Minnesota.

The High Standards define what Minnesota students should know, understand, and be able to do to demonstrate an advanced level of learning. The High Standards are organized into ten learning areas: reading, listening, and viewing; writing and speaking; arts and literature; mathematical applications; inquiry (research skills); scientific applications; people and cultures (social studies); decision making; resource management; and world languages. Public high school students from the class of 2002 and beyond must complete 24 of 48 possible standards from the ten learning areas, unless the district's staff and school board agree to reduce the number. Some standards are required for all students, while in some learning areas students may choose the standards they wish to complete. For more information, visit the Web site at www.cfl.state.mn.us.

Missouri

Missouri currently does not require high school students to pass a proficiency test in order to receive a high school diploma. However, individual school districts may or may not require one.

Nebraska

Nebraska currently does not require high school students to pass a proficiency test in order to receive a high school diploma.

North Dakota

North Dakota currently does not require high school students to pass a proficiency test in order to receive a high school diploma. However, all 12th grade students will participate in the North Dakota 12th Grade Assessment as required by state law. This achievement test is designed to access all 12th grade students in their knowledge and skills in reading and mathematics.

Ohio

Any student graduating from a public or chartered nonpublic high school after September 15, 2000, and before September 15, 2006, must pass writing, reading, mathematics, citizenship, and science tests and meet local curriculum requirements in order to receive a diploma. Students graduating after September 15, 2006, will need to pass the new Ohio Graduation Tests (OGT) and meet curriculum requirements in order to receive a diploma. For more information, visit the Ohio Department of Education Web site at www.ode.state. oh.us or call 877-644-6338.

Oklahoma

Oklahoma currently does not require high school students to pass a proficiency test in order to receive a high school diploma.

South Dakota

South Dakota currently does not require high school students to pass a proficiency test in order to receive a high school diploma.

Wisconsin

A state-developed high school graduation test (HSGT) was first administered in 2002. The use of the HSGT as a criterion for graduation applies to the class of 2004. Students who graduated at the end of the 2003–2004 school year were the first class affected. Other criteria include pupil academic performance and teacher recommendations. The test covers the four academic content areas of English language arts, mathematics, science, and social studies. For more information, call 608-267-3164 or visit www.dpi.state. wi.us/dpi/oea/hsgtdelay.html.

FOUR-YEAR COLLEGES AND UNIVERSITIES

Illinois

American Academy of Art
332 South Michigan Ave, Ste. 300
Chicago, IL 60604-4302
312-461-0600
www.aaart.edu

American InterContinental University Online
5550 Prairie Stone Pkwy, Ste. 400
Hoffman Estates, IL 60192
877-701-3800
www.aiuonline.edu

Argosy University/Chicago
20 South Clark St., Ste. 300
Chicago, IL 60603
800-626-4123
www.argosyu.edu

Argosy University/Schaumburg
1000 North Plaza Dr., Ste. 100
Schaumburg, IL 60173
866-290-2777
www.argosyu.edu

Augustana College
639 38th St.
Rock Island, IL 61201-2296
800-798-8100
www.augustana.edu

Aurora University
347 South Gladstone Ave.
Aurora, IL 60506-4892
800-742-5281
www.aurora.edu

Benedictine University
5700 College Rd.
Lisle, IL 60532-0900
888-829-6363
www.ben.edu

Blackburn College
700 College Ave.
Carlinville, IL 62626-1498
800-233-3550
www.blackburn.edu

Blessing-Rieman College of Nursing
Broadway at 11th St., POB 7005
Quincy, IL 62305-7005
800-877-9140
www.brcn.edu

Bradley University
1501 West Bradley Ave.
Peoria, IL 61625-0002
800-447-6460
www.bradley.edu

Chicago State University
9501 South King Dr.
Chicago, IL 60628
773-995-2513
www.csu.edu

Christian Life College
400 East Gregory St.
Mount Prospect, IL 60056
847-259-1840
www.christianlifecollege.edu

Columbia College Chicago
600 South Michigan Ave.
Chicago, IL 60605-1996
312-663-1600
www.colum.edu

Concordia University
7400 Augusta St.
River Forest, IL 60305-1499
800-285-2668
www.curf.edu

DePaul University
1 East Jackson Blvd
Chicago, IL 60604-2287
312-362-8650
www.depaul.edu

DeVry University
1221 North Swift Rd.
Addison, IL 60101-6106
800-346-5420
www.devry.edu

DeVry University
18624 West Creek Dr.
Tinley Park, IL 60477
877-305-8184
www.devry.edu

DeVry University
3300 North Campbell Ave.
Chicago, IL 60618-5994
800-383-3879
www.devry.edu

Dominican University
7900 West Division St.
River Forest, IL 60305-1099
800-828-8475
www.dom.edu

Eastern Illinois University
600 Lincoln Ave.
Charleston, IL 61920-3099
800-252-5711
www.eiu.edu

East-West University
816 South Michigan Ave.
Chicago, IL 60605-2103
312-939-0111
www.eastwest.edu

Elmhurst College
190 Prospect Ave.
Elmhurst, IL 60126-3296
800-697-1871
www.elmhurst.edu

Eureka College
300 East College Ave.
Eureka, IL 61530-1500
888-4-EUREKA
www.eureka.edu

Governors State University
One University Pkwy
University Park, IL 60466-0975
708-534-3148
www.govst.edu

Greenville College
315 East College, PO Box 159
Greenville, IL 62246-0159
800-345-4440
www.greenville.edu

Harrington College of Design
200 West Madison St.
Chicago, IL 60606
877-939-4975
www.interiordesign.edu

Hebrew Theological College
7135 North Carpenter Rd.
Skokie, IL 60077-3263
847-982-2500
www.htcnet.edu

Illinois College
1101 West College Ave.
Jacksonville, IL 62650-2299
866-464-5265
www.ic.edu

Illinois Institute of Technology
3300 South Federal St.
Chicago, IL 60616-3793
800-448-2329
www.iit.edu

Illinois State University
Normal, IL 61790-2200
309-438-2181
www.ilstu.edu

Illinois Wesleyan University
PO Box 2900
Bloomington, IL 61702-2900
800-332-2498
www.iwu.edu

International Academy of Design & Technology
One North State St., Ste. 400
Chicago, IL 60602-9736
877-ACADEMY
www.iadtchicago.edu

Judson College
1151 North State St.
Elgin, IL 60123-1498
800-839-5376
www.judsoncollege.edu

Kendall College
900 North Branch St.
Chicago, IL 60622
877-588-8860
www.kendall.edu

Knox College
2 East South St.
Galesburg, IL 61401
800-678-KNOX
www.knox.edu

Lake Forest College
555 North Sheridan Rd.
Lake Forest, IL 60045-2399
800-828-4751
www.lakeforest.edu

Lakeview College of Nursing
903 North Logan Ave.
Danville, IL 61832
217-443-5238
www.lakeviewcol.edu

Lewis University
One University Pkwy
Romeoville, IL 60446
800-897-9000
www.lewisu.edu

Lexington College
310 South Peoria St., Ste. 512
Chicago, IL 60607-3534
312-226-6294
lexingtoncollege.edugeneral-education.htm

Lincoln Christian College
100 Campus View Dr.
Lincoln, IL 62656-2167
888-522-5228
www.lccs.edu

Loyola University Chicago
820 North Michigan Ave.
Chicago, IL 60611-2196
800-262-2373
www.luc.edu

MacMurray College
447 East College Ave.
Jacksonville, IL 62650
217-479-7056
www.mac.edu

McKendree College
701 College Rd.
Lebanon, IL 62254-1299
800-232-7228
www.mckendree.edu

Midstate College
411 West Northmoor Rd.
Peoria, IL 61614
309-692-4092
www.midstate.edu

Millikin University
1184 West Main St.
Decatur, IL 62522-2084
800-373-7733
www.millikin.edu

Monmouth College
700 East Brd.way
Monmouth, IL 61462-1998
800-747-2687
www.monm.edu

Moody Bible Institute
820 North LaSalle Blvd
Chicago, IL 60610-3284
800-967-4MBI
www.moody.edu

NAES College
2838 West Peterson Ave.
Chicago, IL 60659-3813
773-761-5000
www.naes.edu

National-Louis University
122 South Michigan Ave.
Chicago, IL 60603
800-443-5522
www.nl.edu

North Central College
30 North Brainard St,
PO Box 3063
Naperville, IL 60566-7063
800-411-1861
www.noctrl.edu

North Park University
3225 West Foster Ave.
Chicago, IL 60625-4895
800-888-NPC8
www.northpark.edu

Northeastern Illinois University
5500 North St Louis Ave.
Chicago, IL 60625-4699
773-442-4000
www.neiu.edu

Northern Illinois University
De Kalb, IL 60115-2854
815-753-0446
www.niu.edu

Northwestern University
Evanston, IL 60208
847-491-7271
www.northwestern.edu

Olivet Nazarene University
One University Ave.
Bourbonnais, IL 60914-2271
800-648-1463
www.olivet.edu

Principia College
One Maybeck Pl.
Elsah, IL 62028-9799
800-277-4648 Ext. 2802
www.prin.educollege/

Quincy University
1800 College Ave.
Quincy, IL 62301-2699
800-688-4295
www.quincy.edu

Robert Morris College
401 South State St.
Chicago, IL 60605
800-RMC-5960
www.robertmorris.edu

Rockford College
5050 East State St.
Rockford, IL 61108-2393
800-892-2984
www.rockford.edu

Roosevelt University
430 South Michigan Ave.
Chicago, IL 60605-1394
877-APPLYRU
www.roosevelt.edu

Rush University
600 South Paulina
Chicago, IL 60612-3832
312-942-7100
www.rushu.rush.edu

Saint Anthony College of Nursing
5658 East State St.
Rockford, IL 61108-2468
815-395-5100
www.sacn.edu

Saint Francis Medical Center College of Nursing
511 NE Greenleaf St.
Peoria, IL 61603-3783
309-624-8980
www.sfmccon.edu

Saint Xavier University
3700 West 103rd St.
Chicago, IL 60655-3105
800-462-9288
www.sxu.edu

School of the Art Institute of Chicago
37 South Wabash
Chicago, IL 60603-3103
800-232-SAIC
www.artic.edusaic/

Shimer College
PO Box 500
Waukegan, IL 60079-0500
800-215-7173
www.shimer.edu

Southern Illinois University Carbondale
Carbondale, IL 62901-4701
618-453-2908
www.siu.edusiuc/

Southern Illinois University Edwardsville
Edwardsville, IL 62026-0001
800-447-SIUE
www.siue.edu

St. Augustine College
1333-1345 West Argyle
Chicago, IL 60640-3501
773-878-7989
www.staugustinecollege.edu

St. John's College
421 North Ninth St.
Springfield, IL 62702-5317
217-525-5628
www.st-johns.org/education/schoolsursing/

Telshe Yeshiva–Chicago
3535 West Foster Ave.
Chicago, IL 60625-5598
773-463-7738

The Illinois Institute of Art
350 North Orleans
Chicago, IL 60654
800-351-3450
www.ilic.artinstitutes.edu

The Illinois Institute of Art-Schaumburg
1000 Plaza Dr.
Schaumburg, IL 60173
800-314-3450
www.ilis.artinstitutes.edu

Trinity Christian College
6601 West College Dr.
Palos Heights, IL 60463-0929
800-748-0085
www.trnty.edu

Trinity College of Nursing and Health Sciences
2122-25th Ave.
Rock Island, IL 91201
309-779-7812
www.trinitycollegeqc.edu

Trinity International University
2065 Half Day Rd.
Deerfield, IL 60015-1284
800-822-3225
www.tiu.edu

University of Chicago
5801 Ellis Ave.
Chicago, IL 60637-1513
773-702-8650
www.uchicago.edu

University of Illinois at Chicago
601 South Morgan St.
Chicago, IL 60607-7128
312-996-4350
www.uic.edu

University of Illinois at Springfield
One University Plaza
Springfield, IL 62703-5407
888-977-4847
www.uis.edu

University of Illinois at Urbana–Champaign
601 East John St.
Champaign, IL 61820
217-333-0302
www.uiuc.edu

University of
Phoenix–Chicago Campus
1500 McConner Pkwy,
Ste. 700
Schaumburg, IL 60173-4399
800-228-7240
www.phoenix.edu

University of St. Francis
500 Wilcox St.
Joliet, IL 60435-6169
800-735-3500
www.stfrancis.edu

VanderCook College of
Music
3140 South Federal St.
Chicago, IL 60616-3731
800-448-2655
www.vandercook.edu

West Suburban College of
Nursing
3 Erie Court
Oak Park, IL 60302
708-763-6530
www.wscn.edu

Western Illinois University
1 University Cr.
Macomb, IL 61455-1390
877-742-5948
www.wiu.edu

Wheaton College
501 East College Ave.
Wheaton, IL 60187-5593
800-222-2419
www.wheaton.edu

Indiana

Anderson University
1100 East Fifth St.
Anderson, IN 46012-3495
800-428-6414
www.anderson.edu

Ball State University
2000 University Ave.
Muncie, IN 47306-1099
800-482-4BSU
www.bsu.edu

Bethel College
1001 West McKinley Ave.
Mishawaka, IN 46545-5591
800-422-4101
www.bethel-in.edu

Butler University
4600 Sunset Ave.
Indianapolis, IN 46208-3485
888-940-8100
www.butler.edu

Calumet College of Saint
Joseph
2400 New York Ave.
Whiting, IN 46394-2195
877-700-9100
www.ccsj.edu

Crossrd.s Bible College
601 North Shortridge Rd.
Indianapolis, IN 46219
800-273-2224
www.crossrd.s.edu

DePauw University
313 South Locust St.
Greencastle, IN 46135-0037
800-447-2495
www.depauw.edu

Earlham College
801 National Rd. West
Richmond, IN 47374-4095
800-327-5426
www.earlham.edu

Franklin College
101 Branigin Blvd
Franklin, IN 46131-2623
800-852-0232
www.franklincollege.edu

Goshen College
1700 South Main St.
Goshen, IN 46526-4794
800-348-7422
www.goshen.edu

Grace College
200 Seminary Dr.
Winona Lake, IN 46590-1294
800-54 GRACE
www.grace.edu

Hanover College
PO Box 108
Hanover, IN 47243-0108
800-213-2178
www.hanover.edu

Huntington College
2303 College Ave.
Huntington, IN 46750-1299
800-642-6493
www.huntington.edu

Indiana Institute of
Technology
1600 East Washington Blvd
Fort Wayne, IN 46803-1297
888-666-TECH
www.indianatech.edu

Indiana State University
210 North Seventh St.
Terre Haute, IN 47809-1401
800-742-0891
web.indstate.edu

Indiana University
Bloomington
107 S. Indiana Ave.
Bloomington, IN 47405-7000
812-855-0661
www.iub.edu

Indiana University East
2325 Chester Blvd
Richmond, IN 47374-1289
800-959-EAST
www.iu.edu

Indiana University Kokomo
PO Box 9003
Kokomo, IN 46904-9003
888-875-4485
www.indiana.edu

Indiana University
Northwest
3400 Brd.way
Gary, IN 46408-1197
800-968-7486
www.iun.edu

Indiana University South
Bend
1700 Mishawaka Ave., PO
Box 7111
South Bend, IN 46634-7111
877-GO-2-IUSB
www.indiana.edu

Indiana University
Southeast
4201 Grant Line Rd.
New Albany, IN 47150-6405
812-941-2212
www.iu.edu

Indiana University–Purdue
University Fort Wayne
2101 East Coliseum Blvd
Fort Wayne, IN 46805-1499
260-481-6812
www.ipfw.edu

Indiana University–Purdue
University Indianapolis
355 North Lansing
Indianapolis, IN 46202-2896
317-274-4591
www.indiana.edu

Indiana Wesleyan University
4201 South Washington St.
Marion, IN 46953-4974
800-332-6901
www.indwes.edu

Manchester College
604 East College Ave.
North Manchester, IN 46962-
1225
800-852-3648
www.manchester.edu

Marian College
3200 Cold Spring Rd.
Indianapolis, IN 46222-1997
317-955-6300
www.marian.edu

Martin University
2171 Avondale Pl., PO Box
18567
Indianapolis, IN 46218-3867
317-543-3237
www.martin.edu

Oakland City University
143 North Lucretia St.
Oakland City, IN 47660-1099
800-737-5125
www.oak.edu

Purdue University
West Lafayette, IN 47907
765-494-1776
www.purdue.edu

Purdue University Calumet
2200 169th St.
Hammond, IN 46323-2094
219-989-2213
www.calumet.purdue.edu

Purdue University North
Central
1401 South US Highway 421
Westville, IN 46391-9542
219-785-5458
www.pnc.edu

Rose-Hulman Institute of
Technology
5500 Wabash Ave.
Terre Haute, IN 47803-3999
800-248-7448
www.rose-hulman.edu

Saint Joseph's College
U.S. Highway 231, PO Box 890
Rensselaer, IN 47978
800-447-8781
www.saintjoe.edu

Saint Mary-of-the-Woods College
Saint Mary-of-the-Woods, IN 47876
800-926-SMWC
www.smwc.edu

Saint Mary's College
Notre Dame, IN 46556
800-551-7621
www.saintmarys.edu

Taylor University
236 West Reade Ave.
Upland, IN 46989-1001
800-882-3456
www.tayloru.edu

Taylor University Fort Wayne
1025 West Rudisill Blvd
Fort Wayne, IN 46807-2197
800-233-3922
fwtaylor.edu

Tri-State University
1 University Ave.
Angola, IN 46703-1764
800-347-4TSU
www.tristate.edu

University of Evansville
1800 Lincoln Ave.
Evansville, IN 47722-0002
800-423-8633
www.evansville.edu

University of Indianapolis
1400 East Hanna Ave.
Indianapolis, IN 46227-3697
800-232-8634
www.uindy.edu

University of Notre Dame
Notre Dame, IN 46556
574-631-7505
www.nd.edu

University of Saint Francis
2701 Spring St.
Fort Wayne, IN 46808-3994
800-729-4732
www.sf.edu

University of Southern Indiana
8600 University Blvd
Evansville, IN 47712-3590
800-467-1965
www.usi.edu

Valparaiso University
651 South College Ave.
Valparaiso, IN 46383-6493
888-GO-VALPO
www.valpo.edu

Wabash College
PO Box 352
Crawfordsville, IN 47933-0352
800-345-5385
www.wabash.edu

Iowa

Allen College
1825 Logan Ave.
Waterloo, IA 50703
319-226-2002
www.allencollege.edu

Briar Cliff University
3303 Rebecca St.
Sioux City, IA 51104-0100
800-662-3303
www.briarcliff.edu

Buena Vista University
610 West Fourth St.
Storm Lake, IA 50588
800-383-9600
www.bvu.edu

Central College
812 University St.
Pella, IA 50219-1999
800-458-5503
www.central.edu

Clarke College
1550 Clarke Dr.
Dubuque, IA 52001-3198
800-383-2345
www.clarke.edu

Coe College
1220 1st Ave., NE
Cedar Rapids, IA 52402-5092
877-225-5263
www.coe.edu

Cornell College
600 First St. West
Mount Vernon, IA 52314-1098
800-747-1112
www.cornellcollege.edu

Divine Word College
102 Jacoby Dr. SW
Epworth, IA 52045-0380
800-553-3321
www.dwci.edu

Dordt College
498 4th Ave., NE
Sioux Center, IA 51250-1697
800-343-6738
www.dordt.edu

Drake University
2507 University Ave.
Des Moines, IA 50311-4516
800-44DRAKE
www.drake.edu

Emmaus Bible College
2570 Asbury Rd.
Dubuque, IA 52001-3097
800-397-2425
www.emmaus.edu

Faith Baptist Bible College and Theological Seminary
1900 Northwest 4th St.
Ankeny, IA 50021-2152
888-FAITH 4U
www.faith.edu

Graceland University
1 University Pl.
Lamoni, IA 50140
866-GRACELAND
www.graceland.edu

Grand View College
1200 Grandview Ave.
Des Moines, IA 50316-1599
800-444-6083
www.gvc.edu

Grinnell College
1121 Park St.
Grinnell, IA 50112-1690
800-247-0113
www.grinnell.edu

Hamilton Technical College
1011 East 53rd St.
Davenport, IA 52807-2653
563-386-3570
www.hamiltontechcollege.com

Iowa State University of Science and Technology
Ames, IA 50011
800-262-3810
www.iastate.edu

Iowa Wesleyan College
601 North Main St.
Mount Pleasant, IA 52641-1398
800-582-2383
www.iwc.edu

Loras College
1450 Alta Vista
Dubuque, IA 52004-0178
800-245-6727
www.loras.edu

Luther College
700 College Dr.
Decorah, IA 52101-1045
800-458-8437
www.luther.edu

Maharishi University of Management
1000 North 4th St.
Fairfield, IA 52557
800-369-6480
www.mum.edu

Mercy College of Health Sciences
928 Sixth Ave.
Des Moines, IA 50309-1239
800-637-2994
www.mchs.edu

Morningside College
1501 Morningside Ave.
Sioux City, IA 51106-1751
800-831-0806
www.morningside.edu

Mount Mercy College
1330 Elmhurst Dr., NE
Cedar Rapids, IA 52402-4797
800-248-4504
www.mtmercy.edu

Northwestern College
101 Seventh St., SW
Orange City, IA 51041-1996
800-747-4757
www.nwciowa.edu

Palmer College of Chiropractic
1000 Brady St.
Davenport, IA 52803-5287
800-722-3648
www.palmer.edu

Simpson College
701 North C St.
Indianola, IA 50125-1297
800-362-2454
www.simpson.edu

St. Ambrose University
518 West Locust St.
Davenport, IA 52803-2898
800-383-2627
www.sau.edu

The Franciscan University of the Prairies
400 North Bluff Blvd,
PO Box 2967
Clinton, IA 52733-2967
800-242-4153
www.tfu.edu

The University of Iowa
Iowa City, IA 52242-1316
800-553-4692
www.uiowa.edu

University of Dubuque
2000 University Ave.
Dubuque, IA 52001-5099
563-589-3214
www.dbq.edu

University of Northern Iowa
1227 West 27th St.
Cedar Falls, IA 50614
800-772-2037
www.uni.edu

Upper Iowa University
605 Washington St., Box 1857
Fayette, IA 52142-1857
800-553-4150
www.uiu.edu

Vennard College
PO Box 29
University Park, IA 52595
800-686-8391
www.vennard.edu

Waldorf College
106 South 6th St.
Forest City, IA 50436-1713
800-292-1903
www.waldorf.edu

Wartburg College
100 Wartburg Blvd,
PO Box 1003
Waverly, IA 50677-0903
800-772-2085
www.wartburg.edu

William Penn University
201 Trueblood Ave.
Oskaloosa, IA 52577-1799
800-779-7366
www.wmpenn.edu

Kansas

Baker University
Box 65
Baldwin City, KS 66006-0065
800-873-4282
www.bakeru.edu

Barclay College
607 North Kingman
Haviland, KS 67059-0288
800-862-0226
www.barclaycollege.edu

Benedictine College
1020 North 2nd St.
Atchison, KS 66002-1499
800-467-5340
www.benedictine.edu

Bethany College
421 North First St.
Lindsborg, KS 67456-1897
800-826-2281
www.bethanylb.edu

Bethel College
300 East 27th St.
North Newton, KS 67117
800-522-1887
www.bethelks.edu

Central Christian College of Kansas
1200 South Main,
PO Box 1403
McPherson, KS 67460-5799
800-835-0078
www.centralchristian.edu

Emporia State University
1200 Commercial St.
Emporia, KS 66801-5087
877-468-6378
www.emporia.edu

Fort Hays State University
600 Park St.
Hays, KS 67601-4099
800-628-FHSU
www.fhsu.edu

Friends University
2100 West University St.
Wichita, KS 67213
800-577-2233
www.friends.edu

Haskell Indian Nations University
155 Indian Ave., #5031
Lawrence, KS 66046-4800
785-749-8454
www.haskell.edu

Kansas State University
Manhattan, KS 66506
785-532-6250
www.ksu.edu

Kansas Wesleyan University
100 East Claflin Ave.
Salina, KS 67401-6196
800-874-1154
www.kwu.edu

Manhattan Christian College
1415 Anderson Ave.
Manhattan, KS 66502-4081
877-246-4622
www.mccks.edu

McPherson College
1600 East Euclid,
PO Box 1402
McPherson, KS 67460-1402
800-365-7402
www.mcpherson.edu

MidAmerica Nazarene University
2030 East College Way
Olathe, KS 66062-1899
800-800-8887
www.mnu.edu

Newman University
3100 McCormick Ave.
Wichita, KS 67213-2097
877-NEWMANU
www.newmanu.edu

Ottawa University
1001 South Cedar
Ottawa, KS 66067-3399
800-755-5200
www.ottawa.edu

Pittsburg State University
1701 South Brd.way
Pittsburg, KS 66762
800-854-7488
www.pittstate.edu

Southwestern College
100 College St.
Winfield, KS 67156-2499
800-846-1543
www.sckans.edu

Sterling College
PO Box 98
Sterling, KS 67579-0098
800-346-1017
www.sterling.edu

Tabor College
400 South Jefferson
Hillsboro, KS 67063
800-822-6799
www.tabor.edu

University of Kansas
Lawrence, KS 66045
785-864-3911
www.ku.edu

University of Saint Mary
4100 South Fourth St. Trafficway
Leavenworth, KS 66048-5082
800-752-7043
www.stmary.edu

Washburn University
1700 SW College Ave.
Topeka, KS 66621
785-231-1010
www.washburn.edu

Wichita State University
1845 North Fairmount
Wichita, KS 67260
800-362-2594
www.wichita.edu

Michigan

Adrian College
110 South Madison St.
Adrian, MI 49221-2575
800-877-2246
www.adrian.edu

Albion College
611 East Porter St.
Albion, MI 49224-1831
800-858-6770
www.albion.edu

Alma College
614 West Superior St.
Alma, MI 48801-1599
800-321-ALMA
www.alma.edu

Andrews University
Berrien Springs, MI 49104
800-253-2874
www.andrews.edu

Aquinas College
1607 Robinson Rd., SE
Grand Rapids, MI 49506-1799
800-678-9593
www.aquinas.edu

Ave Maria College
300 West Forest Ave.
Ypsilanti, MI 48197
866-866-3030
www.avemaria.edu

Baker College of Allen Park
4500 Enterprise Dr.
Allen Park, MI 48101
313-425-3700
www.baker.edu

Baker College of Auburn Hills
1500 University Dr.
Auburn Hills, MI 48326-1586
248-340-0600
www.baker.edu

Baker College of Cadillac
9600 East 13th St.
Cadillac, MI 49601
231-876-3100
www.baker.edu

Baker College of Clinton Township
34950 Little Mack Ave.
Clinton Township, MI 48035-4701
888-272-2842
www.baker.edu

Baker College of Flint
1050 West Bristol Rd.
Flint, MI 48507-5508
800-964-4299
www.baker.edu

Baker College of Jackson
2800 Springport Rd.
Jackson, MI 49202
888-343-3683
www.baker.edu

Baker College of Muskegon
1903 Marquette Ave.
Muskegon, MI 49442-3497
231-777-5207
www.baker.edu

Baker College of Owosso
1020 South Washington St.
Owosso, MI 48867-4400
800-879-3797
www.baker.edu

Baker College of Port Huron
3403 Lapeer Rd.
Port Huron, MI 48060-2597
888-262-2442
www.baker.edu

Calvin College
3201 Burton St., SE
Grand Rapids, MI 49546-4388
800-688-0122
www.calvin.edu

Central Michigan University
Mount Pleasant, MI 48859
888-292-5366
www.cmich.edu

Cleary University
3601 Plymouth Rd.
Ann Arbor, MI 48105-2659
888-5-CLEARY
www.cleary.edu

College for Creative Studies
201 East Kirby
Detroit, MI 48202-4034
800-952-ARTS
www.ccscad.edu

Concordia University
4090 Geddes Rd.
Ann Arbor, MI 48105-2797
800-253-0680
www.cuaa.edu

Cornerstone University
1001 East Beltline Ave., NE
Grand Rapids, MI 49525-5897
800-787-9778
www.cornerstone.edu

Davenport University
643 South Waverly Rd.
Holland, MI 49423
800-643-4630
www.davenport.edu

Davenport University
220 East Kalamazoo St.
Lansing, MI 48933-2197
800-686-1600
www.davenport.edu

Davenport University
415 East Fulton
Grand Rapids, MI 49503
800-724-7708
www.davenport.edu

Davenport University
27650 Dequindre Rd.
Warren, MI 48092-5209
800-724-7708
www.davenport.edu

Davenport University
550 Lake Dr., Ste. B
Lapeer, MI 48446
810-664-9655
www.davenport.edu

Davenport University
2200 Dendrinos Dr.; Ste. 110
Traverse City, MI 49684
231-995-1740
www.davenport.edu

Davenport University
4123 West Main St.
Kalamazoo, MI 49006-2791
800-632-8928
www.davenport.edu

Davenport University
80 Livingston Blvd
Gaylord, MI 49735
888-352-5791
www.davenport.edu

Davenport University
4801 Oakman Blvd
Dearborn, MI 48126-3799
800-815-8023
www.davenport.edu

Eastern Michigan University
Ypsilanti, MI 48197
800-GO TO EMU
www.emich.edu

Ferris State University
901 South State St.
Big Rapids, MI 49307
800-433-7747
www.ferris.edu

Finlandia University
601 Quincy St.
Hancock, MI 49930-1882
877-202-5491
www.finlandia.edu

Grace Bible College
1011 Aldon St. SW,
PO Box 910
Grand Rapids, MI 49509-0910
800-968-1887
7957

Grand Valley State University
1 Campus Dr.
Allendale, MI 49401-9403
800-748-0246
www.gvsu.edu

Great Lakes Christian College
6211 West Willow Highway
Lansing, MI 48917-1299
800-YES-GLCC
www.glcc.edu

Hillsdale College
33 East College St.
Hillsdale, MI 49242-1298
517-607-2327
www.hillsdale.edu

Hope College
141 East 12th St.,
PO Box 9000
Holland, MI 49422-9000
800-968-7850
www.hope.edu

Kalamazoo College
1200 Academy St.
Kalamazoo, MI 49006-3295
800-253-3602
www.kzoo.edu

Kettering University
1700 West Third Ave.
Flint, MI 48504-4898
800-955-4464
www.kettering.edu

Lake Superior State University
650 W Easterday Ave.
Sault Sainte Marie, MI 49783-1626
888-800-LSSU
www.lssu.edu

Lawrence Technological University
21000 West Ten Mile Rd.
Southfield, MI 48075-1058
800-225-5588
www.ltu.edu

Madonna University
36600 Schoolcraft Rd.
Livonia, MI 48150-1173
800-852-4951
www.madonna.edu

Marygrove College
8425 West McNichols Rd.
Detroit, MI 48221-2599
866-313-1297
www.marygrove.edu

Michigan Jewish Institute
25401 Coolidge Highway
Oak Park, MI 48237-1304
248-414-6900
www.mji.edu

Michigan State University
East Lansing, MI 48824
517-355-8332
www.msu.edu

Michigan Technological University
1400 Townsend Dr.
Houghton, MI 49931-1295
888-MTU-1885
www.mtu.edu

Northern Michigan University
1401 Presque Isle Ave.
Marquette, MI 49855-5301
800-682-9797
www.nmu.edu

Northwood University
4000 Whiting Dr.
Midland, MI 48640-2398
800-457-7878
www.northwood.edu

Oakland University
Rochester, MI 48309-4401
800-OAK-UNIV
www.oakland.edu

Olivet College
320 South Main St.
Olivet, MI 49076-9701
800-456-7189
www.olivetcollege.edu

Reformed Bible College
3333 East Beltline, NE
Grand Rapids, MI 49525-9749
800-511-3749
www.reformed.edu

Rochester College
800 West Avon Rd.
Rochester Hills, MI 48307-2764
800-521-6010
www.rc.edu

Sacred Heart Major Seminary
2701 Chicago Blvd
Detroit, MI 48206-1799
313-883-8552
www.archdioceseofdetroit.org/shms/shms.htm

Saginaw Valley State University
7400 Bay Rd.
University Center, MI 48710
800-968-9500
www.svsu.edu

Siena Heights University
1247 East Siena Heights Dr.
Adrian, MI 49221-1796
800-521-0009
www.sienahts.edu

Spring Arbor University
106 East Main St.
Spring Arbor, MI 49283-9799
800-968-0011
www.arbor.edu

University of Detroit Mercy
4001 W McNichols Rd,
PO Box 19900
Detroit, MI 48219-0900
800-635-5020
www.udmercy.edu

University of Michigan
Ann Arbor, MI 48109
734-764-7433
www.umich.edu

University of Michigan–Dearborn
4901 Evergreen Rd.
Dearborn, MI 48128-1491
313-593-5100
www.umd.umich.edu

University of Michigan–Flint
303 East Kearsley St.
Flint, MI 48502-1950
810-762-3434
www.flint.umich.edu

University of Phoenix–Metro Detroit Campus
5480 Corporate Dr., Ste. 260
Troy, MI 48098-2623
800-834-2438
www.phoenix.edu

University of Phoenix–West Michigan Campus
318 River Ridge Dr. NW
Grand Rapids, MI 49544-1683
800-228-7240
www.phoenix.edu

Walsh College of Accountancy and Business Administration
3838 Livernois Rd.,
PO Box 7006
Troy, MI 48007-7006
248-823-1209
www.walshcollege.edu

Wayne State University
656 West Kirby St.
Detroit, MI 48202
313-577-3581
www.wayne.edu

Western Michigan University
1903 West Michigan Ave.
Kalamazoo, MI 49008-5202
269-387-2000
www.wmich.edu

Yeshiva Geddolah of Greater Detroit Rabbinical College
24600 Greenfield
Oak Park, MI 48237-1544

Minnesota

Argosy University win Cities
1515 Central Pkwy
Eagan, MN 55121
888-844-2004
www.argosyu.edu

Argosy University win Cities
1515 Central Pkwy
Eagan, MN 55121
888-844-2004
www.argosyu.edu

Augsburg College
2211 Riverside Ave.
Minneapolis, MN 55454-1351
800-788-5678
www.augsburg.edu

Bemidji State University
1500 Birchmont Dr., NE
Bemidji, MN 56601-2699
800-652-9747
www.bemidjistate.edu

Bethany Lutheran College
700 Luther Dr.
Mankato, MN 56001-6163
800-944-3066
www.blc.edu

Bethel University
3900 Bethel Dr.
St. Paul, MN 55112-6999
800-255-8706
www.bethel.edu

Capella University
222 South Ninth St., 20th Fl
Minneapolis, MN 55402
888-CAPELLA
www.capellauniversity.edu

Carleton College
One North College St.
Northfield, MN 55057-4001
800-995-2275
www.carleton.edu

College of Saint Benedict
37 South College Ave.
Saint Joseph, MN 56374-2091
800-544-1489
www.csbsju.edu

College of St. Catherine
2004 Randolph Ave.
St. Paul, MN 55105-1789
651-690-6505
www.stkate.edu

College of St. Catherine–Minneapolis
601 25th Ave. South
Minneapolis, MN 55454-1494
800-945-4599
www.stkate.edu

College of Visual Arts
344 Summit Ave.
St. Paul, MN 55102-2124
800-224-1536
www.cva.edu

Concordia College
901 South 8th St.
Moorhead, MN 56562
800-699-9897
www.concordiacollege.edu

Concordia University, St. Paul
275 Syndicate St. North
St. Paul, MN 55104-5494
800-333-4705
8633

Crossrd.s College
920 Mayowood Rd., SW
Rochester, MN 55902-2382
800-456-7651
www.crossrd.scollege.edu

Crown College
8700 College View Dr.
St. Bonifacius, MN 55375-9001
800-68-CROWN
www.crown.edu

Gustavus Adolphus College
800 West College Ave.
St. Peter, MN 56082-1498
800-GUSTAVU(S)
www.gustavus.edu

Hamline University
1536 Hewitt Ave.
St. Paul, MN 55104-1284
800-753-9753
www.hamline.edu

Macalester College
1600 Grand Ave.
St. Paul, MN 55105-1899
800-231-7974
www.macalester.edu

Martin Luther College
1995 Luther Court
New Ulm, MN 56073
507-354-8221
www.mlc-wels.edu

Metropolitan State University
700 East 7th St.
St. Paul, MN 55106-5000
651-793-1303
www.metrostate.edu

Minneapolis College of Art and Design
2501 Stevens Ave. South
Minneapolis, MN 55404-4347
800-874-6223
www.mcad.edu

Minnesota State University Mankato
228 Wiecking Center
Mankato, MN 56001
800-722-0544
www.mnsu.edu

Minnesota State University Moorhead
1104 7th Ave. South
Moorhead, MN 56563-0002
800-593-7246
www.mnstate.edu

National American University
1500 West Highway 36
Roseville, MN 55113-4035
651-644-1265
www.national.edu

North Central University
910 Elliot Ave.
Minneapolis, MN 55404-1322
800-289-6222
www.northcentral.edu

Northwestern College
3003 Snelling Ave. North
St. Paul, MN 55113-1598
800-827-6827
www.nwc.edu

Oak Hills Christian College
1600 Oak Hills Rd., SW
Bemidji, MN 56601-8832
888-751-8670
www.oakhills.edu

Pillsbury Baptist Bible College
315 South Grove Ave.
Owatonna, MN 55060-3097
800-747-4557
www.pillsbury.edu

Saint John's University
PO Box 2000
Collegeville, MN 56321
800-544-1489
www.csbsju.edu

Saint Mary's University of Minnesota
700 Terrace Heights
Winona, MN 55987-1399
800-635-5987
www.smumn.edu

Southwest Minnesota State University
1501 State St.
Marshall, MN 56258-1598
800-642-0684
www.southwest.msus.edu

St. Cloud State University
720 4th Ave. South
St. Cloud, MN 56301-4498
877-654-7278
www.stcloudstate.edu

St. Olaf College
1520 St Olaf Ave.
Northfield, MN 55057-1098
800-800-3025
www.stolaf.edu

The Art Institutes International Minnesota
15 South 9th St.
Minneapolis, MN 55402-3137
800-777-3643
www.aim.artinstitutes.edu

The College of St. Scholastica
1200 Kenwood Ave.
Duluth, MN 55811-4199
800-249-6412
www.css.edu

University of Minnesota, Crookston
2900 University Ave.
Crookston, MN 56716-5001
800-862-6466
www.crk.umn.edu

University of Minnesota, Duluth
10 University Dr.
Duluth, MN 55812-2496
800-232-1339
www.d.umn.edu

University of Minnesota, Morris
600 East 4th St.
Morris, MN 56267-2134
800-992-8863
www.mrs.umn.edu

University of Minnesota, Twin Cities Campus
100 Church St., SE
Minneapolis, MN 55455-0213
800-752-1000
www.umn.edutc/

University of St. Thomas
2115 Summit Ave.
St. Paul, MN 55105-1096
800-328-6819
www.stthomas.edu

Winona State University
PO Box 5838
Winona, MN 55987-5838
800-DIAL WSU
www.winona.msus.edu

Missouri

Avila University
11901 Wornall Rd.
Kansas City, MO 64145-1698
800-GO-AVILA
www.avila.edu

Baptist Bible College
628 East Kearney
Springfield, MO 65803-3498
417-268-6000
www.bbcnet.edu

Calvary Bible College and Theological Seminary
15800 Calvary Rd.
Kansas City, MO 64147-1341
800-326-3960
www.calvary.edu

Central Bible College
3000 North Grant Ave.
Springfield, MO 65803-1096
800-831-4222
www.cbcag.edu

Central Christian College of the Bible
911 Urbandale Dr. East
Moberly, MO 65270-1997
660-263-3900
www.cccb.edu

Central Methodist University
411 Central Methodist Square
Fayette, MO 65248-1198
660-248-6247
www.cmc.edu

Central Missouri State University
PO Box 800
Warrensburg, MO 64093
660-543-4290
www.cmsu.edu

Cleveland Chiropractic College-Kansas City Campus
6401 Rockhill Rd.
Kansas City, MO 64131-1181
800-467-2252
www.cleveland.edu

College of the Ozarks
PO Box 17
Point Lookout, MO 65726
800-222-0525
www.cofo.edu

Columbia College
1001 Rogers St.
Columbia, MO 65216-0002
800-231-2391
www.ccis.edudepartments/distanceeducation

Conception Seminary College
PO Box 502
Conception, MO 64433-0502
660-944-2886
www.conceptionabbey.org/

Culver-Stockton College
1 College Hill
Canton, MO 63435-1299
800-537-1883
www.culver.edu

Deaconess College of Nursing
6150 Oakland Ave.
St. Louis, MO 63139-3215
800-942-4310
www.deaconess.edu

DeVry University
11224 Holmes Rd.
Kansas City, MO 64131-3698
800-821-3766
www.devry.edu

Drury University
900 North Benton Ave.
Springfield, MO 65802-3791
800-922-2274
www.drury.edu

Evangel University
1111 North Glenstone
Springfield, MO 65802-2191
417-865-2811
www.evangel.edu

Fontbonne University
6800 Wydown Blvd
St. Louis, MO 63105-3098
314-889-1400
www.fontbonne.edu

Global University of the Assemblies of God
1211 South Glenstone Ave.
Springfield, MO 65804
800-443-1083
www.globaluniversity.edu

Hannibal-LaGrange College
2800 Palmyra Rd.
Hannibal, MO 63401-1999
800-HLG-1119
www.hlg.edu

Harris-Stowe State College
3026 Laclede Ave.
St. Louis, MO 63103-2136
314-340-3301
www.hssc.edu

Jewish Hospital College of Nursing and Allied Health
306 S. Kingshighway Blvd
St. Louis, MO 63110-1091
314-454-7538
www.jhconah.edu

Kansas City Art Institute
4415 Warwick Blvd
Kansas City, MO 64111-1874
800-522-5224
www.kcai.edu

Kansas City College of Legal Studies
402 E. Bannister Rd., Ste. A
Kansas City, MO 64131
877-582-3963
www.metropolitancollege.edu

Lester L. Cox College of Nursing and Health Sciences
1423 North Jefferson
Springfield, MO 65802
417-269-3038
www.coxcollege.edu

Lincoln University
820 Chestnut
Jefferson City, MO 65102
800-521-5052
www.lincolnu.edu

Lindenwood University
209 S. Kingshighway
St. Charles, MO 63301-1695
636-949-4949
www.lindenwood.edu

Logan University-College of Chiropractic
1851 Schoettler Rd., Box 1065
Chesterfield, MO 63006-1065
800-533-9210
www.logan.edu

Maryville University of Saint Louis
13550 Conway Rd.
St. Louis, MO 63141-7299
800-627-9855
www.maryville.edu

Messenger College
PO Box 4050
Joplin, MO 64803
417-624-7070
www.messengercollege.edu

Missouri Baptist University
One College Park Dr.
St. Louis, MO 63141-8660
877-434-1115
www.mobap.edu

Missouri Southern State University
3950 East Newman Rd.
Joplin, MO 64801-1595
866-818-MSSU
www.mssu.edu

Missouri Tech
1167 Corporate Lake Dr.
St. Louis, MO 63132-1716
314-569-3600
www.motech.edu

Missouri Valley College
500 East College
Marshall, MO 65340-3197
660-831-4157
www.moval.edu

Missouri Western State College
4525 Downs Dr.
St. Joseph, MO 64507-2294
800-662-7041
www.mwsc.edu

National American University
4200 Blue Ridge Blvd
Kansas City, MO 64133-1612
816-353-4554
www.national.edu

Northwest Missouri State University
800 University Dr.
Maryville, MO 64468-6001
800-633-1175
www.nwmissouri.edu

Ozark Christian College
1111 North Main St.
Joplin, MO 64801-4804
800-299-4622
www.occ.edu

Park University
8700 NW River Park Dr.
Parkville, MO 64152-3795
800-745-7275
www.park.edu

Research College of Nursing
2300 East Meyer Blvd
Kansas City, MO 64132
800-842-6776
www.researchcollege.edu

Rockhurst University
1100 Rockhurst Rd.
Kansas City, MO 64110-2561
800-842-6776
www.rockhurst.edu

Saint Louis University
221 North Grand Blvd
St. Louis, MO 63103-2097
800-758-3678
www.slu.edu

Saint Luke's College
4426 Wornall Rd.
Kansas City, MO 64111
816-932-2073
www.saintlukescollege.edu

Southeast Missouri State University
One University Plaza
Cape Girardeau, MO 63701-4799
573-651-2590
www.semo.edu

Southwest Baptist University
1600 University Ave.
Bolivar, MO 65613-2597
800-526-5859
www.sbuniv.edu

Southwest Missouri State University
901 South National
Springfield, MO 65804-0094
800-492-7900
www.smsu.edu

St. Louis Christian College
1360 Grandview Dr.
Florissant, MO 63033-6499
800-887-SLCC
www.slcc4ministry.edu

St. Louis College of Pharmacy
4588 Parkview Pl.
St. Louis, MO 63110-1088
314-446-8313
www.stlcop.edu

Stephens College
1200 East Brd.way
Columbia, MO 65215-0002
800-876-7207
www.stephens.edu

Truman State University
100 East Normal St.
Kirksville, MO 63501-4221
660-785-4114
www.truman.edu

University of Missouri–Columbia
Columbia, MO 65211
573-882-7786
www.missouri.edu

University of Missouri–Kansas City
5100 Rockhill Rd.
Kansas City, MO 64110-2499
800-775-8652
www.umkc.edu

University of Missouri–Rolla
1870 Miner Cr.
Rolla, MO 65409-0910
800-522-0938
www.umr.edu

University of Missouri–St. Louis
One University Blvd
St. Louis, MO 63121
314-516-5460
www.umsl.edu

University of Phoenix–
Kansas City Campus
901 East 104th St., Ste. 301
Kansas City, MO 64131-4517
800-228-7240
www.phoenix.edu

University of Phoenix–
St. Louis Campus
Riverport Lakes West, 13801
Riverport Dr., Ste. 100
St. Louis, MO 63043-4828
800-228-7240
www.phoenix.edu

Washington University in
St. Louis
1 Brookings Dr.
St. Louis, MO 63130-4899
800-638-0700
www.wustl.edu

Webster University
470 East Lockwood Ave.
St. Louis, MO 63119-3194
800-75-ENROL
www.webster.edu

Westminster College
501 Westminster Ave.
Fulton, MO 65251-1299
800-475-3361
www.westminster-mo.edu

William Jewell College
500 College Hill
Liberty, MO 64068-1843
800-753-7009
www.jewell.edu

William Woods University
One University Ave.
Fulton, MO 65251-1098
800-995-3159
www.williamwoods.edu

Nebraska

Bellevue University
1000 Galvin Rd. South
Bellevue, NE 68005-3098
800-756-7920
www.bellevue.edu

Chadron State College
1000 Main St.
Chadron, NE 69337
308-432-6263
www.csc.edu

Clarkson College
101 South 42nd St.
Omaha, NE 68131-2739
800-647-5500
www.clarksoncollege.edu

College of Saint Mary
1901 South 72nd St.
Omaha, NE 68124-2377
800-926-5534
www.csm.edu

Concordia University
800 North Columbia Ave.
Seward, NE 68434-1599
800-535-5494
www.cune.edu

Creighton University
2500 California Plaza
Omaha, NE 68178-0001
800-282-5835
www.creighton.edu

Dana College
2848 College Dr.
Blair, NE 68008-1099
800-444-3262
www.dana.edu

Doane College
1014 Boswell Ave.
Crete, NE 68333-2430
800-333-6263
www.doane.edu

Grace University
1311 South Ninth St.
Omaha, NE 68108
800-383-1422
www.graceuniversity.edu

Hastings College
800 North Turner Ave.
Hastings, NE 68901-7696
800-532-7642
www.hastings.edu

Midland Lutheran College
900 North Clarkson St.
Fremont, NE 68025-4200
800-642-8382
www.mlc.edu

Nebraska Christian College
1800 Syracuse Ave.
Norfolk, NE 68701-2458
402-379-5000
www.nechristian.edu

Nebraska Methodist College
8501 West Dodge Rd.
Omaha, NE 68114-3426
800-335-5510
www.methodistcollege.edu

Nebraska Wesleyan
University
5000 Saint Paul Ave.
Lincoln, NE 68504-2796
800-541-3818
www.nebrwesleyan.edu

Peru State College
PO Box 10
Peru, NE 68421
402-872-2221
www.peru.edu

Union College
3800 South 48th St.
Lincoln, NE 68506-4300
800-228-4600
www.ucollege.edu

University of Nebraska at
Kearney
905 West 25th St.
Kearney, NE 68849-0001
800-532-7639
www.unk.edu

University of Nebraska at
Omaha
6001 Dodge St.
Omaha, NE 68182
402-554-2416
www.unomaha.edu

University of Nebraska
Medical Center
Nebraska Medical Center
Omaha, NE 68198
800-626-8431
www.unmc.edu

University of
Nebraska–Lincoln
14th and R Streets
Lincoln, NE 68588
800-742-8800
www.unl.edu

Wayne State College
1111 Main St.
Wayne, NE 68787
402-375-7234
www.wsc.edu

York College
1125 East 8th St.
York, NE 68467
800-950 9675
www.york.edu

North Dakota

Dickinson State University
291 Campus Dr.
Dickinson, ND 58601-4896
800-279-4295
www.dsu.nodak.edu

Jamestown College
6000 College Lane
Jamestown, ND 58405
800-336-2554
www.jc.edu

Mayville State University
330 3rd St., NE
Mayville, ND 58257-1299
800-437-4104
www.mayvillestate.edu

Medcenter One College of
Nursing
512 North 7th St.
Bismarck, ND 58501-4494
701-323-6271
medcenterone.com/
collegeursing.htm

Minot State University
500 University Ave. West
Minot, ND 58707-0002
800-777-0750
www.minotstateu.edu

North Dakota State
University
1301 North University Ave.
Fargo, ND 58105
800-488-NDSU
www.ndsu.edu

Trinity Bible College
50 South 6th Ave.
Ellendale, ND 58436-7150
888-TBC-2DAY
www.trinitybiblecollege.edu

University of Mary
7500 University Dr.
Bismarck, ND 58504-9652
800-288-6279
www.umary.edu

University of North Dakota
Grand Forks, ND 58202
800-CALL UND
www.und.nodak.edu

Valley City State University
101 College St., SW
Valley City, ND 58072
800-532-8641
www.vcsu.edu

Ohio

Allegheny Wesleyan College
2161 Woodsdale Rd.
Salem, OH 44460
800-292-3153
www.awc.edu

Antioch College
795 Livermore St.
Yellow Springs, OH 45387-1697
800-543-9436
www.antioch-college.edu

Antioch University McGregor
800 Livermore St.
Yellow Springs, OH 45387-1609
937-769-1818
www.mcgregor.edu

Art Academy of Cincinnati
1125 Saint Gregory St.
Cincinnati, OH 45202-1799
513-562-8744
www.artacademy.edu

Ashland University
401 College Ave.
Ashland, OH 44805-3702
800-882-1548
www.ashland.edu

Baldwin-Wallace College
275 Eastland Rd.
Berea, OH 44017-2088
440-826-2222
www.bw.edu

Bluffton University
1 University Dr.
Bluffton, OH 45817
800-488-3257
www.bluffton.edu

Bowling Green State University
Bowling Green, OH 43403
419-372-2086
www.bgsu.edu

Bryant and Stratton College
1700 East 13th St.
Cleveland, OH 44114-3203
216-771-1700
www.bryantstratton.edu

Capital University
2199 East Main St.
Columbus, OH 43209-2394
800-289-6289
www.capital.edu

Case Western Reserve University
10900 Euclid Ave.
Cleveland, OH 44106
216-368-4450
www.cwru.edu

Cedarville University
251 North Main St.
Cedarville, OH 45314-0601
800-CEDARVILLE
www.cedarville.edu

Central State University
1400 Brush Row Rd.,
PO Box 1004
Wilberforce, OH 45384
937-376-6348
www.centralstate.edu

Cincinnati Bible College and Seminary
2700 Glenway Ave.,
PO Box 04320
Cincinnati, OH 45204-3200
800-949-4CBC
www.cincybible.edu

Circleville Bible College
1476 Lancaster Pike,
PO Box 458
Circleville, OH 43113-9487
800-701-0222
www.biblecollege.edu

Cleveland Institute of Music
11021 East Blvd
Cleveland, OH 44106-1776
216-795-3107
www.cim.edu

Cleveland State University
2121 Euclid Ave.
Cleveland, OH 44115
888-CSU-OHIO
www.csuohio.edu

College of Mount St. Joseph
5701 Delhi Rd.
Cincinnati, OH 45233-1670
800-654-9314
www.msj.edu

Columbus College of Art & Design
107 North Ninth St.
Columbus, OH 43215-1758
877-997-2223
www.ccad.edu

David N. Myers University
112 Prospect Ave.
Cleveland, OH 44115-1096
800-424-3953
www.dnmyers.edu

Defiance College
701 North Clinton St.
Defiance, OH 43512-1610
800-520-4632
www.defiance.edu

Denison University
Granville, OH 43023
800-DENISON
www.denison.edu

DeVry University
1350 Alum Creek Dr.
Columbus, OH 43209-2705
800-426-2206
www.devry.edu

Franciscan University of Steubenville
1235 University Blvd
Steubenville, OH 43952-1763
800-783-6220
www.franciscan.edu

Franklin University
201 South Grant Ave.
Columbus, OH 43215-5399
877-341-6300
www.franklin.edu

God's Bible School and College
1810 Young St.
Cincinnati, OH 45202-6838
800-486-4637
www.gbs.edu

Heidelberg College
310 East Market St.
Tiffin, OH 44883-2462
800-434-3352
www.heidelberg.edu

Hiram College
Box 67
Hiram, OH 44234-0067
800-362-5280
www.hiram.edu

John Carroll University
20700 North Park Blvd
University Heights, OH 44118-4581
216-397-4294
www.jcu.edu

Kent State University
PO Box 5190
Kent, OH 44242-0001
800-988-KENT
www.kent.edu

Kenyon College
Gambier, OH 43022-9623
800-848-2468
8956

Lake Erie College
391 West Washington St.
Painesville, OH 44077-3389
800-916-0904
www.lec.edu

Laura and Alvin Siegal College of Judaic Studies
26500 Shaker Blvd
Beachwood, OH 44122-7116
888-336-2257
www.siegalcollege.edu

Lourdes College
6832 Convent Blvd
Sylvania, OH 43560-2898
800-878-3210
www.lourdes.edu

Malone College
515 25th St., NW
Canton, OH 44709-3897
800-521-1146
www.malone.edu

Marietta College
215 Fifth St.
Marietta, OH 45750-4000
800-331-7896
www.marietta.edu

MedCentral College of Nursing
335 Glessner Ave.
Mansfield, OH 44903
877-656-4360
www.medcentral.edu

Miami University
Oxford, OH 45056
513-529-5040
www.muohio.edu

Mount Carmel College of Nursing
127 South Davis Ave.
Columbus, OH 43222
614-234-5800
www.mccn.edu

Mount Union College
1972 Clark Ave.
Alliance, OH 44601-3993
800-992-6682
www.muc.edu

Mount Vernon Nazarene University
800 Martinsburg Rd.
Mount Vernon, OH 43050-9500
866-462-6868
www.mvnu.edu

Muskingum College
163 Stormont St.
New Concord, OH 43762
800-752-6082
www.muskingum.edu

Notre Dame College
4545 College Rd.
South Euclid, OH 44121-4293
800-632-1680
www.notredamecollege.edu

Oberlin College
173 West Lorain St.
Oberlin, OH 44074
800-622-OBIE
www.oberlin.edu

Ohio Dominican University
1216 Sunbury Rd.
Columbus, OH 43219-2099
800-854-2670
www.ohiodominican.edu

Ohio Northern University
525 South Main
Ada, OH 45810-1599
888-408-4ONU
www.onu.edu

Ohio University
Athens, OH 45701-2979
740-593-4100
www.ohio.edu

Ohio University–Chillicothe
571 West Fifth St.,
PO Box 629
Chillicothe, OH 45601-0629
740-774-7200
www.ohio.educhillicothe/

Ohio University–Eastern
45425 National Rd.
St. Clairsville, OH 43950-9724
740-593-4120
www.eastern.ohiou.edu

Ohio University–Lancaster
1570 Granville Pike
Lancaster, OH 43130-1097
888-446-4468
www.ohiou.edulancaster/

Ohio University–Southern Campus
1804 Liberty Ave.
Ironton, OH 45638-2214
800-626-0513
www.ohiou.edu

Ohio University–Zanesville
1425 Newark Rd.
Zanesville, OH 43701-2695
740-588-1439
www.zanesville.ohiou.edu

Ohio Wesleyan University
61 South Sandusky St.
Delaware, OH 43015
800-922-8953
www.owu.edu

Otterbein College
1 Otterbein College
Westerville, OH 43081
800-488-8144
www.otterbein.edu

Pontifical College Josephinum
7625 North High St.
Columbus, OH 43235-1498
888-252-5812
www.pcj.edu

Shawnee State University
940 Second St.
Portsmouth, OH 45662-4344
800-959-2SSU
www.shawnee.edu

The Cleveland Institute of Art
11141 East Blvd
Cleveland, OH 44106-1700
800-223-4700
www.cia.edu

The College of Wooster
1189 Beall Ave.
Wooster, OH 44691-2363
800-877-9905
www.wooster.edu

The Ohio State University
190 North Oval Mall
Columbus, OH 43210
614-247-6281
www.osu.edu

The Ohio State University at Lima
4240 Campus Dr.
Lima, OH 45804-3576
419-995-8220
www.lima.ohio-state.edu

The Ohio State University at Marion
1465 Mount Vernon Ave.
Marion, OH 43302-5695
740-389-6786
www.marion.ohio-state.edu

The Ohio State University–Mansfield Campus
1680 University Dr.
Mansfield, OH 44906-1599
419-755-4226
www.mansfield.ohio-state.edu

The Ohio State University–Newark Campus
1179 University Dr.
Newark, OH 43055-1797
614-366-9333
www.newark.osu.edu

The University of Akron
302 Buchtel Common
Akron, OH 44325-0001
800-655-4884
www.uakron.edu

The University of Findlay
1000 North Main St.
Findlay, OH 45840-3653
800-548-0932
www.findlay.edu

Tiffin University
155 Miami St.
Tiffin, OH 44883-2161
800-968-6446
www.tiffin.edu

Tri-State Bible College
506 Margaret St.,
PO Box 445
South Point, OH 45680-8402
740-377-2520
www.tsbc.edu

Union Institute & University
440 East McMillan St.
Cincinnati, OH 45206-1925
800-486-3116
www.tui.edu

University of Cincinnati
2624 Clifton Ave.
Cincinnati, OH 45221
513-556-4100
www.uc.edu

University of Dayton
300 College Park
Dayton, OH 45469-1300
800-837-7433
www.udayton.edu

University of Phoenix–Cleveland Campus
5005 Rockside Rd., Ste. 325
Independence, OH 44131-2194
480-557-1712
www.phoenix.edu

University of Rio Grande
218 North College Ave.
Rio Grande, OH 45674
740-245-7208
www.rio.edu

University of Toledo
2801 West Bancroft
Toledo, OH 43606-3390
419-530-5737
www.utoledo.edu

Urbana University
579 College Way
Urbana, OH 43078-2091
800-7-URBANA
www.urbana.edu

Ursuline College
2550 Lander Rd.
Pepper Pike, OH 44124-4398
888-URSULINE
www.ursuline.edu

Walsh University
2020 East Maple St., NW
North Canton, OH 44720-3396
800-362-8846
www.walsh.edu

Wilberforce University
1055 North Bickett Rd.
Wilberforce, OH 45384
800-367-8568
www.wilberforce.edu

Wilmington College
Pyle Center Box 1185
Wilmington, OH 45177
800-341-9318
www.wilmington.edu

Wittenberg University
PO Box 720
Springfield, OH 45501-0720
800-677-7558
www.wittenberg.edu

Wright State University
3640 Colonel Glenn Highway
Dayton, OH 45435
800-247-1770
www.wright.edu

Xavier University
3800 Victory Pkwy
Cincinnati, OH 45207
800-344-4698
www.xu.edu

Youngstown State University
One University Plaza
Youngstown, OH 44555-0001
877-468-6978
www.ysu.edu

Oklahoma

Bacone College
2299 Old Bacone Rd.
Muskogee, OK 74403-1597
888-682-5514
www.bacone.edu

Cameron University
2800 West Gore Blvd
Lawton, OK 73505-6377
888-454-7600
www.cameron.edu

East Central University
1100 East 14th St.
Ada, OK 74820-6899
580-332-8000
www.ecok.edu

Hillsdale Free Will Baptist College
3701 South I35, PO Box 7208
Moore, OK 73160-1208
405-912-9006
www.hc.edu

Langston University
PO Box 907
Langston, OK 73050-0907
405-466-3428
www.lunet.edu

Metropolitan College
2901 North Classen Blvd, Ste. 200
Oklahoma City, OK 73106
405-843-1000
www.metropolitancollege.edu

Metropolitan College
4528 South Sheridan Rd., Ste. 105
Tulsa, OK 74145-1011
918-627-9300
www.metropolitancollege.edu

Mid-America Christian University
3500 Southwest 119th St.
Oklahoma City, OK 73170-4504
405-392-3241
www.macu.edu

Northeastern State University
600 North Grand
Tahlequah, OK 74464-2399
918-456-5511
www.nsuok.edu

Northwestern Oklahoma State University
709 Oklahoma Blvd
Alva, OK 73717-2799
580-327-8550
www.nwosu.edu

Oklahoma Baptist University
500 West University
Shawnee, OK 74804
800-654-3285
www.okbu.edu

Oklahoma Christian University
PO Box 11000
Oklahoma City, OK 73136-1100
405-425-5050
www.oc.edu

Oklahoma City University
2501 North Blackwelder
Oklahoma City, OK 73106-1402
800-633-7242
www.okcu.edu

Oklahoma Panhandle State University
PO Box 430
Goodwell, OK 73939-0430
800-664-6778
www.opsu.edu

Oklahoma State University
Stillwater, OK 74078
800-852-1255
www.okstate.edu

Oklahoma Wesleyan University
2201 Silver Lake Rd.
Bartlesville, OK 74006-6299
866-222-8226
www.okwu.edu

Oral Roberts University
7777 South Lewis Ave.
Tulsa, OK 74171-0001
800-678-8876
www.oru.edu

Rogers State University
1701 West Will Rogers Blvd
Claremore, OK 74017-3252
800-256-7511
www.rsu.edu

Southeastern Oklahoma State University
1405 North 4th Ave.
Durant, OK 74701-0609
800-435-1327
www.sosu.edu

Southern Nazarene University
6729 Northwest 39th Expwy.
Bethany, OK 73008
800-648-9899
www.snu.edu

Southwestern Christian University
PO Box 340
Bethany, OK 73008-0340
405-789-7661
www.swcu.edu

Southwestern Oklahoma State University
100 Campus Dr.
Weatherford, OK 73096-3098
580-774-3782
www.swosu.edu

St. Gregory's University
1900 West MacArthur Dr.
Shawnee, OK 74804-2499
888-STGREGS
www.stgregorys.edu

University of Central Oklahoma
100 North University Dr.
Edmond, OK 73034-5209
800-254-4215
www.ucok.edu

University of Oklahoma
660 Parrington Oval
Norman, OK 73019-0390
800-234-6868
www.ou.edu

University of Oklahoma Health Sciences Center
PO Box 26901
Oklahoma City, OK 73190
405-271-2359
www.ouhsc.edu

University of Phoenix–Oklahoma City Campus
6501 North Brd.way Extension, Ste. 100
Oklahoma City, OK 73116-8244
800-228-7240
www.phoenix.edu

University of Phoenix–Tulsa Campus
10810 East 45th St., Ste. 103
Tulsa, OK 74146-3801
800-228-7240
www.phoenix.edu

University of Science and Arts of Oklahoma
1727 West Alabama
Chickasha, OK 73018
800-933-8726
www.usao.edu

University of Tulsa
600 South College Ave.
Tulsa, OK 74104-3189
800-331-3050
www.utulsa.edu

South Dakota

Augustana College
2001 South Summit Ave.
Sioux Falls, SD 57197
800-727-2844
www.augie.edu

Black Hills State University
1200 University St.
Spearfish, SD 57799
800-255-2478
www.bhsu.edu

Colorado Technical University Sioux Falls Campus
3901 West 59th St.
Sioux Falls, SD 57108
605-361-0200
www.ctu-siouxfalls.com

Dakota State University
820 North Washington
Madison, SD 57042-1799
888-DSU-9988
www.dsu.edu

Dakota Wesleyan University
1200 West University Ave.
Mitchell, SD 57301-4398
800-333-8506
www.dwu.edu

Mount Marty College
1105 West 8th St.
Yankton, SD 57078-3724
800-658-4552
www.mtmc.edu

National American University
321 Kansas City St.
Rapid City, SD 57701
800-843-8892
www.national.edu

National American University–Sioux Falls Branch
2801 South Kiwanis Ave.
Sioux Falls, SD 57105-4293
800-388-5430
www.national.edu

Northern State University
1200 South Jay St.
Aberdeen, SD 57401-7198
800-678-5330
www.northern.edu

Oglala Lakota College
490 Piya Wiconi Rd.
Kyle, SD 57752-0490
605-455-2321
www.olc.edu

Presentation College
1500 North Main St.
Aberdeen, SD 57401-1299
800-437-6060
www.presentation.edu

Si Tanka University
333 9th St. SW
Huron, SD 57350-2798
800-710-7159
www.sitanka.edu

Sinte Gleska University
PO Box 490
Rosebud, SD 57570-0490
605-747-2263
www.sinte.edu

South Dakota School of Mines and Technology
501 East Saint Joseph
Rapid City, SD 57701-3995
800-544-8162
www.sdsmt.edu

South Dakota State University
PO Box 2201
Brookings, SD 57007
800-952-3541
www.sdstate.edu

The University of South Dakota
414 East Clark St.
Vermillion, SD 57069-2390
877-269-6837
www.usd.edu

University of Sioux Falls
1101 West 22nd St.
Sioux Falls, SD 57105-1699
800-888-1047
www.usiouxfalls.edu

Wisconsin

Alverno College
3400 South 43rd St., PO Box 343922
Milwaukee, WI 53234-3922
800-933-3401
www.alverno.edu

Bellin College of Nursing
725 South Webster Ave, PO Box 23400
Green Bay, WI 54305-3400
800-236-8707
www.bcon.edu

Beloit College
700 College St.
Beloit, WI 53511-5596
800-9-BELOIT
www.beloit.edu

Cardinal Stritch University
6801 North Yates Rd.
Milwaukee, WI 53217-3985
800-347-8822
www.stritch.edu

Carroll College
100 North East Ave.
Waukesha, WI 53186-5593
800-CARROLL
www.cc.edu

Carthage College
2001 Alford Park Dr.
Kenosha, WI 53140-1994
800-351-4058
www.carthage.edu

Columbia College of Nursing
2121 East Newport Ave.
Milwaukee, WI 53211-2952
800-321-6265
www.ccon.edu

Concordia University Wisconsin
12800 North Lake Shore Dr.
Mequon, WI 53097-2402
888-628-9472
www.cuw.edu

Edgewood College
1000 Edgewood College Dr.
Madison, WI 53711-1997
800-444-4861
www.edgewood.edu

Lakeland College
PO Box 359
Sheboygan, WI 53082-0359
920-565-1588
www.lakeland.edu

Lawrence University
PO Box 599
Appleton, WI 54912-0599
800-227-0982
www.lawrence.edu

Maranatha Baptist Bible College
745 West Main St.
Watertown, WI 53094
800-622-2947
www.mbbc.edu

Marian College of Fond du Lac
45 South National Ave.
Fond du Lac, WI 54935-4699
920-923-7650
www.mariancollege.edu

Marquette University
PO Box 1881
Milwaukee, WI 53201-1881
800-222-6544
9615

Milwaukee Institute of Art and Design
273 East Erie St.
Milwaukee, WI 53202-6003
888-749-MIAD
www.miad.edu

Milwaukee School of Engineering
1025 North Brd.way
Milwaukee, WI 53202-3109
800-332-6763
www.msoe.edu

Mount Mary College
2900 North Menomonee River Pkwy
Milwaukee, WI 53222-4597
414-258-4810
www.mtmary.edu

Northland College
1411 Ellis Ave.
Ashland, WI 54806-3925
800-753-1040
www.northland.edu

Ripon College
300 Seward St., PO Box 248
Ripon, WI 54971
800-947-4766
www.ripon.edu

Silver Lake College
2406 South Alverno Rd.
Manitowoc, WI 54220-9319
920-684-5955
www.sl.edu

St. Norbert College
100 Grant St.
De Pere, WI 54115-2099
800-236-4878
www.snc.edu

University of Phoenix–Wisconsin Campus
20075 Watertower Blvd
Brookfield, WI 53045-6608
800-228-7240
www.phoenix.edu

University of Wisconsin–Eau Claire
PO Box 4004
Eau Claire, WI 54702-4004
715-836-5415
www.uwec.edu

University of Wisconsin–Green Bay
2420 Nicolet Dr.
Green Bay, WI 54311-7001
888-367-8942
www.uwgb.edu

University of Wisconsin–La Crosse
1725 State St.
La Crosse, WI 54601-3742
608-785-8939
www.uwlax.edu

University of Wisconsin–Madison
500 Lincoln Dr.
Madison, WI 53706-1380
608-262-3961
www.wisc.edu

University of Wisconsin–Milwaukee
PO Box 413
Milwaukee, WI 53201-0413
414-229-3800
www.uwm.edu

University of Wisconsin–Oshkosh
800 Algoma Blvd
Oshkosh, WI 54901
920-424-0202
www.uwosh.edu

University of Wisconsin–Parkside
900 Wood Rd., Box 2000
Kenosha, WI 53141-2000
262-595-2757
www.uwp.edu

University of Wisconsin–Platteville
1 University Plaza
Platteville, WI 53818-3099
800-362-5515
www.uwplatt.edu

University of Wisconsin–River Falls
410 South Third St.
River Falls, WI 54022-5001
715-425-3500
www.uwrf.edu

University of Wisconsin–Stevens Point
2100 Main St.
Stevens Point, WI 54481-3897
715-346-2441
www.uwsp.edu

University of Wisconsin–Stout
Menomonie, WI 54751
715-232-2639
www.uwstout.edu

University of Wisconsin–Superior
Belknap and Catlin, PO Box 2000
Superior, WI 54880-4500
715-394-8298
www.uwsuper.edu

University of Wisconsin–Whitewater
800 West Main St.
Whitewater, WI 53190-1790
262-472-1440
www.uww.edu

Viterbo University
900 Viterbo Dr.
La Crosse, WI 54601-4797
800-VITERBO
www.viterbo.edu

Wisconsin Lutheran College
8800 West Bluemound Rd.
Milwaukee, WI 53226-9942
888-WIS LUTH
www.wlc.edu

TWO-YEAR COLLEGES

Illinois

Black Hawk College
6600 34th Ave.
Moline, IL 61265-5899
309-796-5043
www.bhc.edu

Career Colleges of Chicago
11 East Adams St., 2nd Fl.
Chicago, IL 60603-6301
312-895-6217
www.careerchi.com

Carl Sandburg College
2400 Tom L. Wilson Blvd.
Galesburg, IL 61401-9576
309-341-5234
www.sandburg.edu

City Colleges of Chicago,
Harold Washington College
30 East Lake St.
Chicago, IL 60601-2449
312-553-6006
hwashington.ccc.edu

City Colleges of Chicago,
Harry S. Truman College
1145 West Wilson Ave.
Chicago, IL 60640-5616
773-907-4720
www.trumancollege.cc

City Colleges of Chicago,
Kennedy-King College
6800 South Wentworth Ave.
Chicago, IL 60621-3733
773-602-5080
kennedyking.ccc.edu

City Colleges of Chicago,
Malcolm X College
1900 West Van Buren St.
Chicago, IL 60612-3145
312-850-7120
malcolmx.ccc.edu

City Colleges of Chicago,
Olive-Harvey College
10001 South Woodlawn Ave.
Chicago, IL 60628-1645
773-291-6359
oliveharvey.ccc.edu

City Colleges of Chicago,
Richard J. Daley College
7500 South Pulaski Rd.
Chicago, IL 60652-1242
daley.ccc.edu

City Colleges of Chicago,
Wilbur Wright College
4300 N. Narragansett Ave.
Chicago, IL 60634-1591
773-481-8207
wright.ccc.edu

College of DuPage
425 Fawell Blvd.
Glen Ellyn, IL 60137-6599
630-942-2442
www.cod.edu

College of Lake County
19351 West Washington St.
Grayslake, IL 60030-1198
847-543-2384
www.clcillinois.edu

Danville Area Community
College
2000 East Main St.
Danville, IL 61832-5199
217-443-8800
www.dacc.cc.il.us

Elgin Community College
1700 Spartan Dr.
Elgin, IL 60123-7193
847-214-7914
www.elgin.edu

Fox College
4201 West 93rd St.
Oak Lawn, IL 60453
866-636-7711
www.foxcollege.com

Gem City College
PO Box 179
Quincy, IL 62301
217-222-0391
www.gemcitycollege.com

Heartland Community
College
1500 West Raab Rd.
Normal, IL 61761
309-268-8000
www.heartland.edu

Highland Community
College
2998 West Pearl City Rd.
Freeport, IL 61032-9341
815-235-6121
www.highland.edu

Illinois Central College
One College Dr.
East Peoria, IL 61635-0001
309-694-5784
www.icc.edu

Illinois Eastern Community
Colleges, Frontier
Community College
Frontier Dr.
Fairfield, IL 62837-2601
618-842-3711
www.iecc.edu/fcc/

Illinois Eastern Community
Colleges, Lincoln Trail
College
11220 State Hwy. 1
Robinson, IL 62454
618-544-8657
www.iecc.edu/ltc

Illinois Eastern Community
Colleges, Olney Central
College
305 North West St.
Olney, IL 62450
618-395-7777
www.iecc.edu/occ

Illinois Eastern Community
Colleges, Wabash Valley
College
2200 College Dr.
Mount Carmel, IL 62863-
2657
618-262-8641
www.iecc.edu/wvc

Illinois Valley Community
College
815 N. Orlando Smith Ave.
Oglesby, IL 61348-9692
815-224-0437
www.ivcc.edu

ITT Technical Institute
1401 Feehanville Dr.
Mount Prospect, IL 60056
847-375-8800
www.itt-tech.edu

ITT Technical Institute
600 Holiday Plaza Dr.
Matteson, IL 60443
708-747-2571
www.itt-tech.edu

ITT Technical Institute
7040 High Grove Blvd.
Burr Ridge, IL 60521
630-455-6470
www.itt-tech.edu

John A. Logan College
700 Logan College Rd.
Carterville, IL 62918-9900
618-985-3741
www.jal.cc.il.us

John Wood Community
College
1301 South 48th St.
Quincy, IL 62305-8736
217-641-4339
www.jwcc.edu

Joliet Junior College
1215 Houbolt Rd.
Joliet, IL 60431-8938
815-280-2493
www.jjc.edu

Kankakee Community
College
PO Box 888
Kankakee, IL 60901-0888
815-802-8520
www.kcc.cc.il.us

Kaskaskia College
27210 College Rd.
Centralia, IL 62801-7878
618-545-3066
www.kaskaskia.edu

Kishwaukee College
21193 Malta Rd.
Malta, IL 60150-9699
815-825-2086
www.kishwaukeecollege.edu

Lake Land College
5001 Lake Land Blvd.
Mattoon, IL 61938-9366
217-234-5378
www.lakelandcollege.edu

Lewis and Clark Community
College
5800 Godfrey Rd.
Godfrey, IL 62035-2466
618-468-5100
www.lc.edu

Lincoln College
300 Keokuk St.
Lincoln, IL 62656-1699
800-569-0556
www.lincolncollege.edu

Lincoln College
715 West Raab Rd.
Normal, IL 61761
800-569-0558
www.lincolncollege.edu/
normal/

Lincoln Land Community College
5250 Shepherd Rd.,
PO Box 19256
Springfield, IL 62794-9256
217-786-2243
www.llcc.cc.il.us

MacCormac College
506 South Wabash Ave.
Chicago, IL 60605-1667
312-922-1884
www.maccormac.edu

McHenry County College
8900 US Hwy. 14
Crystal Lake, IL 60012-2761
815-479-7620
www.mchenry.edu

Moraine Valley Community College
10900 South 88th Ave.
Palos Hills, IL 60465-0937
708-974-5346
www.morainevalley.edu

Morrison Institute of Technology
701 Portland Ave.
Morrison, IL 61270-0410
815-772-7218
www.morrison.tec.il.us

Morton College
3801 South Central Ave.
Cicero, IL 60804-4398
708-656-8000
www.morton.edu

Northwestern Business College
4829 North Lipps Ave.
Chicago, IL 60630-2298
800-396-5613
www.northwesternbc.edu

Oakton Community College
1600 East Golf Rd.
Des Plaines, IL 60016-1268
847-635-1629
www.oakton.edu

Parkland College
2400 West Bradley Ave.
Champaign, IL 61821-1899
217-351-2558
www.parkland.edu

Prairie State College
202 South Halsted St.
Chicago Heights, IL 60411-8226
708-709-3516
www.prairiestate.edu

Rend Lake College
468 North Ken Gray Parkway
Ina, IL 62846-9801
618-437-5321
www.rlc.edu

Richland Community College
One College Park
Decatur, IL 62521-8513
217-875-7200
www.richland.edu

Rock Valley College
3301 North Mulford Rd.
Rockford, IL 61114-5699
800-973-7821
www.rockvalleycollege.edu

Rockford Business College
730 North Church St.
Rockford, IL 61103
815-965-8616
www.rbcsuccess.com

Sauk Valley Community College
173 Illinois Route 2
Dixon, IL 61021
815-288-5511
www.svcc.edu

Shawnee Community College
8364 Shawnee College Rd.
Ullin, IL 62992-2206
618-634-3200
www.shawnee.cc.il.us

South Suburban College
15800 South State St.
South Holland, IL 60473-1270
708-596-2000
www.southsuburbancollege.edu

Southeastern Illinois College
3575 College Rd.
Harrisburg, IL 62946-4925
866-338-2742
www.sic.edu

Southwestern Illinois College
2500 Carlyle Rd.
Belleville, IL 62221-5899
618-235-2700
www.southwestern.cc.il.us

Spoon River College
23235 North County 22
Canton, IL 61520-9801
309-649-6305
www.spoonrivercollege.net

Springfield College in Illinois
1500 North Fifth St.
Springfield, IL 62702-2694
800-635-7289
www.sci.edu

Taylor Business Institute
200 North Michigan Ave., Ste. 301
Chicago, IL 60601

The College of Office Technology
1514-20 West Division St., Second Fl.
Chicago, IL 60622
773-278-0042
www.cotedu.edu

The Cooking and Hospitality Institute of Chicago
361 West Chestnut
Chicago, IL 60610-3050
312-873-2064
www.chicnet.org

Triton College
2000 5th Ave.
River Grove, IL 60171-1995
800-942-7404
www.triton.cc.il.us

Waubonsee Community College
Route 47 at Waubonsee Dr.
Sugar Grove, IL 60554-9799
630-466-7900
www.waubonsee.edu

Westwood College–Chicago Du Page
7155 Janes Ave.
Woodridge, IL 60517
630-434-8244
www.westwood.edu

Westwood College–Chicago Loop Campus
17 N. State St., Ste. 1500
Chicago, IL 60602
312-739-0850
www.westwood.edu

Westwood College–Chicago O'Hare Airport
4825 N. Scott St., Ste. 100
Schiller Park, IL 60176
847-928-0200
www.westwood.edu

Westwood College–Chicago River Oaks
80 River Oaks Dr., Ste. D-49
Calumet City, IL 60409
708-832-1988
www.westwood.edu

William Rainey Harper College
1200 West Algonquin Rd.
Palatine, IL 60067-7398
847-925-6206
www.harpercollege.edu

Worsham College of Mortuary Science
495 Northgate Parkway
Wheeling, IL 60090-2646
847-808-8444
www.worshamcollege.com

Indiana

American Trans Air Aviation Training Academy
7251 West McCarty St.
Indianapolis, IN 46241
800-241-9699
www.aviationtraining.net/

Ancilla College
Union Rd., PO Box 1
Donaldson, IN 46513
574-936-8898
www.ancilla.edu

College of Court Reporting
111 West Tenth St., Ste. 111
Hobart, IN 46342
219-942-1459
www.ccredu.com

Commonwealth Business College
325 East US Hwy. 20
Michigan City, IN 46360
219-877-3100
www.cbcaec.com

Commonwealth Business College
1000 E. 80th Place, Ste. 101, N
Merrillville, IN 46410
219-769-3321
www.cbcaec.com

Davenport University
7121 Grape Rd.
Granger, IN 46530
800-277-8447
www.davenport.edu

Holy Cross College
PO Box 308,
54515 State Rd., 933 North
Notre Dame, IN 46556-0308
574-239-8400
www.hcc-nd.edu

Indiana Business College
411 West Riggin Rd.
Muncie, IN 47303
800-IBC-GRAD
www.ibcschools.edu

Indiana Business College
550 East Washington St.
Indianapolis, IN 46204
800-IBC-GRAD
www.ibcschools.edu

International Business College
5699 Covington Lane
Fort Wayne, IN 46804
800-589-6363
www.ibcfortwayne.edu

International Business College
7205 Shadeland Station
Indianapolis, IN 46256
317-213-2320
www.intlbusinesscollege.com

ITT Technical Institute
4919 Coldwater Rd.
Fort Wayne, IN 46825-5532
800-866-4488
www.itt-tech.edu

ITT Technical Institute
10999 Stahl Rd.
Newburgh, IN 47630-7430
812-858-1600
www.itt-tech.edu

ITT Technical Institute
9511 Angola Court
Indianapolis, IN 46268-1119
800-937-4488
www.itt-tech.edu

Ivy Tech State College–Bloomington
3116 Canterbury Court
Bloomington, IN 47404
812-332-1559
www.ivytech.edu

Ivy Tech State College–Central Indiana
1 West 26th St., PO Box 1763
Indianapolis, IN 46206-1763
317-921-4882
www.ivytech.edu

Ivy Tech State College–Columbus
4475 Central Ave.
Columbus, IN 47203-1868
800-922-4838
www.ivytech.edu

Ivy Tech State College–Eastcentral
4301 South Cowan Rd., PO Box 3100
Muncie, IN 47302-9448
765-289-2291
www.ivytech.edu

Ivy Tech State College–Kokomo
1815 East Morgan St, PO Box 1373
Kokomo, IN 46903-1373
765-459-0561
www.ivytech.edu

Ivy Tech State College–Lafayette
3101 South Creasy Lane
Lafayette, IN 47905-5266
765-772-9116
www.ivytech.edu

Ivy Tech State College–North Central
220 Dean Johnson Blvd.
South Bend, IN 46601
574-289-7001
www.ivytech.edu

Ivy Tech State College–Northeast
3800 North Anthony Blvd.
Fort Wayne, IN 46805-1430
800-859-4882
www.ivytech.edu

Ivy Tech State College–Northwest
1440 East 35th Ave.
Gary, IN 46409-1499
219-981-1111
www.ivytech.edu

Ivy Tech State College–Southcentral
8204 Hwy. 311
Sellersburg, IN 47172-1829
812-246-3301
www.ivytech.edu

Ivy Tech State College–Southeast
590 Ivy Tech Dr., PO Box 209
Madison, IN 47250-1883
812-265-2580
www.ivytech.edu

Ivy Tech State College–Southwest
3501 First Ave.
Evansville, IN 47710-3398
812-429-1430
www.ivytech.edu

Ivy Tech State College–Wabash Valley
7999 US Hwy. 41, South
Terre Haute, IN 47802
812-298-2300
www.ivytech.edu

Ivy Tech State College–Whitewater
2325 Chester Blvd.
Richmond, IN 47374-1220
765-966-2656
www.ivytech.edu

Lincoln Technical Institute
1201 Stadium Dr.
Indianapolis, IN 46202-2194
800-554-4465
www.lincolntech.com

Mid-America College of Funeral Service
3111 Hamburg Pike
Jeffersonville, IN 47130-9630
800-221-6158
www.mid-america.edu

Professional Careers Institute
7302 Woodland Dr.
Indianapolis, IN 46278
317-299-6001
www.pcicareers.com

Sawyer College
6040 Hohman Ave.
Hammond, IN 46320
219-844-0100
www.sawyercollege.edu

The Brown Mackie College–South Bend Campus
1030 East Jefferson Blvd.
South Bend, IN 46617-3123
800-743-2447
www.brownmackie.edu/locations.asp?locid=2

Vincennes University
1002 North First St.
Vincennes, IN 47591-5202
812-888-4313
www.vinu.edu

Vincennes University Jasper Campus
850 College Ave.
Jasper, IN 47546-9393
800-809-VUJC
vujc.vinu.edu

Iowa

AIB College of Business
2500 Fleur Dr.
Des Moines, IA 50321-1799
800-444-1921
www.aib.edu

Clinton Community College
1000 Lincoln Blvd.
Clinton, IA 52732-6299
563-244-7007
www.eicc.edu/ccc/

Des Moines Area Community College
2006 South Ankeny Blvd.
Ankeny, IA 50021-8995
515-964-6216
www.dmacc.edu

Ellsworth Community College
1100 College Ave.
Iowa Falls, IA 50126-1199
800-ECC-9235
www.iavalley.cc.ia.us/ecc/

Hamilton College
3165 Edgewood Parkway, SW
Cedar Rapids, IA 52404
800-728-0481
www.hamiltonia.edu

Hawkeye Community College
PO Box 8015
Waterloo, IA 50704-8015
800-670-4769
www.hawkeyecollege.edu

Indian Hills Community College
525 Grandview Ave., Building #1
Ottumwa, IA 52501-1398
800-726-2585
www.ihcc.cc.ia.us

Iowa Central Community College
330 Ave. M
Fort Dodge, IA 50501-5798
515-576-0099
www.iccc.cc.ia.us

Iowa Lakes Community College
19 South 7th St.
Estherville, IA 51334-2295
800-521-5054
www.iowalakes.edu

Iowa Western Community College
2700 College Rd., Box 4-C
Council Bluffs, IA 51502
800-432-5852
www.iwcc.edu

Kaplan College
1801 East Kimberly Rd., Ste. 1
Davenport, IA 52807-2095
563-441-2496
www.kaplancollegeia.com

Kirkwood Community College
PO Box 2068
Cedar Rapids, IA 52406-2068
800-332-2055
www.kirkwood.cc.ia.us

Marshalltown Community College
3700 South Center St.
Marshalltown, IA 50158-4760
866-622-4748
www.marshalltowncommunitycollege.com/

Muscatine Community College
152 Colorado St.
Muscatine, IA 52761-5396
563-288-6012
www.eicc.edu

North Iowa Area Community College
500 College Dr.
Mason City, IA 50401-7299
888-GO NIACC
www.niacc.edu

Northeast Iowa Community College
Box 400
Calmar, IA 52132-0480
800-728-CALMAR
www.nicc.edu

Northwest Iowa Community College
603 West Park St.
Sheldon, IA 51201-1046
800-352-4907
www.nwicc.edu

Scott Community College
500 Belmont Rd.
Bettendorf, IA 52722-6804
563-441-4007
www.eicc.edu/scc/

Southeastern Community College, North Campus
1500 West Agency St.,
PO Box 180
West Burlington, IA 52655-0180
319-752-2731
www.secc.cc.ia.us

Southeastern Community College, South Campus
335 Messenger Rd.,
PO Box 6007
Keokuk, IA 52632-6007
319-752-2731
www.secc.cc.ia.us

Southwestern Community College
1501 West Townline St.
Creston, IA 50801
800-247-4023
www.swcc.cc.ia.us

St. Luke's College
2720 Stone Park Blvd.
Sioux City, IA 51104
800-352-4660
stlukescollege.org

Vatterott College
6100 Thornton Ave., Ste. 290
Des Moines, IA 50321
800-353-7264
www.vatterott-college.edu

Western Iowa Tech Community College
4647 Stone Ave.,
PO Box 5199
Sioux City, IA 51102-5199
712-274-6400
www.witcc.com

Kansas

Allen County Community College
1801 North Cottonwood St.
Iola, KS 66749-1607
620-365-5116
www.allencc.net

Barton County Community College
245 Northeast 30th Rd.
Great Bend, KS 67530-9283
800-722-6842
www.bartonccc.edu

Butler County Community College
901 South Haverhill Rd.
El Dorado, KS 67042-3280
316-321-2222
www.butlercc.edu

Cloud County Community College
2221 Campus Dr.,
PO Box 1002
Concordia, KS 66901-1002
800-729-5101
www.cloud.edu

Coffeyville Community College
400 West 11th St.
Coffeyville, KS 67337-5063
620-251-7700
www.coffeyville.edu

Colby Community College
1255 South Range
Colby, KS 67701-4099
785-462-4690
www.colbycc.edu

Cowley County Community College and Area Vocational–Technical School
125 South Second,
PO Box 1147
Arkansas City, KS 67005-1147
800-593-CCCC
www.cowley.cc.ks.us

Dodge City Community College
2501 North 14th Ave.
Dodge City, KS 67801-2399
316-225-1321
www.dccc.cc.ks.us

Donnelly College
608 North 18th St.
Kansas City, KS 66102-4298
913-621-8769
www.donnelly.edu

Fort Scott Community College
2108 South Horton
Fort Scott, KS 66701
800-874-3722
www.fortscott.edu

Garden City Community College
801 Campus Dr.
Garden City, KS 67846-6399
620-276-7611
www.gcccks.edu

Hesston College
Box 3000
Hesston, KS 67062-2093
800-995-2757
www.hesston.edu

Highland Community College
606 West Main St.
Highland, KS 66035
785-442-6020
www.highlandcc.edu

Hutchinson Community College and Area Vocational School
1300 North Plum St.
Hutchinson, KS 67501-5894
800-289-3501
www.hutchcc.edu

Independence Community College
Brookside Dr. and College Ave.,
PO Box 708
Independence, KS 67301-0708
800-842-6063
www.indycc.edu

Johnson County Community College
12345 College Blvd.
Overland Park, KS 66210-1299
913-469-8500
www.johnco.cc.ks.us

Kansas City Kansas Community College
7250 State Ave.
Kansas City, KS 66112-3003
913-288-7694
www.kckcc.edu

Labette Community College
200 South 14th St.
Parsons, KS 67357-4299
620-421-6700
www.labette.edu

Manhattan Area Technical College
3136 Dickens Ave.
Manhattan, KS 66503-2499
800-352-7575
www.matc.net

Neosho County Community College
800 West 14th St.
Chanute, KS 66720-2699
800-729-6222
www.neosho.edu

North Central Kansas Technical College
PO Box 507
Beloit, KS 67420
800-658-4655
www.ncktc.tec.ks.us

Pratt Community College
348 NE State Rd. 61
Pratt, KS 67124-8317
620-672-5641
www.prattcc.edu

Seward County Community College
PO Box 1137
Liberal, KS 67905-1137
800-373-9951
www.sccc.edu

The Brown Mackie College
2106 South 9th St.
Salina, KS 67401-2810
800-365-0433
www.bmcaec.com

The Brown Mackie College–Lenexa Campus
9705 Lenexa Dr.
Lenexa, KS 66215
800-635-9101
www.bmcaec.com

Wichita Area Technical College
301 South Grove St.
Wichita, KS 67211
316-677-9559
www.wichitatech.com

Michigan

Alpena Community College
666 Johnson St.
Alpena, MI 49707-1495
989-358-7339
www.alpenacc.edu

Bay de Noc Community College
2001 North Lincoln Rd.
Escanaba, MI 49829-2511
800-221-2001
www.baydenoc.cc.mi.us

Bay Mills Community College
12214 West Lakeshore Dr.
Brimley, MI 49715
800-844-BMCC
www.bmcc.edu

Davenport University
3930 Traxler Court
Bay City, MI 48706
800-968-4416
www.davenport.edu

Davenport University
3555 East Patrick Rd.
Midland, MI 48642
800-968-4860
www.davenport.edu

Delta College
1961 Delta Rd.
University Center, MI 48710
989-686-9449
www.delta.edu

Glen Oaks Community College
62249 Shimmel Rd.
Centreville, MI 49032-9719
888-994-7818
www.glenoaks.edu

Gogebic Community College
E-4946 Jackson Rd.
Ironwood, MI 49938
906-932-4231
www.gogebic.edu

Grand Rapids Community College
143 Bostwick Ave., NE
Grand Rapids, MI 49503-3201
616-234-4100
www.grcc.edu

Henry Ford Community College
5101 Evergreen Rd.
Dearborn, MI 48128-1495
313-845-9615
www.hfcc.edu

ITT Technical Institute
4020 Sparks Dr., SE
Grand Rapids, MI 49546
616-956-1060
www.itt-tech.edu

ITT Technical Institute
1522 East Big Beaver Rd.
Troy, MI 48083-1905
248-524-1800
www.itt-tech.edu

ITT Technical Institute
1905 South Haggerty Rd.
Canton, MI 48188-2025
800-247-4477
www.itt-tech.edu

Jackson Community College
2111 Emmons Rd.
Jackson, MI 49201-8399
888-522-7344
www.jackson.cc.mi.us

Kalamazoo Valley Community College
PO Box 4070
Kalamazoo, MI 49003-4070
269-488-4207
www.kvcc.edu

Kellogg Community College
450 North Ave.
Battle Creek, MI 49017-3397
269-965-3931
www.kellogg.edu

Kirtland Community College
10775 North St Helen Rd.
Roscommon, MI 48653-9699
989-275-5000
www.kirtland.edu

Lake Michigan College
2755 East Napier
Benton Harbor, MI 49022-1899
269-927-8198
www.lmc.cc.mi.us

Lansing Community College
PO Box 40010
Lansing, MI 48901-7210
800-644-4LCC
www.lcc.edu

Lewis College of Business
17370 Meyers Rd.
Detroit, MI 48235-1423
313-862-6300
www.lewiscollege.edu

Macomb Community College
14500 East Twelve Mile Rd.
Warren, MI 48088-3896
866-622-6624
www.macomb.edu

Mid Michigan Community College
1375 South Clare Ave.
Harrison, MI 48625-9447
989-386-6660
www.midmich.cc.mi.us

Monroe County Community College
1555 South Raisinville Rd.
Monroe, MI 48161-9047
734-384-4261
www.monroeccc.edu

Montcalm Community College
2800 College Dr.
Sidney, MI 48885-9723
989-328-1206
www.montcalm.edu

Mott Community College
1401 East Court St.
Flint, MI 48503-2089
810-762-0316
www.mcc.edu

Muskegon Community College
221 South Quarterline Rd.
Muskegon, MI 49442-1493
231-777-0261
www.muskegon.cc.mi.us

North Central Michigan College
1515 Howard St.
Petoskey, MI 49770-8717
888-298-6605
www.ncmc.cc.mi.us

Northwestern Michigan College
1701 East Front St.
Traverse City, MI 49686-3061
800-748-0566
www.nmc.edu

Oakland Community College
2480 Opdyke Rd.
Bloomfield Hills, MI 48304-2266
248-341-2186
www.oaklandcc.edu

Saginaw Chippewa Tribal College
2274 Enterprise Dr.
Mount Pleasant, MI 48858
989-775-4123
www.sagchip.org/tribal college

Schoolcraft College
18600 Haggerty Rd.
Livonia, MI 48152-2696
734-462-4426
www.schoolcraft.edu

Southwestern Michigan College
58900 Cherry Grove Rd.
Dowagiac, MI 49047-9793
800-456-8675
www.swmich.edu

St. Clair County Community College
323 Erie St., PO Box 5015
Port Huron, MI 48061-5015
810-989-5500
www.sc4.edu

Washtenaw Community College
4800 East Huron River Dr., PO Box D-1
Ann Arbor, MI 48106
734-973-3315
www.wccnet.edu

Wayne County Community College District
801 West Fort St.
Detroit, MI 48226-3010
313-496-2884
www.wcccd.edu

West Shore Community College
PO Box 277, 3000 North Stiles Rd.
Scottville, MI 49454-0277
231-845-6211
www.westshore.edu/

Minnesota

Academy College
1101 East 78th St., Ste. 100
Minneapolis, MN 55420
800-292-9149
www.academycollege.edu

Alexandria Technical College
1601 Jefferson St.
Alexandria, MN 56308-3707
888-234-1222
www.alextech.edu

Anoka Technical College
1355 West Hwy. 10
Anoka, MN 55303
763-576-4746
www.ank.tec.mn.us

Anoka-Ramsey Community College
11200 Mississippi Blvd., NW
Coon Rapids, MN 55433-3470
763-427-2600
www.anokaramsey.edu

Anoka-Ramsey Community College, Cambridge Campus
300 Polk St. South
Cambridge, MN 55008-5706
763-689-7028
www.anokaramsey.edu

Brown College
1440 Northland Dr.
Mendota Heights, MN 55120
800-6BROWN6
www.browncollege.edu

Central Lakes College
501 West College Dr.
Brainerd, MN 56401-3904
218-828-2525
www.clcmn.edu

Century College
3300 Century Ave. North
White Bear Lake, MN 55110
800-228-1978
www.century.cc.mn.us

Dakota County Technical College
1300 East 145th St.
Rosemount, MN 55068
877-YES-DCTC
www.dctc.edu

Duluth Business University
4724 Mike Colalillo Dr.
Duluth, MN 55807
800-777-8406
www.dbumn.edu

Dunwoody College of Technology
818 Dunwoody Blvd.
Minneapolis, MN 55403
800-292-4625
www.dunwoody.edu

Fond du Lac Tribal and Community College
2101 14th St.
Cloquet, MN 55720
800-657-3712
www.fdltcc.edu

Globe College
7166 North 10th St.
Oakdale, MN 55128
651-714-7313
www.globecollege.com

Hennepin Technical College
9000 Brooklyn Blvd.
Brooklyn Park, MN 55445
763-488-2415
www.hennepintech.edu

Herzing College, Lakeland Medical–Dental Division
5700 West Brd.way
Minneapolis, MN 55428
763-535-3000
us.herzing.edu/lakeland

Herzing College, Minneapolis Drafting School Division
5700 West Brd.way
Minneapolis, MN 55428
800-878-DRAW
www.herzing.edu

Hibbing Community College
1515 East 25th St.
Hibbing, MN 55746-3300
800-224-4HCC
www.hcc.mnscu.edu

Inver Hills Community College
2500 East 80th St.
Inver Grove Heights, MN 55076-3224
651-450-8572
www.ih.cc.mn.us

Itasca Community College
1851 Hwy. 169 East
Grand Rapids, MN 55744
800-996-6422
www.itascacc.edu

Lake Superior College
2101 Trinity Rd.
Duluth, MN 55811
800-432-2884
www.lsc.mnscu.edu

Leech Lake Tribal College
PO Box 180
Cass Lake, MN 56633-0180
888-829-4240
www.lltc.org

Mesabi Range Community and Technical College
1001 Chestnut St. West
Virginia, MN 55792-3448
218-749-0314
www.mr.mnscu.edu

Minneapolis Business College
1711 West County Rd. B
Roseville, MN 55113
800-279-5200
www.mplsbusinesscollege.com

Minneapolis Community and Technical College
1501 Hennepin Ave.
Minneapolis, MN 55403-1779
612-659-1328
www.mctc.mnscu.edu

Minnesota School of Business–Brooklyn Center
5910 Shingle Creek Parkway
Brooklyn Center, MN 55430
763-585-7777
www.msbcollege.edu

Minnesota School of Business–Plymouth
1455 Country Rd. 101 North
Minneapolis, MN 55447
763-476-2000
www.msbcollege.edu

Minnesota School of Business–Richfield
1401 West 76th St.
Richfield, MN 55423
612-861-2000
www.msbcollege.edu

Minnesota State College–Southeast Technical
1250 Homer Rd., PO Box 409
Winona, MN 55987
800-372-8164
www.southeastmn.edu

Minnesota State Community and Technical College–Fergus Falls
1414 College Way
Fergus Falls, MN 56537-1009
888-MY-MSCTC
www.minnesota.edu

Minnesota West Community and Technical College
1314 North Hiawatha Ave.
Pipestone, MN 56164
800-658-2330
www.mnwest.mnscu.edu

Musictech College
19 Exchange St. East
Saint Paul, MN 55101
800-594-9500
www.musictech.edu

Normandale Community College
9700 France Ave. South
Bloomington, MN 55431-4399
866-880-8740
www.normandale.edu

North Hennepin Community College
7411 85th Ave. North
Brooklyn Park, MN 55445-2231
763-424-0713
www.nhcc.mnscu.edu

Northland Community and Technical College–Thief River Falls
1101 Hwy. One East
Thief River Falls, MN 56701
800-959-6282
www.northlandcollege.edu

Northwest Technical College
905 Grant Ave., SE
Bemidji, MN 56601-4907
800-942-8324
bemidji.ntcmn.edu

Northwest Technical Institute
11995 Singletree Lane
Eden Prairie, MN 55344-5351
800-443-4223
www.nti.edu

Pine Technical College
900 4th St. SE
Pine City, MN 55063
800-521-7463
www.ptc.tec.mn.us

Rainy River Community College
1501 Hwy. 71
International Falls, MN 56649
800-456-3996
www.rrcc.mnscu.edu

Rasmussen College Eagan
3500 Federal Dr.
Eagan, MN 55122-1346
800-852-6367
www.rasmussen.edu

Rasmussen College Mankato
501 Holly Lane
Mankato, MN 56001-6803
507-625-6556
www.rasmussen.edu

Rasmussen College Minnetonka
12450 Wayzata Blvd., Ste. 315
Minnetonka, MN 55305-1928
952-545-2000
www.rasmussen.edu

Rasmussen College St. Cloud
226 Park Ave. South
St. Cloud, MN 56301-3713
320-251-5600
www.rasmussen.edu

Ridgewater College
PO Box 1097
Willmar, MN 56201-1097
800-722-1151
www.ridgewater.mnscu.edu

Riverland Community College
1900 8th Ave., NW
Austin, MN 55912
800-247-5039
www.riverland.cc.mn.us

Rochester Community and Technical College
851 30th Ave., SE
Rochester, MN 55904-4999
507-280-3509
www.roch.edu

Saint Paul College–A Community & Technical College
235 Marshall Ave.
St. Paul, MN 55102-1800
800-227-6029
www.saintpaul.edu

South Central Technical College
1920 Lee Blvd.
North Mankato, MN 56003
507-389-7334
www.sctc.mnscu.edu

St. Cloud Technical College
1540 Northway Dr.
St. Cloud, MN 56303-1240
320-308-5089
www.sctc.edu

Vermilion Community College
1900 East Camp St.
Ely, MN 55731-1996
800-657-3608
www.vcc.edu/

Missouri

Allied College
500 Northwest Plaza Tower, Ste. 400
Saint Ann, MO 63074
314-739-4450
www.alliedmedicalcollege.com

Blue River Community College
1501 West Jefferson St.
Blue Springs, MO 64015
816-655-6118
www.kcmetro.edu

Cottey College
1000 West Austin
Nevada, MO 64772
888-526-8839
www.cottey.edu

Crowder College
601 Laclede Ave.
Neosho, MO 64850-9160
866-238-7788
www.crowdercollege.net

East Central College
1964 Prairie Dell Rd.
Union, MO 63084
636-583-5195
www.eastcentral.edu

Hickey College
940 West Port Plaza, Ste. 101
St. Louis, MO 63146
800-777-1544
www.hickeycollege.com

IHM Health Studies Center
2500 Abbott Place
St. Louis, MO 63143-2636
314-768-1234
www.ihmhealthstudies.com

ITT Technical Institute
1930 Meyer Drury Dr.
Arnold, MO 63010
888-488-1082
www.itt-tech.edu

ITT Technical Institute
13505 Lakefront Dr.
Earth City, MO 63045-1412
800-235-5488
www.itt-tech.edu

Jefferson College
1000 Viking Dr.
Hillsboro, MO 63050-2441
636-797-3000
www.jeffco.edu

Linn State Technical College
One Technology Dr.
Linn, MO 65051-9606
800-743-TECH
www.linnstate.edu

Longview Community College
500 Southwest Longview Rd.
Lee's Summit, MO 64081-2105
816-672-2249
www.kcmetro.edu

Maple Woods Community College
2601 Northeast Barry Rd.
Kansas City, MO 64156-1299
816-437-3108
www.kcmetro.edu

Metro Business College
1202 East State Route 72
Rolla, MO 65401
800-467-0785
www.metrobusinesscollege.edu

Metro Business College
1732 North Kingshwy.
Cape Girardeau, MO 63701
573-334-9181
www.metrobusinesscollege.edu

Metro Business College
1407 Southwest Blvd.
Jefferson City, MO 65109
800-467-0786
www.metrobusinesscollege.edu

Metropolitan Community College-Business & Technology College
1775 Universal Ave.
Kansas City, MO 64120
800-841-7158
www.mccbtc.com

Midwest Institute
10910 Manchester Rd.
Kirkwood, MO 63122
www.midwestinstitute.com

Mineral Area College
PO Box 1000
Park Hills, MO 63601-1000
573-518-2206
www.mineralarea.edu

Missouri College
10121 Manchester Rd.
St. Louis, MO 63122-1583
314-821-7700
www.mocollege.com

Moberly Area Community College
101 College Ave.
Moberly, MO 65270-1304
800-622-2070
www.macc.edu

North Central Missouri College
1301 Main St.
Trenton, MO 64683-1824
800-880-6180
www.ncmc.cc.mo.us

Ozarks Technical Community College
PO Box 5958
Springfield, MO 65801
417-895-7136
www.otc.edu

Patricia Stevens College
330 N. Fourth St., Ste. 306
St. Louis, MO 63102
800-871-0949
www.patriciastevens
college.edu

Penn Valley Community
College
3201 Southwest Trafficway
Kansas City, MO 64111
816-759-4101
www.kcmetro.edu

Pinnacle Career Institute
15329 Kensington Ave.
Kansas City, MO 64147-1212
816-331-5700
www.pcitraining.edu

Ranken Technical College
4431 Finney Ave.
St. Louis, MO 63113
866-4RANKEN
www.ranken.edu

Saint Charles Community
College
4601 Mid Rivers Mall Dr.
St. Peters, MO 63376-0975
636-922-8229
www.stchas.edu

Sanford-Brown College
75 Village Square
Hazelwood, MO 63042
314-731-5200
www.sanford-brown.edu

Sanford-Brown College
1203 Smizer Mill Rd.
Fenton, MO 63026
800-456-7222
www.sanford-brown.edu

Sanford-Brown College
3555 Franks Dr.
St. Charles, MO 63301
636-949-2620
www.sanford-brown.edu

Sanford-Brown College
520 East 19th Ave.
North Kansas City, MO 64116
800-456-7222
www.sanford-brown.edu

Southeast Missouri Hospital
College of Nursing and
Health Sciences
1819 Broadway
Cape Girardeau, MO 63701
534-334-6825
www.southeastmissouri
hospital.com/college/

Southwest Missouri State
University–West Plains
128 Garfield
West Plains, MO 65775
417-255-7955
www.wp.smsu.edu

Springfield College
1010 West Sunshine
Springfield, MO 65807-2488
800-475-2669
www.Springfield-college.
com

St. Louis Community
College at Florissant Valley
3400 Pershall Rd.
St. Louis, MO 63135-1499
314-595-4258
www.stlcc.edu

St. Louis Community
College at Forest Park
5600 Oakland Ave.
St. Louis, MO 63110-1316
314-644-9131
www.stlcc.edu

St. Louis Community
College at Meramec
11333 Big Bend Blvd.
Kirkwood, MO 63122-5720
314-984-7609
www.stlcc.edu

State Fair Community
College
3201 West 16th St.
Sedalia, MO 65301-2199
877-311-SFCC
www.sfcc.cc.mo.us

Three Rivers Community
College
2080 Three Rivers Blvd.
Poplar Bluff, MO 63901-2393
573-840-9604
www.trcc.edu

Vatterott College
3925 Industrial Dr.
St. Ann, MO 63074-1807
800-345-6018
www.vatterott-college.edu

Vatterott College
12970 Maurer Industrial Dr.
St. Louis, MO 63127
314-843-4200
www.vatterott-college.edu

Vatterott College
3131 Frederick Ave.
St. Joseph, MO 64506
800-282-5327
www.vatterott-college.com

Vatterott College
1258 East Trafficway St.
Springfield, MO 65802
800-766-5829
www.vatterott-college.com

Wentworth Military
Academy and Junior College
1880 Washington Ave.
Lexington, MO 64067
660-259-2221
www.wma1880.org

Nebraska

Central Community
College–Columbus Campus
4500 63rd St., PO Box 1027
Columbus, NE 68602-1027
402-562-1296
www.cccneb.edu

Central Community College–
Grand Island Campus
PO Box 4903
Grand Island, NE 68802-4903
308-398-7406
www.cccneb.edu

Central Community College–
Hastings Campus
PO Box 1024
Hastings, NE 68902-1024
402-461-2428
www.cccneb.edu

Hamilton College-Lincoln
1821 K St., PO Box 82826
Lincoln, NE 68501-2826
402-474-5315
www.hamiltonlincoln.com

Hamilton College-Omaha
3350 North 90th St.
Omaha, NE 68134
800-642-1456
www.hamiltonomaha.edu

ITT Technical Institute
9814 M St.
Omaha, NE 68127-2056
800-677-9260
www.itt-tech.edu

Little Priest Tribal College
PO Box 270
Winnebago, NE 68071
402-878-2380
www.lptc.bia.edu

Metropolitan Community
College
PO Box 3777
Omaha, NE 68103-0777
800-228-9553
www.mccneb.edu

Mid-Plains Community
College
601 West State Farm Rd.
North Platte, NE 69101
800-658-4348
www.mpcca.cc.ne.us

Myotherapy Institute
6020 South 58th St.
Lincoln, NE 68516
800-896-3363
www.myomassage.net

Nebraska College of
Technical Agriculture
RR3, Box 23A
Curtis, NE 69025-9205
800-3CURTIS
www.ncta.unl.edu

Nebraska Indian Community
College
PO Box 428
Macy, NE 68039-0428
888-843-6432
www.thenicc.edu

Northeast Community
College
801 East Benjamin Ave,
PO Box 469
Norfolk, NE 68702-0469
402-844-7258
www.northeastcollege.com

Southeast Community
College, Beatrice Campus
4771 W. Scott Rd.
Beatrice, NE 68310-7042
800-233-5027
www.southeast.edu

Southeast Community
College, Lincoln Campus
8800 O St.
Lincoln, NE 68520-1299
800-642-4075
www.southeast.edu

Southeast Community
College, Milford Campus
600 State St.
Milford, NE 68405-8498
800-933-7223
www.southeast.edu

The Creative Center
10850 Emmet St.
Omaha, NE 68164
888-898-1789
www.thecreativecenter.com

Vatterott College
225 North 80th St.
Omaha, NE 68114
402-392-1300
www.vatterott-college.edu

Western Nebraska
Community College
371 College Dr.
Sidney, NE 69162
800-348-4435
www.wncc.net

North Dakota

Aakers Business College
4012 19th Ave., SW
Fargo, ND 58103
800-817-0009
www.aakers-college.com

Bismarck State College
PO Box 5587
Bismarck, ND 58506-5587
800-445-5073
www.bismarckstate.edu

Cankdeska Cikana
Community College
PO Box 269
Fort Totten, ND 58335-0269
701-766-1342
www.littlehoop.cc

Fort Berthold Community
College
PO Box 490
New Town, ND 58763-0490
701-627-3665
www.fbcc.bia.edu

Lake Region State College
1801 College Dr. North
Devils Lake, ND 58301-1598
800-443-1313
www.lrsc.nodak.edu

Minot State University–
Bottineau Campus
105 Simrall Blvd.
Bottineau, ND 58318-1198
800-542-6866
www.misu-b.nodak.edu

North Dakota State College
of Science
800 North Sixth St.
Wahpeton, ND 58076
800-342-4325
www.ndscs.nodak.edu

Sitting Bull College
1341 92nd St.
Fort Yates, ND 58538-9701
701-854-3864
www.sittingbull.edu

Turtle Mountain Community
College
Box 340
Belcourt, ND 58316-0340
701-477-5605
www.turtle-mountain.
cc.nd.us

United Tribes Technical
College
3315 University Dr.
Bismarck, ND 58504-7596
701-255-3285
www.uttc.edu

Williston State College
Box 1326
Williston, ND 58802-1326
888-863-9455
www.wsc.nodak.edu

Ohio

Academy of Court Reporting
2044 Euclid Ave.
Cleveland, OH 44115
216-861-3222
www.acr.edu

AEC Southern Ohio College
1320 West Maple St., NW
North Canton, OH 44720-
2854
330-494-1214
www.socaec.com

AEC Southern Ohio College,
Akron Campus
2791 Mogadore Rd.
Akron, OH 44312-1596
330-733-8766
www.socaec.com

AEC Southern Ohio College,
Findlay Campus
1637 Tiffin Ave.
Findlay, OH 45840
800-842-3687
www.socaec.com

Antonelli College
124 East Seventh St.
Cincinnati, OH 45202-2592
800-505-4338
www.antonellic.com

Belmont Technical College
120 Fox Shannon Place
St. Clairsville, OH 43950-
9735
740-695-9500
www.btc.edu

Bowling Green State
University–Firelands College
One University Dr.
Huron, OH 44839-9791
419-433-5560
www.firelands.bgsu.edu

Bradford School
2469 Stelzer Rd.
Columbus, OH 43219
800-678-7981
www.bradfordschool
columbus.edu

Bryant and Stratton College
27557 Chardon Rd.
Willoughby Hills, OH 44092
440-444-6800
www.bryantstratton.edu

Bryant and Stratton College
12955 Snow Rd.
Parma, OH 44130-1013
216-265-3151
www.bryantstratton.edu

Central Ohio Technical
College
1179 University Dr.
Newark, OH 43055-1767
740-366-9222
www.cotc.edu

Chatfield College
20918 State Route 251
St. Martin, OH 45118-9705
513-875-3344
www.chatfield.edu

Cincinnati College of
Mortuary Science
645 West North Bend Rd.
Cincinnati, OH 45224-1462
513-761-2020
www.ccms.edu

Cincinnati State Technical
and Community College
3520 Central Parkway
Cincinnati, OH 45223-2690
513-569-1640
www.cincinnatistate.edu

Clark State Community
College
570 East Leffel Lane,
PO Box 570
Springfield, OH 45501-0570
937-328-6027
www.clarkstate.edu

Cleveland Institute of
Electronics
1776 East Seventeenth St.
Cleveland, OH 44114-3636
800-243-6446
www.cie-wc.edu

College of Art Advertising
4343 Bridgetown Rd.
Cincinnati, OH 45211-4427
937-294-0592
www.collegeofartadvertising.
com

Columbus State Community
College
Box 1609
Columbus, OH 43216-1609
800-621-6407
www.cscc.edu

Cuyahoga Community
College
700 Carnegie Ave.
Cleveland, OH 44115-2878
800-954-8742
www.tri-c.edu

Davis College
4747 Monroe St.
Toledo, OH 43623-4307
800-477-7021
daviscollege.edu

Edison State Community
College
1973 Edison Dr.
Piqua, OH 45356-9253
937-778-8600
www.edisonohio.edu

ETI Technical College of
Niles
2076 Youngstown-Warren Rd.
Niles, OH 44446-4398
330-652-9919
www.eti-college.com

Gallipolis Career College
1176 Jackson Pike, Ste. 312
Gallipolis, OH 45631
800-214-0452
www.gallipoliscareercollege.
com

Hocking College
3301 Hocking Parkway
Nelsonville, OH 45764-9588
740-753-3591
www.hocking.edu

Hondros College
4140 Executive Parkway
Westerville, OH 43081-3855
800-783-0095
www.hondroscollege.com

International College of Brd.casting
6 South Smithville Rd.
Dayton, OH 45431-1833
937-258-8251
www.icbcollege.com

ITT Technical Institute
3781 Park Mill Run Dr.
Hilliard, OH 43026
888-483-4888
www.itt-tech.edu

ITT Technical Institute
3325 Stop 8 Rd.
Dayton, OH 45414-3425
937-454-2267
www.itt-tech.edu

ITT Technical Institute
1030 North Meridian Rd.
Youngstown, OH 44509-4098
800-832-5001
www.itt-tech.edu

ITT Technical Institute
14955 Sprague Rd.
Strongsville, OH 44136
800-331-1488
www.itt-tech.edu

ITT Technical Institute
4750 Wesley Ave.
Norwood, OH 45212
800-314-8324
www.itt-tech.edu

James A. Rhodes State College
4240 Campus Dr.
Lima, OH 45804-3597
419-995-8050
www.rhodesstate.edu

Jefferson Community College
4000 Sunset Blvd.
Steubenville, OH 43952-3598
740-264-5591
www.jcc.edu

Kent State University, Ashtabula Campus
3325 West 13th St.
Ashtabula, OH 44004-2299
440-964-4217
www.ashtabula.kent.edu

Kent State University, East Liverpool Campus
400 East 4th St.
East Liverpool, OH 43920-3497
330-382-7414
www.kenteliv.kent.edu

Kent State University, Geauga Campus
14111 Claridon-Troy Rd.
Burton, OH 44021-9500
440-834-4187
www.geauga.kent.edu

Kent State University, Salem Campus
2491 State Route 45 South
Salem, OH 44460-9412
330-332-0361
www.salem.kent.edu

Kent State University, Stark Campus
6000 Frank Ave., NW
Canton, OH 44720-7599
330-244-3259
www.stark.kent.edu

Kent State University, Trumbull Campus
4314 Mahoning Ave., NW
Warren, OH 44483-1998
330-847-0571
www.trumbull.kent.edu

Kent State University, Tuscarawas Campus
330 University Dr., NE
New Philadelphia, OH 44663-9403
330-339-3391
www.tusc.kent.edu

Kettering College of Medical Arts
3737 Southern Blvd.
Kettering, OH 45429-1299
800-433-5262
www.kcma.edu

Lakeland Community College
7700 Clocktower Dr.
Kirtland, OH 44094-5198
440-525-7230
www.lakeland.cc.oh.us

Lorain County Community College
1005 Abbe Rd., North
Elyria, OH 44035
800-995-5222
www.lorainccc.edu

Marion Technical College
1467 Mount Vernon Ave.
Marion, OH 43302-5694
740-389-4636
www.mtc.edu

Mercy College of Northwest Ohio
2221 Madison Ave.
Toledo, OH 43624-1132
888-80-Mercy
www.mercycollege.edu

Miami University Hamilton
1601 Peck Blvd.
Hamilton, OH 45011-3399
513-785-3111
www.ham.muohio.edu

Miami University–Middletown Campus
4200 East University Blvd.
Middletown, OH 45042-3497
513-727-3346
www.mid.muohio.edu

Miami–Jacobs College
PO Box 1433
Dayton, OH 45401-1433
937-461-5174
www.miamijacobs.edu

North Central State College
2441 Kenwood Circle,
PO Box 698
Mansfield, OH 44901-0698
419-755-4896
www.ncstatecollege.edu

Northwest State Community College
22-600 State Route 34
Archbold, OH 43502-9542
419-267-5511
www.nscc.cc.oh.us

Ohio Business College
4020 Milan Rd.
Sandusky, OH 44870-5894
888-627-8345
www.ohiobusinesscollege.com

Ohio Business College
1907 North Ridge Rd.
Lorain, OH 44055
888-514-3126
www.ohiobusinesscollege.com

Ohio College of Massotherapy
225 Heritage Woods Dr.
Akron, OH 44321
330-665-1084
www.ocm.edu

Ohio Institute of Photography and Technology
2029 Edgefield Rd.
Dayton, OH 45439-1917
800-932-9698
www.oipt.com

Ohio Technical College
1374 East 51st St.
Cleveland, OH 44103
800-322-7000
www.ohiotechnicalcollege.com

Ohio Valley College of Technology
16808 St. Clair Ave.,
PO Box 7000
East Liverpool, OH 43920
330-385-1070
www.ovct.edu

Owens Community College
PO Box 10000
Toledo, OH 43699-1947
800-GO-OWENS
www.owens.edu

Owens Community College
300 Davis St.
Findlay, OH 45840
800-FINDLAY
www.owens.edu

Professional Skills Institute
20 Arco Dr.
Toledo, OH 43607
419-531-9610
www.proskills.com

Remington College–Cleveland Campus
14445 Brd.way Ave.
Cleveland, OH 44125
216-475-7520
www.remingtoncollege.edu

Remington College–Cleveland West Campus
26350 Brookpark Rd.
North Olmstead, OH 44070
440-777-2560
www.remingtoncollege.edu

RETS Tech Center
555 East Alex Bell Rd.
Centerville, OH 45459
800-837-7387
www.retstechcenter.com

Rosedale Bible College
2270 Rosedale Rd.
Irwin, OH 43029-9501
740-857-1311
www.rosedalebible.org

School of Advertising Art
1725 East David Rd.
Kettering, OH 45440-1612
877-300-9326
www.saacollege.com

Sinclair Community College
444 West Third St.
Dayton, OH 45402-1460
937-512-3060
www.sinclair.edu

Southeastern Business College
504 McCarty Lane
Jackson, OH 45640
740-286-1554
www.careersohio.com

Southeastern Business College
1855 Western Ave.
Chillicothe, OH 45601-1038
740-774-6300
www.careersohio.com

Southeastern Business College
1522 Sheridan Dr.
Lancaster, OH 43130-1303
740-687-6126
www.careersohio.com

Southern State Community College
100 Hobart Dr.
Hillsboro, OH 45133-9487
937-393-3431
www.sscc.edu

Southwestern College of Business
111 West First St.
Dayton, OH 45402-3003
937-224-0061
www.swcollege.net

Southwestern College of Business
149 Northland Blvd.
Cincinnati, OH 45246-1122
513-874-0432
www.swcollege.net

Southwestern College of Business
632 Vine St., Ste. 200
Cincinnati, OH 45202-4304
513-421-3212
www.swcollege.net

Southwestern College of Business
201 East Second St.
Franklin, OH 45005
937-746-6633
www.swcollege.net

Stark State College of Technology
6200 Frank Ave., NW
Canton, OH 44720-7299
800-797-8275
www.starkstate.edu

Stautzenberger College
5355 Southwyck Blvd.
Toledo, OH 43614
800-552-5099
www.sctoday.com

Technology Education College
288 South Hamilton Rd.
Columbus, OH 43213-2087
800-838-3233
www.teceducation.com

Terra State Community College
2830 Napoleon Rd.
Fremont, OH 43420-9670
419-334-8400
www.terra.edu

The Art Institute of Cincinnati
1171 East Kemper Rd.
Cincinnati, OH 45246
513-751-1206
www.theartinstituteofcincinnati.com

The Brown Mackie College–Cincinnati Campus
1011 Glendale-Milford Rd.
Cincinnati, OH 45215
513-771-2424
www.brownmackie.edu/locations.asp?locid=6

The Ohio State University Agricultural Technical Institute
1328 Dover Rd.
Wooster, OH 44691
330-264-3911
www.ati.ohio-state.edu

The University of Akron–Wayne College
1901 Smucker Rd.
Orrville, OH 44667-9192
800-221-8308
www.wayne.uakron.edu/

Trumbull Business College
3200 Ridge Rd.
Warren, OH 44484
330-369-3200
www.tbc-trumbullbusiness.com

University of Cincinnati Clermont College
4200 Clermont College Dr.
Batavia, OH 45103-1785
513-732-5247
www.clc.uc.edu

University of Cincinnati Raymond Walters College
9555 Plainfield Rd.
Cincinnati, OH 45236-1007
513-745-5700
www.rwc.uc.edu

University of Northwestern Ohio
1441 North Cable Rd.
Lima, OH 45805-1498
419-227-3141
www.unoh.edu

Vatterott College
5025 East Royalton Rd.
Brd.view Heights, OH 44147
800-864-5644
www.vatterott-college.edu

Virginia Marti College of Art and Design
11724 Detroit Ave.,
PO Box 580
Lakewood, OH 44107-3002
216-221-8584
www.vmcad.edu

Washington State Community College
710 Colegate Dr.
Marietta, OH 45750-9225
740-374-8716
www.wscc.edu

Wright State University, Lake Campus
7600 State Route 703
Celina, OH 45822-2921
419-586-0324
www.wright.edu/lake/

Zane State College
1555 Newark Rd.
Zanesville, OH 43701-2626
740-454-2501
www.zanestate.edu

Oklahoma

Carl Albert State College
1507 South McKenna
Poteau, OK 74953-5208
918-647-1301
www.casc.cc.ok.us

Connors State College
Route 1 Box 1000
Warner, OK 74469-9700
918-463-2931
www.connorsstate.edu

Eastern Oklahoma State College
1301 West Main
Wilburton, OK 74578-4999
918-465-2361
www.eosc.edu

Murray State College
One Murray Campus
Tishomingo, OK 73460-3130
580-371-2371
www.mscok.edu

Northeastern Oklahoma Agricultural and Mechanical College
200 I St., NE
Miami, OK 74354-6434
918-540-6212
www.neoam.cc.ok.us

Northern Oklahoma College
1220 East Grand Ave.,
PO Box 310
Tonkawa, OK 74653-0310
800-429-5715
www.north-ok.edu

Oklahoma City Community College
7777 South May Ave.
Oklahoma City, OK 73159-4419
405-682-7515
www.okccc.edu

Oklahoma State University, Oklahoma City
900 North Portland
Oklahoma City, OK 73107-6120
405-945-3287
www.osuokc.edu

Oklahoma State University, Okmulgee
1801 East Fourth St.
Okmulgee, OK 74447-3901
800-722-4471
www.osu-okmulgee.edu

Platt College
309 South Ann Arbor Ave.
Oklahoma City, OK 73128
405-946-7799
www.plattcollege.org

Platt College
3801 South Sheridan Rd.
Tulsa, OK 74145-111
918-663-9000
www.plattcollege.org

Redlands Community College
1300 S. Country Club Rd.
El Reno, OK 73036-5304
405-262-2552
www.redlandscc.edu

Rose State College
6420 Southeast 15th St.
Midwest City, OK 73110-2799
405-733-7673
www.rose.edu

Seminole State College
PO Box 351
Seminole, OK 74818-0351
405-382-9272
www.ssc.cc.ok.us

Southwestern Oklahoma State University at Sayre
409 East Mississippi St.
Sayre, OK 73662-1236
580-928-5533
www.swosu.edu/sayre/

Spartan College of Aeronautics and Technology
8820 East Pine St.,
PO Box 582833
Tulsa, OK 74158-2833
918-836-6886
www.spartan.edu

Tulsa Community College
6111 East Skelly Dr.
Tulsa, OK 74135-6198
918-595-7811
www.tulsacc.edu

Tulsa Welding School
2545 East 11th St.
Tulsa, OK 74104-3909
800-WELD-PRO
www.weldingschool.com

Vatterott College
555 South Memorial Dr.
Tulsa, OK 74112
888-857-4016
www.vatterott-college.edu

Vatterott College
4629 Northwest 23rd St.
Oklahoma City, OK 73127
888-948-0088
www.vatterott-college.edu

Western Oklahoma State College
2801 North Main St.
Altus, OK 73521-1397
580-477-7720
www.wosc.edu

South Dakota

Kilian Community College
300 East 6th St.
Sioux Falls, SD 57103
800-888-1147
www.kilian.edu

Lake Area Technical Institute
230 11th St. Northeast
Watertown, SD 57201
800-657-4344
www.lati.tec.sd.us

Mitchell Technical Institute
821 North Capital
Mitchell, SD 57301
800-952-0042
mti.tec.sd.us

Sisseton-Wahpeton Community College
Old Agency Box 689
Sisseton, SD 57262
605-698-3966
www.swc.tc

Southeast Technical Institute
2320 N. Career Ave.
Sioux Falls, SD 57107-1301
605-367-6115
www.southeasttech.com

Western Dakota Technical Institute
800 Mickelson Dr.
Rapid City, SD 57703
800-544-8765
www.westerndakotatech.org

Wisconsin

Blackhawk Technical College
PO Box 5009
Janesville, WI 53547-5009
800-472-0024
www.blackhawk.edu

Bryant and Stratton College
1300 North Jackson St.
Milwaukee, WI 53202-2608
414-276-5200
www.bryantstratton.edu

Chippewa Valley Technical College
620 West Clairemont Ave.
Eau Claire, WI 54701-6162
800-547-2882
www.cvtc.edu

College of Menominee Nation
PO Box 1179
Keshena, WI 54135
715-799-5600
www.menominee.edu

Fox Valley Technical College
1825 North Bluemound,
PO Box 2277
Appleton, WI 54912-2277
920-735-5643
www.fvtc.edu

Gateway Technical College
3520 30th Ave.
Kenosha, WI 53144-1690
262-564-3224
www.gtc.edu

Herzing College
5218 East Terrace Dr.
Madison, WI 53718
800-582-1227
www.herzing.edu

ITT Technical Institute
6300 West Layton Ave.
Greenfield, WI 53220-4612
414-282-9494
www.itt-tech.edu

ITT Technical Institute
470 Security Blvd.
Green Bay, WI 54313
888-884-3626
www.itt-tech.edu

Lac Courte Oreilles Ojibwa Community College
13466 West Trepania Rd.
Hayward, WI 54843-2181
888-526-6221
www.lco-college.edu

Lakeshore Technical College
1290 North Ave.
Cleveland, WI 53015-1414
888-GO TO LTC
www.gotoltc.com

Madison Area Technical College
3550 Anderson St.
Madison, WI 53704-2599
608-246-6212
madison.tec.wi.us

Madison Media Institute
2702 Agriculture Dr., Ste. 1
Madison, WI 53718
800-236-4997
www.madisonmedia.com

Mid-State Technical College
500 32nd St. North
Wisconsin Rapids, WI 54494-5599
888-575-6782
www.mstc.edu

Milwaukee Area Technical College
700 West State St.
Milwaukee, WI 53233-1443
414-297-6274
www.matc.edu

Moraine Park Technical College
235 North National Ave,
PO Box 1940
Fond du Lac, WI 54936-1940
920-929-2126
www.morainepark.edu

Nicolet Area Technical College
Box 518
Rhinelander, WI 54501-0518
715-365-4451
www.nicoletcollege.edu

Northcentral Technical College
1000 West Campus Dr.
Wausau, WI 54401-1899
715-675-3331
www.ntc.edu

Northeast Wisconsin Technical College
2740 W Mason St.,
PO Box 19042
Green Bay, WI 54307-9042
800-422-6982
www.nwtc.edu

Southwest Wisconsin Technical College
1800 Bronson Blvd.
Fennimore, WI 53809-9778
608-822-3262
www.southwest.edu

University of Wisconsin–Baraboo/Sauk County
1006 Connie Rd.
Baraboo, WI 53913-1015
608-356-8351
baraboo-sauk.uwc.edu

University of Wisconsin–Barron County
1800 College Dr.
Rice Lake, WI 54868-2497
715-234-8024
www.barron.uwc.edu

University of Wisconsin–Fond du Lac
400 University Dr.
Fond du Lac, WI 54935
920-929-3606
www.fdl.uwc.edu

University of Wisconsin–Fox Valley
1478 Midway Rd.
Menasha, WI 54952
888-INFOUWC
www.uwfoxvalley.uwc.edu

University of Wisconsin–Manitowoc
705 Viebahn St.
Manitowoc, WI 54220-6699
920-683-4708
www.manitowoc.uwc.edu

University of Wisconsin–Marathon County
518 South Seventh Ave.
Wausau, WI 54401-5396
888-367-8962
www.uwmc.uwc.edu

University of Wisconsin–Marinette
750 West Bay Shore
Marinette, WI 54143-4299
715-735-4301
www.uwc.edu/mnt/

University of Wisconsin–Marshfield/Wood County
2000 West 5th St.
Marshfield, WI 54449
715-389-6500
marshfield.uwc.edu

University of Wisconsin–Richland
1200 Hwy. 14 West
Richland Center, WI 53581
608-647-8422
richland.uwc.edu

University of Wisconsin–Rock County
2909 Kellogg Ave.
Janesville, WI 53546-5699
888-INFO-UWC
rock.uwc.edu

University of Wisconsin–Sheboygan
One University Dr.
Sheboygan, WI 53081-4789
920-459-6633
www.sheboygan.uwc.edu

University of Wisconsin–Washington County
400 University Dr.
West Bend, WI 53095-3699
262-335-5201
www.washington.uwc.edu

University of Wisconsin–Waukesha
1500 University Dr.
Waukesha, WI 53188-2799
262-521-5200
www.waukesha.uwc.edu

Waukesha County Technical College
800 Main St.
Pewaukee, WI 53072-4601
888-892-WCTC
www.wctc.edu

Western Wisconsin Technical College
304 6th St. North,
PO Box C-908
La Crosse, WI 54602-0908
800-248-9982
www.wwtc.edu

Wisconsin Indianhead Technical College
505 Pine Ridge Dr.
Shell Lake, WI 54871
800-243-9482
www.witc.edu

VOCATIONAL/CAREER COLLEGES

Iowa

AIB College of Business
2500 Fleur Dr.
Des Moines, IA 50321-1799
515-244-4221
www.aib.edu

Hamilton College
1924 D St. SW
Cedar Rapids, IA 52404
319-363-0481
www.hamiltonia.edu

Hamilton College-Mason City Branch
100 First St., NW
Mason City, IA 50401
641-423-2530

Hamilton Technical College
1011 East 53rd St.
Davenport, IA 52807-2653
319-386-3570
www.hamiltontechcollege.com

Hawkeye Community College
PO Box 8015
Waterloo, IA 50704-8015
319-296-4000
www.hawkeyecollege.edu

Indian Hills Community College
525 Grandview Ave., Building #1
Ottumwa, IA 52501-1398
515-683-5153
www.ihcc.cc.ia.us

Iowa Central Community College
330 Ave. M
Fort Dodge, IA 50501-5798
515-576-7201 Ext. 4800
www.iccc.cc.ia.us

Iowa Lakes Community College
19 South 7th St.
Estherville, IA 51334-2295
712-362-7946
www.iowalakes.edu

Iowa Western Community College
2700 College Rd., Box 4-C
Council Bluffs, IA 51502
712-325-3277
www.iwcc.edu

La' James College of Hairstyling
6322 University Ave.
Cedar Falls, IA 50613
800-779-8589
www.lajames.net

La' James College of Hairstyling
211 West 53rd St.
Davenport, IA 52807
800-779-8589
www.lajames.net

La' James College of Hairstyling
6336 Hickman Rd.
Des Moines, IA 50322
800-779-8589
www.lajames.net

La' James College of Hairstyling
2604 First Ave., S
Fort Dodge, IA 50501
515-576-3119

La' James College of Hairstyling
227 East Market St.
Iowa City, IA 52240
800-779-8589
www.lajames.net

La' James College of Hairstyling and Cosmetology
24 Second Ave., NE
Mason City, IA 50401
641-424-2161

Marshalltown Community College
3700 South Center St.
Marshalltown, IA 50158-4760
641-752-4643
www.marshalltown communitycollege.com

Mercy College of Health Sciences
928 Sixth Ave.
Des Moines, IA 50309-1239
515-643-6605
www.mchs.edu

North Iowa Area Community College
500 College Dr.
Mason City, IA 50401-7299
641-422-4245
www.niacc.edu

Northwest Iowa Community College
603 West Park St.
Sheldon, IA 51201-1046
712-324-5061 Ext. 124
www.nwicc.cc.ia.us

Professional Cosmetology Institute
627 Main St.
Ames, IA 50010
515-232-7250 Ext. 2

Southeastern Community College, North Campus
1500 West Agency St.
PO Box 180
West Burlington, IA 52655-0180
319-752-2731 Ext. 8234
www.secc.cc.ia.us

Illinios

Altamore School of Cosmetology
7904 North Second St.
Machesney Park, IL 61115
815-633-1771

Beck Area Career Center-Red Bud
6137 Beck Rd.
Red Bud, IL 62278
618-473-2222

Bell Mar Beauty College
5717 West Cermak
Cicero, IL 60804
708-863-6644

Blessing Hospital-School of Medical Lab Technicians
Brd.way at 11th St.
Quincy, IL 62305
217-223-8400 Ext. 6205

Cannella School of Hair Design
12840 South Western Ave.
Blue Island, IL 60406
708-388-4949

Cannella School of Hair Design
4269 South Archer Ave.
Chicago, IL 60632
773-890-0412

Cannella School of Hair Design
4217 West North Ave.
Chicago, IL 60639
773-278-4477

Cannella School of Hair Design
6614 South Halsted St.
Chicago, IL 60620
773-846-6700

Cannella School of Hair Design
9012 South Commercial
Chicago, IL 60617
773-221-4700

Cannella School of Hair Design
113-117 West Chicago St.
Elgin, IL 60120
773-523-7211

Cannella School of Hair Design
191 North York Rd.
Elmhurst, IL 60126
312-523-7211

Capital Area School of Practical Nursing
2201 Toronto Rd.
Springfield, IL 62707
217-585-2160

Capri Garfield Ridge School of Beauty Culture
6301 South Washtenaw
Chicago, IL 60629
773-778-0882

Center For Employment Training-Chicago
3301 West Arthington, Ste. 101
Chicago, IL 60624
408-287-7924

Christian Life College
400 East Gregory St.
Mt. Prospect, IL 60056
847-259-1840

Coiffure School of Cosmetology Arts and Sciences, Inc.
402 East Main St.
Belleville, IL 62220
618-233-6850

Du Quoin Beauty College
202 South Washington St.
Du Quoin, IL 62832
618-542-9777

Educators of Beauty
122 Wright St.
La Salle, IL 61301
800-610-2300

Educators of Beauty
128 South Fifth St.
Rockford, IL 61104
800-424-7678

Educators of Beauty
211 East Third St.
Sterling, IL 61081
800-642-5169
www.educatorsofbeauty.com

Hair Professional Career College, Inc.
1734 Sycamore Rd.
De Kalb, IL 60115
815-756-3596
www.beautyschool.com/hairpros

Hair Professionals Academy of Cosmetology
440 Airport Rd., Ste. C
Elgin, IL 60123
847-622-7871

Hair Professionals Academy of Cosmetology
1145 East Butterfield Rd.
Wheaton, IL 60187
630-653-6630

Heartland School of Business
49 North Central Park Pl.
Jacksonville, IL 62650
630-434-8244

Hebrew Theological College
7135 North Carpenter Rd.
Skokie, IL 60077-3263
847-982-2500 Ext. 126
www.htcnet.edu

Illinois Center For Brd.casting
200 West 22nd St., Ste. 202
Lombard, IL 60148
708-916-1700

John Amico School of Hair Design
15301 South Cicero
Oak Forest, IL 60452
708-687-7800

John Wood Community College
1301 South 48th St.
Quincy, IL 62305-8736
217-224-6564 Ext. 4338
www.jwcc.edu

Kankakee Academy of Hair Design
100 East 115th St.
Chicago, IL 60628
773-468-8666

Kankakee Community College
PO Box 888
Kankakee, IL 60901-0888
815-933-0242
www.kankakeecc.org

La' James College of Hairstyling
485 42nd Ave.
East Moline, IL 61244
309-755-1313
www.lajames.net

Lamonts International School of Cosmetology
60 and 64 East Elm St.
Canton, IL 61520
309-647-4224

MacDaniel's Beauty School
5228 North Clark St.
Chicago, IL 60640
773-561-2376

Ms. Roberts Academy of Beauty Culture-Villa Park
17 East Park Blvd
Villa Park, IL 60181
708-941-3880

Niles School of Cosmetology
8057 North Milwaukee Ave.
Niles, IL 60714
847-965-8061

Oehrlein School of Cosmetology, Inc.
100 Meadow Ave.
East Peoria, IL 61611
309-699-1561

Professionals Choice Hair Design Academy
2719 West Jefferson St.
Joliet, IL 60435
815-741-8224
www.pchairdesign.com

St. Augustine College
1333-1345 West Argyle
Chicago, IL 60640-3501
773-878-8756 Ext. 343
www.staugustinecollege.edu

The Chicago School of Massage Therapy
2918 North Lincoln Ave.
Chicago, IL 60657
773-477-9444

Trend Beauty College
21 Town and County Shopping Center
Marion, IL 62959
618-997-3138

Trend Setter's College of Cosmetology
665 West Brd.way
Bradley, IL 60915
815-932-5049

Worsham College
495 Northgate Pkwy
Wheeling, IL 60090-2646
847-808-8444

Indiana

Apex School of Beauty Culture
333 Jackson St.
Anderson, IN 46016
765-642-7560

Commonwealth Business College
1000 East 80th Pl., Ste. 101, N
Merrillville, IN 46410
219-769-3321
www.cbcaec.com

Don Roberts Beauty School
1354 West Lincoln Way
Valparaiso, IN 46385
219-462-5189

Hair Fashions by Kaye Beauty College
6316 East 82nd St.
Indianapolis, IN 46250
317-576-0224

Hair Fashions by Kaye Beauty College
1111 South 10th St.
Noblesville, IN 46060
317-773-6189

Indiana Business College
140 East 53rd St.
Anderson, IN 46013
765-644-7514
www.ibcschools.com

Indiana Business College
2222 Poshard Dr.
Columbus, IN 47203-1843
812-379-9000
www.ibcschools.com

Indiana Business College
4601 Theatre Dr.
Evansville, IN 47715-4601
812-476-6000
www.ibcschools.com

Indiana Business College
6413 North Clinton St.
Fort Wayne, IN 46825
219-471-7667
www.ibcschools.com

Indiana Business College
550 East Washington St.
Indianapolis, IN 46204
317-264-5656
www.ibcschools.com

Indiana University-Purdue University Indianapolis
355 North Lansing
Indianapolis, IN 46202-2896
317-274-4591
www.indiana.edu

International Business College
5699 Covington Lane
Fort Wayne, IN 46804
453-459-4535 Ext. 4535
www.bradfordschools.com

Ivy Tech State College-Central Indiana
1 West 26th St., PO Box 1763
Indianapolis, IN 46206-1763
317-921-4823
www.ivytech.edu

Ivy Tech State College-Columbus
4475 Central Ave.
Columbus, IN 47203-1868
812-372-9925 Ext. 129
www.ivytech.edu

Ivy Tech State College-Eastcentral
4301 South Cowan Rd., PO Box 3100
Muncie, IN 47302-9448
765-289-2291 Ext. 334
www.ivytech.edu

Ivy Tech State College-Kokomo
1815 East Morgan St,
PO Box 1373
Kokomo, IN 46903-1373
765-459-0561 Ext. 316
www.ivytech.edu

Ivy Tech State College-Lafayette
3101 South Creasy Lane
Lafayette, IN 47905-5266
765-772-9100 Ext. 118
www.ivytech.edu

Ivy Tech State College-Northeast
3800 North Anthony Blvd
Fort Wayne, IN 46805-1430
219-482-9171 Ext. 4255
www.ivytech.edu

Ivy Tech State College-Southwest
3501 First Ave.
Evansville, IN 47710-3398
812-426-2865 Ext. 1433
www.ivytech.edu

Ivy Tech State College-Wabash Valley
7999 US Hwy 41, South
Terre Haute, IN 47802
812-299-1121 Ext. 2320
www.ivytech.edu

J. Everett Light Career Center
1901 East 86 St.
Indianapolis, IN 46240
317-259-5265 Ext. 4017

J. Michael Harrold Beauty Academy
2232 Wabash Ave.
Terre Haute, IN 47807
812-234-2932

Lincoln Technical Institute
1201 Stadium Dr.
Indianapolis, IN 46202-2194
317-632-5553
www.lincolntech.com

Marion Community Schools Tucker Area Vocational Tech Center
107 South Pennsylvania Ave.
Marion, IN 46952
765-664-9091

Merrillville Beauty College
48 West 67th Pl.
Merrillville, IN 46410
219-769-2232

Oakland City University
143 North Lucretia St.
Oakland City, IN 47660-1099
812-749-4781
www.oak.edu

PJ's College of Cosmetology
1414 Blackiston Mill Rd.
Clarksville, IN 47129
317-846-6444

PJ's College of Cosmetology
2026 Stafford Rd.
Plainfield, IN 46168
317-846-6444

Ruade's School of Beauty Culture
5317 Coldwater Rd.
Ft Wayne, IN 46825-5444
219-483-2466 Ext. 303

Saint Josephs College
PO Box 889
Rensselaer, IN 47978
219-866-6170

Sawyer College
6040 Hohman Ave.
Hammond, IN 46320
219-931-0436
www.sawyercollege.com

Sawyer College
3803 East Lincoln Hwy
Merrillville, IN 46410
219-947-4555
www.sawyercollege.edu

Kansas

Academy of Hair Design
115 South Fifth St.
Salina, KS 67401
785-825-8155

American Academy of Hair Design
901 SW 37th St.
Topeka, KS 66611
785-267-5800

American Institute of Baking
1213 Bakers Way
Manhattan, KS 66502
785-537-4750 Ext. 179
www.aibonline.org

Bryan Career College
1527 SW Fairlawn Rd.
Topeka, KS 66604
785-272-0889

Classic College of Hair Design
1675 South Rock Rd.
Wichita, KS 67207
316-681-2288

Crums Beauty College
512 Poyntz Ave., Box 663
Manhattan, KS 66502
785-776-4794

Garden City Community College
801 Campus Dr.
Garden City, KS 67846-6399
620-276-9608
www.gccc.cc.ks.us

Hays Academy of Hair Design
119 West Tenth St.
Hays, KS 67601
913-628-3981

Kansas School of Hair Styling
1207 East Douglas Ave.
Wichita, KS 67211-1693
316-264-4891

Pratt Community College
348 NE State Rd. 61
Pratt, KS 67124-8317
620-672-5641 Ext. 217
www.prattcc.edu

Seward County Community College
Box 1137
Liberal, KS 67905-1137
620-629-2710
www.sccc.cc.ks.us

Superior School of Hairstyling
1215 East Santa Fe St.
Olathe, KS 66061
913-782-4004

The Brown Mackie College
2106 South 9th St.
Salina, KS 67401-2810
800-365-0433
www.bmcaec.com

Vernons Kansas School of Cosmetology-Central
501 East Pawnee, Ste. 525
Wichita, KS 67211
316-265-2629
www.globalads.commalla/vernons

Washburn University
1700 SW College Ave.
Topeka, KS 66621
785-231-1010 Ext. 1030
www.washburn.edu

Xenon International School of Hair Design
3804 West Douglas
Wichita, KS 67203
316-943-5516

Michigan

Academy of Court Reporting
26111 Evergreen Rd.,Ste. 101
Southfield, MI 48076-4481
313-353-4880

Baker College Center for Graduate Studies
1116 West Bristol Rd.
Flint, MI 48507-9843
810-766-4390
www.online.baker.edu

Baker College of Jackson
2800 Springport Rd.
Jackson, MI 49202
517-788-7800 Ext. 4555
www.baker.edu

Baker College of Port Huron
3403 Lapeer Rd.
Port Huron, MI 48060-2597
810-985-7000
www.baker.edu

Bayshire Beauty Academy
917 Saginaw St.
Bay City, MI 48708
989-894-2431

Chic University of Cosmetology
1735 Four Mile, NE
Grand Rapids, MI 49525
616-363-9853

Detroit Business Institute-Southfield
23077 Greenfield Rd.,
Ste. LL28
Southfield, MI 48075
248-552-6300

Douglas J. Educational Center
333 Albert St., Ste. 110
East Lansing, MI 48823
517-333-9656
www.douglasj.com

Hillsdale Beauty College
64 Waldron St.
Hillsdale, MI 49242
517-437-4670

Kalamazoo Beauty Academy
DBA Wright Beauty Academy
6666 Lovers Lane
Portage, MI 49002
616-321-8708

Lawton School
20755 Greenfield Rd., #300
Southfield, MI 48075
248-569-7787 Ext. 110

Michigan College of Beauty
15233 South Dixie Hwy
Monroe, MI 48161
734-241-8877

Michigan Jewish Institute
25401 Coolidge Hwy
Oak Park, MI 48237-1304
248-414-6900
www.mji.edu

Mr. Belas School of
Cosmetology, Incorporated
29475 John R. St.
Madison Heights, MI 48071
248-543-1584

Northwestern Michigan
College
1701 East Front St.
Traverse City, MI 49686-3061
231-995-1054
www.nmc.edu

Northwestern Technological
Institute
24567 Northwestern Hwy,
Ste. 200
Southfield, MI 48075
248-358-4006

Port Huron Cosmetology
College
5620 Dixie Hwy
Waterford, MI 48329
248-623-9494

Ross Medical Education
Center
4703 Washtenaw
Ann Arbor, MI 48108-1411
734-434-7320

Ross Medical Education
Center
1036 Gilbert St.
Flint, MI 48532
810-230-1100

Ross Medical Education
Center
2035 28th St., SE
Grand Rapids, MI 49508
616-243-3070

Ross Medical Education
Center
950 West Norton Ave.
Roosevelt Park, MI 49441
231-739-1531

Ross Medical Education
Center
26417 Hoover Rd.
Warren, MI 48089-1190
586-574-0830

Ross Technical Institute
5757 Whitmore Lake Rd.,
Ste. 800
Brighton, MI 48116
810-227-0160

SER Business and Technical
Institute
9301 Michigan Ave.
Detroit, MI 48210-2095
313-846-2240 Ext. 226

Sharp's Academy of
Hairstyling
115 Main St.
Flushing, MI 48433
810-659-3348

Travel Education Institute-
Warren Campus
30100 Van Dyke Ave.,Ste. 200
Warren, MI 48093
810-751-5634
www.travinst.com

Virginia Farrell Beauty
School
22925 Woodward Ave.
Ferndale, MI 48220
248-424-9123

West Shore Community
College
PO Box 277,
3000 North Stiles Rd.
Scottville, MI 49454-0277
231-845-6211 Ext. 3117
www.westshore.edu

WIA School of Practical
Nursing
735 Griswold St.
Detroit, MI 48226-3275
313-596-7580

Wright Beauty Academy
492 Capital, SW
Battle Creek, MI 49015
616-964-4016

Minnesota

Academy Education Center,
Inc.
3050 Metro Dr., Ste. 200
Minneapolis, MN 55425
952-851-0066

Alexandria Technical College
1601 Jefferson St.
Alexandria, MN 56308-3707
320-762-4520
www.alextech.org

Aveda Institute-Minneapolis
400 Central Ave.
Minneapolis, MN 55414
612-378-7404
www.aveda.com

Cosmetology Careers
Unlimited-Duluth
121 West Superior St.
Duluth, MN 55802
218-722-7484
www.coscareers.com

Fergus Falls Community
College
1414 College Way
Fergus Falls, MN 56537-1009
218-739-7516
www.ffcc.edu

Globe College
7166 North 10th St.
Oakdale, MN 55128
651-730-5100
www.globecollege.com

Hibbing Community College
1515 East 25th St.
Hibbing, MN 55746-3300
218-262-7207
www.hcc.mnscu.edu

High-Tech Institute
5701 Shingle Creek Pkwy,
Ste. 200
Brooklyn Center, MN 55430
763-560-9700
www.high-techinstitute.com

Inver Hills Community
College
2500 East 80th St.
Inver Grove Heights, MN
55076-3224
651-450-8504
www.ih.cc.mn.us

Itasca Community College
1851 Hwy 169 East
Grand Rapids, MN 55744
218-327-4468
www.it.cc.mn.us

Lake Superior College
2101 Trinity Rd.
Duluth, MN 55811
218-733-5903
www.lsc.mnscu.edu

Lakeland Medical-Dental
Academy, Inc.
1402 West Lake St.
Minneapolis, MN 55408
612-827-5656
www.lakelandacademy.com

Mayo School of Health
Sciences
Siebens Building
200 First St., SW
Rochester, MN 55905
507-284-3678
www.mayo.edumshs

McConnell School, Inc.
1201 Marquette Ave. Ste. 100
Minneapolis,
MN 55403-2456
612-332-4238
www.mcconnellschool.com

Minneapolis Drafting School
5700 West Brd.way
Minneapolis,
MN 55428-3548
763-535-8843 Ext. 224
www.mplsdrafting.com

Minnesota Cosmetology
Education Center, Inc.
704 Marie Ave.
South St. Paul, MN 55075
651-450-6102 Ext. 11
www.mncosmetology.com

Minnesota School of
Business-Brooklyn Center
5910 Shingle Creek Pkwy
Brooklyn Center, MN 55430
763-566-7777
www.msbcollege.com

Minnesota School of
Business-Richfield
1401 West 76th St.
Richfield, MN 55423
612-861-2000
www.msbcollege.edu

Musictech College
19 Exchange St. East
Saint Paul, MN 55101
651-291-0177 Ext. 2379
www.musictech.com

National American University
112 West Market
Bloomington, MN 55425
605-394-4827

Normandale Community College
9700 France Ave. South
Bloomington, MN 55431-4399
952-487-8210
www.normandale.edu

North Hennepin Community College
7411 85th Ave. North
Brooklyn Park, MN 55445-2231
763-424-0721
www.nhcc.mnscu.edu

Oliver Thein Beauty School
150 Cobblestone Lane
Burnsville, MN 55337
612-435-3882
www.oliverthein.com

Pillsbury Baptist Bible College
315 South Grove Ave.
Owatonna, MN 55060-3097
507-451-2710 Ext. 274
www.pillsbury.edu

Pine Technical College
900 4th St. SE
Pine City, MN 55063
320-629-5100
www.ptc.tec.mn.us

Rasmussen College-Mankato Campus
501 Holly Lane
Mankato, MN 56001-9938
507-625-6556

Ritas-Moorhead Beauty School
17 South Fourth St.
Moorhead, MN 56560
218-236-7201

St. Cloud Regency Beauty Academy
912 West Saint Germain St.
St. Cloud, MN 56301
320-251-0500 Ext. 102

Vermilion Community College
1900 East Camp St.
Ely, MN 55731-1996
218-365-7224
www.vcc.edu

Missouri

Boonslick Area Vocational-Technical School
1694 Ashley Rd.
Boonville, MO 65233
660-882-5306
www.bavts.boonville.k12.mo.us

Bryan Career College
1700 South Campbell Ave., #L
Springfield, MO 65807
417-862-5700

Central College of Cosmetology
Business Loop I44
St. Robert, MO 65583
573-336-3888

Chillicothe Beauty Academy, Inc.
505 Elm St.
Chillicothe, MO 64601
816-646-4198

Columbia Beauty Academy
1729 West Brd.way
Columbia, MO 65203

Crowder College
601 Laclede Ave.
Neosho, MO 64850-9160
417-451-3223 Ext. 5466
www.crowdercollege.net

Franklin Technology Center
2020 Iowa St.
Joplin, MO 64804
417-659-4400

Grabber School of Hair Design
14560 Manchester, Ste. 25
Ballwin, MO 63011
636-227-4440

Grand River Technical School
1200 Fair St.
Chillicothe, MO 64601
660-646-3414

House of Heavilin Beauty College
5720 Troost Ave.
Kansas City, MO 64110-2826
816-523-2471

Jerry's School of Hairstyling, Inc.
217 North Ninth St.
Columbia, MO 65201
573-449-7527

Lester L. Cox College of Nursing and Health Science
1423 North Jefferson
Springfield, MO 65802
417-269-3069

Metro Business College of Cape Girardeau
1732 North Kings Hwy
Cape Girardeau, MO 63701
573-334-9181

Midwest Institute
10910 Manchester Rd.
Kirkwood, MO 63122
314-965-8363
www.midwestinstitutue.com

Midwestern Baptist Theological Seminary
5001 North Oak Trafficway
Kansas City, MO 64118-4697
800-944-6287
www.mbts.edu

National Academy of Beauty Arts
157 Concord Plaza
St. Louis, MO 63128
314-842-3616

Neosho Beauty College
116 North Wood St.
Neosho, MO 64850
417-451-7216

Nevada Regional Technical Center
900 West Ashland
Nevada, MO 64772
417-448-2090

New Dimension School of Hair Design
705 Illinois St., Ste. 12
Joplin, MO 64801
417-782-2875

Nichols Career Center
609 Union
Jefferson City, MO 65101
573-659-3100

North County Technical Special School District
1700 Derhake Rd.
Florissant, MO 63033
314-989-7900

Northwest Technical School
1515 South Munn
Maryville, MO 64468
660-562-3022
www.nts.tec.mo.us

Patricia Stevens College
330 North Fourth St., Ste. 306
St. Louis, MO 63102
314-421-0949 Ext. 12
www.patriciastevens college.com

Patsy and Rob's Academy of Beauty
18 NW Plaza
St. Ann, MO 63074
314-298-8804

Pinnacle Career Institute
15329 Kensington Ave.
Kansas City, MO 64147-1212
816-331-5700
www.pcitraining.com

Salem College of Hairstyling
1051 Kings Hwy
Rolla, MO 65401
573-368-3136

St. Louis Hair Academy, Inc.
3701 Kossuth Ave.
St. Louis, MO 63107
314-533-3125

Stage One
904 Brd.way
Cape Girardeau, MO 63701
314-335-5078

Vatterott College
5898 North Main St.
Joplin, MO 64801
417-781-5633
www.vatterott-college.com

Waynesville Technical Academy
810 Roosevelt
Waynesville, MO 65583

North Dakota

Aakers Business College
4012 19th Ave., SW
Fargo, ND 58103
701-277-3889
www.aakers-college.com

Cankdeska Cikana Community College
PO Box 269
Fort Totten, ND 58335-0269
701-766-1342
www.littlehoop.cc/

Lake Region State College
1801 College Dr. North
Devils Lake, ND 58301-1598
701-662-1514
www.lrsc.nodak.edu

Minot State University-Bottineau Campus
105 Simrall Blvd
Bottineau, ND 58318-1198
701-228-5426
www.misu-b.nodak.edu

RD Hairstyling College, Inc.
124 North Fourth St.
Bismarck, ND 58501
701-223-8804

Ohio

AEC Southern Ohio College, Cincinnati Campus
1011 Glendale-Milford Rd.
Cincinnati, OH 45215
513-771-2424
www.socaec.com

Beatrice Academy of Beauty
10500 Cedar Ave.
Cleveland, OH 44106
216-421-2313

Carousel Beauty College
125 East Second St.
Dayton, OH 45402
937-223-3572

Carousel Beauty College
3120 Woodman Dr.
Kettering, OH 45420
937-223-3572 Ext. 227

Carousel Beauty College
633 South Breiel Blvd
Middletown, OH 45044
937-223-3572

Carousel of Miami Valley Beauty College
7809 Waynetowne Blvd
Huber Heights, OH 45424
937-223-3572 Ext. 227

Central School of Practical Nursing, Inc.
4600 Carnegie Ave.
Cleveland, OH 44103
216-391-8434

Charmayne Beauty Academy
20880 Southgate Park Blvd
Maple Heights, OH 44137
216-662-4090

ETI Technical College of Niles
2076 Youngstown-Warren Rd.
Niles, OH 44446-4398
330-652-9919
www.eti-college.com

Fairview Beauty Academy
22610 Lorain Rd.
Fairview Park, OH 44126
216-734-5555

Gerbers Akron Beauty School
33 Shiawassee Ave.
Fairlawn, OH 44333
330-867-6200

Hamrick Truck Driving School
1156 Medina Rd.
Medina, OH 44256-9615
440-239-2229

Hobart Institute of Welding Technology
400 Trade Square, E
Troy, OH 45373
937-332-5215
www.welding.org

International College of Brd.casting
6 South Smithville Rd.
Dayton, OH 45431-1833
937-258-8251 Ext. 202

Moore University of Hair Design
6011 Montgomery Rd.
Cincinnati, OH 45213
513-531-3100

Nationwide Beauty Academy
5300 Westpointe Plaza
Columbus, OH 43228
614-252-5252

Northern Institute of Cosmetology
667-669 Brd.way
Lorain, OH 44052
440-244-4282

Ohio Business College
4020 Milan Rd.
Sandusky, OH 44870-5894
419-627-8345
www.ohiobusinesscollege.com

Ohio Center For Brd.casting
4790 Red Bank Exwy, Ste. 102
Cincinnati, OH 45227
513-271-6060

Ohio Center For Brd.casting
9000 Sweet Valley Dr.
Valley View, OH 44125
216-447-9117

Ohio Hi Point Joint Vocational School District
2280 St., Rt. 540
Bellefontaine, OH 43311-9594
937-599-6275 Ext. 210

Omni Technical School
924 East Tallmadge Ave.
Akron, OH 44310
330-633-3102

Paramount Beauty Academy
1745 11th St.
Portsmouth, OH 45662
740-353-2436

Parma School of Practical Nursing
6726 Ridge Rd.
Parma, OH 44129
440-885-2364

Portage Lakes Career Center-W. Howard Nicol School of Practical Nursing
4401 Shriver Rd. PO Box 248
Green, OH 44232-0248
330-896-8105

Practical Nurse Program of Canton City Schools
1253 Third St., SE
Canton, OH 44707-4798
330-453-3271

Raphaels School of Beauty Culture
1324 Youngstown Warren Rd.
Niles, OH 44446
330-652-1559

Raphaels School of Beauty Culture, Inc.
2635 Elm Rd., NE
Warren, OH 44483-2905
330-395-4999

Raphaels School of Beauty Culture, Inc.
3035 Belmont Ave.
Youngstown, OH 44505
330-759-9604

School of Advertising Art
1725 East David Rd.
Kettering, OH 45440-1612
937-294-0592
www.saacollege.com

Southern Ohio College
1637 Tiffin
Findlay, OH 45840
419-423-2211

Toledo Academy of Beauty Culture-North
4801 Lewis Ave.
Toledo, OH 43612
419-478-6660

Toledo School of Practical Nursing
1602 Washington St.
Whitney Building
Toledo, OH 43624
419-244-8301

TriState Travel School
4600 Montgomery Rd.
Ste. 106
Cincinnati, OH 45212
513-841-5588

Trumbull Business College
3200 Ridge Rd.
Warren, OH 44484
330-369-3200
www.tbc-trumbullbusiness.com

Western Hills School of Beauty and Hair Design
6490 Glenway
Cincinnati, OH 45211
513-574-3818

Willoughby-Eastlake School of Practical Nursing
25 Public Square
Willoughby, OH 44094
440-946-7085 Ext. 5093

Oklahoma

Advance Barber College
5301 S. Pennsylvania Ave.
Oklahoma City, OK 73119
405-631-3399

American Brd.casting School
4511 SE 29th St.
Oklahoma City, OK 73115
405-672-6511

American Brd.casting School
7016 South Utica Ave.
Tulsa, OK 74136
918-499-2271
www.radioschool.com

Beauty Technical College, Inc.
1600 Downing
Tahlequah, OK 74465
918-456-9431

Broken Arrow Beauty College
400 South Elm Pl.
Broken Arrow, OK 74012
918-251-9660

CC's Cosmetology College
4439 NW 50th
Oklahoma City, OK 73112
405-943-2300

CC's Cosmetology College
11630 East 21
Tulsa, OK 74129
918-234-9444

Chisholm Trail Area Vocational Technical Center
Rt. 1, Box 60
Omega, OK 73764
405-729-8324

Claremore Beauty College
200 North Cherokee
Claremore, OK 74017
918-341-4370

Connors State College
Rt. 1 Box 1000
Warner, OK 74469-9700
918-463-2931 Ext. 6241
www.connors.cc.ok.us

Metropolitan College of Legal Studies
4528 South Sheridan Rd., Ste. 105
Tulsa, OK 74145
918-627-9300

Northeast Area Vocational Technical School
Hwy 20,
6 Miles West of Pryor
Pryor, OK 74362
918-825-5555 Ext. 2111

Northwest Technology Center
1801 South 11th St.
Alva, OK 73717
580-327-0344
www.nwt.tec.ok.us

Poteau Beauty College
2601 North Brd.way
Poteau, OK 74953
918-647-4119

Pryor Beauty College
330 West Graham
Pryor, OK 74361
918-825-2795

School of Hair Design
1437 SE Washington
Idabel, OK 74745
580-286-7840

Shawnee Beauty College
410 E. Main St.
Shawnee, OK 74801
405-275-3182

Southern School of Beauty
140 West Main St.
Durant, OK 74701
580-924-1049

Southwestern Christian University
PO Box 340
Bethany, OK 73008-0340
405-789-7661 Ext. 3449
www.swcu.edu

Stillwater Beauty Academy
1684 Cimmaron Plaza
Stillwater, OK 74075
405-377-4100

Technical Institute of Cosmetology Arts and Sciences
2909A South Sheridan Rd.
Tulsa, OK 74129
918-660-8828 Ext. 11

Woodward Beauty College
502 Texas
Woodward, OK 73801
580-256-7535

Yukon Beauty College
1231 South 11th St.
Yukon, OK 73099
405-354-3172

South Dakota

Kilian Community College
300 East 6th St.
Sioux Falls, SD 57103
605-336-1711
www.kilian.edu

Wisconsin

Gill-Tech Academy of Hair Design
423 West College Ave.
Appleton, WI 54911
920-739-8684
www.gill-tech.com

Lac Courte Oreilles Ojibwa Community College
13466 West Trepania Rd.
Hayward, WI 54843-2181
715-634-4790 Ext. 104
www.geocities.comathens/acropolis/4551/

Lakeshore Technical College
1290 North Ave.
Cleveland, WI 53015-1414
920-458-4183 Ext. 162
www.gotoltc.com

Madison Area Technical College
3550 Anderson St.
Madison, WI 53704-2599
608-246-6221
www.madison.tec.wi.us

Martin's School of Hair Design
2310 West College Ave.
Appleton, WI 54914
920-832-8686 Ext. 112

Martin's School of Hair Design
2575 West Mason St.
Green Bay, WI 54304
920-494-1430 Ext. 112

Nicolet Area Technical College
Box 518
Rhinelander, WI 54501-0518
715-365-4451
www.nicoletcollege.edu

Scientific College of Beauty
326 Pearl St.
La Crosse, WI 54601
608-784-4702

Scientific College of Beauty and Barbering
310 Westgate Mall
Madison, WI 53711
608-271-4204

St. Lukes Medical Center-School of Diagnostic Medical Sonography
2900 West Oklahoma Ave.
Milwaukee, WI 53215
414-649-6689

University of Wisconsin-Parkside
900 Wood Rd., Box 2000
Kenosha, WI 53141-2000
262-595-2241
www.uwp.edu

Waukesha County Technical College
800 Main St.
Pewaukee, WI 53072-4601
414-691-5200
www.wctc.edu

Wisconsin Indianhead Technical College
1019 South Knowles Ave.
New Richmond, WI 54017
715-468-2815 Ext. 2280
www.witc.tec.wi.us

SCHOLARSHIPS AND FINANCIAL AID

Illinois

Italian Catholic Federation, Inc.

Renewable awards for high school students who are residents of California, Illinois, Arizona and Nevada and plan to pursue postsecondary education. Must have minimum 3.2 GPA. Must be a U.S. citizen, Catholic, and of Italian descent or if non-Italian the student's parents or grandparents must be members of the Federation for the student to qualify. Applicants must submit the last two pages of parents' income tax return, along with other required materials as listed on the application. **Award:** Scholarship for use in freshman, sophomore, junior, or senior years; renewable. **Number:** 170–200. **Amount:** $400–$1000. **Eligibility Requirements:** Applicant must be Roman Catholic; of Italian heritage; high school student; planning to enroll or expecting to enroll full-time at a two-year or four-year institution or university and resident of Arizona, California, Illinois, or Nevada. Available to U.S. citizens. **Application Requirements:** Application, essay, references, transcript. **Application Deadline:** March 15. **Contact:** Scholarship Director, Italian Catholic Federation, Inc., 675 Hegenberger Road, Suite 230, Oakland, CA 94621. **Phone:** 510-633-9058

Hispanic College Fund, Inc.

Scholarships ranging from $500 to $2500 are available for full-time undergraduate students of Hispanic origin who reside in any of the following Burlington Northern Santa Fe-served states: Arizona, Colorado, Illinois, Missouri, New Mexico, California and Texas. Must be pursuing a bachelor's degree in accounting, economics, engineering, finance, information systems, marketing or a related major. Minimum GPA of 3.0. **Award:** Scholarship for use in freshman, sophomore, junior, or senior years; not renewable. **Number:** 10. **Amount:** $500–$2500. **Eligibility Requirements:** Applicant must be Hispanic; enrolled or expecting to enroll full-time at a two-year or four-year institution or university and resident of Arizona, California, Colorado, Illinois, Missouri, New Mexico, or Texas. Applicant must have 3.0 GPA or higher. Available to U.S. citizens. **Application Requirements:** Application, essay, financial need analysis, references, transcript. **Application Deadline:** April 15. **Contact:** Stina Augustsson, Program Manager, Hispanic College Fund, Inc., 1717 Pennsylvania Avenue, NW, Suite 460, Washington, DC 20006. **Phone:** 202-296-5400. **E-mail:** hcf-info@hispanicfund.org

American Legion, Department of Illinois

Multi-level oratorical contest with winners advancing to next level. Open to students in 9th–12th grades of any accredited high school in Illinois. Seniors must be in attendance as of 1/1. Fifteen prizes in the form of tuition scholarships from $75–$1,600 will be awarded. Contact local American Legion Post or Department Headquarters for complete information and applications, which will be available in the fall. **Award:** Scholarship for use in freshman year; not renewable. **Number:** 15. **Amount:** $75–$1600. **Eligibility Requirements:** Applicant must be high school student; age 20 or under; planning to enroll or expecting to enroll full or part-time at a two-year, four-year, or technical institution or university and resident of Illinois. Available to U.S. citizens. **Application Requirements:** Application, applicant must enter a contest, transcript. **Application Deadline:** January 15. **Contact:** American Legion, Department of Illinois, PO Box 2910, Bloomington, IL 61702

American Legion, Department of Illinois, Boy Scout/Explorer Scholarship

American Legion, Department of Illinois, Boy Scout/Explorer Scholarship<rx;91265>
Scholarship for a graduating high school senior who is a qualified senior Boy Scout or Explorer and a resident of Illinois. Must write a 500-word essay on Legion's Americanism and Boy Scout programs. Deadline: April 30. **Award:** Scholarship for use in freshman year; not renewable. **Number:** 5. **Amount:** $200–$1000. **Eligibility Requirements:** Applicant must be high school student; planning to enroll or expecting to enroll full or part-time at a two-year, four-year, or technical institution or university and resident of Illinois. Applicant or parent of applicant must be member of Boy Scouts. Available to U.S. and non-U.S. citizens. **Application Requirements:** Application, applicant must enter a contest, essay. **Application Deadline:** April 30. **Contact:** American Legion Boy Scout Chairman, Department Headquarters, American Legion, Department of Illinois, PO Box 2910, Bloomington, IL 61702

American Legion, Department of Illinois Scholarships

Twenty $1000 scholarships for graduating students of Illinois high schools. May be used at any accredited college, university, trade or technical school. Applicant must be a child or grandchild of members of the American Legion Illinois. Awards will be based on academic merit and financial need. Applications available September 15 and must be returned prior to March 15. **Award:** Scholarship for use in freshman year; not renewable. **Number:** 20. **Amount:** $1000. **Eligibility Requirements:** Applicant must be high school student; planning to enroll or expecting to enroll full or part-time at a two-year, four-year, or technical institution or university and resident of Illinois. Applicant or parent of applicant must be member of American Legion or Auxiliary. Available to U.S. citizens. **Application Requirements:** Application, financial need analysis, photo, test scores, transcript. **Application Deadline:** March 14. American Legion, Department of Illinois, PO Box 2910 Bloomington, IL 61702

AMVETS Department of Illinois

Applicant must be an Illinois high school sophomore, junior, or senior. Provide a copy of driver's license and a copy of certificate of completion of driver's education. **Award:** Scholarship for use in freshman, sophomore, junior, or senior years; renewable. **Number:** 3. **Amount:** $500–$1500. **Eligibility Requirements:** Applicant must be high school student; age 16-18; planning to enroll or expecting to enroll full-time at a two-year, four-year, or technical institution or university and resident of

Illinois. Available to U.S. citizens. **Application Requirements:** Application, applicant must enter a contest, driver's license, certificate of completion of driver's education. **Application Deadline:** March 1. **Contact:** Sara Van Dyke, Scholarship Director, AMVETS Department of Illinois, 2200 South Sixth Street, Springfield, IL 62703-3496. **Phone:** 217-528-4713. **E-mail:** scholarship@amvetsillinois.com

AMVETS Service Foundation Scholarship Award

Applicant must be an Illinois high school senior. Must submit ACT scores and IRS 1040 form. Must be the child or grandchild of an honorably discharged veteran who served after September 15, 1940, or is currently serving in the military. Renewable award of $1000. **Award:** Scholarship for use in freshman, sophomore, junior, or senior years; renewable. **Number:** 30. **Amount:** $1000. **Eligibility Requirements:** Applicant must be high school student; age 17-18; planning to enroll or expecting to enroll full-time at a two-year, four-year, or technical institution or university and resident of Illinois. Available to U.S. citizens. Applicant or parent must meet one or more of the following requirements: general military experience; retired from active duty; disabled or killed as a result of military service; prisoner of war; or missing in action. **Application Requirements:** Application, financial need analysis, test scores, transcript, IRS 1040 form. **Application Deadline:** March 1. **Contact:** Sara Van Dyke, Scholarship Director, AMVETS Department of Illinois, 2200 South Sixth Street, Springfield, IL 62703-3496. **Phone:** 217-528-4713. **E-mail:** scholarship@amvetsillinois.com

Boys and Girls Clubs of Chicago

Boys and Girls Clubs of Chicago scholarships are awarded to graduating high school seniors who are local Club members. Scholarships are based upon academic achievement, Club involvement, financial need, and personal interviews. Students are asked to maintain their grades, seek internships and job opportunities, and lend guidance to younger children. **Award:** Scholarship for use in freshman, sophomore, junior, or senior years; renewable. **Number:** varies. **Amount:** $3000–$5000. **Eligibility Requirements:** Applicant must be high school student; planning to enroll or expecting to enroll full or part-time at a two-year, four-year, or technical institution or university and resident of Illinois. Applicant or parent of applicant must be member of Boys or Girls Club. Applicant must have 2.5 GPA or higher. Available to U.S. citizens. **Contact:** LaKesha Nelson, Project Director, Boys and Girls Clubs of Chicago, 550 West Van Buren Street, Suite 350, Chicago, IL 60607. **Phone:** 312-235-8000. **E-mail:** lnelson@bgcc.org

Bradley M. Swanson Memorial Scholarship Fund

The Bradley M. Swanson Memorial Scholarship was established to award scholarships to those students whose high school class rank is in the top 15th to 30th percentile, have maintained a 2.5 GPA, and a composite minimum ACT score of 25 with no ACT subject area score below 24. Must be a U.S. citizen. Application forms may be requested via **E-mail:** johnmarswa@worldnet.att.net **Award:** Scholarship for use in freshman, sophomore, junior, or senior years; not renewable. **Number:** 1–3. **Amount:** $500–$1000. **Eligibility Requirements:** Applicant must be enrolled or expecting to enroll full-time at a four-year institution or university and resident of Illinois, Iowa, Minnesota, South Dakota, or Wisconsin. Applicant must have 2.5 GPA or higher. Available to U.S. citizens. **Application Requirements:** Application, essay, self-addressed stamped envelope, test scores, transcript, class rank. **Application Deadline:** January 30. **Contact:** Marilyn Swanson, Director, Bradley M. Swanson Memorial Scholarship Fund, 3408 Deer Path Road, Rockford, IL 61107. **Phone:** 815-877-5939.

Community Banker Association of Illinois

Essay competition open to Illinois high school seniors who are sponsored by a CBAI member bank. Student bank employees, plus immediate families of bank employees, board members, stockholders, CBAI employees, and judges are ineligible. For more details see **Web site:** www.cbai.com. **Award:** Scholarship for use in freshman year; not renewable. **Number:** up to 13. **Amount:** $1000–$4000. **Eligibility Requirements:** Applicant must be high school student; planning to enroll or expecting to enroll full-time at a two-year, four-year, or technical institution or university and resident of Illinois. Available to U.S. citizens. **Application Requirements:** Applicant must enter a contest, essay. **Application Deadline:** February 9. **Contact:** Andrea Cusick, Senior Vice President of Communications, Community Banker Association of Illinois, Attn: CBAI Foundation for Community Banking, 901 Community Drive, Springfield, IL 62703-5184. **Phone:** 217-529-2265. **E-mail:** cbaicom@cbai.com

Community Banker Association of Illinois Children of Community Banking Scholarship

Eligible Illinois community banks can submit one name for each $1,000 they have donated to the CBAI Foundation. Children of eligible community bankers and part-time bank employees entering freshman year of higher education are eligible. Winner determined by drawing. Must be Illinois resident. **Award:** Scholarship for use in freshman year; not renewable. **Number:** 1. **Amount:** $1000–$4000. **Eligibility Requirements:** Applicant must be high school student; planning to enroll or expecting to enroll full-time at a two-year, four-year, or technical institution or university and resident of Illinois. Applicant or parent of applicant must be member of Community Banker Association of Illinois. Applicant or parent of applicant must have employment or volunteer experience in banking. Available to U.S. citizens. **Application Requirements: Application Deadline:** August 15. **Contact:** Andrea Cusick, Senior Vice President of Communications, Community Banker Association of Illinois, Attn: CBAI Foundation for Community Banking, 901 Community Drive, Springfield, IL 62703-5184. **Phone:** 217-529-2265. **E-mail:** cbaicom@cbai.com

Golden Apple Foundation

100 scholars are selected annually. Scholars receive $7,000 a year for 4 years. Applicants must be between 17 and 21 and maintain a GPA of 2.5. Eligible applicants must be residents of Illinois studying in Illinois. Recipients must agree to teach in high-need Illinois schools. **Award:** Forgivable loan

for use in freshman, sophomore, junior, or senior years; renewable. **Number:** up to 100. **Amount:** $7000. **Eligibility Requirements:** Applicant must be age 17-21; enrolled or expecting to enroll full-time at a four-year institution or university; resident of Illinois and studying in Illinois. Applicant must have 2.5 GPA or higher. Available to U.S. and non-U.S. citizens. **Application Requirements:** Application, autobiography, essay, interview, photo, references, test scores, transcript. **Application Deadline:** December 1. **Contact:** Pat Kilduff, Director of Recruitment and Placement, Golden Apple Foundation, 8 South Michigan Avenue, Suite 700, Chicago, IL 60603-3318. **Phone:** 312-407-0006 Ext. 105. **E-mail:** kilduff@goldenapple.org

Higher Education License Plate Program–HELP

Need-based grants for students at institutions participating in program whose funds are raised by sale of special license plates commemorating the institutions. Deadline: June 30. Must be Illinois resident. **Award:** Grant for use in freshman, sophomore, junior, or senior years; not renewable. **Number:** 175–200. **Amount:** up to $2000. **Eligibility Requirements:** Applicant must be enrolled or expecting to enroll full or part-time at a two-year or four-year institution or university; resident of Illinois and studying in Illinois. Available to U.S. and non-U.S. citizens. **Application Requirements:** Financial need analysis. **Application Deadline:** June 30. **Contact:** David Barinholtz, Client Information, Illinois Student Assistance Commission (ISAC), 1755 Lake Cook Road, Deerfield, IL 60015-5209. **Phone:** 847-948-8500 Ext. 2385. **E-mail:** cssupport@isac.org

Illinois Congress of Parents and Teachers

This scholarship is for a student studying in the field of education or an education-related degree program, which requires certification from Illinois State Board of Education. Must be an Illinois resident. Must rank in upper quarter of class. Award for high school seniors graduating from any Illinois public high school. Applications available at every public high school in the counseling office/career center starting in January, or see **Web site:** www.illinoispta.org. **Award:** Scholarship for use in freshman year; not renewable. **Number:** 44. **Amount:** $500–$1000. **Eligibility Requirements:** Applicant must be high school student; planning to enroll or expecting to enroll full-time at a four-year institution or university and resident of Illinois. Available to U.S. citizens. **Application Requirements:** Application, essay, photo, references, self-addressed stamped envelope, transcript. **Application Deadline:** March 1. **Contact:** See high school counselor.

Illinois Future, Inc.

Award for Illinois students whose parent or guardian has suffered permanent disability or death as the result of a work-related accident as adjucated with Illinois Industrial Commission. Must be U.S. citizen under 22 years of age and an Illinois resident. Please send a SASE ($.60 postage required) along with phone number in order to receive an application. **Award:** Scholarship for use in freshman, sophomore, junior, or senior years; renewable. **Number:** 2. **Amount:** $2000. **Eligibility Requirements:** Applicant must be age 21 or under; enrolled or expecting to enroll full-time at a two-year, four-year, or technical institution or university and resident of Illinois. Available to U.S. citizens. **Application Requirements:** Application, financial need analysis, references, self-addressed stamped envelope, test scores, transcript. **Application Deadline:** Continuous. **Contact:** Margie Putzler, Office Manager, Illinois Future, Inc., 821 West Galena Boulevard, Aurora, IL 60506, **Phone:** 630-264-7300, **Fax:** 630-897-8637

Illinois Monetary Award Program

Award for eligible students attending Illinois public universities, private colleges and universities, community colleges, and some proprietary institutions. Applicable only to tuition and fees. Based on financial need. Applicants are encouraged to apply as soon after January 1st as possible. **Award:** Grant for use in freshman, sophomore, junior, or senior years; not renewable. **Number:** 135,000–145,000. **Amount:** up to $4968. **Eligibility Requirements:** Applicant must be enrolled or expecting to enroll full or part-time at a two-year, four-year, or technical institution or university; resident of Illinois and studying in Illinois. Available to U.S. and non-U.S. citizens. **Application Requirements:** Financial need analysis. **Application Deadline:** Continuous. **Contact:** David Barinholtz, Client Information, Illinois Student Assistance Commission (ISAC), 1755 Lake Cook Road, Deerfield, IL 60015-5209. **Phone:** 847-948-8500 Ext. 2385. **E-mail:** cssupport@isac.org

Illinois National Guard Grant Program

Award for qualified National Guard personnel which pays tuition and fees at Illinois public universities and community colleges. Must provide documentation of service. Applications are due October 1 of the academic year for full year, March 1 for second/third term, or June 15 for the summer term. **Award:** Grant for use in freshman, sophomore, junior, senior, graduate, or postgraduate years; renewable. **Number:** 2000–3000. **Amount:** $1300–$1700. **Eligibility Requirements:** Applicant must be enrolled or expecting to enroll full or part-time at a two-year or four-year institution or university; resident of Illinois and studying in Illinois. Available to U.S. and non-U.S. citizens. Applicant must have served in the Air Force National Guard or Army National Guard. **Application Requirements:** Application, documentation of service. **Application Deadline:** varies. **Contact:** David Barinholtz, Client Information, Illinois Student Assistance Commission (ISAC), 1755 Lake Cook Road, Deerfield, IL 60015-5209. **Phone:** 847-948-8500 Ext. 2385. **E-mail:** cssupport@isac.org

Illinois Restaurant Association Educational Foundation

Scholarship available to Illinois residents enrolled in a food service management, culinary arts, or hospitality management concentration in an accredited program of a two- or four-year college or university. Must be a U.S. citizen. **Award:** Scholarship for use in freshman, sophomore, junior, senior, graduate, or postgraduate years; not renewable. **Number:** 50–70. **Amount:** $500–$10,000. **Eligibility Requirements:** Applicant must be enrolled or expecting to enroll full or part-time at a two-year, four-year, or technical institution or university and resident of Illinois. Applicant or parent of applicant must have employment or volunteer experience in food service or hospitality/hotel administration/operations. Available to U.S. citizens. **Application Requirements:** Application, essay, photo, references, transcript. **Application Deadline:** May 15. **Contact:** Roxanne Charles, Program and Operations Manager, Illinois Restaurant Association, Educational Foundation, 200 North LaSalle, Suite 880, Chicago, IL 60601-1014. **Phone:** 312-787-4000. **E-mail:** roxannec@illinoisrestaurants.org

Illinois Student Assistance Commission (ISAC)

Award for dependents of police, fire, and corrections officers killed or disabled in line of duty. Provides for tuition and fees at approved Illinois institutions. Must be resident of Illinois. Continuous deadline. Provide proof of status. **Award:** Grant for use in freshman, sophomore, junior, senior, graduate, or postgraduate years; renewable. **Number:** 50–55. **Amount:** $3000–$4000. **Eligibility Requirements:** Applicant must be enrolled or expecting to enroll at a two-year, four-year, or technical institution or university; resident of Illinois and studying in Illinois. Applicant or parent of applicant must have employment or volunteer experience in police/firefighting. Available to U.S. and non-U.S. citizens. **Application Requirements:** Application, proof of status. **Application Deadline:** Continuous. **Contact:** David Barinholtz, Client Information, Illinois Student, Assistance Commission (ISAC), 1755 Lake Cook Road, Deerfield, IL 60015-5209. **Phone:** 847-948-8500 Ext. 2385. **E-mail:** cssupport@isac.org

Illinois Veteran Grant Program–IVG

Award for qualified veterans for tuition and fees at Illinois public universities and community colleges. Must provide documentation of service (DD214). **Award:** Grant for use in freshman, sophomore, junior, senior, or graduate years; renewable. **Number:** 11,000–13,000. **Amount:** $1400–$1600. **Eligibility Requirements:** Applicant must be enrolled or expecting to enroll full or part-time at a two-year or four-year institution or university; resident of Illinois and studying in Illinois. Available to U.S. and non-U.S. citizens. Applicant must have general military experience. **Application Requirements:** Application, documentation of service. **Application Deadline:** Continuous. **Contact:** David Barinholtz, Client Information, Illinois Student Assistance Commission (ISAC), 1755 Lake Cook Road, Deerfield, IL 60015-5209. **Phone:** 847-948-8500 Ext. 2385. **E-mail:** cssupport@isac.org

Italian-American Chamber of Commerce Midwest

One-time awards for Illinois residents of Italian descent. Available to high school seniors and college students for use at a four-year institution. Applicants must have a 3.5 GPA. Must reside in Cook, Du Page, Kane, Lake, McHenry, or Will counties in Illinois. **Award:** Scholarship for use in freshman, sophomore, junior, or senior years; not renewable. **Number:** 1. **Amount:** up to $1000. **Eligibility Requirements:** Applicant must be of Italian heritage; enrolled or expecting to enroll full-time at a four-year institution and resident of Illinois. Applicant must have 3.5 GPA or higher. Available to U.S. citizens. **Application Requirements:** Application, autobiography, essay, photo, references, self-addressed stamped envelope, transcript. **Application Deadline:** May 31. **Contact:** Frank Pugno, Scholarship Chairman, Italian-American Chamber of Commerce Midwest, 30 South Michigan Avenue, #504, Chicago, IL 60603. **Phone:** 312-553-9137 Ext. 13. **E-mail:** info.chicago@italchambers.net

Merit Recognition Scholarship (MRS) Program

Award for Illinois high school seniors graduating in the top 5% of their class and attending Illinois postsecondary institution. Students scoring in the top 5% in one of the college entrance tests among Illinois residents are also eligible. Contact for application procedures. **Award:** Scholarship for use in freshman year; not renewable. **Number:** 5000–6000. **Amount:** up to $1000. **Eligibility Requirements:** Applicant must be high school student; planning to enroll or expecting to enroll full or part-time at a two-year or four-year institution or university; resident of Illinois and studying in Illinois. Applicant must have 3.5 GPA or higher. Available to U.S. and non-U.S. citizens. **Application Requirements:** Application. **Application Deadline:** Continuous. **Contact:** David Barinholtz, Client Information, Illinois Student Assistance Commission (ISAC), 1755 Lake Cook Road, Deerfield, IL 60015-5209. **Phone:** 847-948-8500 Ext. 2385. **E-mail:** cssupport@isac.org

Robert C. Byrd Honors Scholarship

Available to Illinois residents who are graduating high school seniors. Based on outstanding academic merit. Awards are renewable up to four years. Must be accepted on a full-time basis as an undergraduate student. **Award:** Scholarship for use in freshman, sophomore, junior, or senior years; renewable. **Number:** 1100–1200. **Amount:** up to $1500. **Eligibility Requirements:** Applicant must be high school student; planning to enroll or expecting to enroll full-time at a two-year or four-year institution or university and resident of Illinois. Applicant must have 3.5 GPA or higher. Available to U.S. and non-U.S. citizens. **Application Requirements:** Test scores, transcript. **Application Deadline:** varies. **Contact:** David Barinholtz, Client Information, Illinois Student Assistance Commission (ISAC), 1755 Lake Cook Road, Deerfield, IL 60015-5209. **Phone:** 847-948-8500 Ext. 2385. **E-mail:** cssupport@isac.org

Mellinger Educational Foundation

Scholarships for undergraduates residing in western Illinois and eastern Iowa. **Award:** Scholarship for use in freshman, sophomore, junior, or senior years; renewable. **Number:** 300–350. **Amount:** $300–$1200. **Eligibility Requirements:** Applicant must be enrolled or expecting to enroll full or part-time at a two-year, four-year, or technical institution or university and resident of Illinois or Iowa. Available to U.S. citizens. **Application Requirements:** Application, financial need analysis, test scores, transcript. **Application Deadline:** May 1. **Contact:** David Fleming, President, Mellinger Educational Foundation, 1025 East Broadway, Box 770, Monmouth, IL 61462. **Phone:** 309-734-2419. **Fax:** 309-734-4435

Swiss Benevolent Society of Chicago
Renewable scholarship for full-time students of documented Swiss descent. College students need a 3.5 GPA. High school students need a 26 on ACT or 1,050 on SAT. Must live in Illinois or southern Wisconsin. Applications may be requested after December 15. **Award:** Scholarship for use in freshman, sophomore, junior, or senior years; renewable. **Number:** 30. **Amount:** $750–$2500. **Eligibility Requirements:** Applicant must be of Swiss heritage; enrolled or expecting to enroll full-time at an institution or university and resident of Illinois or Wisconsin. Applicant must have 3.5 GPA or higher. Available to U.S. citizens. **Application Requirements:** Application, essay, self-addressed stamped envelope, test scores, transcript. **Application Deadline:** March 15. **Contact:** Education Committee Swiss Benevolent Society of Chicago, PO Box 2137, Chicago, IL 60690-2137. **E-mail:** education@sbschicago.org

Township Officials of Illinois
The TOI scholarships are awarded to graduating Illinois high school seniors who have a B average or above, have demonstrated an active interest in school activities, who have submitted an essay on "The Importance of Township Government," high school transcript, and letters of recommendation. Students must attend Illinois institutions, either four-year or junior colleges. Must be full-time student. **Award:** Scholarship for use in freshman year; not renewable. **Number:** 10. **Amount:** $2000. **Eligibility Requirements:** Applicant must be high school student; planning to enroll or expecting to enroll full-time at a two-year or four-year institution or university; resident of Illinois and studying in Illinois. Applicant must have 3.0 GPA or higher. Available to U.S. citizens. **Application Requirements:** Application, essay, references, test scores, transcript. **Application Deadline:** March 1. **Contact:** Bryan Smith, Editor and Executive Director, Township Officials of Illinois, 408 South 5th Street, Springfield, IL 62701-1804. **Phone:** 217-744-2212. **E-mail:** bryantoi@toi.org

Indiana

American Legion Auxiliary, Department of Indiana
One-time award for Indiana residents who are high school seniors planning to continue their education. Award is primarily based on need. Contact local units for application and deadline information. **Award:** Scholarship for use in freshman year; not renewable. **Number:** 2. **Eligibility Requirements:** Applicant must be high school student; planning to enroll or expecting to enroll at a two-year, four-year, or technical institution or university and resident of Indiana. Available to U.S. citizens. **Application Requirements:** Application, essay, financial need analysis, self-addressed stamped envelope, transcript. **Application Deadline:** varies. **Contact:** Ms. Sue Liford, Department Secretary and Treasurer American Legion Auxiliary, Department of Indiana, 777 North Meridian, Room 107, Indianapolis, IN 46204

American Legion, Department of Indiana
Oratorical contest open to students in grades 9-12 of any accredited Indiana high school. Speech contests begin in November at post level and continue on to national competition. Contact local American Legion post for deadline and application details. **Award:** Prize for use in freshman year; not renewable. **Number:** 4–8. **Amount:** $500–$1200. **Eligibility Requirements:** Applicant must be high school student; age 19 or under; planning to enroll or expecting to enroll full or part-time at a two-year, four-year, or technical institution or university; resident of Indiana and must have an interest in public speaking. Available to U.S. and Canadian citizens. **Application Requirements:** Application, applicant must enter a contest. **Application Deadline:** varies. **Contact:** B.J. McWilliams, Program Coordinator, American Legion, Department of Indiana, 777 North Meridan Street, Room 104, Indianapolis, IN 46204, **Phone:** 317-630-1264. **E-mail:** bjmcwilliams@indlegion.org

Frank W. McHale Memorial Scholarships
One-time award for Indiana high school juniors who recently participated in the Boys State Program. Must be nominated by Boys State official. Write for more information and deadline. **Award:** Scholarship for use in freshman, sophomore, junior, or senior years; not renewable. **Number:** 3. **Amount:** $1500–$2000. **Eligibility Requirements:** Applicant must be high school student; planning to enroll or expecting to enroll full or part-time at a two-year, four-year, or technical institution or university; male; resident of Indiana and must have an interest in leadership. Available to U.S. citizens. **Application Requirements:** Application. **Application Deadline:** June 1. **Contact:** B.J. McWilliams, Program Coordinator, American Legion, Department of Indiana, 777 North Meridan Street, Room 104, Indianapolis, IN 46204. **Phone:** 317-630-1264. **E-mail:** bjmcwilliams@indlegion.org

Greater Lafayette Community Foundation
Scholarship is for four years of full tuition and fees at the accredited Indiana college or university of the recipient's choice, plus $800 per year for required books and equipment. Must be a resident of Tippecanoe County, Indiana. Minimum 2.75 GPA required. Visit **Web site:** www.glcfonline.org for more information. **Award:** Scholarship for use in freshman, sophomore, junior, or senior years; not renewable. **Number:** 6. **Amount:** $6250–$25,000. **Eligibility Requirements:** Applicant must be enrolled or expecting to enroll full-time at a four-year institution or university; resident of Indiana and studying in Indiana. Available to U.S. citizens. **Application Requirements:** Application, essay, financial need analysis, interview, references, test scores, transcript. **Application Deadline:** varies. **Contact:** Carol Crochet, Program Director, Greater Lafayette Community Foundation, 1114 State Street, PO Box 225, Lafayette, IN 47902-0225. **Phone:** 765-742-9078 Ext. 225. **E-mail:** carol@glcfonline.org

Indiana Broadcasters Association
Must be majoring in broadcasting, electronic media or journalism. Must maintain a 3.0 GPA and be a resident of Indiana. One-time award for full-time undergraduate study in Indiana. **Award:** Scholarship for use in freshman, sophomore, junior, or senior years; not

renewable. **Number:** up to 14. **Amount:** $500–$2000. **Eligibility Requirements:** Applicant must be high school student; planning to enroll or expecting to enroll full-time at a two-year, four-year, or technical institution or university; resident of Indiana and studying in Indiana. Applicant must have 3.0 GPA or higher. Available to U.S. and non-U.S. citizens. **Application Requirements:** Application, essay, references, transcript. **Application Deadline:** March 2. **Contact:** Gwen C. Piening, Scholarship Administrator, Indiana Broadcasters Association, 3003 East 98th Street, Suite 161, Indianapolis, IN 46280. **Phone:** 317-573-0119. **E-mail:** indba@aol.com

Indiana Freedom of Choice Grant

The Freedom of Choice Grant is a need-based, tuition-restricted program for students attending Indiana private institutions seeking a first undergraduate degree. It is awarded in addition to the Higher Education Award. Students (and parents of dependent students) who are U.S. citizens and Indiana residents must file the FAFSA yearly by the March 10 deadline. **Award:** Grant for use in freshman, sophomore, junior, or senior years; not renewable. **Number:** 10,000–11,830. **Amount:** $200–$5915. **Eligibility Requirements:** Applicant must be enrolled or expecting to enroll full-time at a four-year institution or university; resident of Indiana and studying in Indiana. Available to U.S. citizens. **Application Requirements:** Application, financial need analysis, FAFSA. **Application Deadline:** March 10. **Contact:** Grants Counselor, State Student Assistance Commission of Indiana (SSACI), 150 West Market Street, Suite 500, Indianapolis, IN 46204-2805. **Phone:** 317-232-2350. **E-mail:** grants@ssaci.state.in.us

Indiana Health Care Foundation

One-time award of up to $1500 for Indiana residents studying nursing at an institution in Indiana, Ohio, Kentucky, Illinois or Michigan. Minimum 2.5 GPA. Application deadline May 1. **Award:** Scholarship for use in freshman, sophomore, junior, senior, graduate, or postgraduate years; not renewable. **Number:** varies. **Amount:** $750–$1500. **Eligibility Requirements:** Applicant must be enrolled or expecting to enroll full or part-time at a two-year, four-year, or technical institution or university; resident of Indiana and studying in Illinois, Indiana, Kentucky, Michigan, or Ohio. Applicant must have 2.5 GPA or higher. Available to U.S. citizens. **Application Requirements:** Application, essay, interview, references, transcript. **Application Deadline:** May 1. **Contact:** Tamara Noel, Executive Director, Indiana Health Care Foundation, One North Capitol, Suite 1115, Indianapolis, IN 46204. **Phone:** 317-636-6406. **E-mail:** tnoel@ihca.org

Indiana Higher Education Award

The Higher Education Award is a need-based, tuition-restricted program for students attending Indiana public, private, or proprietary institutions seeking a first undergraduate degree. Students (and parents of dependent students) who are U.S. citizens and Indiana residents must file the FAFSA yearly by the March 10 deadline. **Award:** Grant for use in freshman, sophomore, junior, or senior years; not renewable. **Number:** 38,000–43,660. **Amount:** $200–$4700. **Eligibility Requirements:** Applicant must be enrolled or expecting to enroll full-time at a two-year, four-year, or technical institution or university; resident of Indiana and studying in Indiana. Available to U.S. citizens. **Application Requirements:** Application, financial need analysis, FAFSA. **Application Deadline:** March 10. **Contact:** Grants Counselor, State Student Assistance Commission of Indiana (SSACI), 150 West Market Street, Suite 500, Indianapolis, IN 46204-2805. **Phone:** 317-232-2350. **E-mail:** grants@ssaci.state.in.us

Indiana Minority Teacher and Special Education Services Scholarship Program

For Black or Hispanic students seeking teaching certification or for students seeking special education teaching certification or occupational or physical therapy certification. Must be a U.S. citizen and Indiana resident enrolled full-time in an eligible Indiana institution. Must teach in an Indiana-accredited elementary or secondary school after graduation. Contact institution for application and deadline. Minimum 2.0 GPA required. **Award:** Scholarship for use in freshman, sophomore, junior, or senior years; not renewable. **Number:** 280–370. **Amount:** $1000–$4000. **Eligibility Requirements:** Applicant must be Black (non-Hispanic) or Hispanic; enrolled or expecting to enroll full-time at a four-year institution or university; resident of Indiana and studying in Indiana. Available to U.S. citizens. **Application Requirements:** Application, financial need analysis. **Application Deadline:** Continuous. **Contact:** Ms. Yvonne Heflin, Director, Special Programs, State Student Assistance Commission of Indiana (SSACI), 150 West Market Street, Suite 500, Indianapolis, IN 46204-2805. **Phone:** 317-232-2350. **E-mail:** grants@ssaci.state.in.us

Indiana Nursing Scholarship Fund

Need-based tuition funding for nursing students enrolled full- or part-time at an eligible Indiana institution. Must be a U.S. citizen and an Indiana resident and have a minimum 2.0 GPA or meet the minimum requirements for the nursing program. Upon graduation, recipients must practice as a nurse in an Indiana health care setting for two years. **Award:** Scholarship for use in freshman, sophomore, junior, or senior years; not renewable. **Number:** 490–690. **Amount:** $200–$5000. **Eligibility Requirements:** Applicant must be enrolled or expecting to enroll full or part-time at a two-year or four-year institution or university; resident of Indiana and studying in Indiana. Available to U.S. citizens. **Application Requirements:** Application, financial need analysis. **Application Deadline:** Continuous. **Contact:** Ms. Yvonne Heflin, Director, Special Programs, State Student Assistance Commission of Indiana (SSACI), 150 West Market Street, Suite 500, Indianapolis, IN 46204-2805. **Phone:** 317-232-2350

Marion D. and Eva S. Peeples Foundation Trust Scholarship Program

Award for study in nursing, dietetics, and teaching in industrial arts. Applicant must reapply each year for renewal. Recipient must maintain 2.5 GPA and take at least 12 credit hours per semester. Minimum 1100 on SAT if high school student. Must be Indiana resident and attending an Indiana school. **Award:** Scholarship for use in freshman, sophomore, junior, or senior years; not renewable. **Number:** 15–30. **Amount:** $500–$4000.

Eligibility Requirements: Applicant must be enrolled or expecting to enroll full-time at a two-year, four-year, or technical institution or university; resident of Indiana and studying in Indiana. Applicant must have 2.5 GPA or higher. Available to U.S. citizens. **Application Requirements:** Application, autobiography, financial need analysis, interview, references, self-addressed stamped envelope, test scores, transcript. **Application Deadline:** March 1. **Contact:** Sonya Baker-Hallett, Scholarship Director, Marion D. and Eva S. Peeples Foundation Trust Scholarship Program, 398 South Main Street, Franklin, IN 46131.
Phone: 317-738-2213.
E-mail: sonyah@jccf.org

Pacers Foundation, Inc.

The Pacers Teamup Scholarship presented by Miller Lite is awarded to Indiana high school seniors for their first year of undergraduate study at any accredited four-year college or university or two-year college or junior college. Primary selection criteria is student involvement in community service. **Award:** Scholarship for use in freshman year; not renewable. **Number:** 5. **Amount:** $2000. **Eligibility Requirements:** Applicant must be high school student; planning to enroll or expecting to enroll full-time at a two-year or four-year institution or university and resident of Indiana. Available to U.S. citizens. **Application Requirements:** Application, essay, references, transcript. **Application Deadline:** March 1. **Contact:** Sarah Furimsky, Coordinator, Pacers Foundation, Inc., 125 South Pennsylvania Street, Indianapolis, IN 46204. **Phone:** 317-917-2864.
E-mail: foundation@pacers.com

Part-time Grant Program

Program is designed to encourage part-time undergraduates to start and complete their associate or baccalaureate degrees or certificates by subsidizing part-time tuition costs. It is a term-based award that is based on need. State residency requirements must be met and a FAFSA must be filed. Eligibility is determined at the institutional level subject to approval by SSACI. **Award:** Grant for use in freshman, sophomore, junior, or senior years; not renewable. **Number:** 4680–6700. **Amount:** $50–$4000. **Eligibility Requirements:** Applicant must be enrolled or expecting to enroll part-time at a two-year, four-year, or technical institution or university; resident of Indiana and studying in Indiana. Available to U.S. citizens. **Application Requirements:** Application, financial need analysis. **Application Deadline:** Continuous. **Contact:** Grants Counselor, State Student Assistance Commission of Indiana (SSACI), 150 West Market Street, Suite 500, Indianapolis, IN 46204-2805.
Phone: 317-232-2350.
E-mail: grants@ssaci.state.in.us

State Student Assistance Commission of Indiana (SSACI)

Scholarship is designed to recognize academic achievement and requires a minimum SAT score of 1300 or ACT score of 31, or recent GED score of 65. The scholarship is awarded equally among Indiana's congressional districts. The amount of the scholarship varies depending upon federal funding and is automatically renewed if the institution's satisfactory academic progress requirements are met. **Award:** Scholarship for use in freshman, sophomore, junior, or senior years; renewable. **Number:** 550–570. **Amount:** $1500. **Eligibility Requirements:** Applicant must be enrolled or expecting to enroll full-time at a two-year or four-year institution or university and resident of Indiana. Applicant must have 3.5 GPA or higher. Available to U.S. citizens. **Application Requirements:** Application, test scores, transcript. **Application Deadline:** April 24. **Contact:** Ms. Yvonne Heflin, Director, Special Programs, State Student Assistance Commission of Indiana (SSACI), 150 West Market Street, Suite 500, Indianapolis, IN 46204-2805.
Phone: 317-232-2350

Twenty-first Century Scholars Award

Income-eligible 7th graders who enroll in the program, fulfill a pledge of good citizenship, and complete the Affirmation Form are guaranteed tuition for four years at any participating public institution. If the student attends a private institution, the state will award an amount comparable to that of a public institution. If the student attends a participating proprietary school, the state will award a tuition scholarship equal to that of Ivy Tech State College. FAFSA and affirmation form must be filed yearly by March 10. Applicant must be resident of Indiana. **Award:** Scholarship for use in freshman, sophomore, junior, or senior years; not renewable. **Number:** 2800–8100. **Amount:** $1000–$6516. **Eligibility Requirements:** Applicant must be enrolled or expecting to enroll full-time at a two-year, four-year, or technical institution or university; resident of Indiana and studying in Indiana. Applicant must have 2.5 GPA or higher. Available to U.S. citizens. **Application Requirements:** Application, financial need analysis, affirmation form. **Application Deadline:** March 10. **Contact:** Twenty-first Century Scholars Program Counselors, State Student Assistance Commission of Indiana (SSACI), 150 West Market Street, Suite 500, Indianapolis, IN 46204-2805. **Phone:** 317-233-2100

Iowa

American Legion, Department of Iowa

Three one-time award for Eagle Scouts who are residents of Iowa. Must be a high school student with minimum 2.5 GPA. **Award:** Scholarship for use in freshman year; not renewable. **Number:** 3. **Amount:** $400–$2000. **Eligibility Requirements:** Applicant must be high school student; planning to enroll or expecting to enroll full-time at a two-year or four-year institution or university; male and resident of Iowa. Applicant or parent of applicant must be member of Boy Scouts. Applicant must have 2.5 GPA or higher. Available to U.S. citizens. **Application Deadline:** February 1. **Contact:** Program Director, American Legion, Department of Iowa, 720 Lyon Street, Des Moines, IA 50309

American Legion Department of Iowa Outstanding Senior Baseball Player

One-time award for Iowa residents who participated in the American Legion Senior Baseball Program and display outstanding sportsmanship, athletic ability, and proven academic achievements. Must be recommended by Baseball Committee. **Award:** Scholarship for use in freshman,

sophomore, junior, or senior years; not renewable. **Number:** 1. **Amount:** $750–$1500. **Eligibility Requirements:** Applicant must be high school student; age 15-18; planning to enroll or expecting to enroll full-time at a two-year, four-year, or technical institution or university; resident of Iowa and must have an interest in athletics/sports. Applicant must have 3.5 GPA or higher. **Application Requirements:** Application. **Application Deadline:** June 1. **Contact:** Program Director
American Legion, Department of Iowa, 720 Lyon Street, Des Moines, IA 50309

Grand Lodge of Iowa, AF and AM

Scholarships are awarded based on scholastics, school and community activity, and leadership. Applicants are selected to be interviewed based on their written application. Recipients are selected based on those interviews. **Award:** Scholarship for use in freshman year; not renewable. **Number:** 60–70. **Amount:** $2000. **Eligibility Requirements:** Applicant must be high school student; planning to enroll or expecting to enroll full-time at a two-year, four-year, or technical institution or university and resident of Iowa. Available to U.S. and non-U.S. citizens. **Application Requirements:** Application, autobiography, interview, references, transcript. **Application Deadline:** February 1. **Contact:** William Crawford, Grand Secretary, Grand Lodge of Iowa, AF and AM, PO Box 279, Cedar Rapids, IA 52406-0279. **Phone:** 319-365-1438. **E-mail:** gs@gl-iowa.org

Herbert Hoover Presidential Library Association

Only juniors in an Iowa high school or home school program may apply. Grades and test scores are not evaluated. Applicants are chosen on the basis of project proposals they submit. Those chosen complete their project and make a presentation. All receive $750. Three are chosen for $5000 award. **Award:** Scholarship for use in freshman or sophomore years; not renewable. **Number:** 18. **Amount:** $750–$5000. **Eligibility Requirements:** Applicant must be high school student; planning to enroll or expecting to enroll full-time at a two-year or four-year institution and resident of Iowa. Available to U.S. and non-U.S. citizens. **Application Requirements:** Application, references, project proposal. **Application Deadline:** March 31. **Contact:** Patricia Hand, Academic Programs Manager, Herbert Hoover Presidential Library Association, PO Box 696, West Branch, IA 52358-0696. **Phone:** 319-643-5327. **E-mail:** info@hooverassociation.org

Iowa College Student Aid Commission

Up to four scholarships ranging from $500 to $1000 will be awarded to students graduating from an Iowa high school. Must actively participate at the Iowa State Fair. For more details see **Web site:** www.iowacollegeaid.org. **Award:** Scholarship for use in freshman year; not renewable. **Number:** up to 4. **Amount:** $500–$1000. **Eligibility Requirements:** Applicant must be high school student; planning to enroll or expecting to enroll at an institution or university; resident of Iowa and studying in Iowa. Available to U.S. citizens. **Application Requirements:** Application, essay, financial need analysis, references, transcript. **Application Deadline:** May 1. **Contact:** Brenda Easter, Director, Special Programs, Iowa College Student Aid Commission, 200 10th Street, 4th Floor, Des Moines, IA 50309-3609. **Phone:** 515-242-3380

Iowa Division of Vocational Rehabilitation Services

Provides vocational rehabilitation services to individuals with disabilities who need these services in order to maintain, retain, or obtain employment compatible with their disabilities. Must be Iowa resident. **Award:** Grant for use in freshman, sophomore, junior, senior, graduate, or postgraduate years; renewable. **Number:** up to 5000. **Amount:** $500–$4000. **Eligibility Requirements:** Applicant must be enrolled or expecting to enroll full or part-time at a two-year, four-year, or technical institution or university and resident of Iowa. Applicant must be hearing impaired, learning disabled, physically disabled, or visually impaired. Available to U.S. and non-U.S. citizens. **Application Requirements:** Application, interview. **Application Deadline:** Continuous. **Contact:** Ralph Childers, Policy and Workforce Initiatives Coordinator, Iowa Division of Vocational Rehabilitation Services, Division of Vocational Rehabilitation Services, 510 East 12th Street, Des Moines, IA 50319. **Phone:** 515-281-4151. **E-mail:** rchilders@dvrs.state.ia.us

Iowa Foster Child Grants

Grants renewable up to four years will be awarded to students graduating from an Iowa high school who are in Iowa foster care under the care and custody of the Iowa Department of Human Service. Must have a minimum GPA of 2.25 and have applied to an accredited Iowa college or university. For more details see **Web site:** www.iowacollegeaid.org. **Award:** Grant for use in freshman year; renewable. **Number:** varies. **Amount:** $2000–$4200. **Eligibility Requirements:** Applicant must be high school student; planning to enroll or expecting to enroll at a two-year or four-year institution or university; resident of Iowa and studying in Iowa. Available to U.S. citizens. **Application Requirements:** Application. **Application Deadline:** April 15. **Contact:** Brenda Easter, Director, Special Programs, Iowa College Student Aid Commission, 200 10th Street, 4th Floor, Des Moines, IA 50309-3609. **Phone:** 515-242-3380

Iowa Grants

Statewide need-based program to assist high-need Iowa residents. Recipients must demonstrate a high level of financial need to receive awards ranging from $100 to $1,000. Awards are prorated for students enrolled for less than full-time. Awards must be used at Iowa postsecondary institutions. **Award:** Grant for use in freshman, sophomore, junior, or senior years; not renewable. **Number:** varies. **Amount:** $100–$1000. **Eligibility Requirements:** Applicant must be enrolled or expecting to enroll full or part-time at a two-year, four-year, or technical institution or university; resident of Iowa and studying in Iowa. Available to U.S. citizens. **Application Requirements:** Application, financial need analysis. **Application Deadline:** Continuous. **Contact:** Julie Leeper, Director, State Student Aid Programs, Iowa College Student Aid Commission, 200 10th Street, 4th Floor, Des Moines, IA 50309-3609. **Phone:** 515-242-3370. **E-mail:** icsac@max.state.ia.us

Iowa National Guard Education Assistance Program

Program provides postsecondary tuition assistance to members of Iowa National Guard Units. Must study at a postsecondary institution in Iowa.

Contact for additional information. **Award:** Grant for use in freshman, sophomore, junior, or senior years; not renewable. **Number:** varies. **Amount:** up to $1200. **Eligibility Requirements:** Applicant must be enrolled or expecting to enroll full or part-time at a two-year, four-year, or technical institution or university; resident of Iowa and studying in Iowa. Available to U.S. citizens. Applicant must have served in the Air Force National Guard or Army National Guard. **Application Requirements:** Application. **Application Deadline:** Continuous. **Contact:** Julie Leeper, Director, State Student Aid Programs, Iowa College Student Aid Commission, 200 10th Street, 4th Floor, Des Moines, IA 50309-3609. **Phone:** 515-242-3370. **E-mail:** icsac@max.state.ia.us

Iowa Teacher Forgivable Loan Program

Forgivable loan assists students who will teach in Iowa secondary schools. Must be an Iowa resident attending an Iowa postsecondary institution. Contact for additional information. **Award:** Forgivable loan for use in freshman, sophomore, junior, or senior years; not renewable. **Number:** varies. **Amount:** $2686. **Eligibility Requirements:** Applicant must be enrolled or expecting to enroll full or part-time at a four-year institution or university; resident of Iowa and studying in Iowa. Applicant or parent of applicant must have employment or volunteer experience in teaching. Available to U.S. citizens. **Application Requirements:** Application, financial need analysis. **Application Deadline:** Continuous. **Contact:** Brenda Easter, Special Programs Administrator, Iowa College Student Aid Commission, 200 10th Street, 4th Floor, Des Moines, IA 50309-3609. **Phone:** 515-242-3380. **E-mail:** icsac@max.state.ia.us

Iowa Tuition Grant Program

Program assists students who attend independent postsecondary institutions in Iowa. Iowa residents currently enrolled, or planning to enroll, for at least three semester hours at one of the eligible Iowa postsecondary institutions may apply. Awards currently range from $100 to $4000. Grants may not exceed the difference between independent college and university tuition and fees and the average tuition and fees at the three public Regent universities. **Award:** Grant for use in freshman, sophomore, junior, or senior years; not renewable. **Number:** varies. **Amount:** $100–$4000. **Eligibility Requirements:** Applicant must be enrolled or expecting to enroll full or part-time at a two-year or four-year institution; resident of Iowa and studying in Iowa. Available to U.S. citizens. **Application Requirements:** Application, financial need analysis. **Application Deadline:** July 1. **Contact:** Julie Leeper, Director, State Student Aid Programs, Iowa College Student Aid Commission, 200 10th Street, 4th Floor, Des Moines, IA 50309-3609. **Phone:** 515-242-3370. **E-mail:** icsac@max.state.ia.us

Oratorical Contest Scholarship

Three awards granted in oratorical contest. Must be resident of Iowa. **Award:** Prize for use in freshman, sophomore, junior, or senior years; not renewable. **Number:** 3. **Amount:** $400–$2000. **Eligibility Requirements:** Applicant must be enrolled or expecting to enroll full-time at a two-year or four-year institution or university; resident of Iowa and must have an interest in public speaking. Available to U.S. citizens. **Application Requirements:** Applicant must enter a contest. **Application Deadline:** varies. **Contact:** Program Director, American Legion, Department of Iowa, 720 Lyon Street, Des Moines, IA 50309

Robert C. Byrd Honors Scholarship

Scholarships up to $1500 are awarded to exceptionally able Iowa high school seniors who show promise of continued academic excellence. Must have a minimum of a 28 ACT or 1240 SAT, a 3.5 GPA and rank in the top 10% of the student's high school graduating class. For more details see **Web site:** www.iowacollegeaid.org. **Award:** Scholarship for use in freshman year; renewable. **Number:** up to 70. **Amount:** up to $1500. **Eligibility Requirements:** Applicant must be high school student; planning to enroll or expecting to enroll at an institution or university and resident of Iowa. Applicant must have 3.5 GPA or higher. Available to U.S. citizens. **Application Requirements:** Application, test scores, transcript. **Application Deadline:** February 1. **Contact:** Brenda Easter, Director, Special Programs, Iowa College Student Aid Commission, 200 10th Street, 4th Floor, Des Moines, IA 50309-3609. **Phone:** 515-242-3380

Kansas

American Legion, Department of Kansas

Oratorical contest open to students in 9th, 10th, 11th, and 12th grades of any accredited Kansas high school. Speech contests begin in January at post level and continue on to national competition. Contact local American Legion for deadlines. **Award:** Prize for use in freshman year; not renewable. **Number:** 4. **Amount:** $150–$1500. **Eligibility Requirements:** Applicant must be high school student; age 20 or under; planning to enroll or expecting to enroll at an institution or university; resident of Kansas and must have an interest in public speaking. Applicant or parent of applicant must be member of American Legion or Auxiliary. Available to U.S. citizens. **Application Requirements:** Application, applicant must enter a contest, photo, references. **Contact:** Sallie Stewart, Scholarship Administrator, American Legion, Department of Kansas, 1314 SouthwestTopeka Boulevard.Topeka, KS 66612-1886

Kansas National Guard Educational Assistance Program

Service scholarship for enlisted soldiers in the Kansas National Guard. Pays up to 100% of tuition and fees based on funding. Must attend a state-supported institution. Recipients will be required to serve in the KNG for three months for every semester of benefits after the last payment of state tuition assistance. Must not have over 15 years of service at time of application. Deadlines are January 15 and August 20. Contact KNG Education Services Specialist for further information. Must be Kansas resident. **Award:** Scholarship for use in freshman, sophomore, junior, or senior years; not renewable. **Number:** up to 400. **Amount:** $250–$3500. **Eligibility Requirements:** Applicant must be enrolled or expecting to enroll full or part-time at a two-year, four-year, or technical institution or university; resident of Kansas and studying in Kansas. Available to U.S. citizens. Applicant must have served in the Air Force National Guard or Army National Guard. **Application Requirements:** Application. **Application Deadline:** varies. **Contact:** Steve Finch, Education Services Specialist Kansas National Guard Educational Assistance Program,

Attn: AGKS-DOP-ESO, The Adjutant General of Kansas, 2800 South West, Topeka Boulevard, Topeka, KS 66611-1287. **Phone:** 785-274-1060. **E-mail:** steve.finch@ks.ngb.army.mil

Michigan

American Cancer Society, Inc.-Great Lakes Division

Scholarships for Michigan and Indiana residents who have had a diagnosis of cancer before the age of 21. Applicant must be under 21 at time of application. To be used for undergraduate degrees at any accredited Michigan or Indiana college or university. Deadline: mid-April. Open to U.S. citizens only. **Award:** Scholarship for use in freshman, sophomore, junior, or senior years; renewable. **Number:** up to 72. **Amount:** $1000. **Eligibility Requirements:** Applicant must be age 17-20; enrolled or expecting to enroll full-time at a two-year, four-year, or technical institution or university; resident of Indiana or Michigan and studying in Indiana or Michigan. Available to U.S. citizens. **Application Requirements:** Application, essay, financial need analysis, references, test scores, transcript. **Application Deadline:** April 16. **Contact:** Deb Dillingham, Director of Quality of Life, American Cancer Society, Inc.-Great Lakes Division, 1755 Abbey Road, East Lansing, MI 48823. **Phone:** 800-723-0360. **E-mail:** deb.dillingham@cancer.org

American Legion Auxiliary, Department of Michigan

One-time scholarship for son or daughter of veterans who were in Armed Forces during eligibility dates for American Legion membership. Must be high school senior in Michigan. Only one candidate per Unit. Applicant must complete fifty hours of volunteer service in the community. Submit essay of no more than 1000 words on a specified topic. **Award:** Scholarship for use in freshman year; not renewable. **Number:** 3. **Amount:** $1000–$2500. **Eligibility Requirements:** Applicant must be high school student; planning to enroll or expecting to enroll full or part-time at a two-year or four-year institution or university and resident of Michigan. Available to U.S. citizens. Applicant or parent must meet one or more of the following requirements: general military experience; retired from active duty; disabled or killed as a result of military service; prisoner of war; or missing in action. **Application Requirements:** Application, essay, financial need analysis, references, test scores, transcript, fifty hours of volunteer service. **Application Deadline:** March 10. **Contact:** Leisa Eldred, Scholarship Coordinator, American Legion Auxiliary, Department of Michigan, 212 North Verlinden Avenue, Lansing, MI 48915. **Phone:** 517-371-4720 Ext. 19. **E-mail:** michalaux@voyager.net

American Legion, Department of Michigan

Oratorical contest open to students in 9th-12th grades of any accredited Michigan high school or state accredited home school. Five one-time awards of varying amounts. Speech contests begin in January at zone level and continue on to national competition. Contact for deadlines and application details. **Award:** Prize for use in freshman year; not renewable. **Number:** 5. **Amount:** $600–$1000. **Eligibility Requirements:** Applicant must be high school student; age 20 or under; planning to enroll or expecting to enroll full or part-time at a two-year, four-year, or technical institution or university; resident of Michigan and must have an interest in public speaking. Available to U.S. citizens. **Application Requirements:** Application, applicant must enter a contest. **Application Deadline:** January 31. **Contact:** Deanna Clark, Program Secretary, American Legion, Department of Michigan, 212 North Verlinden Avenue, Lansing, MI 48915, **Phone:** 517-371-4720 Ext. 25. **E-mail:** programs@michiganlegion.org

Coleman A. Young Foundation

Renewable award to Detroit area high school seniors who demonstrate leadership qualities. Minimum 2.5 GPA required. Must be single and U.S. citizen. Aimed at students who would not ordinarily qualify for traditional scholarships. Must be enrolled full-time in a four year college in Michigan or attend an accredited, historically black institution. **Award:** Scholarship for use in freshman, sophomore, junior, or senior years; renewable. **Number:** 5–10. **Amount:** up to $20,000. **Eligibility Requirements:** Applicant must be high school student; planning to enroll or expecting to enroll full-time at a four-year institution or university; single and resident of Michigan. Applicant must have 2.5 GPA or higher. Available to U.S. citizens. **Application Requirements:** Application, essay, financial need analysis, interview, references, test scores, transcript. **Application Deadline:** April 1. **Contact:** Thelma Bush, Program Manager, Coleman A. Young Foundation, 2111 Woodward Avenue, Suite 600, Detroit, MI 48201. **Phone:** 313-962-2200. **E-mail:** thelmabush@cayf.org

Lawrence P. Doss Scholarship Foundation

Renewable scholarships are available to residents of Michigan who are seniors graduating from a high school in the greater Detroit area. Must be pursuing a degree in accounting, finance, management or business. Financial need considered. For more details see **Web site:** www.lawrencepdossfnd.org. **Award:** Scholarship for use in freshman, sophomore, junior, or senior years; renewable. **Number:** 5. **Amount:** $5000. **Eligibility Requirements:** Applicant must be high school student; planning to enroll or expecting to enroll full-time at a four-year institution or university; single and resident of Michigan. Applicant must have 2.5 GPA or higher. Available to U.S. citizens. **Application Requirements:** Application, essay, financial need analysis, interview, references, test scores, transcript. **Application Deadline:** March 15. **Contact:** Lawrence P. Doss Scholarship Foundation, 7 Oak Station, PO Box 351037, Detroit, MI 48325

Michigan Bureau of Student Financial Assistance

Awards limited to tuition. Must maintain a C average and meet the college's academic progress requirements. Must file Free Application for Federal Student Aid. Deadline: March 1. Must be Michigan resident. Renewable award of $1300 for undergraduate study at a Michigan institution. **Award:** Scholarship for use in freshman, sophomore, junior, or senior years; renewable. **Number:** varies. **Amount:** $100–$1300. **Eligibility Requirements:** Applicant must be enrolled or expecting to enroll at a two-year or four-year institution or university; resident of Michigan and studying in Michigan. Available to U.S. citizens.

Application Requirements: Application, financial need analysis, test scores, FAFSA. **Application Deadline:** March 1. **Contact:** Scholarship and Grant Director, Michigan Bureau of Student Financial Assistance, PO Box 30466, Lansing, MI 48909

Michigan Educational Opportunity Grant

Need-based program for Michigan residents who are at least half-time undergraduates attending public Michigan colleges. Must maintain good academic standing. Deadline determined by college. Award of up to $1000. **Award:** Grant for use in freshman, sophomore, junior, or senior years; not renewable. **Number:** varies. **Amount:** up to $1000. **Eligibility Requirements:** Applicant must be enrolled or expecting to enroll full or part-time at a two-year or four-year institution or university; resident of Michigan and studying in Michigan. Available to U.S. citizens. **Application Requirements:** Application, financial need analysis. **Application Deadline:** varies. **Contact:** Program Director, Michigan Bureau of Student Financial Assistance, PO Box 30466, Lansing, MI 48909-7966

Michigan Merit Award

Scholarship for students scoring well on state's standardized assessment tests. Students will have four years from high school graduation to use the award. **Award:** Scholarship for use in freshman year; not renewable. **Number:** varies. **Amount:** $1000–$2500. **Eligibility Requirements:** Applicant must be high school student; planning to enroll or expecting to enroll full or part-time at a two-year, four-year, or technical institution or university and resident of Michigan. Available to U.S. citizens. **Application Requirements:** Test scores. **Contact:** Program Director, Michigan Bureau of Student, Financial Assistance, PO Box 30466, Lansing, MI 48909-7966

Michigan Nursing Scholarship

For students enrolled in an LPN, associate degree in nursing, or bachelor of science in nursing programs. Colleges determine application procedure and select recipients. Recipients must fulfill in-state work commitment or repay scholarship. **Award:** Scholarship for use in freshman, sophomore, junior, or senior years; renewable. **Number:** varies. **Amount:** up to $4000. **Eligibility Requirements:** Applicant must be enrolled or expecting to enroll full or part-time at a two-year or four-year institution or university; resident of Michigan and studying in Michigan. Available to U.S. citizens. **Contact:** Program Director, Michigan Bureau of Student Financial Assistance, PO Box 30466, Lansing, MI 48909-7966

Michigan Society of Professional Engineers

Grant of $2000 for engineering student demonstrating an interest in the fields of manufacturing and industry. Preference given to a student attending Lawrence Technical University and majoring in manufacturing engineering. Must be a member of MSPE Student Chapter or a state member-at-large. Minimum 3.0 GPA required. Restricted to Michigan residents attending Michigan schools. Academic Fields/Career Goals: Chemical Engineering; Civil Engineering; Engineering/Technology; Mechanical Engineering. **Award:** Grant for use in freshman, sophomore, junior, or senior years; not renewable. **Number:** 1. **Amount:** $2000. **Eligibility Requirements:** Applicant must be enrolled or expecting to enroll full-time at an institution or university; resident of Michigan and studying in Michigan. Applicant or parent of applicant must be member of Michigan Society of Professional Engineers. Applicant must have 3.0 GPA or higher. Available to U.S. citizens. **Application Requirements:** Application, essay, references, transcript. **Application Deadline:** varies. **Contact:** Scholarship Coordinator, Michigan Society of Professional Engineers, PO Box 15276, Lansing, MI 48901-5276. **Phone:** 517-487-9388. **E-mail:** mspe@voyager.net

Michigan Society of Professional Engineers Undesignated Grant

Grant of $2000 for a top-ranking student enrolled in an ABET-accredited engineering program at a Michigan college or university. Renewal based on academic performance and approval of both the MSPE Scholarship Trust and Dean of School. Must be a member of MSPE student chapter or state member-at-large. Minimum 3.0 GPA required. Must be a Michigan resident. **Award:** Grant for use in freshman, sophomore, junior, or senior years; renewable. **Number:** 1. **Amount:** $2000. **Eligibility Requirements:** Applicant must be enrolled or expecting to enroll at an institution or university; resident of Michigan and studying in Michigan. Applicant or parent of applicant must be member of Michigan Society of Professional Engineers. Applicant must have 3.0 GPA or higher. Available to U.S. citizens. **Application Requirements:** Application, essay, references, test scores, transcript. **Application Deadline:** varies. **Contact:** Scholarship Coordinator, Michigan Society of Professional Engineers, PO Box 15276, Lansing, MI 48901-5276. **Phone:** 517-487-9388. **E-mail:** mspe@voyager.net

Michigan Society of Professional Engineers 1980 National Society of Professional Engineers Annual Meeting Committee Grant

One $2000 grant for a Michigan high school senior to study engineering at an ABET-accredited college or university in Michigan. Minimum 3.0 GPA required for grades 11 and 12. **Award:** Grant for use in freshman year; not renewable. **Number:** 1. **Amount:** $2000. **Eligibility Requirements:** Applicant must be high school student; planning to enroll or expecting to enroll full-time at an institution or university; resident of Michigan and studying in Michigan. Applicant must have 3.0 GPA or higher. Available to U.S. citizens. **Application Requirements:** Application, test scores, transcript. **Application Deadline:** varies. **Contact:** Scholarship Coordinator, Michigan Society of Professional Engineers, PO Box 15276, Lansing, MI 48901-5276. **Phone:** 517-487-9388. **E-mail:** mspe@voyager.net

Michigan Society of Professional Engineers Abrams Grant

One $3000 grant for a top ranking student interested in pursuing a career in civil or surveying engineering. Must be a Michigan resident enrolled in an ABET-accredited program at a Michigan college or university. Minimum 3.0 GPA required. Applicant must be a member of MSPE student chapter or a state member-at-large. **Award:** Grant for use in freshman, sophomore, junior, or senior years; not renewable.

Number: 1. **Amount:** $3000. **Eligibility Requirements:** Applicant must be enrolled or expecting to enroll full-time at an institution or university; resident of Michigan and studying in Michigan. Applicant or parent of applicant must be member of Michigan Society of Professional Engineers. Applicant must have 3.0 GPA or higher. Available to U.S. citizens. **Application Requirements:** Application, essay, references, transcript. **Application Deadline:** varies. **Contact:** Scholarship Coordinator, Michigan Society of Professional Engineers, PO Box 15276, Lansing, MI 48901-5276. **Phone:** 517-487-9388. **E-mail:** mspe@voyager.net

Michigan Society of Professional Engineers Auxiliary Grant

One $1000 grant for high ranking Michigan high school seniors interested in pursuing a career in engineering and planning to attend an ABET-accredited college or university in Michigan. Preference given to a son or daughter of an MSPE member. Minimum 3.0 GPA required in grades 11 and 12. **Award:** Grant for use in freshman year; not renewable. **Number:** 1. **Amount:** $1000. **Eligibility Requirements:** Applicant must be high school student; planning to enroll or expecting to enroll full-time at a four-year institution or university; resident of Michigan and studying in Michigan. Applicant or parent of applicant must be member of Michigan Society of Professional Engineers. Applicant must have 3.0 GPA or higher. Available to U.S. citizens. **Application Requirements:** Application, test scores, transcript. **Application Deadline:** varies. **Contact:** Scholarship Coordinator, Michigan Society of Professional Engineers, PO Box 15276, Lansing, MI 48901-5276. **Phone:** 517-487-9388. **E-mail:** mspe@voyager.net

Michigan Society of Professional Engineers Harry R. Ball, P.E. Grant

One $2000 grant for a Michigan high school student to study engineering at an ABET-accredited college or university in Michigan. Minimum 3.0 GPA required in grades 11 and 12. Submit application to local MSPE Chapter Chair. **Award:** Grant for use in freshman year; not renewable. **Number:** 1. **Amount:** $2000. **Eligibility Requirements:** Applicant must be high school student; planning to enroll or expecting to enroll full-time at an institution or university; resident of Michigan and studying in Michigan. Applicant must have 3.0 GPA or higher. Available to U.S. citizens. **Application Requirements:** Application, test scores, transcript. **Application Deadline:** varies. **Contact:** Scholarship Coordinator, Michigan Society of Professional Engineers, PO Box 15276, Lansing, MI 48901-5276. **Phone:** 517-487-9388. **E-mail:** mspe@voyager.net

Michigan Society of Professional Engineers Kenneth B. Fishbeck, P.E. Memorial Grant

One $1000 grant for a Michigan high school student to study engineering at an ABET-accredited college or university in Michigan. Minimum 3.0 GPA required in grades 11 and 12. Submit application to local MSPE Chapter Chair. Applicants should demonstrate qualifications of high merit and professional ethics. **Award:** Grant for use in freshman year; not renewable. **Number:** 1. **Amount:** $1000. **Eligibility Requirements:** Applicant must be high school student; planning to enroll or expecting to enroll full-time at an institution or university; resident of Michigan and studying in Michigan. Applicant must have 3.0 GPA or higher. Available to U.S. citizens. **Application Requirements:** Application, test scores, transcript. **Application Deadline:** varies. **Contact:** Scholarship Coordinator, Michigan Society of Professional Engineers, PO Box 15276, Lansing, MI 48901-5276. **Phone:** 517-487-9388. **E-mail:** mspe@voyager.net

Michigan Society of Professional Engineers Scholarship Trust Grant

One $2000 grant for Michigan high school senior planning to pursue a career in engineering at a Michigan ABET-accredited college or university. Minimum 3.0 GPA for grades 11 and 12 required. **Award:** Grant for use in freshman year; not renewable. **Number:** 1. **Amount:** $2000. **Eligibility Requirements:** Applicant must be high school student; planning to enroll or expecting to enroll full-time at an institution or university; resident of Michigan and studying in Michigan. Applicant must have 3.0 GPA or higher. Available to U.S. citizens. **Application Requirements:** Application, test scores, transcript. **Application Deadline:** varies. **Contact:** Scholarship Coordinator, Michigan Society of Professional Engineers, PO Box 15276, Lansing, MI 48901-5276. **Phone:** 517-487-9388. **E-mail:** mspe@voyager.net

Michigan Tuition Grants

Need-based program. Students must attend a Michigan private, nonprofit, degree-granting college. Must file the Free Application for Federal Student Aid and meet the college's academic progress requirements. Deadline: March 1. Must be Michigan resident. Renewable award of $2000. **Award:** Grant for use in freshman, sophomore, junior, or senior years; renewable. **Number:** varies. **Amount:** $100–$2750. **Eligibility Requirements:** Applicant must be enrolled or expecting to enroll at a two-year or four-year institution or university; resident of Michigan and studying in Michigan. Available to U.S. citizens. **Application Requirements:** Application, financial need analysis, FAFSA. **Application Deadline:** March 1. **Contact:** Scholarship and Grant Director, Michigan Bureau of Student Financial Assistance, PO Box 30466, Lansing, MI 48909-7966

MSPE Auxiliary Grant for Undergraduate Study

One grant of $1000 will be awarded to a student interested in pursuing a career in engineering. Preference is given to a son/daughter of an MSPE member, but is not required to apply. **Award:** Grant for use in freshman, sophomore, junior, or senior years; not renewable. **Number:** 1. **Amount:** $1000. **Eligibility Requirements:** Applicant must be enrolled or expecting to enroll full-time at an institution or university; resident of Michigan and studying in Michigan. Applicant must have 3.0 GPA or higher. Available to U.S. citizens. **Application Requirements:** Application, essay, references, transcript. **Application Deadline:** varies. **Contact:** Scholarship Coordinator, Michigan Society of Professional Engineers, PO Box 15276, Lansing, MI 48901-5276. **Phone:** 517-487-9388. **E-mail:** mspe@voyager.net

Robert E. Folmsbee, P.E. Memorial Grant

One $2000 grant for a top-ranking student interested in pursuing a career in construction engineering. Preference given to a construction engineering student interested in general fields of construction engineering. Restricted to Michigan students attending Michigan postsecondary institutions. Must be a member of MSPE student chapter or state member-at-large. Minimum 3.0 GPA required. **Award:** Grant for use in freshman, sophomore, junior, or senior years; not renewable. **Number:** 1. **Amount:** $2000. **Eligibility Requirements:** Applicant must be enrolled or expecting to enroll full-time at an institution or university; resident of Michigan and studying in Michigan. Applicant or parent of applicant must be member of Michigan Society of Professional Engineers. Applicant must have 3.0 GPA or higher. Available to U.S. citizens. **Application Requirements:** Application, essay, references, test scores, transcript. **Application Deadline:** varies. **Contact:** Scholarship Coordinator, Michigan Society of Professional Engineers, PO Box 15276, Lansing, MI 48901-5276. **Phone:** 517-487-9388. **E-mail:** mspe@voyager.net

Tuition Incentive Program (TIP)

Award for Michigan residents who receive or have received Medicaid for required period of time through the Family Independence Agency. Scholarship provides two years tuition towards an associate's degree at a Michigan college or university. Apply before graduating from high school or earning General Education Development diploma. **Award:** Scholarship for use in freshman or sophomore years; renewable. **Number:** varies. **Eligibility Requirements:** Applicant must be high school student; planning to enroll or expecting to enroll full or part-time at a two-year or four-year institution or university; resident of Michigan and studying in Michigan. Available to U.S. citizens. **Application Requirements:** Application, financial need analysis. **Application Deadline:** Continuous. **Contact:** Program Director Michigan Bureau of Student Financial Assistance, PO Box 30466, Lansing, MI 48909

Recreational Boating Industries Educational Foundation

Scholarships are awarded to students pursuing a degree that will eventually lead to a career in the recreational boating industry. Applicants must be residents of Michigan. Selection will be based on transcript, recommendations, an essay and financial need. **Award:** Scholarship for use in freshman, sophomore, junior, or senior years; not renewable. **Number:** 10–30. **Amount:** $250–$1000. **Eligibility Requirements:** Applicant must be enrolled or expecting to enroll full or part-time at a two-year or four-year institution or university and resident of Michigan. Available to U.S. citizens. **Application Requirements:** Application, essay, financial need analysis, references, transcript. **Application Deadline:** March 15. **Contact:** Mary Sherman, Administrator, Recreational Boating Industries Educational Foundation, 32398 Five Mile Road, Livonia, MI 48154-6109. **Phone:** 734-261-0123. **E-mail:** msherm@mbia.org

Minnesota

American Legion, Department of Minnesota

Oratorical contest open to students in 9th-12th grades of any accredited Minnesota high school. Speech contests begin in January at post level and continue to national competition. Contact local American Legion Post for deadlines and application details. Four one-time awards of varying amounts. **Award:** Scholarship for use in freshman year; not renewable. **Number:** 4. **Amount:** $500–$1200. **Eligibility Requirements:** Applicant must be high school student; planning to enroll or expecting to enroll full or part-time at a two-year, four-year, or technical institution or university; resident of Minnesota and must have an interest in public speaking. Available to U.S. citizens. **Application Requirements:** Application, applicant must enter a contest. **Application Deadline:** varies. **Contact:** Jennifer Kelley, Program Coordinator, American Legion, Department of Minnesota, 20 West 12th Street, Room 300-A, St. Paul, MN 55155. **Phone:** 651-291-1800

Midwestern Higher Education Compact

MSEP is a reduced tuition exchange program that is open to students in Kansas, Michigan, Minnesota, Missouri, Nebraska, and North Dakota. To be eligible, student must be a legal resident of one of these 6 states and going to an institution in one of the other 5 states. Student must be considered an out-of-state student attending a participating college or university. Students are to apply directly to the college or university. There is no universal application form; each institution varies. See MSEP Web site (www.mhec.org) for complete details, including a list of participating colleges and universities. **Award:** Grant for use in freshman, sophomore, junior, senior, or graduate years; renewable. **Number:** varies. **Amount:** varies. **Eligibility Requirements:** Applicant must be enrolled or expecting to enroll full or part-time at a two-year, four-year, or technical institution or university; resident of Kansas, Michigan, Minnesota, Missouri, Nebraska, or North Dakota and studying in Kansas, Michigan, Minnesota, Missouri, Nebraska, or North Dakota. Available to U.S. citizens. **Application Requirements:** Application. **Application Deadline:** varies. **Contact:** Ms. Jennifer Dahlquist, Program Officer, Midwestern Higher Education Compact, 1300 South Second Street, Suite 130, Minneapolis, MN 55454-1079. **Phone:** 612-626-1602. **E-mail:** jenniferd@mhec.org

Minnesota Broadcasters Association

One-time scholarships to Minnesota residents interested in broadcasting who are planning to enter broadcasting or other work in electronic media. Minimum 2.5 GPA is required. Submit proof of enrollment at an accredited postsecondary institution. **Award:** Scholarship for use in freshman, sophomore, junior, senior, or graduate years; not renewable. **Number:** 10. **Amount:** $1500. **Eligibility Requirements:** Applicant must be enrolled or expecting to enroll full-time at a four-year institution or university; resident of Minnesota and must have an interest in designated field specified by sponsor. Applicant must have 2.5 GPA or higher. Available to U.S. citizens. **Application Requirements:** Application, essay, references, transcript. **Application Deadline:** May 31.

Contact: Megan Eischen, Member Services Coordinator, Minnesota Broadcasters Association, 3033 Excelsior Boulevard, Suite 301, Minneapolis, MN 55416-4675.
Phone: 612-926-8123.
E-mail: meischen@minnesotabroadcasters.com

Minnesota Higher Education Services Office

Need-based grant program available for Minnesota residents attending Minnesota colleges. Student covers 46% of cost with remainder covered by Pell Grant, parent contribution and state grant. Students apply with FAFSA and college administers the program on campus. **Award:** Grant for use in freshman, sophomore, junior, or senior years; not renewable. **Number:** 71,000–75,000. **Amount:** $100–$7662. **Eligibility Requirements:** Applicant must be age 17; enrolled or expecting to enroll full or part-time at a two-year, four-year, or technical institution or university; resident of Minnesota and studying in Minnesota. Available to U.S. citizens. **Application Requirements:** Application, financial need analysis. **Application Deadline:** varies. **Contact:** Minnesota Higher Education Services Office, 1450 Energy Park Drive, Suite 350, St. Paul, MN 55108.
Phone: 651-642-0567 Ext. 1

Postsecondary Child Care Grant Program-Minnesota

One-time grant available for students not receiving MFIP. Based on financial need. Cannot exceed actual child care costs or maximum award chart (based on income). Must be Minnesota resident. For use at Minnesota two- or four-year school, including public technical colleges. **Award:** Grant for use in freshman, sophomore, junior, or senior years; not renewable. **Number:** varies. **Amount:** $100–$2200. **Eligibility Requirements:** Applicant must be enrolled or expecting to enroll full or part-time at a two-year, four-year, or technical institution or university; resident of Minnesota and studying in Minnesota. Available to U.S. citizens. **Application Requirements:** Application, financial need analysis. **Application Deadline:** Continuous. **Contact:** Minnesota Higher Education Services Office, 1450 Energy Park Drive, Suite 350, St. Paul, MN 55108-5227.
Phone: 651-642-0567 Ext. 1

Minnesota Indian Scholarship Office

One time award for Minnesota Native-American. Applicant must be one quarter Native-American and a resident of Minnesota. Must re-apply for scholarship annually. **Award:** Scholarship for use in freshman, sophomore, junior, or senior years; not renewable. **Number:** varies. **Amount:** up to $3300. **Eligibility Requirements:** Applicant must be American Indian/Alaska Native; enrolled or expecting to enroll full or part-time at a two-year, four-year, or technical institution or university; resident of Minnesota and studying in Minnesota. Available to U.S. citizens. **Application Requirements:** Application, financial need analysis. **Application Deadline:** July 1. **Contact:** Lea Perkins, Director, Minnesota Indian Scholarship Office, Minnesota Department of Education, 1500 Highway 36W, Roseville, MN 55113-4266.
Phone: 800-657-3927.
E-mail: fl.indianeducation@state.mn.us

Minnesota Soybean Research and Promotion Council

Up to eight $1000 scholarships are available to graduating high school seniors who are residents of Minnesota. Must demonstrate activity in agriculture with plans to study in an agricultural related program. For more details see **Web site:** www.mnsoybean.org. **Award:** Scholarship for use in freshman year; not renewable. **Number:** up to 8. **Amount:** $1000. **Eligibility Requirements:** Applicant must be high school student; planning to enroll or expecting to enroll full or part-time at a two-year, four-year, or technical institution or university and resident of Minnesota. Applicant or parent of applicant must have employment or volunteer experience in agriculture or farming. **Application Requirements:** Application, references, self-addressed stamped envelope, transcript. **Application Deadline:** March 29. **Contact:** J J. Morgan, Scholarship Coordinator, Minnesota Soybean Research and Promotion Council, 360 Pierce Avenue, Suite 110, North Mankato, MN 56003,
Phone: 888-896-9678.
E-mail: jj@mnsoybean.com

Playwrights' Center

The Playwrights' Center's Many Voices programs enrich the American theater by offering playwriting residencies to artists of color. Must be U.S. citizen. **Award:** Grant for use in freshman, sophomore, junior, senior, graduate, or postgraduate years; not renewable. **Number:** 8. **Amount:** $1200–$2000. **Eligibility Requirements:** Applicant must be American Indian/Alaska Native, Asian/Pacific Islander, Black (non-Hispanic), or Hispanic; enrolled or expecting to enroll full or part-time at a two-year, four-year, or technical institution or university; resident of Minnesota; studying in Minnesota and must have an interest in writing. Available to U.S. citizens. **Application Requirements:** Application. **Application Deadline:** July 31. **Contact:** Stacey Parshall, Many Voices Coordinator, Playwrights' Center, 2301 Franklin Avenue East, Minneapolis, MN 55406.
Phone: 612-332-7481 Ext. 10.
E-mail: staceyp@pwcenter.org

Printing Industry of Minnesota Education Foundation

The PIMEF offers $1,000-2,000 renewable scholarships to full-time students enrolled in two- or four-year institutions and technical colleges offering degrees in the print communications discipline. Applicant must be a Minnesota resident and be committed to a career in the print communications industry. Minimum 3.0 GPA required. Priority given to children of PIM member company employees. **Award:** Scholarship for use in freshman, sophomore, junior, or senior years; renewable. **Number:** 10–15. **Amount:** $1000–$2000. **Eligibility Requirements:** Applicant must be enrolled or expecting to enroll full-time at a two-year, four-year, or technical institution; resident of Minnesota and studying in Minnesota, New York, or Wisconsin. Applicant must have 3.0 GPA or higher. Available to U.S. citizens. **Application Requirements:** Application, essay, references, test scores, transcript, copy of college admission form, proof of admission. **Application Deadline:** April 15. **Contact:** Lisa Elfrink, Scholarship Fund Program Coordinator, Printing Industry of Minnesota Education Foundation, 2829 University Avenue SE, Suite 750, Minneapolis, MN 55414-3248.
Phone: 612-379-6014.
E-mail: lelfrink@pimn.org

Vincent L. Hawkinson Foundation for Peace and Justice

The scholarship is awarded to students who have demonstrated a commitment to peace and justice. This generally involves participation in a peace and justice project, leadership and participation in a peace organization, or serving as a role model. The scholarship selection committee of the Foundation uses essays and letters of reference to screen candidates and a personal interview in Minneapolis to select a winner. Applicant must either reside or study in Iowa, Minnesota, North Dakota, South Dakota, or Wisconsin. **Award:** Scholarship for use in freshman, sophomore, junior, senior, or graduate years; not renewable. **Number:** 1–6. **Amount:** $500–$1500. **Eligibility Requirements:** Applicant must be enrolled or expecting to enroll full-time at a two-year or four-year institution or university; resident of Iowa, Minnesota, North Dakota, South Dakota, or Wisconsin and studying in Iowa, Minnesota, North Dakota, South Dakota, or Wisconsin. Available to U.S. and non-U.S. citizens. **Application Requirements:** Application, essay, interview, references, transcript. **Application Deadline:** April 1. **Contact:** Vincent L. Hawkinson Foundation for Peace and Justice, Grace University Lutheran Church, 324 Harvard Street SE, Minneapolis, MN 55414. **Phone:** 612-331-8125

WAMSO-Minnesota Orchestra Volunteer Association

Created in 1956, the contest is designed to discover and encourage exceptional young talented musicians ages 15-26 through a regional competition. Applicants submit taped performances. From that group, selected participants compete in the semi-finals with finalists advancing to the last round. Applicant must play an instrument which has a permanent chair in the Minnesota orchestra. Only students or legal residents of Michigan, Minnesota, Iowa, Illinois, Kansas, Missouri, Nebraska, North Dakota, South Dakota, Indiana, Wisconsin, Ontario and Manitoba are eligible. Application fee is $65. **Award:** Prize for use in freshman, sophomore, junior, senior, graduate, or postgraduate years; not renewable. **Number:** 9–14. **Amount:** $500–$5250. **Eligibility Requirements:** Applicant must be age 15-26; enrolled or expecting to enroll at an institution or university; resident of Illinois, Indiana, Iowa, Kansas, Manitoba, Michigan, Minnesota, Missouri, Nebraska, North Dakota, Ontario, South Dakota, or Wisconsin and must have an interest in music. Available to U.S. and non-U.S. citizens. **Application Requirements:** Application, applicant must enter a contest, taped performance of specific repertoire. Fee: $65. **Application Deadline:** September 15. **Contact:** YAC Chair, WAMSO-Minnesota, Orchestra Volunteer Association, Orchestra Hall, 1111 Nicollet Mall, Minneapolis, MN 55403-2477. **Phone:** 612-371-5654. **E-mail:** wamso@mnorch.org

Missouri

American Legion Auxiliary, Department of Missouri

$500 scholarship awarded to high school graduate who has chosen to study nursing. $250 will be awarded each semester upon receipt of verification from the college that student is enrolled. The applicant must be a resident of Missouri and a member of a veteran's family. The applicant must be validated by the sponsoring unit. Check with sponsoring unit for details on required recommendation letters. **Award:** Scholarship for use in freshman year; renewable. **Number:** 1. **Amount:** $500–$1000. **Eligibility Requirements:** Applicant must be high school student; planning to enroll or expecting to enroll at a two-year, four-year, or technical institution or university and resident of Missouri. Applicant or parent of applicant must be member of American Legion or Auxiliary. Available to U.S. citizens. Applicant or parent must meet one or more of the following requirements: general military experience; retired from active duty; disabled or killed as a result of military service; prisoner of war; or missing in action. **Application Requirements:** Application, photo. **Application Deadline:** April 1. **Contact:** Kim Merchant, Department Secretary/Treasurer, American Legion Auxiliary, Department of Missouri, 600 Ellis Boulevard, Jefferson City, MO 65101-1615. **Phone:** 573-636-9133. **E-mail:** dptmoala@socket.net

American Legion, Department of Missouri

One-time award of $1000 given out to a male and female that attended a full session of the American Legion Boys/Girls State of Missouri or a full session of the Department's Cadet Patrol Academy in Jefferson City. Applicant must be Missouri resident. **Award:** Scholarship for use in freshman year; not renewable. **Number:** 2. **Amount:** $1000. **Eligibility Requirements:** Applicant must be high school student; age 21 or under; planning to enroll or expecting to enroll full-time at a four-year institution or university; single and resident of Missouri. Available to U.S. citizens. Applicant or parent must meet one or more of the following requirements: general military experience; retired from active duty; disabled or killed as a result of military service; prisoner of war; or missing in action. **Application Requirements:** Application, financial need analysis, test scores. **Application Deadline:** April 20. **Contact:** Scholarship Information, American Legion, Department of Missouri, PO Box 179, Jefferson City, MO 65102. **Phone:** 573-893-2353

Asthma and Allergy Foundation of America (AAFA) Greater Kansas City Chapter

The Berri Mitchel Memorial Scholarship provides four scholarships to greater Kansas City area high school seniors who have a history of asthma, have succeeded academically, and have shown an interest in their school and community. **Award:** Scholarship for use in freshman year; not renewable. **Number:** 4. **Amount:** $1000. **Eligibility Requirements:** Applicant must be high school student; planning to enroll or expecting to enroll full or part-time at a two-year, four-year, or technical institution or university and resident of Kansas or Missouri. Applicant must be physically disabled. Available to U.S. citizens. **Application Requirements:** Application, essay, references, transcript. **Application Deadline:** March 1. **Contact:** Michelle Cook, Director of Community Education, Asthma and Allergy Foundation of America (AAFA) Greater Kansas City Chapter, 9140 Ward Parkway, Suite 120, Kansas City, MO 64114. **Phone:** 816-333-6608. **E-mail:** info@aafakc.org

Marguerite Ross Barnett Memorial Scholarship

Applicant must be employed (at least 20 hours per week) and attending school part-time. Must be Missouri resident and enrolled at a participating Missouri postsecondary school. Awards not available during summer term. Minimum age is 18. **Award:** Scholarship for use in freshman, sophomore, junior, or senior years; not renewable. **Number:** varies. **Amount:** $900–$1700. **Eligibility Requirements:** Applicant must be age 18; enrolled or expecting to enroll part-time at a two-year or four-year institution or university; resident of Missouri and studying in Missouri. Available to U.S. citizens. **Application Requirements:** Application, financial need analysis. **Application Deadline:** April 1. **Contact:** MDHE Information Center, Missouri Department of Higher Education, 3515 Amazonas Drive, Jefferson City, MO 65109. **Phone:** 800-473-6757 Ext. 1. **E-mail:** icweb@dhe.mo.gov

Missouri College Guarantee Program

Available to Missouri residents attending Missouri colleges full-time. Minimum 2.5 GPA required. Must have participated in high school extracurricular activities. **Award:** Scholarship for use in freshman, sophomore, junior, or senior years; not renewable. **Number:** varies. **Amount:** $100–$4900. **Eligibility Requirements:** Applicant must be enrolled or expecting to enroll full-time at a two-year or four-year institution or university; resident of Missouri and studying in Missouri. Applicant must have 2.5 GPA or higher. Available to U.S. citizens. **Application Requirements:** Financial need analysis, test scores. **Application Deadline:** April 1. **Contact:** MDHE Information Center, Missouri Department of Higher Education, 3515 Amazonas Drive, Jefferson City, MO 65109. **Phone:** 800-473-6757 Ext. 1. **E-mail:** icweb@dhe.mo.gov

Missouri Department of Elementary and Secondary Education

Award may be used any year up to four years at an approved, participating Missouri institution. Scholarship is for minority Missouri residents in teaching programs. Recipients must commit to teach for five years in a Missouri public elementary or secondary school. Graduate students must teach math or science. Otherwise, award must be repaid. **Award:** Scholarship for use in freshman, sophomore, junior, senior, or graduate years; renewable. **Number:** 100. **Amount:** $3000. **Eligibility Requirements:** Applicant must be American Indian/Alaska Native, Asian/Pacific Islander, Black (non-Hispanic), or Hispanic; enrolled or expecting to enroll full-time at a two-year or four-year institution or university; resident of Missouri and studying in Missouri. Applicant must have 3.0 GPA or higher. Available to U.S. citizens. **Application Requirements:** Application, essay, financial need analysis, references, test scores, transcript. **Application Deadline:** February 15. **Contact:** Laura Harrison, Administrative Assistant II, Missouri Department of Elementary and Secondary Education, PO Box 480, Jefferson City, MO 65102-0480. **Phone:** 573-751-1668. **E-mail:** laura.harrison@dese.mo.gov

Missouri Department of Higher Education

Available to Missouri residents attending Missouri colleges or universities full-time. Must be undergraduates with financial need. May reapply for up to a maximum of ten semesters. Free Application for Federal Student Aid (FAFSA) or a renewal must be received by the federal processor by April 1 to be considered. **Award:** Grant for use in freshman, sophomore, junior, or senior years; not renewable. **Number:** varies. **Amount:** $100–$1500. **Eligibility Requirements:** Applicant must be enrolled or expecting to enroll full-time at a two-year, four-year, or technical institution or university; resident of Missouri and studying in Missouri. Available to U.S. citizens. **Application Requirements:** Financial need analysis. **Application Deadline:** April 1. **Contact:** MDHE Information Center, Missouri Department of Higher Education, 3515 Amazonas Drive, Jefferson City, MO 65109. **Phone:** 800-473-6757 Ext. 1. **E-mail:** icweb@dhe.mo.gov

Missouri Higher Education Academic Scholarship (Bright Flight)

Awards of $2000 for Missouri high school seniors. Must be in top 3% of Missouri SAT or ACT scorers. Must attend Missouri institution as full-time undergraduate. May reapply for up to ten semesters. Must be Missouri resident and U.S. citizen. **Award:** Scholarship for use in freshman, sophomore, junior, or senior years; not renewable. **Number:** varies. **Amount:** $2000. **Eligibility Requirements:** Applicant must be high school student; planning to enroll or expecting to enroll full-time at a two-year, four-year, or technical institution or university; resident of Missouri and studying in Missouri. Available to U.S. citizens. **Application Requirements:** Test scores. **Application Deadline:** July 31. **Contact:** MDHE Information Center, Missouri Department of Higher Education, 3515 Amazonas Drive, Jefferson City, MO 65109. **Phone:** 800-473-6757 Ext. 1. **E-mail:** icweb@dhe.mo.gov

Missouri Teacher Education Scholarship (General)

Nonrenewable award for Missouri high school seniors or Missouri resident college students. Must attend approved teacher training program at a participating Missouri institution. Must rank in top 15 % of high school class on ACT/SAT. Merit-based award. Recipients must commit to teach in Missouri for five years at a public elementary or secondary school or award must be repaid. **Award:** Scholarship for use in freshman, sophomore, junior, or senior years; not renewable. **Number:** 200–240. **Amount:** $2000. **Eligibility Requirements:** Applicant must be enrolled or expecting to enroll full-time at a two-year or four-year institution or university; resident of Missouri and studying in Missouri. Applicant must have 3.5 GPA or higher. Available to U.S. citizens. **Application Requirements:** Application, essay, references, test scores, transcript. **Application Deadline:** February 15. **Contact:** Laura Harrison, Administrative Assistant II, Missouri Department of Elementary and Secondary Education, PO Box 480, Jefferson City, MO 65102-0480. **Phone:** 573-751-1668. **E-mail:** laura.harrison@dese.mo.gov

National Federation of the Blind of Missouri

Awards are based on achievement, commitment to community and financial need. Recipients must be legally blind. Amount of money each year

available for program will vary. **Award:** Scholarship for use in freshman, sophomore, junior, senior, graduate, or postgraduate years; not renewable. **Number:** up to 2. **Amount:** $500–$1500. **Eligibility Requirements:** Applicant must be enrolled or expecting to enroll full or part-time at a two-year, four-year, or technical institution or university and resident of Missouri. Applicant must be visually impaired. Available to U.S. citizens. **Application Requirements:** Application, autobiography, essay, financial need analysis, interview, references, transcript. **Application Deadline:** February 1. **Contact:** Mr. Gary Wunder, President, National Federation of the Blind of Missouri, 3910 Tropical Lane, Columbia, MO 65202.
Phone: 573-874-1774.
E-mail: president@nfbmo.org

Robert C. Byrd Honors Scholarship

Award for Missouri high school seniors who are residents of Missouri. The amount of the award per student each year depends on the amount the state is allotted by the U.S. Department of Education. The highest amount of award per student is $1500. Students must rank in top 10% of high school class and score in top 10% of ACT test. **Award:** Scholarship for use in freshman year; renewable. **Number:** 100–150. **Amount:** $1100–$1500. **Eligibility Requirements:** Applicant must be high school student; planning to enroll or expecting to enroll full-time at a two-year, four-year, or technical institution or university and resident of Missouri. Applicant must have 3.5 GPA or higher. Available to U.S. and non-Canadian citizens. **Application Requirements:** Application, test scores, transcript, 7th semester transcripts. **Application Deadline:** April 15. **Contact:** Laura Harrison, Administrative Assistant II, Missouri Department of Elementary and Secondary Education, PO Box 480, Jefferson City, MO 65102-0480.
Phone: 573-751-1668.
E-mail: laura.harrison@mo.dese.gov

Rural Missouri, Inc.

The grant is from the Department of Labor. Renewable grant to low income seasonal farm workers and their dependents for tuition assistance. Must be a resident of Missouri. Must be paid wages for doing farm work. High school seniors may apply. Must attend a Missouri school. Minimum 2.5 GPA required. **Award:** Grant for use in freshman, sophomore, junior, or senior years; renewable. **Number:** varies. **Amount:** up to $3000. **Eligibility Requirements:** Applicant must be age 16; enrolled or expecting to enroll at a two-year, four-year, or technical institution or university; resident of Missouri and studying in Missouri. Applicant or parent of applicant must have employment or volunteer experience in agriculture, farming, or migrant worker. Applicant must have 2.5 GPA or higher. **Application Requirements:** Application. **Application Deadline:** Continuous. **Contact:** Lynn Hatfield, Program Director, Rural Missouri, Inc., 1014 Northeast Drive, Jefferson City, MO 65109. **Phone:** 800-234-4971
E-mail: lynn@rmiinc.org

United Negro College Fund

Must enroll in UNCF Member College or University. Must have minimum 3.3 GPA after sophomore year and minimum 3.5 GPA after junior year. Please visit Web site for more information: www.uncf.org. **Award:** Scholarship for use in freshman year; renewable. **Number:** varies. **Amount:** $5000. **Eligibility Requirements:** Applicant must be Black (non-Hispanic); enrolled or expecting to enroll at a four-year institution or university and resident of Missouri. Applicant must have 3.0 GPA or higher. Available to U.S. citizens. **Application Requirements:** Application, financial need analysis, FAFSA, SAR. **Application Deadline:** varies. **Contact:** Program Services Department, United Negro College Fund, 8260 Willow Oaks Corporate Drive. Fairfax, VA 22031

Nebraska

American Legion, Department of Nebraska

Several one-time awards ranging from $100 to $1000 for high school students who are residents of Nebraska. Must submit speech. Must have minimum of 2.5 GPA. Must be between the ages of 14–19. **Award:** Prize for use in freshman year; not renewable. **Number:** up to 19. **Amount:** $100–$1000. **Eligibility Requirements:** Applicant must be high school student; age 14-19; planning to enroll or expecting to enroll full-time at a two-year, four-year, or technical institution or university; resident of Nebraska and must have an interest in public speaking. Applicant must have 2.5 GPA or higher. Available to U.S. citizens. **Application Requirements:** Application, applicant must enter a contest, autobiography, financial need analysis, photo, references, transcript. **Application Deadline:** November 1. **Contact:** Burdette Burkhart, Activities Director, American Legion, Department of Nebraska, PO Box 5205, Lincoln, NE 68505-0205. **Phone:** 402-464-6338.
E-mail: actdirlegion@alltel.net

Bryan/LGH Medical Center West Auxiliary Junior Volunteer Scholarship

Scholarship for graduating seniors from high school who have volunteered at least 150 hours at Bryan/LGH Medical Center West in Lincoln, NE. **Award:** Scholarship for use in freshman year; not renewable. **Number:** 1. **Amount:** $1000. **Eligibility Requirements:** Applicant must be high school student; planning to enroll or expecting to enroll full-time at a two-year, four-year, or technical institution or university and resident of Nebraska. Applicant must have 2.5 GPA or higher. Available to U.S. citizens. **Application Requirements:** Application, essay, test scores, transcript, verification of volunteer hours. **Application Deadline:** April 15. **Contact:** Application available at Web site..

Duncan E. and Lillian M. McGregor Scholarship

Scholarship for graduating seniors or former graduates of the high schools in Ansley, Arcadia, Gibbon, Ord, Shelton, or Sargent high schools in Nebraska. Must have resided in a community served by the Nebraska Central Telephone Company during his/her high school education. **Award:** Scholarship for use in freshman, sophomore, junior, or senior years; not renewable. **Number:** 80–100. **Amount:** $500–$1000. **Eligibility Requirements:** Applicant must be enrolled or expecting to enroll full-time at a two-year, four-year, or technical institution or university and resident of Nebraska. Applicant must have 2.5 GPA or higher. Available to U.S. citizens. **Application Requirements:** Application, financial need analysis, test scores, transcript. **Application Deadline:** April 15. **Contact:** Application available at Web site.

Gallup Organization/Cornhusker State Games

One-time award for Nebraska students who are participants in the Cornhusker State Games. For use at a Nebraska postsecondary institution. See Web site at www.cornhuskerstategames.com for further details. **Award:** Scholarship for use in freshman, sophomore, junior, senior, graduate, or postgraduate years; not renewable. **Number:** 5. **Amount:** $1000. **Eligibility Requirements:** Applicant must be enrolled or expecting to enroll full or part-time at a two-year, four-year, or technical institution or university; resident of Nebraska and studying in Nebraska. Available to U.S. citizens. **Application Requirements:** Application, applicant must enter a contest, essay, transcript. **Application Deadline:** June 23. **Contact:** Dave Mlnarik, Executive Director, Gallup Organization/Cornhusker State Games, PO Box 82411, 2202 South 11th Street, Lincoln, NE 68501. **E-mail:** dmlnarik@cornhuskerstategames.com

George Watters-Nebraska Petroleum Marketers Association Scholarship

Scholarship for any Nebraska high school graduating senior to attend any two- or four-year postsecondary institution in Nebraska. Must be in upper 33% of class, and demonstrate academic achievement and leadership. Sponsored by Nebraska Petroleum Marketers who makes the selection process and determines application deadline. Applicants must be the son or daughter of any Nebraska Petroleum Marketer and Convenience Store Association member, or the son or daughter of a Nebraska Petroleum Marketers and Convenience Store Association's full- or part-time employee. **Award:** Scholarship for use in freshman year; not renewable. **Number:** 3. **Amount:** $1000–$1500. **Eligibility Requirements:** Applicant must be high school student; planning to enroll or expecting to enroll full-time at a two-year, four-year, or technical institution or university; resident of Nebraska; studying in Nebraska and must have an interest in leadership. Applicant or parent of applicant must have employment or volunteer experience in designated career field. Applicant must have 3.0 GPA or higher. Available to U.S. citizens. **Application Requirements:** Application, references, transcript. **Application Deadline:** March 1. **Contact:** Application available at Web site..

Harry and Lenora Richardson-National Association of Postmasters of the United States Scholarship

Scholarship for a graduating senior who is the child, grandchild, or member of the Nebraska Chapter, National Association of Postmaster of the United States or the Nebraska Branch, National League of Postmasters of the United States. Applicants must demonstrate academic achievement and participation in extracurricular and community activities. Must be a Nebraska resident. Must attend a Nebraska college or university. **Award:** Scholarship for use in freshman year; not renewable. **Number:** 1. **Amount:** $1000. **Eligibility Requirements:** Applicant must be high school student; planning to enroll or expecting to enroll full-time at a two-year or four-year institution or university; resident of Nebraska and studying in Nebraska. Applicant or parent of applicant must have employment or volunteer experience in federal/postal service. Applicant must have 2.5 GPA or higher. Available to U.S. citizens. **Application Requirements:** Application, autobiography, references, transcript. **Application Deadline:** April 1. **Contact:** Application available at Web site.

Harry and Lenora Richardson-Nebraska Branch of the National League of Postmasters Scholarship

Scholarship for a graduating senior who is the child, grandchild, or member of the Nebraska Chapter, National Association of Postmasters of the United States, or the Nebraska Branch, National League of Postmasters of the United States. Applicants must demonstrate academic achievement and participation in extracurricular and community activities. Must be a Nebraska resident. Must attend a Nebraska college or university. **Award:** Scholarship for use in freshman year; not renewable. **Number:** 1. **Amount:** $1000. **Eligibility Requirements:** Applicant must be high school student; planning to enroll or expecting to enroll full-time at a two-year or four-year institution or university; resident of Nebraska and studying in Nebraska. Applicant or parent of applicant must have employment or volunteer experience in federal/postal service. Applicant must have 2.5 GPA or higher. Available to U.S. citizens. **Application Requirements:** Application, autobiography, references, transcript. **Application Deadline:** March 1. **Contact:** Application available at Web site.

Jennings and Beulah Haggerty Scholarship

Scholarship for graduating seniors from public or private high schools in Lincoln, NE area. Must be in the top third of graduating class, and enroll in a two- or four-year institution in Nebraska. Must demonstrate financial need and academic achievement. Applications must be received between April 1 and July 1. **Award:** Scholarship for use in freshman year; not renewable. **Number:** 10–20. **Amount:** $500–$1000. **Eligibility Requirements:** Applicant must be high school student; planning to enroll or expecting to enroll full-time at a two-year, four-year, or technical institution or university; resident of Nebraska and studying in Nebraska. Applicant must have 3.0 GPA or higher. Available to U.S. citizens. **Application Requirements:** Application, essay, financial need analysis, interview, references, test scores, transcript. **Application Deadline:** July 1. **Contact:** Application available at Web site.

Knights of Ak-Sar-Ben

Scholarships are awarded to outstanding and talented graduates of "Heartland" (Nebraska and Western Iowa) high schools. Must be a graduating high school senior with a minimum 2.5 GPA, who plans on attending a college or university within the Ak-Sar-Ben region. For more details and an application see **Web site:** www.aksarben.org. **Award:** Scholarship for use in freshman, sophomore, junior, or senior years; renewable. **Number:** 20. **Amount:** $10,000. **Eligibility Requirements:** Applicant must be high school student; planning to enroll or expecting to enroll full-time at a four-year institution or university and resident of Iowa or Nebraska. Applicant must have 2.5 GPA or higher. Available to U.S. citizens. **Application Requirements:** Application, essay, financial need analysis, references, test scores, transcript. **Application Deadline:** February 11. **Contact:** Application available at Web site.: www.aksarben.org

Knights of Ak-Sar-Ben One-Year Community College Scholarship.

Scholarships available to applicants from Nebraska and Western Iowa (Heartland) who plan to attend a community college in the region. Applications will be due into the office of the community college to which the student is applying by March 19. For more details and the application, visit the **Web site:** www.aksarben.org **Award:** Scholarship for use in freshman year; not renewable. **Number:** up to 12. **Amount:** $1000. **Eligibility Requirements:** Applicant must be enrolled or expecting to enroll full-time at a two-year institution; resident of Iowa or Nebraska and studying in Iowa or Nebraska. Available to U.S. citizens. **Application Requirements:** Application. **Application Deadline:** March 19. **Contact:** Sandy Heather, Development Assistant, Knights of Ak-Sar-Ben, 302 South 36th Street, Suite 800, Omaha, NE 68131. **Phone:** 402-554-9600 Ext. 106. **E-mail:** heather@aksarben.org

Lincoln Community Foundation

Scholarship for graduating seniors from Thayer County high schools in Nebraska; namely Hebron, Deshler, Chester, Bruning, and Davenport. Need not excel academically. Must demonstrate financial need. Scholarship may be renewed for no more than five years for any one recipient. **Award:** Scholarship for use in freshman year; renewable. **Number:** 3. **Amount:** $5000. **Eligibility Requirements:** Applicant must be high school student; planning to enroll or expecting to enroll full-time at a two-year, four-year, or technical institution or university and resident of Nebraska. Available to U.S. citizens. **Application Requirements:** Application, financial need analysis, test scores, transcript. **Application Deadline:** April 30. **Contact:** Application available at Web site.

Louis C. and Amy E. Nuernberger Memorial Scholarship

Scholarship for high school graduates who have been employed at the Wakefield Health Care Center in Wakefield, NE for at least one year. **Award:** Scholarship for use in freshman, sophomore, junior, or senior years; renewable. **Number:** 1. **Amount:** $5000–$10,000. **Eligibility Requirements:** Applicant must be enrolled or expecting to enroll full-time at a two-year, four-year, or technical institution or university and resident of Nebraska. Applicant or parent of applicant must have employment or volunteer experience in designated career field. Applicant must have 2.5 GPA or higher. Available to U.S. citizens. **Application Requirements:** Application, essay, test scores, transcript. **Application Deadline:** April 1. **Contact:** Application available at Web site.

Max and Margaret Pumphrey Scholarship

Scholarship for graduating seniors or former graduates of public or private high schools in Lancaster County, NE. Preference given to those attending Nebraska colleges/universities. Must demonstrate financial need and academic success. Applications must be received between April 1 and July 1. **Award:** Scholarship for use in freshman, sophomore, junior, or senior years; not renewable. **Number:** 35–40. **Amount:** $500–$1000. **Eligibility Requirements:** Applicant must be enrolled or expecting to enroll full-time at a two-year, four-year, or technical institution or university and resident of Nebraska. Applicant must have 2.5 GPA or higher. Available to U.S. citizens. **Application Requirements:** Application, essay, financial need analysis, interview, references, test scores, transcript. **Application Deadline:** July 1. **Contact:** Application available at Web site.

Nebraska Department of Education

Up to $1500 each year for up to four years. Must be U.S. citizen and Nebraska resident. Awards designed to promote student excellence and achievement and to recognize able students who show promise of continued excellence. Funded scholars must submit Renewal Application each year. Renewal based on continuing eligibility requirements. Must have minimum ACT score of 30. Please refer to Web site for application and further details: www.nde.state.ne.us/byrd. **Award:** Scholarship for use in freshman, sophomore, junior, or senior years; not renewable. **Number:** 40–45. **Amount:** $1500. **Eligibility Requirements:** Applicant must be high school student; planning to enroll or expecting to enroll full-time at a two-year, four-year, or technical institution or university and resident of Nebraska. Available to U.S. citizens. **Application Requirements:** Application, test scores, transcript. **Application Deadline:** March 15. **Contact:** Robert C. Byrd Scholarship Information, Nebraska Department of Education, 301 Centennial Mall South, PO Box 94987, Lincoln, NE 68509-4987. **Phone:** 402-471-3962

Nebraska Press Association

Award for graduates of Nebraska high schools who have a minimum GPA of 2.5 and are enrolled or planning to enroll in programs in Nebraska colleges or universities leading to careers in print journalism. Two to four awards of $1250. **Award:** Scholarship for use in freshman, sophomore, junior, or senior years; not renewable. **Number:** 2–4. **Amount:** $1250. **Eligibility Requirements:** Applicant must be enrolled or expecting to enroll full-time at a four-year institution or university; resident of Nebraska and studying in Nebraska. Applicant must have 2.5 GPA or higher. Available to U.S. citizens. **Application Requirements:** Application, financial need analysis. **Application Deadline:** March 8. **Contact:** Allen Beermann, Executive Director, Nebraska Press Association, 845 S Street, Lincoln, NE 68508-1226. **Phone:** 402-476-2851. **E-mail:** nebpress@nebpress.com

Nebraska Rural Community Schools Association Scholarship

Scholarships are for students attending schools in Nebraska holding current memberships in NRCSA. Must major in education and demonstrate financial need. Applicants should also demonstrate academic achievement, leadership, character, and initiative. Preferred students will be involved in extracurricular activities. Must be a resident of Nebraska. **Award:** Scholarship for use in freshman year; not renewable. **Number:** 6. **Amount:** $500–$1000. **Eligibility Requirements:** Applicant must be high school student; planning to enroll or expecting to enroll full-time at a two-year or four-year institution or university; resident of Nebraska and studying in Nebraska. Applicant must have 3.5 GPA or higher. Available to U.S. citizens. **Application Requirements:** Application, essay, financial need analysis, references. **Application Deadline:** February 9. **Contact:** Application available at Web site.

P.G. Richardson Masonic Memorial Scholarship

Scholarship for graduating high school seniors who have a family member belonging to Custer Lodge #148 A.F. & A.M. The deadline for applications is March 1. Must be Nebraska resident. **Award:** Scholarship for use in freshman year; not renewable. **Number:** 1. **Amount:** $1000. **Eligibility Requirements:** Applicant must be high school student; planning to enroll or expecting to enroll full-time at a two-year, four-year, or technical institution or university and resident of Nebraska. Applicant must have 2.5 GPA or higher. Available to U.S. citizens. **Application Requirements:** Application, references, test scores, transcript. **Application Deadline:** March 1. **Contact:** Application available at Web site.

Ralph and Jean Cuca Scholarship

Scholarship for graduating high school seniors from a public high school in the greater Lincoln, NE area who demonstrate financial need and academic success. **Award:** Scholarship for use in freshman year; not renewable. **Number:** 1. **Amount:** $500–$1000. **Eligibility Requirements:** Applicant must be high school student; planning to enroll or expecting to enroll full-time at a two-year, four-year, or technical institution or university and resident of Nebraska. Applicant must have 2.5 GPA or higher. Available to U.S. citizens. **Application Requirements:** Application, financial need analysis, references, test scores, transcript. **Application Deadline:** April 1. **Contact:** Application available at Web site.

State of Nebraska Coordinating Commission for Postsecondary Education

Available to undergraduates attending a participating postsecondary institution in Nebraska. Available to Pell Grant recipients only. Nebraska residency required. Awards determined by each participating institution. Contact financial aid office at institution for application and additional information. **Award:** Grant for use in freshman, sophomore, junior, or senior years; not renewable. **Number:** varies. **Amount:** $100–$1032. **Eligibility Requirements:** Applicant must be enrolled or expecting to enroll full or part-time at a two-year, four-year, or technical institution or university; resident of Nebraska and studying in Nebraska. Available to U.S. citizens. **Application Requirements:** Application, financial need analysis. **Application Deadline:** Continuous. **Contact:** Financial Aid Office at college or university.

Thomas C. Woods, Jr. Memorial Scholarship

Scholarships are for graduating seniors or former graduates of any high school in the following counties in Nebraska: Adams, Butler, Cass, Clay, Fillmore, Gage, Hamilton, Jefferson, Johnson, Lancaster, Nemaha, Nucholls, Otoe, Pawnee, Polk, Richardson, Saline, Saunders, Seward, Thayer, Webster, and York. Applicants must be qualified dependents of current ALLTEL employees. Must attend a college/universities in Nebraska. Minimum 2.5 GPA required. **Award:** Scholarship for use in freshman, sophomore, junior, or senior years; not renewable. **Number:** 10–15. **Amount:** $1000–$2000. **Eligibility Requirements:** Applicant must be enrolled or expecting to enroll full-time at a two-year or four-year institution or university; resident of Nebraska and studying in Nebraska. Applicant or parent of applicant must have employment or volunteer experience in designated career field. Applicant must have 2.5 GPA or higher. Available to U.S. citizens. **Application Requirements:** Application, essay, financial need analysis, test scores. **Application Deadline:** April 17. **Contact:** Application available at Web site.

Willa Cather Foundation

Awarded yearly to a Nebraska female high school graduate. Must major in English at any accredited college or university. Must have a minimum 3.0 GPA. **Award:** Scholarship for use in freshman year; not renewable. **Number:** 1. **Amount:** $1000. **Eligibility Requirements:** Applicant must be enrolled or expecting to enroll full-time at a four-year institution or university; female and resident of Nebraska. Applicant must have 3.0 GPA or higher. Available to U.S. citizens. **Application Requirements:** Application, essay, portfolio, references, test scores, transcript. **Application Deadline:** January 31. **Contact:** Betty Kort, Executive Director, Willa Cather Foundation, 413 North Webster, Red Cloud, NE 68970, **Phone:** 402-746-2653. **E-mail:** bkort@gpcom.net

North Dakota

American Indian Science and Engineering Society

Award for high school senior for study of science, business, education, and health administration. Must reside in Arizona, Colorado, Kansas, Minnesota, Montana, North Dakota, New Mexico, Oklahoma, Oregon, South Dakota, Washington, or San Bernadino County, California. Must be at least one quarter American-Indian or Alaska Native and/or member of federally recognized tribe. Minimum 2.0 GPA required. Must be a current AISES member. **Award:** Scholarship for use in freshman, sophomore, junior, or senior years; renewable. **Number:** varies. **Amount:** $2500. **Eligibility Requirements:** Applicant must be American Indian/Alaska Native; high school student; planning to enroll or expecting to enroll at an institution or university and resident of Arizona, California, Colorado, Kansas, Minnesota, Montana, New Mexico, North Dakota, Oklahoma, Oregon, South Dakota, or Washington. Available to U.S. citizens. **Application Requirements:** Application, essay, references, transcript. **Application Deadline:** April 15. **Contact:** Scholarship Information, American Indian Science and Engineering Society, PO Box 9828, Albuquerque, NM 87119-9828. **Phone:** 505-765-1052. **E-mail:** info@aises.org

American Legion, Department of North Dakota

Oratorical contest for high school students in grades 9-12. Contestants must prepare to speak on the topic of the U.S. Constitution. Must graduate from an accredited North Dakota high school. Contest begins at the local level and continues to the national level. Several one-time awards of $100-$1900. **Award:** Prize for use in freshman year; not renewable. **Number:** 38. **Amount:** $100–$1900. **Eligibility Requirements:** Applicant must be high school student; planning to enroll or expecting to enroll at an institution or university; resident of North Dakota and must have an interest in public speaking. Available to U.S. citizens. **Application Requirements:** Application, applicant must enter a contest, speech contest. **Application Deadline:** November 30. **Contact:** American Legion, Department of North Dakota, Box 2666, Fargo, ND 58108-2666. **Phone:** 701-293-3120. **E-mail:** adjutant@ndlegion.org

Hattie Tedrow Memorial Fund Scholarship

Applicants must be a legal resident of North Dakota, a high school senior, and a direct descendent of a veteran with honorable service in the United States military. Send SASE for more information and deadlines. **Award:** Scholarship for use in freshman year; not renewable. **Number:** varies. **Amount:** up to $2000. **Eligibility Requirements:** Applicant must be high school student; planning to enroll or expecting to enroll at an institution or university and resident of North Dakota. Available to U.S. citizens. Applicant or parent must meet one or more of the following requirements: general military experience; retired from active duty; disabled or killed as a result of military service; prisoner of war; or missing in action. **Application Requirements:** Application, self-addressed stamped envelope. **Application Deadline:** April 15. **Contact:** American Legion, Department of North Dakota, PO Box 1055, Indianapolis, IN 46206

North Dakota Department of Public Instruction

Renewable award to exceptionally able high school seniors who show promise of continued excellence in postsecondary education. Must be resident of North Dakota and a U.S. citizen. Deadline second week in April. **Award:** Scholarship for use in freshman, sophomore, junior, or senior years; renewable. **Number:** 10–12. **Amount:** $1500. **Eligibility Requirements:** Applicant must be high school student; planning to enroll or expecting to enroll full-time at a two-year, four-year, or technical institution or university and resident of North Dakota. Available to U.S. citizens. **Application Requirements:** Application, essay, references, test scores, transcript, college acceptance letter. **Application Deadline:** varies. **Contact:** Heidi Bergland, Administrative Assistant, North Dakota Department of Public Instruction, 600 East Boulevard Avenue, Department 201, Bismarck, ND 58505-0440, **Phone:** 701-328-2317. **E-mail:** hbergland@state.nd.us

North Dakota University System

Renewable award to Native-American residents of North Dakota. Priority given to full-time undergraduate students. Minimum 2.0 GPA required. **Award:** Scholarship for use in freshman, sophomore, junior, senior, or graduate years; renewable. **Number:** up to 150. **Amount:** $700–$2000. **Eligibility Requirements:** Applicant must be American Indian/Alaska Native; enrolled or expecting to enroll full-time at a two-year, four-year, or technical institution or university and resident of North Dakota. Available to U.S. citizens. **Application Requirements:** Application, financial need analysis, transcript, proof of tribal enrollment. **Application Deadline:** July 15. **Contact:** Rhonda Schauer, SAA Director, North Dakota University System, 600 East Boulevard, Department 215, Bismarck, ND 58505-0230. **Phone:** 701-328-9661

Ohio

Akron Urban League

This scholarship is designated for 17-19 year-old high school students who are planning on furthering their education. Awards range from $250 to full tuition. Restricted to applicants who are residents of Ohio. **Award:** Scholarship for use in freshman year; renewable. **Number:** 40–45. **Eligibility Requirements:** Applicant must be high school student; age 17-19; planning to enroll or expecting to enroll full-time at a two-year, four-year, or technical institution or university and resident of Ohio. Applicant must have 2.5 GPA or higher. Available to U.S. citizens. **Application Requirements:** Application, essay, financial need analysis, interview, photo, references, test scores, transcript. **Application Deadline:** March 1. **Contact:** Rochelle Fisher, Development Director, Akron Urban League, 250 East Market Street, Akron, OH 44308. **Phone:** 330-434-6996

American Legion Auxiliary, Department of Ohio

Scholarship for children or grandchildren of veterans who served in Armed Forces during eligibility dates for American Legion membership. Must be high school senior, ages 16 to 18, Ohio resident, and U.S. citizen. Award for full-time undergraduate study. One-time award of $1500-$2000. **Award:** Scholarship for use in freshman year; not renewable. **Number:** 2. **Amount:** $1500–$2000. **Eligibility Requirements:** Applicant must be high school student; age 16-18; planning to enroll or expecting to enroll full-time at a two-year or four-year institution or university and resident of Ohio. Available to U.S. citizens. Applicant or parent must meet one or more of the following requirements: general military experience; retired from active duty; disabled or killed as a result of military service; prisoner of war; or missing in action. **Application Requirements:** Application, essay, financial need analysis, references, transcript. **Application Deadline:** March 1. **Contact:** Reva McClure, Department Scholarship Coordinator, American Legion Auxiliary, Department of Ohio, PO Box 2760, Zanesville, OH 43702-2760. **Phone:** 740-452-8245. **E-mail:** ala_pam@rrohio.com

Engineers Foundation of Ohio

Award available to full-time, undergraduate students enrolled or planning to enroll in an ABET-accredited engineering program in an Ohio school or university. Minimum ACT or SAT required. ACT: math-29, English-25, SAT: math-600, verbal-500. Minimum 3.0 GPA required. Must be an Ohio resident and U.S. citizen. Application deadline is in mid-December. Call or go to the Web site for the exact date. **Award:** Scholarship for use in freshman, sophomore, junior, or senior years; renewable. **Number:** 10–14. **Amount:** $500–$2500. **Eligibility Requirements:** Applicant must be enrolled or expecting to enroll full-time at a four-year institution or university; resident of Ohio and studying in Ohio. Applicant must have 3.0 GPA or higher. Available to U.S. citizens. **Application Requirements:** Application, essay, references, test scores, transcript. **Application Deadline:** varies. **Contact:** Pam McClure, Manager of Administration, Engineers Foundation of Ohio, 4795 Evanswood Drive, Suite 201, Columbus, OH 43229-7216. **Phone:** 614-846-1177. **E-mail:** ospe@iwaynet.net

Esperanza, Inc.

The Esperanza Scholarship is a one-year award valid only for full-time tuition and/or books at an accredited college or university. Recipients are eligible to apply yearly until they have completed their curriculum. Award restricted to residents of Cuyahoga or Lorain counties in Ohio. **Award:** Scholarship for use in freshman, sophomore, junior, or senior years; not renewable. **Number:** 50.

Amount: $500–$1250. **Eligibility Requirements:** Applicant must be of Hispanic heritage; enrolled or expecting to enroll full-time at a two-year or four-year institution or university and resident of Ohio. Applicant must have 2.5 GPA or higher. Available to U.S. and non-U.S. citizens. **Application Requirements:** Application, essay, interview, references, test scores, transcript. **Application Deadline:** March 15. **Contact:** Olga Ferrer, Office Assistant, Esperanza, Inc., 4115 Bridge Avenue, Room 108, Cleveland, OH 44113. **Phone:** 216-651-7178. **E-mail:** hope4ed@aol.com

Fuhrmann Orchards

One-time award for Ohio residents studying horticulture or agribusiness at any two- or four-year postsecondary institution in the U.S. Must be a U.S. citizen. Must be a graduate of an Ohio high school. Write for more information. **Award:** Scholarship for use in freshman, sophomore, junior, or senior years; not renewable. **Number:** up to 2. **Amount:** $600–$1000. **Eligibility Requirements:** Applicant must be enrolled or expecting to enroll full-time at a two-year or four-year institution and resident of Ohio. Available to U.S. citizens. **Application Requirements:** Application, essay, transcript. **Application Deadline:** May 15. **Contact:** Paul W. Fuhrmann, Partner, Fuhrmann Orchards, 510 Hansgen-Morgan Road, Wheelersburg, OH 45694

James C. Caldwell Scholarship

Renewable scholarships for minority residents of the greater Toledo, Ohio area for use in undergraduate study in a college or university. Must maintain 3.0 GPA. Must be African-American, Asian-American, Hispanic-American or Native American. Write for application and enclose a self-addressed stamped envelope. **Award:** Scholarship for use in freshman, sophomore, junior, or senior years; renewable. **Number:** up to 20. **Amount:** varies. **Eligibility Requirements:** Applicant must be American Indian/Alaska Native, Asian/Pacific Islander, Black (non-Hispanic), or Hispanic; enrolled or expecting to enroll at a four-year institution or university and resident of Ohio. Applicant must have 3.0 GPA or higher. Available to U.S. citizens. **Application Requirements:** Application, self-addressed stamped envelope, transcript. **Application Deadline:** Continuous. **Contact:** Executive Director, James C. Caldwell Scholarship, PO Box 80056, Toledo, OH 43608

Ohio Association of Career Colleges and Schools

Renewable award to full-time students attending a trade/technical institution in Ohio. Must be U.S. citizen. Minimum 2.5 GPA required. Must be graduating high school senior. **Award:** Scholarship for use in freshman or sophomore years; renewable. **Number:** 80. **Amount:** $2600–$13,448. **Eligibility Requirements:** Applicant must be high school student; planning to enroll or expecting to enroll full-time at a technical institution; resident of Ohio and studying in Ohio. Applicant must have 2.5 GPA or higher. Available to U.S. citizens. **Application Requirements:** Application, essay, references, transcript. **Application Deadline:** March 5. **Contact:** Max Lerner, Executive Director, Ohio Association of Career Colleges and Schools, 1857 Northwest Boulevard, The Annex, Columbus, OH 43212. **Phone:** 614-487-8180

Ohio Board of Regents

Award for academically outstanding Ohio residents planning to attend an approved Ohio college. Must be a high school senior intending to enroll full-time. Award is renewable for up to four years. Must rank in upper quarter of class or have a minimum GPA of 3.5. **Award:** Scholarship for use in freshman, sophomore, junior, or senior years; renewable. **Number:** 1000. **Amount:** $2205. **Eligibility Requirements:** Applicant must be high school student; planning to enroll or expecting to enroll full-time at a two-year or four-year institution; resident of Ohio and studying in Ohio. Applicant must have 3.5 GPA or higher. Available to U.S. citizens. **Application Requirements:** Application, test scores, transcript. **Application Deadline:** February 23. **Contact:** Sarina Wilks, Program Administrator, Ohio Board of Regents, PO Box 182452, Columbus, OH 43218-2452 **Phone:** 614-752-9528. **E-mail:** swilks@regents.state.oh.us

Ohio Instructional Grant

Award for low- and middle-income Ohio residents attending an approved college or school in Ohio or Pennsylvania. Must be enrolled full-time and have financial need. Average award is $630. May be used for any course of study except theology. **Award:** Grant for use in freshman, sophomore, junior, or senior years; renewable. **Number:** varies. **Amount:** $78–$5466. **Eligibility Requirements:** Applicant must be enrolled or expecting to enroll full-time at a two-year or four-year institution or university; resident of Ohio and studying in Ohio or Pennsylvania. Available to U.S. citizens. **Application Requirements:** Application, financial need analysis. **Application Deadline:** October 1. **Contact:** Charles Shahid, Assistant Director, Ohio Board of Regents, PO Box 182452 Columbus, OH 43218-2452. **Phone:** 614-644-5959. **E-mail:** cshahid@regents.state.oh.us

Ohio Student Choice Grant Program

Renewable award available to Ohio residents attending private colleges within the state. Must be enrolled full-time in a bachelor's degree program. Do not apply to state. Check with financial aid office of college. **Award:** Grant for use in freshman, sophomore, junior, or senior years; renewable. **Number:** varies. **Amount:** up to $1002. **Eligibility Requirements:** Applicant must be enrolled or expecting to enroll full-time at a four-year institution; resident of Ohio and studying in Ohio. Available to U.S. citizens. **Application Requirements:** **Application Deadline:** Continuous. **Contact:** Barbara Metheney, Program Administrator, Ohio Board of Regents, PO Box 182452, Columbus, OH 43218-2452. **Phone:** 614-752-9535. **E-mail:** bmethene@regents.state.oh.us

Ohio Civil Service Employees Association

Up to twelve scholarships worth up to $1000 will be awarded to eligible union members, spouses and their dependent children. For more details see **Web site:** www.ocsea.org. **Award:** Scholarship for use in freshman year; not renewable. **Number:** 8–12. **Amount:** $250–$1000. **Eligibility Requirements:** Applicant must be enrolled or expecting to enroll full or part-time at a two-year, four-year, or technical institution or university and resident of Ohio. Applicant or parent of applicant must be member of Ohio Civil Service Employee Association. Available to U.S. citizens. **Application Requirements:** Application, essay, references, transcript, proof of enrollment. **Application Deadline:** April 2. **Contact:** Les Best Scholarship Program, Ohio Civil Service Employees Association, 390 Worthington Road, Suite A, Westerville, OH 43082-8331. **Phone:** 614-865-4740

Ohio Department of Education

Renewable award for graduating high school seniors who demonstrate outstanding academic achievement. Each Ohio high school receives applications by January of each year. School can submit one application for every 200 students in the senior class. **Award:** Scholarship for use in freshman, sophomore, junior, or senior years; renewable. **Number:** varies. **Amount:** up to $1500. **Eligibility Requirements:** Applicant must be high school student; planning to enroll or expecting to enroll at a two-year or four-year institution or university and resident of Ohio. Applicant must have 3.5 GPA or higher. Available to U.S. citizens. **Application Requirements:** Application, test scores. **Application Deadline:** varies. **Contact:** Byrd Program Office, Ohio Department of Education, 25 South Front Street, Second Floor, Columbus, OH 43215. **Phone:** 614-466-4590

Ohio Newspapers Foundation

A $1,000 scholarship will be awarded to a northern Ohio high school senior who plans to pursue a newspaper journalism career. Applicants must be enrolled in a high school in Cuyahoga, Lorain, Huron, Erie, Wood, Geauge, Sandusky, Ottawa, or Lucas County. The applicant must be enrolled in an accredited Ohio college or university at the time the award is distributed. A minimum high school GPA of 3.0 (B) is required. **Award:** Scholarship for use in freshman year; not renewable. **Number:** 1. **Amount:** $1000. **Eligibility Requirements:** Applicant must be high school student; planning to enroll or expecting to enroll at an institution or university; resident of Ohio and studying in Ohio. Applicant must have 3.0 GPA or higher. Available to U.S. citizens. **Application Requirements:** Application, autobiography, financial need analysis, references, transcript. **Application Deadline:** March 31. **Contact:** Kathleen Pouliot, Secretary, Ohio Newspapers Foundation, 1335 Dublin Road, Suite 216-B, Columbus, OH 43215-7038. **Phone:** 614-486-6677. **E-mail:** kpouliot@ohionews.org

Ohio Newspapers Foundation Minority Scholarship

Three $1,500 scholarships will be awarded to minority high school seniors who plan to pursue a newspaper journalism career. Applicants must be enrolled in an accredited Ohio college or university. A minimum high school GPA of 2.5 (C+) is required. Applicants must be African-American, Hispanic, Asian-American or American-Indian. **Award:** Scholarship for use in freshman year; not renewable. **Number:** 3. **Amount:** $1500. **Eligibility Requirements:** Applicant must be American Indian/Alaska Native, Asian/Pacific Islander, Black (non-Hispanic), or Hispanic; high school student; planning to enroll or expecting to enroll at an institution or university; resident of Ohio and studying in Ohio. Applicant must have 2.5 GPA or higher. Available to U.S. citizens. **Application Requirements:** Application, autobiography, essay, transcript. **Application Deadline:** March 31. **Contact:** Kathleen Pouliot, Secretary, Ohio Newspapers Foundation, 1335 Dublin Road, Suite 216-B, Columbus, OH 43215-7038. **Phone:** 614-486-6677. **E-mail:** kpouliot@ohionews.org

Oklahoma

Oklahoma State Regents for Higher Education

Open to outstanding Oklahoma high school graduates who agree to teach in shortage areas. Must rank in top 15% of graduating class or score above 85th percentile on ACT or similar test, or be accepted in an educational program. Students nominated by institution. Reapply to renew. Must attend college/university in Oklahoma. Contact institution's financial aid office for application deadline. **Award:** Scholarship for use in freshman, sophomore, junior, senior, or graduate years; not renewable. **Number:** varies. **Amount:** up to $1500. **Eligibility Requirements:** Applicant must be enrolled or expecting to enroll full or part-time at a two-year or four-year institution or university; resident of Oklahoma and studying in Oklahoma. Available to U.S. and non-U.S. citizens. **Application Requirements:** Application, essay, test scores, transcript. **Application Deadline:** Continuous. **Contact:** Oklahoma State Regents for Higher Education, PO Box 108850, Oklahoma City, OK 73101-8850, **Phone:** 800-858-1840

Oklahoma Tuition Aid Grant

Award for Oklahoma residents enrolled at an Oklahoma institution at least part time each semester in a degree program. May be enrolled in two- or four-year or approved vocational-technical institution. Award of up to $1000 per year. Application is made through FAFSA. **Award:** Grant for use in freshman, sophomore, junior, senior, or graduate years; renewable. **Number:** 23,000. **Amount:** $200–$1000. **Eligibility Requirements:** Applicant must be enrolled or expecting to enroll full or part-time at a two-year, four-year, or technical institution or university; resident of Oklahoma and studying in Oklahoma. Available to U.S. citizens. **Application Requirements:** Application, financial need analysis, FAFSA. **Application Deadline:** April 30. **Contact:** Oklahoma State Regents for Higher Education, PO Box 3020, Oklahoma City, OK 73101-3020. **Phone:** 405-225-9456. **E-mail:** otaginfo@otag.org

Regional University Baccalaureate Scholarship

Renewable award for Oklahoma residents attending one of 11 participating Oklahoma public universities. Must have an ACT composite score of at least 30 or be a National Merit semifinalist or commended student. In addition to the award amount, each recipient will receive a resident tuition waiver from the institution. Must maintain a 3.25 GPA. **Award:** Scholarship for use in freshman, sophomore, junior, or senior years; renewable. **Number:** varies. **Amount:** $3000. **Eligibility Requirements:** Applicant must be enrolled or expecting to enroll full-time at an institution or university; resident of Oklahoma and studying in Oklahoma. Available to U.S. and non-U.S. citizens. **Application Requirements:** Application. **Application Deadline:** varies. **Contact:** Oklahoma State Regents for Higher Education, PO Box 108850, Oklahoma City, OK 73101-8850. **Phone:** 800-858-1840. **E-mail:** studentinfo@osrhe.edu

William P. Willis Scholarship

Renewable award for Oklahoma residents attending an Oklahoma institution. Contact institution financial aid office for application deadline. **Award:** Scholarship for use in freshman, sophomore, junior, or senior years; renewable. **Number:** 32. **Amount:** $2000–$3000. **Eligibility Requirements:** Applicant must be enrolled or expecting to enroll full-time at a two-year or four-year institution or university; resident of Oklahoma and studying in Oklahoma. Available to U.S. and non-U.S. citizens. **Application Requirements: Application Deadline:** varies. **Contact:** Oklahoma State Regents for Higher Education, PO Box 108850, Oklahoma City, OK 73101-8850.
Phone: 800-858-1840.
E-mail: studentinfo@osrhe.edu

South Dakota

American Legion, Department of South Dakota

Provide a 8-10 minute oration on some phase of the U.S. Constitution. Be prepared to speak extemporaneously for 3.5 minutes on specified articles or amendments. Compete at Local, District, and State levels. State winner goes on to National Contest and opportunity to win $18,000 in scholarships. Contact local American Legion post for contest dates. **Award:** Prize for use in freshman, sophomore, junior, or senior years; not renewable. **Number:** 1–4. **Amount:** $100–$1000. **Eligibility Requirements:** Applicant must be high school student; age 19 or under; planning to enroll or expecting to enroll full or part-time at a two-year, four-year, or technical institution or university and resident of South Dakota. Available to U.S. citizens. **Application Requirements:** Applicant must enter a contest, oration. **Application Deadline:** varies. **Contact:** Ronald Boyd, Department Adjutant, American Legion, Department of South Dakota, PO Box 67, Watertown, SD 57201. **Phone:** 605-886-3604.
E-mail: sdlegion@dailypost.com

South Dakota Board of Regents

Scholarship for graduating South Dakota high school seniors to pursue a career in elementary education at a South Dakota public university. University must be one of the following: BHSU, BSU, NSU or USD. Applicants must have a cumulative GPA of 3.0 after three years of high school. One-time award. **Award:** Scholarship for use in freshman year; not renewable. **Number:** 2. **Amount:** $1000. **Eligibility Requirements:** Applicant must be high school student; planning to enroll or expecting to enroll at an institution or university; resident of South Dakota and studying in South Dakota. Applicant must have 3.0 GPA or higher. **Application Requirements:** Application, essay, references, test scores, transcript. **Application Deadline:** February 25. **Contact:** South Dakota Board of Regents, 306 East Capitol Avenue, Suite 200, Pierre, SD 57501-3159

South Dakota Department of Education

For South Dakota residents in their senior year of high school. Must have a minimum 3.5 GPA and a minimum ACT score of 30 or above. Awards are renewable up to four years. Contact high school guidance office for more details. **Award:** Scholarship for use in freshman, sophomore, junior, or senior years; renewable. **Number:** up to 80. **Amount:** $1500. **Eligibility Requirements:** Applicant must be high school student; planning to enroll or expecting to enroll full-time at a two-year, four-year, or technical institution or university and resident of South Dakota. Applicant must have 3.5 GPA or higher. Available to U.S. citizens. **Application Requirements:** Application, test scores, transcript. **Application Deadline:** May 1. **Contact:** Roxie Thielen, Financial Aid Administrator, South Dakota Department of Education, 700 Governors Drive, Pierre, SD 57501-2291.
Phone: 605-773-5669.
E-mail: roxie.thielen@state.sd.us

Wisconsin

American Legion Auxiliary, Department of Wisconsin

One-time award of $1000. For a student to qualify, the mother of the applicant or the applicant must be a member of an Auxiliary unit. Must send with completed application: certification of an American Legion Auxiliary Unit President, copy of proof that veteran was in service (i.e. discharge papers), letters of recommendation, transcripts, and essay. Must have minimum 3.5 GPA, show financial need, and be a resident of Wisconsin. Refer questions to Department Secretary, (608) 745-0124. Applications available on **Web site:** www.legion-aux.org. **Award:** Scholarship for use in freshman, sophomore, junior, senior, or graduate years; not renewable. **Number:** 2. **Amount:** $1000. **Eligibility Requirements:** Applicant must be enrolled or expecting to enroll full or part-time at a four-year institution or university and resident of Wisconsin. Applicant or parent of applicant must be member of American Legion or Auxiliary. Applicant must have 3.5 GPA or higher. Available to U.S. citizens. **Application Requirements:** Application, essay, financial need analysis, references, transcript. **Application Deadline:** March 15. **Contact:** Kim Henderson, Scholarship Information, American Legion Auxiliary, Department of Wisconsin, PO Box 140, Portage, WI 53901-0140. **Phone:** 608-745-0124.
E-mail: membership@amlegionauxwi.org

Great Lakes Hemophilia Foundation

Scholarship for Wisconsin residents who have a bleeding disorder such as hemophilia, Von Willebrand disease, or a platelet function disorder. Consideration is also given to family members. It can also be used to retrain adults with bleeding disorders who can no longer function in chosen field due to health complications. Write for an application. **Award:** Scholarship for use in freshman, sophomore, junior, or senior years; not renewable. **Number:** 5–6. **Amount:** $1000. **Eligibility Requirements:** Applicant must be enrolled or expecting to enroll full or part-time at a two-year, four-year, or technical institution or university and resident of Wisconsin. Applicant must be physically disabled. Available to U.S. citizens. **Application Requirements:** Application, essay, references, self-addressed stamped envelope, transcript. **Application Deadline:** Continuous. **Contact:** Eva Cribben, Program Services Coordinator, Great Lakes Hemophilia Foundation, PO Box 0704, Milwaukee, WI 53201-0704.
Phone: 414-257-0200.
E-mail: ecribben@glhf.org

H.S. and Angelina Lewis Scholarships

One-time award of $1000. Applicant must be a daughter, son, wife, or widow of a veteran. Granddaughters and great-granddaughters of veterans who are auxiliary members may also apply. Must send with completed application: certification of an American Legion Auxiliary Unit President, copy of proof that veteran was in service (i.e. discharge papers), letters of recommendation, transcripts and essay. Must have minimum 3.5 GPA, show financial need, and be a resident of Wisconsin. Refer questions to Department Secretary, (608) 745-0124. Applications available on **Web site:** www.legion-aux.org. **Award:** Scholarship for use in freshman, sophomore, junior, senior, or graduate years; not renewable. **Number:** 6. **Amount:** $1000. **Eligibility Requirements:** Applicant must be enrolled or expecting to enroll full or part-time at a four-year institution or university and resident of Wisconsin. Applicant or parent of applicant must be member of American Legion or Auxiliary. Applicant must have 3.5 GPA or higher. Available to U.S. citizens. **Application Requirements:** Application, essay, financial need analysis, references, transcript. **Application Deadline:** March 15. **Contact:** Kim Henderson, Scholarship Information, American Legion Auxiliary, Department of Wisconsin, PO Box 140, Portage, WI 53901-0140. **Phone:** 608-745-0124. **E-mail:** membership@amlegionauxwi.org

Merit and Memorial Scholarships

One-time award of $1000. Applicant must be a daughter, son, wife, or widow of a veteran. Granddaughters and great granddaughters of veterans who are auxiliary members may also apply. Must send with completed application: certification of an American Legion Auxiliary Unit President, copy of proof that veteran was in service (i.e. discharge papers), letters of recommendation, transcripts, and essay. Must have minimum 3.5 GPA, show financial need, and be a resident of Wisconsin. Refer questions to Department Secretary, (608) 745-0124. Applications available on **Web site:** www.legion-aux.org. **Award:** Scholarship for use in freshman, sophomore, junior, senior, or graduate years; not renewable. **Number:** 6. **Amount:** $1000. **Eligibility Requirements:** Applicant must be enrolled or expecting to enroll full or part-time at a four-year institution or university and resident of Wisconsin. Applicant or parent of applicant must be member of American Legion or Auxiliary. Applicant must have 3.5 GPA or higher. Available to U.S. citizens. **Application Requirements:** Application, essay, financial need analysis, references, transcript. **Application Deadline:** March 15. **Contact:** Kim Henderson, Scholarship Information, American Legion Auxiliary, Department of Wisconsin, PO Box 140, Portage, WI 53901-0140. **Phone:** 608-745-0124. **E-mail:** membership@amlegionauxwi.org

ShopKo Stores, Inc.

Must live within 100 miles of a ShopKo store. Scholars selected on the basis of academic record, potential to succeed, leadership, and participation in school and community activities, honors, work, experience, a statement of educational and career goals, and an outside appraisal. Financial need is not considered. **Award:** Scholarship for use in freshman, sophomore, junior, or senior years; not renewable. **Number:** 100–110. **Amount:** $1000. **Eligibility Requirements:** Applicant must be enrolled or expecting to enroll full-time at a two-year, four-year, or technical institution or university and resident of California, Colorado, Idaho, Illinois, Iowa, Michigan, Minnesota, Montana, Nebraska, Nevada, Oregon, South Dakota, Utah, Washington, or Wisconsin. Available to U.S. citizens. **Application Requirements:** Application, essay, photo, references, self-addressed stamped envelope, transcript. **Application Deadline:** December 1. **Contact:** Amy Anderson, Communications Specialist, ShopKo Stores, Inc., 700 Pilgrim Way, PO Box 19060, Green Bay, WI 54307-9060. **Phone:** 920-429-4328. **E-mail:** aanderso@shopko.com

State President's Scholarships

One-time award of $1000. In order for student to qualify, the mother of the applicant or the applicant must be a member of an Auxiliary unit. Must send with completed application: certification of an American Legion Auxiliary Unit President, copy of proof that veteran was in service (i.e. discharge papers), letters of recommendation, transcripts, and essay. Must have minimum 3.5 GPA, show financial need, and be a resident of Wisconsin. Refer questions to Department Secretary, (608) 745-0124. Applications available on **Web site:** www.legion-aux.org. **Award:** Scholarship for use in freshman, sophomore, junior, senior, or graduate years; not renewable. **Number:** 3. **Amount:** $1000. **Eligibility Requirements:** Applicant must be enrolled or expecting to enroll full or part-time at a four-year institution or university and resident of Wisconsin. Applicant or parent of applicant must be member of American Legion or Auxiliary. Applicant must have 3.5 GPA or higher. Available to U.S. citizens. **Application Requirements:** Application, essay, financial need analysis, references, transcript. **Application Deadline:** March 15. **Contact:** Kim Henderson, Scholarship Information, American Legion Auxiliary, Department of Wisconsin, PO Box 140, Portage, WI 53901-0140. **Phone:** 608-745-0124. **E-mail:** membership@amlegionauxwi.org

Talent Incentive Program Grant

Assists residents of Wisconsin who are attending a nonprofit institution in Wisconsin and have substantial financial need. Must meet income criteria, be considered economically and educationally disadvantaged and be enrolled at least half-time. Please refer to Web site for further details: www.heab.state.wi.us **Award:** Grant for use in freshman, sophomore, junior, or senior years; renewable. **Number:** varies. **Amount:** $250–$1800. **Eligibility Requirements:** Applicant must be enrolled or expecting to enroll full or part-time at a two-year, four-year, or technical institution or university; resident of Wisconsin and studying in Wisconsin. Available to U.S. citizens. **Application Requirements:** Financial need analysis, nomination. **Application Deadline:** Continuous. **Contact:** John Whitt, Program Coordinator, Wisconsin Higher Educational Aids Board, PO Box 7885, Madison, WI 53707-7885. **Phone:** 608-266-1665. **E-mail:** john.whitt@heab.state.wi.us

Teacher of the Visually Impaired Loan Program

Provides forgivable loans to students who enroll in programs that lead to be certified as a teacher of the visually impaired or an orientation and mobility instructor. Must be a Wisconsin resident. For study in Wisconsin, Illinois, Iowa, Michigan, and Minnesota. Please refer to Web site for further details: www.heab.state.wi.us **Award:** Forgivable loan for use in freshman, sophomore, junior, senior, graduate, or postgraduate years; not renewable. **Number:** varies. **Amount:** $250–$10,000. **Eligibility Requirements:** Applicant must be enrolled or expecting to enroll full or part-time at a two-year, four-year, or technical institution or university; resident of Wisconsin and studying in Illinois, Iowa, Michigan, Minnesota, or Wisconsin. Available to U.S. citizens. **Application Requirements:** Application, financial need analysis. **Application Deadline:** Continuous. **Contact:** John Whitt, Program Coordinator, Wisconsin Higher Educational Aids Board, PO Box 7885, Madison, WI 53707-7885. **Phone:** 608-266-0888. **E-mail:** john.whitt@heab.state.wi.us

Wisconsin Academic Excellence Scholarship

Renewable award for high school seniors with the highest GPA in graduating class. Must be a Wisconsin resident. Award covers tuition for up to four years. Must maintain 3.0 GPA for renewal. Scholarships of up to $2250 each. Must attend a nonprofit Wisconsin institution full-time. Please refer to Web site for further details: www.heab.state.wi.us **Award:** Scholarship for use in freshman, sophomore, junior, or senior years; renewable. **Number:** 3445. **Amount:** up to $2250. **Eligibility Requirements:** Applicant must be enrolled or expecting to enroll full-time at a two-year, four-year, or technical institution or university; resident of Wisconsin and studying in Wisconsin. Applicant must have 3.5 GPA or higher. Available to U.S. citizens. **Application Requirements:** Transcript. **Application Deadline:** Continuous. **Contact:** Alice Winters, Program Coordinator, Wisconsin Higher Educational Aids Board, PO Box 7885, Madison, WI 53707-7885. **Phone:** 608-267-2213. **E-mail:** alice.winters@heab.state.wi.us

Wisconsin Congress of Parents and Teachers, Inc.

One-time award to graduating high school seniors from Wisconsin public schools. Must pursue a degree in education. High school must have an active PTA in good standing of the Wisconsin PTA. **Award:** Scholarship for use in freshman year; not renewable. **Number:** 2. **Amount:** $1000. **Eligibility Requirements:** Applicant must be high school student; planning to enroll or expecting to enroll full-time at a four-year institution and resident of Wisconsin. Available to U.S. citizens. **Application Requirements:** Application, essay, interview, references, transcript. **Application Deadline:** January 15. **Contact:** Kim Schwantes, Executive Administrator, Wisconsin Congress of Parents and Teachers, Inc., 4797 Hayes Road, Suite 2, Madison, WI 53704-3256

Wisconsin Department of Veterans Affairs

Open only to Wisconsin veterans. Renewable for continuing study. Contact office for more details. Application deadline is no later than sixty days after the course completion. Veterans may be reimbursed up to 100% of tuition and fees. **Award:** Grant for use in freshman, sophomore, junior, or senior years; renewable. **Number:** varies. **Amount:** $300–$2000. **Eligibility Requirements:** Applicant must be enrolled or expecting to enroll part-time at an institution or university; resident of Wisconsin and studying in Wisconsin. Available to U.S. citizens. Applicant or parent must meet one or more of the following requirements: general military experience; retired from active duty; disabled or killed as a result of military service; prisoner of war; or missing in action. **Application Requirements:** Application. **Application Deadline:** varies. **Contact:** Mike Keatley, Grants Coordinator, Wisconsin Department of Veterans Affairs, PO Box 7843, Madison, WI 53707-7843. **Phone:** 608-266-1311

Wisconsin Foundation for Independent Colleges, Inc.

Award for full-time undergraduate students to attend a WFIC member institution. Must show financial need, have a minimum 3.0 GPA and be a resident of a state within American Family Insurance's service area. See Web site for additional information and application: www.wficweb.org. **Award:** Scholarship for use in freshman, sophomore, junior, or senior years; not renewable. **Number:** up to 20. **Amount:** up to $1000. **Eligibility Requirements:** Applicant must be enrolled or expecting to enroll full-time at a four-year institution; resident of Arizona, Colorado, Idaho, Illinois, Indiana, Iowa, Kansas, Minnesota, Missouri, Nebraska, Nevada, North Dakota, Ohio, Oregon, or South Dakota and studying in Wisconsin. Applicant must have 3.0 GPA or higher. Available to U.S. citizens. **Application Requirements:** Application, essay, financial need analysis, references. **Application Deadline:** April 23. **Contact:** Christy Miller, Programs and Marketing Director, Wisconsin Foundation for Independent Colleges, Inc., 735 North Water Street, Suite 600, Milwaukee, WI 53202, **Phone:** 414-273-5980. **E-mail:** wfic@wficweb.org

Wisconsin First Scholarship Program

Wisconsin First Scholarships are designed to encourage Wisconsin's brightest students to obtain an education, and ultimately pursue a career in Wisconsin. Minimum 3.0 GPA required. Submit listing of academic achievements, merits, honors and awards. Also submit listing of community or campus involvement and number of hours. **Award:** Scholarship for use in freshman, sophomore, junior, or senior years; not renewable. **Number:** varies. **Amount:** $3000. **Eligibility Requirements:** Applicant must be enrolled or expecting to enroll full-time at a four-year institution or university; resident of Wisconsin and studying in Wisconsin. Applicant must have 3.0 GPA or higher. Available to U.S. citizens. **Application Requirements:** Application, autobiography, references, test scores, transcript. **Application Deadline:** March 12. **Contact:** Christy Miller, Marketing Program Manager, Wisconsin Foundation for Independent Colleges, Inc., 735 North Water Street, Suite 600, Milwaukee, WI 53202. **Phone:** 414-273-5980. **E-mail:** wfic@execpc.com

Wisconsin Higher Educational Aids Board

Provides forgivable loans to students enrolled in a nursing program. Must be a Wisconsin resident studying in Wisconsin. Application deadline is last day on which student is enrolled. Please refer to Web site for further details: www.heab.state.wi.us

Award: Forgivable loan for use in freshman, sophomore, junior, or senior years; renewable. **Number:** 150–1800. **Amount:** $250–$3000. **Eligibility Requirements:** Applicant must be enrolled or expecting to enroll full or part-time at a two-year, four-year, or technical institution or university; resident of Wisconsin and studying in Wisconsin. Available to U.S. citizens. **Application Requirements:** Application, financial need analysis. **Contact:** Cindy Lehrman, Program Coordinator, Wisconsin Higher Educational Aids Board, PO Box 7885, Madison, WI 53707-7885. **Phone:** 608-267-2209. **E-mail:** cindy.lehrman@heab.state.wi.us

Wisconsin National Guard Tuition Grant

Renewable award for active members of the Wisconsin National Guard in good standing, who successfully complete a course of study at a qualifying school. Award covers full tuition, excluding fees, not to exceed undergraduate tuition charged by University of Wisconsin-Madison. Must have a minimum 2.0 GPA. **Award:** Grant for use in freshman, sophomore, junior, or senior years; renewable. **Number:** up to 4000. **Amount:** up to $1927. **Eligibility Requirements:** Applicant must be enrolled or expecting to enroll full or part-time at a two-year, four-year, or technical institution or university and resident of Wisconsin. Available to U.S. citizens. Applicant must have served in the Air Force National Guard or Army National Guard. **Application Requirements:** Application. **Application Deadline:** Continuous. **Contact:** Karen Behling, Tuition Grant Administrator, Department of Military Affairs, PO Box 14587, Madison, WI 53708-0587. **Phone:** 608-242-3159. **E-mail:** karen.behling@dma.state.wi.us

Wisconsin Native American Student Grant

Grants for Wisconsin residents who are at least one-quarter American-Indian. Must be attending a college or university within the state. Please refer to Web site for further details: www.heab.state.wi.us **Award:** Grant for use in freshman, sophomore, junior, senior, graduate, or postgraduate years; not renewable. **Number:** varies. **Amount:** $250–$1100. **Eligibility Requirements:** Applicant must be American Indian/Alaska Native; enrolled or expecting to enroll full or part-time at a two-year, four-year, or technical institution or university; resident of Wisconsin and studying in Wisconsin. Available to U.S. citizens. **Application Requirements:** Application, financial need analysis. **Application Deadline:** Continuous. **Contact:** Sandra Thomas, Program Coordinator, Wisconsin Higher Educational Aids Board, PO Box 7885, Madison, WI 53707-7885. **Phone:** 608-266-0888. **E-mail:** sandy.thomas@heab.state.wi.us

Wisconsin Society of Professional Engineers

One-time award for students pursuing full-time study in engineering. Must be a Wisconsin resident and have a minimum GPA of 3.0. **Award:** Scholarship for use in freshman, junior, or senior years; not renewable. **Number:** 4. **Amount:** $1000–$1500. **Eligibility Requirements:** Applicant must be enrolled or expecting to enroll full-time at a four-year institution or university and resident of Wisconsin. Applicant must have 3.0 GPA or higher. Available to U.S. and non-U.S. citizens. **Application Requirements:** Application, essay, references, self-addressed stamped envelope, test scores, transcript. **Application Deadline:** December 15. **Contact:** Office Manager, Wisconsin Society of Professional Engineers, 7044 South 13th Street, Oak Creek, WI 53154. **E-mail:** e.grochowski@wspe.org

SUMMER OPPORTUNITIES

Iowa

Grinnell Summer Institute

Grinnell, IA
General Information: Coed residential academic program established in 1983.
Contact: Jim Sumner, Dean of Admissions/Financial Aid, Office of Admissions, 1103 Park Street, Grinnell, IA 50112-0810
Phone: 800-247-0113
Fax: 641-269-4800
E-mail: sumnerj@grinnell.edu
Web site: www.grinnell.edu

Iowa Young Writers' Studio

Iowa City, IA
General Information: Coed residential academic program established in 1999.
Contact: Ms. Trish Walsh, Director, 100 Oakdale Campus W310, Iowa City, IA 52242-5000
Phone: 319-335-4209
Fax: 319-335-4039
E-mail: iyws@uiowa.edu
Web site: www.uiowa.edu/~iyws

Illinois

Center for American Archeology/Archeology Field School

Kampsville, IL
General Information: Coed residential academic program established in 1968.
Contact: Mary Pirkl, Director of Education, PO Box 366, Kampsville, IL 62053
Phone: 618-653-4316
Fax: 618-653-4232
E-mail: caa@caa-archeology.org
Web site: www.caa-archeology.org

Center for American Archeology/Past Lifeways Program

Kampsville, IL
General Information: Coed residential and day academic program established in 1968.
Contact: Mary Pirkl, Director of Education, PO Box 366, Kampsville, IL 62053
Phone: 618-653-4316
Fax: 618-653-4232
E-mail: caa@caa-archeology.org
Web site: www.caa-archeology.org

Center for Talent Development Summer Academic Program

Evanston, IL
General Information: Coed residential and day academic program established in 1983.
Contact: Susie Hoffmann, Summer Program Coordinator, 617 Dartmouth Place, Evanston, IL 60208
Phone: 847-491-3782
Fax: 847-467-4283
E-mail: ctd@northwestern.edu
Web site: www.ctd.northwestern.edu

Columbia College Chicago's High School Summer Institute

Chicago, IL
General Information: Coed residential and day academic program established in 1984.
Contact: Ms. Stephanie Strait, Coordinator, Undergraduate Admissions, 600 South Michigan Avenue, Chicago, IL 60605
Phone: 312-344-7134
Fax: 312-344-8024
E-mail: sstrait@colum.edu
Web site: www.colum.edu

Cybercamps–Benedictine University

Lisle, IL
General Information: Coed residential and day academic program established in 1997.
Contact: Cybercamps Information Office, 2401 4th Avenue, Suite 1110, Seattle, WA 98121
Phone: 206-442-4500
Fax: 206-442-4501
E-mail: info@cybercamps.com
Web site: www.cybercamps.com

Cybercamps–Concordia University

River Forest, IL
General Information: Coed residential and day academic program established in 1997.
Contact: Cybercamps Information Office, 2401 4th Avenue, Suite 1110, Seattle, WA 98121
Phone: 206-442-4500
Fax: 206-442-4501
E-mail: info@cybercamps..com
Web site: www.cybercamps.com

Emagination Computer Camps

Lake Forest, IL
General Information: Coed residential and day academic program established in 1982.
Contact: Ms. Kathi Rigg, Director, 110 Winn Street, Suite 207, Woburn, MA 01801
Phone: 888-226-6733
Fax: 781-933-0749
E-mail: camp@computercamps.com
Web site: www.computercamps.com

iD Tech Camps–Lake Forest College

Evanston, IL
General Information: Coed residential and day academic program established in 1999.
Contact: Client Service Representatives, 1885 Winchester Boulevard, Suite 201, Campbell, CA 95008
Phone: 888-709-TECH
Fax: 408-871-2228
E-mail: requests@internaldrive.com
Web site: www.internaldrive.com

iD Tech Camps–Northwestern University

Chicago, IL
General Information: Coed residential and day academic program established in 1999.
Contact: Client Service Representatives, 1885 Winchester Boulevard, Suite 201, Campbell, CA 95008
Phone: 888-709-TECH
Fax: 408-871-2228
E-mail: requests@internaldrive.com
Web site: www.internaldrive.com

Junior Statesmen Summer School–Northwestern University

Evanston, IL
General Information: Coed residential academic program established in 1995.
Contact: Matt Randazzo, National Summer School Director, 400 South El Camino Real, Suite 300, San Mateo, CA 94402
Phone: 650-347-1600
Fax: 650-347-7200
E-mail: jsa@jsa.org
Web site: www.jsa.org

Kendall College Culinary Camp

Chicago, IL
General Information: Coed residential and day arts program established in 1998.
Contact: Office of Admissions, 900 N. North Branch Street, Chicago, IL 60622
Phone: 877-588-8860
Fax: 312-752-2021
E-mail: culinarycamp@kendall.edu
Web site: www.kendall.edu

National Guitar Workshop–Chicago

Elgin, IL
General Information: Coed residential and day arts program established in 1984.
Contact: Emily Flower, Registrar, PO Box 222, Lakeside, CT 06758
Phone: 800-234-6479
Fax: 860-567-0374
E-mail: emily@guitarworkshop.com
Web site: www.guitarworkshop.com

Northwestern University's College Preparation Program

Evanston, IL
General Information: Coed residential and day academic program established in 1987.
Contact: Stephanie Teterycz, Associate Director of Summer Sessions, 405 Church Street, Evanston, IL 60208
Phone: 847-491-4358
Fax: 847-491-3660
E-mail: s_teterycz@northwestern.edu
Web site: www.northwestern.edu/collegeprep

Northwestern University's National High School Institute

Evanston, IL
General Information: Coed residential academic program established in 1931.
Contact: Nick Kanel, Department Assistant, 617 Noyes Street, Evanston, IL 60208
Phone: 800-662-NHSI
Fax: 847-467-1057
E-mail: nhsi@northwestern.edu
Web site: www.northwestern.edu/nhsi

Power Chord Academy

Chicago, IL
General Information: Coed residential academic program.
Contact: Mr. Bryan J. Wrzesinski, 7336 Santa Monica Boulevard, #107, Los Angeles, CA 90046
Phone: 800-897-6677
Fax: 775-306-7923
E-mail: bryan@powerchordacademy.com
Web site: www.powerchordacademy.com

University of Chicago–Insight

Chicago, IL
General Information: Coed residential and day academic program established in 1998.
Contact: Ms. Valerie Huston, Secretary, Summer Session Office, The Graham School of General Studies, Summer Sessions Office, 1427 East 60th Street, Chicago, IL 60637
Phone: 773-702-6033
Fax: 773-702-6814
E-mail: uc-summer@uchicago.edu
Web site: summer.uchicago.edu/

University of Chicago–Research in the Biological Sciences

Chicago, IL
General Information: Coed residential academic program established in 1999.
Contact: Ms. Valerie Huston, Secretary, Summer Session Office, Graham School of General Studies, Summer Sessions Office, 1427 East 60th Street, Chicago, IL 60637
Phone: 773-702-6033
Fax: 773-702-6814
E-mail: uc-summer@uchicago.edu
Web site: summer.uchicago.edu/

University of Chicago–Summer Quarter for High School Students

Chicago, IL
General Information: Coed residential and day academic program established in 1999.
Contact: Ms. Valerie Huston, Secretary, Summer Session Office, Graham School of General Studies, Summer Sessions Office, 1427 East 60th Street, Chicago, IL 60637
Phone: 773-702-6033
Fax: 773-702-6814
E-mail: uc-summer@uchicago.edu
Web site: summer.uchicago.edu

Indiana

Ball State University Summer Journalism Workshops

Muncie, IN
General Information: Coed residential academic program established in 1966.
Contact: Mark Herron, Director, Ball State University, AJ 304, Muncie, IN 47306
Phone: 765-285-8900
Fax: 765-285-7997
E-mail: bsuworkshops@bsu.edu
Web site: www.bsu.edu/web/bsuworkshops

Explore-A-College

Richmond, IN
General Information: Coed residential academic program established in 1982.
Contact: Dee Johnson, Director of Summer Studies, Drawer 188, Richmond, IN 47374-4095
Phone: 800-EARLHAM
Fax: 765-983-1560
E-mail: ballde@earlham.edu
Web site: www.earlham.edu/~eac

Indiana University School of Music College Audition Preparation Workshop

Bloomington, IN
General Information: Coed residential arts program established in 1998.
Contact: Helena Walsh, Registration Coordinator, Office of Special Programs, Indiana University School of Music, Bloomington, IN 47405-7006
Phone: 812-855-6025
Fax: 812-855-9847
E-mail: musicsp@indiana.edu
Web site: www.music.indiana.edu

Indiana University School of Music Piano Academy

Bloomington, IN
General Information: Coed residential arts program established in 1985.
Contact: Helena Walsh, Registration Coordinator, Office of Special Programs, Indiana University School of Music, Bloomington, IN 47405-7006
Phone: 812-855-6025
Fax: 812-855-9847
E-mail: musicsp@indiana.edu
Web site: www.music.indiana.edu/som/piano_academy/

Indiana University School of Music Recorder Academy

Bloomington, IN
General Information: Coed residential arts program established in 1993.
Contact: Helena Walsh, Registration Coordinator, Office of Special Programs, Indiana University School of Music, Bloomington, IN 47405-7006
Phone: 812-855-6025
Fax: 812-855-9847
E-mail: musicsp@indiana.edu
Web site: www.music.indiana.edu/som/special_programs/

Indiana University School of Music String Academy

Bloomington, IN
General Information: Coed residential arts program established in 1984.
Contact: Helena Walsh, Registration Coordinator, Office of Special Programs, Indiana University School of Music, Bloomington, IN 47405-7006
Phone: 812-855-6025
Fax: 812-855-9847
E-mail: musicsp@indiana.edu
Web site: www.indiana.edu/~smsa/

Kansas

Future Astronaut Training Program

Hutchinson, KS
General Information: Coed residential academic program established in 1985.
Contact: Mrs. Laurie Givan, Camp Registrar, 1100 North Plum, Hutchinson, KS 67501
Phone: 800-397-0330 ext. 323
Fax: 620-662-3693
E-mail: laurieg@cosmo.org
Web site: www.cosmo.org

Jayhawk Debate Institute

Lawrence, KS
General Information: Coed residential and day academic program established in 1966.
Contact: Jacob Thompson, Associate Debate Institute Director, Department of Communication Studies, 1440 Jayhawk Boulevard - SB 103 Bailey Hall, Lawrence, KS 66045
Phone: 785-864-9893
Fax: 785-864-5203
E-mail: coms3@raven.cc.ukans.edu
Web site: www.kudebate.org/~coms3/home.html

Kansas Journalism Institute

Lawrence, KS
General Information: Coed residential academic program established in 1963.
Contact: John Hudnall, Director, 200 Stauffer-Flint Hall, 1435 Jayhawk Boulevard, Lawrence, KS 66045
Phone: 785-864-0605
Fax: 785-864-5945
E-mail: kspa@ku.edu
Web site: www.ku.edu/~jschool/kji

KU Jazz Workshop

Lawrence, KS
General Information: Coed residential and day arts program established in 1990.
Contact: James Hudson, Director, 452 Murphy Hall, 1530 Naismith Drive, #452, Lawrence, KS 66045-3120
Phone: 785-864-4730
Fax: 785-864-5023
E-mail: musicamp@ku.edu
Web site: www.ku.edu/~mad/summer/mwmcamp/#content

KU Marching Band Camps

Lawrence, KS
General Information: Coed residential and day arts program established in 1991.
Contact: James Hudson, Director, 452 Murphy Hall, 1530 Naismith Drive, #452, Lawrence, KS 66045-3120
Phone: 785-864-4730
Fax: 785-864-5023
E-mail: musicamp@ku.edu
Web site: www.musiccamp.ku.edu

Mars Academy

Hutchinson, KS
General Information: Coed residential academic program established in 2003.
Contact: Mrs. Laurie Givan, Education Registrar, 1100 North Plum, Hutchinson, KS 67501
Phone: 800-397-0330 ext. 323
Fax: 620-662-3693
E-mail: laurieg@cosmo.org
Web site: www.cosmo.org

University of Kansas–Duke University Talent Identification Program

Lawrence, KS
General Information: Coed residential academic program.
Contact: TIP Program Director, 1121 West Main Street, Durham, NC 27701-2028
Phone: 919-668-9100
Fax: 919-681-7921
E-mail: information@tip.duke.edu
Web site: www.tip.duke.edu/ss/kansas.htm

University of Kansas–Midwestern Music Camp–Junior and Senior Divisions

Lawrence, KS
General Information: Coed residential and day arts program established in 1936.
Contact: James Hudson, Director, 452 Murphy Hall, 1530 Naismith Drive, #452, Lawrence, KS 66045-3120
Phone: 785-864-4730
Fax: 785-864-5023
E-mail: musicamp@ku.edu
Web site: www.musiccamp.ku.edu

University of Kansas–School of Pharmacy Summer Camp

Lawrence, KS
General Information: Coed residential academic program.
Contact: Gene Hotchkiss, Pharmacy Summer Camp Coordinator, School of Pharmacy, 2056 Malott Hall, 1251 Wesoce Hall Drive, Lawrence, KS 66045
Phone: 785-864-3591
E-mail: ghotchkiss@ku.edu
Web site: www2.pharm.ku.edu/phpr/camp/camp.html

Michigan

American Youth Foundation Leadership Conference

Shelby, MI
General Information: Coed residential academic program established in 1925.
Contact: Ms. Lori Greene, Registrar, Miniwanca Education Center, 8845 West Garfield Road, Shelby, MI 49455
Phone: 231-861-4313
Fax: 231-861-5244
E-mail: lori.greene@ayf.com
Web site: www.ayf.com

Cybercamps–University of Michigan

Ann Arbor, MI
General Information: Coed residential and day academic program established in 1997.
Contact: Cybercamps Information Office, 2401 4th Avenue, Suite 1110, Seattle, WA 98121
Phone: 206-442-4500
Fax: 206-442-4501
E-mail: info@cybercamps.com
Web site: www.cybercamps.com

Hillsdale College Summer Science Camps

Hillsdale, MI
General Information: Coed residential academic program established in 1989.
Contact: Dr. Francis X. Steiner, Professor of Biology/Dean of Natural Sciences, Biology Department, Hillsdale, MI 49242

Phone: 517-607-2399
Fax: 517-607-2252
E-mail: fxs@hillsdale.edu
Web site: www.hillsdale.edu

iD Tech Camps–University of Michigan

Ann Arbor, MI
General Information: Coed residential and day academic program established in 1999.
Contact: Client Service Representatives, 1885 Winchester Boulevard, Suite 201, Campbell, CA 95008
Phone: 888-709-TECH
Fax: 408-871-2228
E-mail: requests@internaldrive.com
Web site: www.internaldrive.com

Interlochen Arts Camp

Interlochen, MI
General Information: Coed residential arts program established in 1928.
Contact: Tom Bewley, Director of Admissions, PO Box 199, Interlochen, MI 49643
Phone: 231-276-7472
Fax: 231-276-7464
E-mail: admissions@interlochen.org
Web site: www.interlochen.org/

Michigan State University High School Engineering Institute

East Lansing, MI
General Information: Coed residential academic program established in 1962.
Contact: Jonathan Lembright, Director, High School Engineering Institute, 1410 Engineering Building, East Lansing, MI 48824
Phone: 517-355-6616 ext. 6
Fax: 517-432-1350
E-mail: lembrigh@egr.msu.edu
Web site: www.egr.msu.edu/egr/programs/bachelors/hsei.php

Michigan Technological University American Indian Workshop

Houghton, MI
General Information: Coed residential academic program established in 1988.
Contact: John Lehman, Youth Programs Coordinator, 1400 Townsend Drive, Houghton, MI 49931-1295
Phone: 906-487-2219
Fax: 906-487-3101
E-mail: yp@mtu.edu
Web site: youthprograms.mtu.edu

Michigan Technological University Explorations in Engineering Workshop

Houghton, MI
General Information: Coed residential academic program established in 1988.
Contact: John Lehman, Youth Programs Coordinator, 1400 Townsend Drive, Houghton, MI 49931-1295
Phone: 906-487-2219
Fax: 906-487-3101
E-mail: yp@mtu.edu
Web site: youthprograms.mtu.edu

Michigan Technological University Honors Orchestra Program

Houghton, MI
General Information: Coed residential arts program established in 1994.
Contact: John Lehman, Youth Programs Coordinator, 1400 Townsend Drive, Houghton, MI 49931-1295
Phone: 906-487-2219
Fax: 906-487-3101
E-mail: yp@mtu.edu
Web site: youthprograms.mtu.edu

Michigan Technological University Summer Youth Program

Houghton, MI
General Information: Coed residential and day academic program established in 1973.
Contact: John Lehman, Youth Programs Coordinator, 1400 Townsend Drive, Houghton, MI 49931
Phone: 906-487-2219
Fax: 906-487-3101
E-mail: yp@mtu.edu
Web site: youthprograms.mtu.edu

Summer Discovery at Michigan

Ann Arbor, MI
General Information: Coed residential academic program established in 1991.
Contact: The Musiker Family, Director, 1326 Old Northern Boulevard, Roslyn Village, NY 11576
Phone: 888-878-6637
Fax: 516-625-3438
E-mail: discovery@summerfun.com
Web site: www.summerfun.com

Minnesota

Carleton College Summer Writing Program

Northfield, MN
General Information: Coed residential academic program established in 1976.
Contact: Becky Fineran-Gardner, Director of Summer Academic Programs, 1 North College Street, Northfield, MN 55057-4016
Phone: 507-646-4038
Fax: 507-646-4540
E-mail: swp@carleton.edu
Web site: www.webapps.acs.Carleton.edu/campus/SAP/writing/

Concordia Language Villages–Chinese

Bemidji, MN
General Information: Coed residential academic program established in 1961.
Contact: Alex Loehrer, Assistant Director, Public Relations, 901 South Eighth Street, Moorhead, MN 56562
Phone: 218-299-4544
Fax: 218-299-3807
E-mail: clv@cord.edu
Web site: www.ConcordiaLanguageVillages.org

Concordia Language Villages–Danish

Bemidji, MN
General Information: Coed residential academic program established in 1961.
Contact: Alex Loehrer, Assistant Director, Public Relations, 901 South Eighth Street, Moorhead, MN 56562
Phone: 218-299-4544
Fax: 218-299-3807
E-mail: clv@cord.edu
Web site: www.ConcordiaLanguageVillages.org

Concordia Language Villages–English

Moorhead, MN
General Information: Coed residential academic program established in 1961.
Contact: Alex Loehrer, Assistant Director, Public Relations, 901 South Eighth Street, Moorhead, MN 56562
Phone: 800-222-4750
Fax: 218-299-3807
E-mail: clv@cord.edu
Web site: www.ConcordiaLanguageVillages.org

Concordia Language Villages–Finnish

Bemidji, MN
General Information: Coed residential academic program established in 1961.
Contact: Alex Loehrer, Assistant Director, Public Relations, 901 South Eighth Street, Moorhead, MN 56562
Phone: 218-299-4544 **Fax:** 218-299-3807
E-mail: clv@cord.edu
Web site: www.ConcordiaLanguageVillages.org

Concordia Language Villages–French
Bemidji, MN
General Information: Coed residential academic program established in 1961.
Contact: Alex Loehrer, Assistant Director, Public Relations, 901 South Eighth Street, Moorhead, MN 56562
Phone: 218-299-4544
Fax: 218-299-3807
E-mail: clv@cord.edu
Web site: www.ConcordiaLanguageVillages.org

Concordia Language Villages–French–Camp Holiday
Hackensack, MN
General Information: Coed residential academic program established in 1961.
Contact: Alex Loehrer, Assistant Director, Public Relations, 901 South Eighth Street, Moorhead, MN 56562
Phone: 218-299-4544
Fax: 218-299-3807
E-mail: clv@cord.edu
Web site: www.ConcordiaLanguageVillages.org

Concordia Language Villages–French
Fosston, MN
General Information: Coed residential academic program established in 1961.
Contact: Alex Loehrer, Assistant Director, Public Relations, 901 South Eighth Street, Moorhead, MN 56562
Phone: 218-299-4544
Fax: 218-299-3807
E-mail: clv@cord.edu
Web site: www.ConcordiaLanguageVillages.org

Concordia Language Villages–French Voyageur
Bemidji, MN
General Information: Coed residential academic program established in 1961.
Contact: Alex Loehrer, Assistant Director, Public Relations, 901 South Eighth Street, Moorhead, MN 56562
Phone: 218-299-4544
Fax: 218-299-3807
E-mail: clv@cord.edu
Web site: www.ConcordiaLanguageVillages.org

Concordia Language Villages–German
Bemidji, MN
General Information: Coed residential academic program established in 1961.
Contact: Alex Loehrer, Assistant Director, Public Relations, 901 South Eighth Street, Moorhead, MN 56562
Phone: 218-299-4544
Fax: 218-299-3807
E-mail: clv@cord.edu
Web site: www.ConcordiaLanguageVillages.org

Concordia Language Villages–German–Camp Trowbridge
Vergas, MN
General Information: Coed residential academic program established in 1961.
Contact: Alex Loehrer, Assistant Director, Public Relations, 901 South Eighth Street, Moorhead, MN 56562
Phone: 218-299-4544
Fax: 218-299-3807
E-mail: clv@cord.edu
Web site: www.ConcordiaLanguageVillages.org

Concordia Language Villages–Italian
Hackensack, MN
General Information: Coed residential academic program established in 2003.
Contact: Alex Loehrer, Assistant Director, Public Relations, Hackensack, MN
Phone: 800-222-4750
Fax: 218-299-3807
E-mail: clv@cord.edu
Web site: www.ConcordiaLanguageVillages.org

Concordia Language Villages–Japanese
Dent, MN
General Information: Coed residential academic program established in 1961.
Contact: Alex Loehrer, Assistant Director, Public Relations, 901 South Eighth Street, Moorhead, MN 56562
Phone: 218-299-4544
Fax: 218-299-3807
E-mail: clv@cord.edu
Web site: www.ConcordiaLanguageVillages.org

Concordia Language Villages–Korean
Hackensack, MN
General Information: Coed residential academic program established in 1961.
Contact: Alex Loehrer, Assistant Director, Public Relations, 901 South Eighth Street, Moorhead, MN 56562
Phone: 218-299-4544
Fax: 218-299-3807
E-mail: clv@cord.edu
Web site: www.ConcordiaLanguageVillages.org

Concordia Language Villages–Norwegian
Bemidji, MN
General Information: Coed residential academic program established in 1961.
Contact: Alex Loehrer, Assistant Director, Public Relations, 901 South Eighth Street, Moorhead, MN 56562
Phone: 218-299-4544
Fax: 218-299-3807
E-mail: clv@cord.edu
Web site: www.ConcordiaLanguageVillages.org

Concordia Language Villages–Russian
Vergas, MN
General Information: Coed residential academic program established in 1961.
Contact: Alex Loehrer, Assistant Director, Public Relations, 901 South Eighth Street, Moorhead, MN 56562
Phone: 218-299-4544
Fax: 218-299-3807
E-mail: clv@cord.edu
Web site: www.ConcordiaLanguageVillages.org

Concordia Language Villages–Spanish
Bemidji, MN
General Information: Coed residential academic program established in 1961.
Contact: Alex Loehrer, Assistant Director, Public Relations, 901 South Eighth Street, Moorhead, MN 56562
Phone: 800-222-4750
Fax: 218-299-3807
E-mail: clv@cord.edu
Web site: www.ConcordiaLanguageVillages.org

Concordia Language Villages–Spanish
Maplelag, MN
General Information: Coed residential academic program established in 1961.
Contact: Alex Loehrer, Assistant Director, Public Relations, 901 South Eighth Street, Moorhead, MN 56562
Phone: 218-299-4544
Fax: 218-299-3807
E-mail: clv@cord.edu
Web site: www.ConcordiaLanguageVillages.org

Concordia Language Villages–Spanish–Wilder Forest
Marine on the St. Croix, MN
General Information: Coed residential academic program established in 1961.
Contact: Alex Loehrer, Assistant Director, Public Relations, 901 South

Eighth Street, Moorhead, MN 56562
Phone: 218-299-4544
Fax: 218-299-3807
E-mail: clv@cord.edu
Web site: www.ConcordiaLanguage Villages.org

Concordia Language Villages–Swedish

Bemidji, MN
General Information: Coed residential academic program established in 1961.
Contact: Alex Loehrer, Assistant Director, Public Relations, 901 South Eighth Street, Moorhead, MN 56562
Phone: 218-299-4544
Fax: 218-299-3807
E-mail: clv@cord.edu
Web site: www.ConcordiaLanguage Villages.org

Cybercamps–University of Minnesota

Minneapolis, MN
General Information: Coed residential and day academic program established in 1997.
Contact: Cybercamps Information Office, 2401 4th Avenue, Suite 1110, Seattle, WA 98121
Phone: 206-442-4500
Fax: 206-442-4501
E-mail: info@cybercamps.com
Web site: www.cybercamps.com

iD Tech Camps–University of Minnesota

Minneapolis, MN
General Information: Coed residential and day academic program established in 1999.
Contact: Client Service Representatives, 1885 Winchester Boulevard, Suite 201, Campbell, CA 95008
Phone: 888-709-TECH
Fax: 408-871-2228
E-mail: requests@internaldrive.com
Web site: www.internaldrive.com

Shattuck-St. Mary's Summer Discovery and English Language Institute

Faribault, MN
General Information: Coed residential and day academic program established in 1988.
Contact: Mike Frankenfield, Director of Summer Programs, Box 218, Faribault, MN 55021
Phone: 507-333-1674
Fax: 507-333-1591
E-mail: mfrankenfield@s-sm.org
Web site: www.s-sm.org

Wilderness Dance Camp

Bloomington, MN
General Information: Coed residential arts program established in 1997.
Contact: Ms. Chandra Saign, Director, 10251 Lyndale Avenue South, Bloomington, MN 55420
Phone: 952-884-6009
E-mail: info@dancecamp.org
Web site: www.dancecamp.org/

Missouri

Cybercamps–Washington University

St. Louis, MO
General Information: Coed residential and day academic program established in 1997.
Contact: Cybercamps Information Office, 2401 4th Avenue, Suite 1110, Seattle, WA 98121
Phone: 206-442-4500
Fax: 206-442-4501
E-mail: info@cybercamps.com
Web site: www.cybercamps.com

Washington University High School Summer Scholars Program

St. Louis, MO
General Information: Coed residential academic program established in 1988.
Contact: Ms. Marsha Hussung, Director, High School Summer Scholars Program, Campus Box 1145, 1 Brookings Drive, St. Louis, MO 63130
Phone: 314-935-6834
Fax: 314-935-4847
E-mail: mhussung@wustl.edu
Web site: ucollege.wustl.edu/hssp

Washington University in St. Louis, School of Art–Portfolio Plus

St. Louis, MO
General Information: Coed residential and day arts program established in 2004.
Contact: Belinda Lee, Director, Study Abroad, Washington University in St. Louis, School of Art, Box 1031, One Brookings Drive, St. Louis, MO 63130
Phone: 314-935-8456
Fax: 314-935-4862
E-mail: bslee@art.wustl.edu
Web site: www.artsci.wustl.edu/~artweb/washUSoa/

Wentworth Military Academy Summer School

Lexington, MO
General Information: Coed residential academic program established in 1940.
Contact: Maj. Todd Kitchen, Director of Admissions, 1880 Washington Avenue, Lexington, MO 64067-1799
Phone: 800-962-7682
Fax: 660-259-2677
E-mail: admissions@wma1880.org
Web site: www.wma1880.org

Wentworth Military Academy Summer School–Camp LEAD

Lexington, MO
General Information: Coed residential academic program.
Contact: Maj. Todd Kitchen, Director of Admissions, 1880 Washington Avenue, Lexington, MO 64067
Phone: 800-962-7682
Fax: 660-259-2677
E-mail: admissions@wma1880.org
Web site: www.wma1880.org

Nebraska

Groundwater University

Lincoln, NE
General Information: Coed residential academic program established in 1994.
Contact: Ms. Carla Mansfield, Camp Director, 5561 South 48th Street, #215, Lincoln, NE 68516
Phone: 800-858-4844
Fax: 402-434-2742
E-mail: gu@groundwater.org
Web site: www.groundwater.org

Ohio

Cleveland Institute of Art Pre-College Program

Cleveland, OH
General Information: Coed residential arts program established in 1999.
Contact: Admissions Office, 11141 East Boulevard, Cleveland, OH 44106
Phone: 216-421-7418
Fax: 216-421-7438
E-mail: summer@gate.cia.edu
Web site: www.cia.edu

Cleveland Institute of Art Pre-College Program–Architecture
Cleveland, OH
General Information: Coed residential arts program established in 1999.
Contact: Admissions Office, 11141 East Boulevard, Cleveland, OH 44106
Phone: 216-421-7418
Fax: 216-421-7438
E-mail: summer@gate.cia.edu
Web site: www.cia.edu

Cleveland Institute of Art Pre-College Program–Product and Auto Design
Cleveland, OH
General Information: Coed residential arts program established in 1999.
Contact: Admissions Office, 11141 East Boulevard, Cleveland, OH 44106
Phone: 216-421-7418
Fax: 216-421-7438
E-mail: summer@gate.cia.edu
Web site: www.cia.edu

Cleveland Institute of Art Pre-College Program–Special Effects and Animation
Cleveland, OH
General Information: Coed residential arts program established in 1999.
Contact: Admissions Office, 11141 East Boulevard, Cleveland, OH 44106
Phone: 216-421-7418
Fax: 216-421-7438
E-mail: summer@gate.cia.edu
Web site: www.cia.edu

Friends Music Camp
Barnesville, OH
General Information: Coed residential arts program established in 1980.
Contact: Peg Champney, Director, 61830 Sandy Ridge Road, Barnesville, OH 43713
Phone: 740-425-3655
E-mail: musicfmc@yahoo.com
Web site: www.quaker.org/friends-music-camp/

The Grand River Summer Academy
Austinburg, OH
General Information: Coed residential and day academic program established in 1990.
Contact: Sam Corabi, Director of Admission, 3042 College Street, Austinburg, OH 44010
Phone: 440-275-2811 ext. 25
Fax: 440-275-1825
E-mail: academy@grandriver.org
Web site: www.grandriver.org

Junior Statesmen Symposium on Ohio State Politics and Government
Columbus, OH
General Information: Coed residential academic program established in 1998.
Contact: Matt Randazzo, National Summer School Director, 400 South El Camino Real, Suite 300, San Mateo, CA 94402
Phone: 650-347-1600
Fax: 650-347-7200
E-mail: jsa@jsa.org
Web site: www.jsa.org

Kenyon Review Young Writers
Gambier, OH
General Information: Coed residential academic program established in 1989.
Contact: David Lynn, Walton House, Gambier, OH 43022
Phone: 740-427-5208
Fax: 740-427-5417
E-mail: kenyonreview@kenyon.edu
Web site: www.kenyonreview.org/writing/young/

Kenyon Review Young Writers
Gambier, OH
General Information: Coed residential arts program established in 1989.
Contact: David Lynn, Walton House, Gambier, OH 43022
Phone: 740-427-5208
Fax: 740-427-5417
E-mail: kenyonreview@kenyon.edu
Web site: www.kenyonreview.org/writing/young/

Miami University Junior Scholars Program
Oxford, OH
General Information: Coed residential academic program established in 1982.
Contact: Dr. Robert S. Smith, Director, 301 South Patterson Avenue, Room 202, Oxford, OH 45056-3414
Phone: 513-529-5825
Fax: 513-529-1498
E-mail: juniorscholars@muohio.edu
Web site: www.muohio.edu/JuniorScholars/

National Computer Camps at Notre Dame College
South Euclid, OH
General Information: Coed residential and day academic program.
Contact: Dr. Michael Zabinski, President, PO Box 585, Orange, CT 06477
Phone: 203-795-9667
E-mail: info@nccamp.com
Web site: www.nccamp.com

The Summer Institute for the Gifted at Oberlin College
Oberlin, OH
General Information: Coed residential academic program.
Contact: Dr. Stephen Gessner, Director, River Plaza, 9 West Broad Street, Stamford, CT 06902-3788
Phone: 866-303-4744
Fax: 203-399-5598
E-mail: sig.info@aifs.com
Web site: www.giftedstudy.com

Wright State University Residential Camps and Institutes
Dayton, OH
General Information: Coed residential academic program established in 1990.
Contact: Chris S. Hoffman, Assistant Director, Pre-College Programs, 120 Millet Hall, Wright State University, Dayton, OH 45435-0001
Phone: 937-775-3135
Fax: 937-775-4883
E-mail: precollege@wright.edu
Web site: www.wright.edu/academics/precollege/

Wright State University Residential Camps and Institutes
Dayton, OH
General Information: Coed residential arts program established in 1990.
Contact: Chris S. Hoffman, Assistant Director, Pre-College Programs, 120 Millet Hall, Wright State University, Dayton, OH 45435-0001
Phone: 937-775-3135
Fax: 937-775-4883
E-mail: precollege@wright.edu
Web site: www.wright.edu/academics/precollege/

Wisconsin

American Collegiate Adventures
Madison, WI
General Information: Coed residential academic program.
Contact: Jason Lubar, Director of Summer Programs, 1811 W. North Avenue, Suite 201, Chicago, IL 60622
Phone: 800-509-SUMR
Fax: 773-342-0246
E-mail: info@acasummer.com
Web site: www.acasummer.com

Central Wisconsin Environmental Station–Natural Resources Careers Camp
Amherst Junction, WI
General Information: Coed residential academic program established in 1975.
Contact: Ms. Rebecca Franzen, Program Manager, 10186 County Road MM, Amherst Junction, WI 54407
Phone: 715-824-2428
Fax: 715-824-3201
E-mail: bfranzen@uwsp.edu
Web site: www.uwsp.edu/cnr/cwes

Milwaukee School of Engineering (MSOE)–Discover the Possibilities
Milwaukee, WI
General Information: Coed residential academic program established in 1999.
Contact: Ms. Linda Levandowski, Special Events Coordinator MSOE, 1025 North Broadway, Milwaukee, WI 53202
Phone: 800-332-6763
Fax: 414-277-7475
E-mail: levandow@msoe.edu
Web site: www.msoe.edu/admiss/summer

Milwaukee School of Engineering (MSOE)–Focus on Nursing
Milwaukee, WI
General Information: Coed residential academic program established in 2004.
Contact: Ms. Linda Levandowski, Special Events Coordinator, MSOE, 1025 North Broadway, Milwaukee, WI 53202
Phone: 800-332-6763
Fax: 414-277-7475
E-mail: levandow@msoe.edu
Web site: www.msoe.edu/admiss/summer

Milwaukee School of Engineering (MSOE)–Focus on the Possibilities
Milwaukee, WI
General Information: Coed residential academic program established in 1999.
Contact: Ms. Linda Levandowski, Special Events Coordinator, MSOE, 1025 North Broadway, Milwaukee, WI 53202
Phone: 800-332-6763
Fax: 414-277-7475
E-mail: levandow@msoe.edu
Web site: www.msoe.edu/admiss/summer

Point Arts Camp–Music
Stevens Point, WI
General Information: Coed residential arts program established in 1950.
Contact: Ruth Daniels, Program Assistant, 1101 Reserve Street, CAC 324, Stevens Point, WI 54481
Phone: 715-346-3956
Fax: 715-346-2718
E-mail: rdaniels@uwsp.edu
Web site: www.uwsp.edu/cofac/pointartscamps/

Summer Music Clinic
Madison, WI
General Information: Coed residential arts program established in 1929.
Contact: Anne Aley, Program Manager, 5554 Humanities, 455 North Park Street, Madison, WI 53706
Phone: 608-263-2242
Fax: 608-265-0452
E-mail: maaley@facstaff.wisc.edu
Web site: www.wisc.edu/smc

SuperCamp–University of Wisconsin at Parkside
Kenosha, WI
General Information: Coed residential academic program established in 1981.
Contact: Enrollments Department, 1725 South Coast Highway, Oceanside, CA 92054
Phone: 800-285-3276
Fax: 760-722-3507
E-mail: info@supercamp.com
Web site: www.supercamp.com

Timber-lee Drama Camp
East Troy, WI
General Information: Coed residential arts program established in 1972.
Contact: Mr. Tom Parsons, Director, Human Resources, N8705 Scout Road, East Troy, WI 53120
Phone: 262-642-7348
Fax: 262-642-7517
E-mail: timber-lee@timber-lee.com
Web site: www.timber-lee.com

Timber-lee Science Camp
East Troy, WI
General Information: Coed residential and day academic program established in 1972.
Contact: Mr. Tom Parsons, Director, Human Resources, N8705 Scout Road, East Troy, WI 53120
Phone: 262-642-7345
Fax: 262-642-7517
E-mail: tomp@timber-lee.com
Web site: www.timber-lee.com

University of Wisconsin–Green Bay Biz 4 Youth Camp
Green Bay, WI
General Information: Coed residential and day academic program established in 2004.
Contact: Ms. Mona Christensen, Director of Youth Opportunities, 2420 Nicolet Drive, Green Bay, WI 54311
Phone: 920-465-CAMP (2267)
Fax: 920-465-2552
E-mail: summercamps@uwgb.edu
Web site: www.uwgbsummercamps.com

University of Wisconsin–Green Bay Computer Camp
Green Bay, WI
General Information: Coed residential and day academic program established in 1999.
Contact: Mona Christensen, Director of Youth Opportunities, 2420 Nicolet Drive, Green Bay, WI 54311-7001
Phone: 920-465-CAMP (2267)
Fax: 920-465-2552
E-mail: summercamps@uwgb.edu
Web site: www.uwgbsummercamps.com

University of Wisconsin–Green Bay Ecosystem Investigations
Green Bay, WI
General Information: Coed residential and day academic program established in 2004.
Contact: Ms. Mona Christensen, Director of Youth Opportunities, 2420 Nicolet Drive, Green Bay, WI 54311
Phone: 920-465-CAMP (2267)
Fax: 920-465-2552
E-mail: summercamps@uwgb.edu
Web site: www.uwgbsummercamps.com

University of Wisconsin–Green Bay Space Trek Camp
Green Bay, WI
General Information: Coed residential and day academic program established in 2004.
Contact: Ms. Mona Christensen, Director of Youth Opportunities, 2420 Nicolet Drive, Green Bay, WI 54311
Phone: 920-465-CAMP (2267)
Fax: 920-465-2552
E-mail: summercamps@uwgb.edu
Web site: www.uwgbsummercamps.com

University of Wisconsin–Green Bay Summer Art Studio
Green Bay, WI
General Information: Coed residential and day arts program established in 1957.
Contact: Mona Christensen, Director of Youth Opportunities, 2420 Nicolet Drive, Green Bay, WI 54311-7001
Phone: 920-465-CAMP (2267)
Fax: 920-465-2552
E-mail: summercamps@uwgb.edu
Web site: www.uwgbsummercamps.com

University of Wisconsin–Green Bay Summer Music Camps
Green Bay, WI
General Information: Coed residential and day arts program established in 1965.
Contact: Mona Christensen, Director of Youth Opportunities, 2420 Nicolet Drive, Green Bay, WI 54311-7001
Phone: 920-465-CAMP (2267)
Fax: 920-465-2552
E-mail: summercamps@uwgb.edu
Web site: www.uwgbsummercamps.com

University of Wisconsin–Green Bay Summer Spanish Immersion
Green Bay, WI
General Information: Coed residential and day academic program established in 2003.
Contact: Ms. Mona Christensen, Director of Youth Opportunities, 2420 Nicolet Drive, Green Bay, WI 54311-7001
Phone: 920-465-CAMP
Fax: 920-465-2552
E-mail: summercamps@uwgb.edu
Web site: www.uwgbsummercamps.com

University of Wisconsin–Superior Youthsummer 2005
Superior, WI
General Information: Coed residential and day academic program established in 1972.
Contact: Gregory Burke, Director, Rothwell Student Center, Room 50, PO Box 2000, Superior, WI 54880
Phone: 715-394-8173
Fax: 715-394-8445
E-mail: gburke@uwsuper.edu
Web site: www2.uwsuper.edu/youth

World Affairs Seminar
Whitewater, WI
General Information: Coed residential academic program established in 1977.
Contact: Mr. Frederick R. Luedke, General Manager, 800 West Main Street, University of Wisconsin-Whitewater, Whitewater, WI 53190
Phone: 888-404-4049
Fax: 262-472-5210
E-mail: was@uww.edu
Web site: www.worldaffairsseminar.org

NOTES

NOTES

THOMSON PETERSON'S

Your Everything Education Destination...

Petersons.com

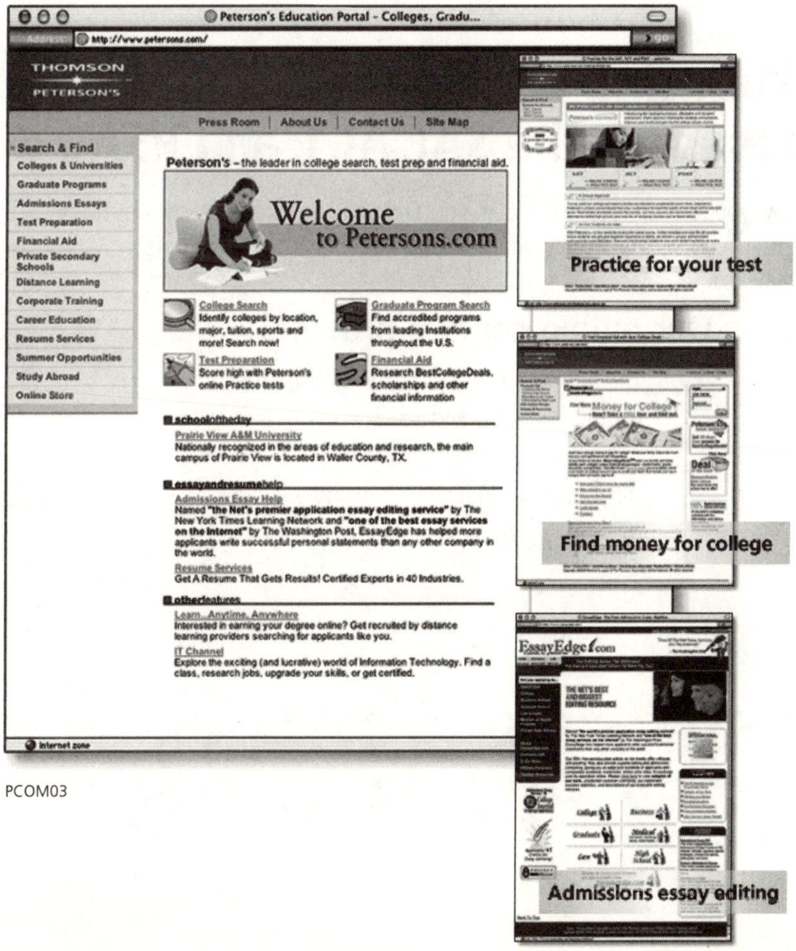

PCOM03

No matter where you're headed, visit the Net's largest, most important education portal.

Whether you're preparing for college, grad school, professional school, or the working world, Petersons.com is your first choice for accurate information and real-world advice.

- Search for the right school
- Find a scholarship
- Take practice admissions tests
- Use interactive courses designed just for you
- Write a better admissions essay with help from Harvard-educated editors

It's your future.

Visit www.petersons.com today!

Get **20% off any book** at Peterson's Online Bookstore

www.petersons.com

Educational Search | Test Preparation | Financial Aid

THOMSON PETERSON'S™

Introducing personalized online courses for the SAT, ACT, and PSAT.

The way you dress. Your college major. Everybody's different, so why take a test-prep course that treats you like everybody else? With Peterson's you don't have to.

Our online courses provide:

- The Internet's only customized preparation for the SAT, ACT, and PSAT
- An interactive study plan based on your individual strengths and weaknesses
- 24/7 access from your own computer

www.PetersonsTestPrep.com

1-877-TEST-PREP

Peterson's TESTPREP™
SAT · ACT · PSAT

PTPC04